My Fellow AMERICANS

THE MOST IMPORTANT SPEECHES OF AMERICA'S PRESIDENTS, FROM GEORGE WASHINGTON TO GEORGE W. BUSH

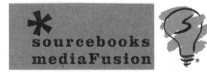

sourcebooks
mediaFusion

An Imprint of Sourcebooks Inc.®
Naperville, Illinois

MICHAEL WALDMAN

CDs NARRATED BY
GEORGE STEPHANOPOULOS

Front cover photos, from left to right: AP/Wide World Photos; AP/Wide World Photos; Corbis Images; Corbis Images; AP/Wide World Photos; AP/Wide World Photos

Back cover photos, from left to right: Corbis Images; Corbis Images; AP/Wide World Photos; Corbis Images; AP/Wide World Photos

Additional Photo Credits and Audio Credits at back

Published by Sourcebooks, Inc.
P.O. Box 4410, Naperville, Illinois 60567-4410
(630) 961-3900
FAX: (630) 961-2168
www.sourcebooks.com

Library of Congress Cataloging-in-Publication Data

My fellow Americans : the most important speeches of America's presidents from George Washington to George W. Bush / [compiled] by Michael Waldman.
p. cm.
Includes bibliographical references.
ISBN 1-4022-0027-7 (alk. paper)
1. Presidents—United States—Messages. 2. Political oratory—United States. 3. United States—Politics and government. I. Waldman, Michael.
J81.4.M93 2003
352.23'8'0973—dc21

2003006879

Printed and bound in the United States of America
QW 10 9 8 7 6 5 4 3 2 1

To my brother Steve

ALSO BY MICHAEL WALDMAN

POTUS Speaks: Finding the Words that Defined the Clinton Presidency
Who Robbed America? A Citizen's Guide to the S & L Scandal
Big Business Reader (2nd ed., edited with Mark Green)
Who Runs Congress? (4th ed., with Mark Green)

CONTENTS

A NOTE ABOUT THE AUDIO

Through the words and voices of its presidents, the history of America comes alive. The audio CDs that accompany and are integrated into this book feature the greatest of those voices, plus a little more. We encourage you to use the book and CDs together to best experience the rich and remarkable history in this collection.

Wherever possible, the greatest speeches of presidents from the recorded era are brought to you as completely as space limitations allowed. Speeches from before recorded sound have been faithfully recreated here by the voice talents of Pat Duke and Roger Mueller. Also, while we were creating this book, we faced the realization that many presidents from the recorded era simply would not have speeches featured in the book itself. In the interest of offering a complete record of presidential voices, these CDs include short audio segments of what we believe to be every president ever recorded, a history that goes all the way back to Benjamin Harrison.

FOREWORD

Once every few years, a dramatic moment draws us together as Americans, sometimes joyous, sometimes calamitous—planes strike the World Trade Center, the *Challenger* space craft blows up before our eyes, young people tear down the Berlin Wall, peace comes after war. We watch, we listen, we wonder. But each time, there is one person to whom we turn to explain and give meaning—our president.

On a summer night during the Great Depression, historians tell us, one could walk through the streets of Baltimore and hear every word Franklin Roosevelt spoke from a fireside in the White House. Families up and down the blocks were gathered 'round their radios, and his voice carried through open windows. Memories of John F. Kennedy's voice crystallizing in the cold air as he spoke during his inaugural remain forever etched. When he was slain, we waited anxiously to hear Lyndon Johnson and were relieved by his humility and his call to continue. When Richard Nixon resigned, we needed to hear Gerald Ford tell us, "Our long national nightmare is over." And as schoolchildren tried to make sense of the *Challenger* explosion, Ronald Reagan wisely recalled for us "the last time we saw them, this morning, as they prepared for the journey and waved good-bye and 'slipped the surly bonds of earth' to 'touch the face of God.'"

Michael Waldman knows as well as anyone the importance of the bully pulpit, having been the chief speechwriter in the Clinton White House. But, as Waldman reminds us, up until the time of Teddy Roosevelt, presidents spoke much less frequently than today. George Washington gave few public addresses, even though he had the finest speechwriting team in history—Jefferson, Hamilton, and Madison. Washington thought his deeds spoke more persuasively than his words. Thomas Jefferson was a shy man who loved to write (he sent endless written messages to his cabinet officers) but spoke only when required: he sent his State of the Union messages to Congress on paper and gave only two major speeches, his first and second inaugurals!

Abraham Lincoln gained political prominence through the power of his oratory. For years after, students studied his Lyceum speech, given as a young man, as well as his "House Divided" speech; his debates with Douglas that lifted him onto the national stage; and his address at Cooper Union that convinced New Yorkers he might be a good nominee for the presidency. Once elected, however, Lincoln refrained from speaking much. His first and second inaugurals, along with the Gettysburg Address, are among the only ones he delivered. At a time when presidential speeches seem two-a-penny, one longs for a day when a speech was both singular and incandescent.

Rereading Lincoln's presidential speeches here, one is reminded how a leader can give deeper and fresher meaning to the American experience through the power of the pen. At Gettysburg, as Garry Wills pointed out in his Pulitzer prize–winning book, *Lincoln at Gettysburg*, Lincoln reinterpreted American history, placing the value of equality on the same plane as liberty. In his second inaugural, as Ronald White has underscored in his book, *Lincoln's Greatest Speech*, Lincoln pointed the nation toward a peace of reconciliation. Both speeches rely upon a theme of America's birth, death, and rebirth—at Gettysburg, cast in secular terms, and in his second inaugural, cast as a spiritual rebirth. The two together are among the most important statements ever made about who we are as a people.

And that's the point. Our presidents not only wear the two traditional hats of head-of-state and head-of-government, they also give us voice as a people. Every speaker must come to know his or her own voice, but power comes when a speaker's authentic voice is also the voice of the people being addressed. Our best presidents have known that instinctively, and they have helped to define who we are, what we are experiencing, and how our experience fits into our great national experiment.

Among the many paintings depicting the signers of the Constitution, gathered in Philadelphia in 1787, one has often intrigued people who work at the White House. It shows most of the signers in detail but others are only sketched in and large patches of white space are left unmarked. More than one president has suggested to audiences that the painter did that for a reason: he wanted to tell each succeeding generation that it is up to it to carry on the work, to complete the canvas. That's what these presidential speeches, collected here with so much care, represent. Each one provides an important brush stroke that paints in yet another piece of the American story.

David Gergen
Cambridge, Massachusetts
July 11, 2003

INTRODUCTION

"Four score and seven years ago"…"A date which will live in infamy"…"Ask not what your country can do for you"…"Mr. Gorbachev, tear down this wall!" From our earliest days, and especially in the past century, presidents have led with their words—using what Theodore Roosevelt called the "bully pulpit" to inspire, rally, and unite the country. By moving ordinary citizens, these speeches moved history. Franklin Roosevelt called the presidency "preeminently a place of moral leadership." As he understood, only a president can speak, with a clear voice, to the whole country—and on behalf of the nation to the world. If you want to understand American history, the great speeches of American presidents are a good place to start. And not just to read them, but to hear them.

From 1995 to 1999, I was director of speechwriting in the White House for President Bill Clinton. I worked on two inaugural addresses, four State of the Unions—all told, editing or writing nearly two thousand speeches. Drawing on that experience, I have selected what I believe to be the forty-three most significant speeches by American presidents, from George Washington to George W. Bush. These are the speeches that made the greatest impact—those most remembered by later generations, or those that will most likely be so recalled. To introduce each speech, I explain the historic context, the goals of the talk, and how it was composed. The text is accompanied by two audio CDs that feature the actual voices of all the presidents since Benjamin Harrison.

A few explanations are in order.

First, these are the complete speeches—some have been edited for length, but more are presented in their entirety. I think it's best to read these speeches in full, to move beyond the familiar soundbites or slogans. Second, this book focuses on those speeches made by presidents while they were in office. There are three exceptions, however: Abraham Lincoln's "House Divided" speech, Theodore Roosevelt's "New Nationalism," and George H.W. Bush's 1988 convention address, each chosen because of the way it illuminates key themes of the presidency of those three men.

Third, you'll notice that most of these speeches date from the twentieth century. Before then, presidents rarely spoke in public. When they did, they didn't ask citizens to support specific policies. Such appeals were considered demagogic. (Indeed, one of the articles of impeachment against President Andrew Johnson actually accused him of going on a speaking tour—not only that, doing so in a "loud voice"!) Congress, rather than the chief executive, ran the country—and the great orators, such as Daniel Webster and Henry Clay, held forth on Capitol Hill. When presidents addressed the public, they usually did so in writing. We have included three of those written addresses—George Washington's "Farewell Address," and two by Andrew Jackson—because their ringing phrases lived beyond the day's controversies.

Social change—and new technologies—transformed the presidency. At the turn of the twentieth century, new national media—wire services, national magazines, photographic reproduction—began to transmit the words and especially pictures of leaders to a wide new audience. The industrial revolution produced a demand for a stronger national government. From the beginning, as Alexander Hamilton urged, the chief executive was the source of "energy." Now the country wanted action. As government grew, so did the presidency.

And from Theodore Roosevelt and Woodrow Wilson forward, chief executives came to see their public speeches as a key tool for leadership. Soon radio would carry the voice of the president directly to millions of citizens. FDR's skill on the medium was key to his success, and to those of other contemporary orators, such as Churchill—and Hitler. Then came the next revolution, and it was televised. The first presidential TV talk aired in 1947. Eisenhower held the first televised press conference in 1955. In the 1960s, the televised presidency truly came of age. Three television networks now had nightly newscasts, and the president was the "star." Presidents often spoke to the country in widely watched, prime-time addresses. Richard Nixon, when he resigned in a speech from his desk, began, "This is the thirty-seventh time I have spoken to you from this office."

The next explosion of technology came in the 1980s and mushroomed in the 1990s—and with it, the president's voice was both more ubiquitous and less commanding. By the end of the century, there were four all-news cable networks (CNN, Fox, MSNBC, and CNBC). But broadcast television networks now balked at giving presidents time to address the public directly. Today, short of war or scandal, the only time a president can be assured of a national TV audience is in the annual State of the Union address. So presidential talk is now a matter not just of quality but quantity. In a typical, non-election year, Harry Truman spoke in public eighty-eight times; Ronald Reagan, 320 times; Bill Clinton, nearly 550 times. (George W. Bush has never had a full year of placid normalcy. He has consciously sought to be less garrulous than his predecessors. Still, he speaks in public nearly every day.) No doubt, as the Internet continues to transform communication, the way presidents lead through words will change, too.

The memorable speeches in this book teach us about our country in several ways. The very first presidential talk,

Washington's inaugural, called our nation a great "experiment." Perhaps a great argument is more like it—a long conversation, stretching over two centuries, about what we stand for.

What is the role of government? From Jefferson and Jackson through to the Roosevelts and JFK and Reagan and Clinton, the presidents have contested, with the demand for a strong hand in the capital alternating with the demand for a minimal state.

What is America's role in the world? Washington warned against "permanent alliances." But Wilson, Franklin Roosevelt, and Truman argued the country must exert global leadership—and the Cold War dominated presidential rhetoric for half a century. Now George W. Bush calls Americans to a new kind of struggle with terrorists and nations that threaten through weapons of mass destruction.

And what of the dilemma of race? In these pages, Lincoln grows from a lawyer's insisting on preserving the union to his second inaugural calling the Civil War God's punishment for the sin of slavery. Lyndon Johnson adopted the civil rights anthem, "We Shall Overcome." But as Bill Clinton preached from the pulpit in Memphis where Martin Luther King Jr. gave his last sermon, legal civil rights are incomplete if our communities are torn by violence and crime.

The best presidential addresses call on our nation to live by its ideals, first (and best) expressed in the preamble to the Declaration of Independence. Time and again, presidents rely for moral authority on what historian Pauline Maier calls our "American scripture." Lincoln at Gettysburg argued that the country's founding vision required us to end slavery. Roosevelt argued that the same ideals required a new strong central government to combat economic inequality. Ronald Reagan quoted those same founders to argue instead for a more limited government. And presidents from Wilson to Roosevelt to Reagan to Bush have sought to extend that vision worldwide.

There are lessons here for aspiring leaders and would-be "great communicators." These speeches—for all their pomp and poetry—are distinguished by their muscularity. They are more than words; they are action. They convey big ideas, often controversial ones. They are memorable not solely because they are eloquent, but because, so often, they pressed people to change their minds. (One recurring theme, in fact, is surprise—presidents knew that by confounding expectation, they kept the initiative in their hands.)

In the end, the fact that we still listen to these words reflects well on our democracy. Usually, presidents cannot command. They can only persuade. For all the majesty of office, they rise only as far as they bring the people with them. True, citizens no longer huddle around the radio, anxiously listening to FDR's latest fireside chat. But in the crowded and dangerous days since September 11, 2001, we again listen intently to the words of our president. In a time of crisis, for all our cynicism, we look to the president for inspiration, information, and direction. This book—along with the CDs that accompany it—gives us a chance to hear for ourselves how, in our best moments, our leaders have challenged our ideas, stirred our hearts, and moved our nation.

Michael Waldman
New York City
April 2003

George
WASHINGTON

1ST PRESIDENT: 1789–1797

Born: February 22, 1732, in Westmoreland County, Virginia

Died: December 14, 1799, in Mount Vernon, Virginia

Disc 1, Tracks 2–3

A DISPLAY of the UNITED STATES of AMERICA

I

"THE AMERICAN EXPERIMENT"

WHEN GEORGE WASHINGTON traveled from Mount Vernon to New York City to take the oath of office, there had never before been a president of the United States. Crowds wild with adulation followed his coach up the East Coast. As Washington crossed the Hudson River to New York City, a band played "God Save the King," with new words honoring the American leader. As James Madison noted ruefully, the selection of Washington as president was the only part of the government that the people truly liked. But what was the presidency? Nobody really knew. Was it like an elected monarch? Was it merely an adjunct to the Congress? On the role and scope of the new office, as on much else, the Constitution was vague. The first chief executive would have to begin to fill in that outline, and he would begin by delivering an inaugural address.

Amid pomp and artillery fusillades, before a large crowd on Wall Street, Washington was sworn in. Then he went indoors to address the Congress. Representative Fisher Ames, a renowned orator in Congress, described the talk:

> It was a very touching scene and quite of the solemn kind. [Washington's] aspect grave, almost to sadness; his modesty, actually shaking; his voice deep, a little tremulous, and so low as to call for close attention; added to the series of objects presented to the mind, and overwhelming it, produced emotions of the most affecting kind upon the members. I...sat entranced. It seemed to me an allegory in which virtue was personified.

Washington, as one historian noted, was a confident military commander, but when it came to assuming the nation's highest civil office, he lost his composure. By this very unsteadiness, he showed the audience he shared their respect for civilian authority. With his endearing stage fright, Washington cloaked the new republican form of government with his own monumental personal standing.

What should an inaugural address say? At first, Washington drafted a long list of legislative recommendations. But as he explained, he decided that would best wait for another occasion—what would become the message on the State of the Union. His diffidence won warm public approval; in fact, it was what audiences of the day expected from a leader. Though they revered Washington, citizens had just fought a revolution against overweening executive authority. Instead of offering a detailed program, Washington spoke instead in broad and sweeping terms about the newly launched country. He understood the president was head of state before he was head of government. Washington also announced he would not take a salary, a bit of showmanship that was likely as popular then as it would be now. As he did in his farewell address later, he warned against factionalism and "party animosity," and urged Americans to think of their country and not just their communities.

The speech took an unmistakable spiritual tone. Over nearly a third of its length, Washington spoke of divine guidance for the new nation. Historians believe that Washington, like Thomas Jefferson and Benjamin Franklin and others of the day, was a deist. He did not follow the doctrine of a church, but held to the Enlightenment view that an indefinable supreme being created the universe. Washington's wartime experiences convinced him that the new nation had been so fortunate in so many ways that it must have been blessed by Providence.

Repeatedly, he argued that public happiness depended on private virtues such as honesty.

Washington knew his generation faced challenges novel and grave. Earlier self-governing republics had ended in failure. None had stretched across a landmass the size of the thirteen states. The new country constantly would have to contend with empires that coveted its land and wealth. Even the Constitution, though better than the improvisational governments of the decade before, was only an outline. Hence the power of Washington's eloquent charge to the citizens: "The preservation of the sacred fire of liberty and the destiny of the republican model of government are justly considered, perhaps, as *deeply*, as *finally*, staked on the experiment intrusted to the hands of the American people." The cause of the new government was the same cause fought for in the Revolution; it was a test of the virtue of the people and of the republican (and, increasingly over the years, of the democratic) idea. These first words spoken by a president fixed the idea of America as an experiment in liberty. The American "experiment" would reappear in Abraham Lincoln's Gettysburg Address (the Civil War was testing whether or not a nation "conceived in liberty" could endure).

The presidency would evolve continuously. For most of the country's first century, Congress would overshadow the White House and its occupants. Only gradually did the chief executive become the prominent and singular figure in American government, expected to initiate policy. But Washington's inaugural fixed one of the chief responsibilities of office: to speak for the nation's core political principles.

George Washington's
FIRST INAUGURAL ADDRESS

hear...
disc 1
track 2

Federal Hall, New York City • April 30, 1789

Fellow-Citizens of the Senate and of the House of Representatives:

Among the vicissitudes incident to life no event could have filled me with greater anxieties than that of which the notification was transmitted by your order, and received on the 14th day of the present month. On the one hand, I was summoned by my country, whose voice I can never hear but with veneration and love, from a retreat which I had chosen with the fondest predilection, and, in my flattering hopes, with an immutable decision, as the asylum of my declining years—a retreat which was rendered every day more necessary as well as more dear to me by the addition of habit to inclination, and of frequent interruptions in my health to the gradual waste committed on it by time. On the other hand, the magnitude and difficulty of the trust to which the voice of my country called me, being sufficient to awaken in the wisest and most experienced of her citizens a distrustful scrutiny into his qualifications, could not but overwhelm with despondence one who (inheriting inferior endowments from nature and unpracticed in the duties of civil administration) ought to be peculiarly conscious of his own deficiencies. In this conflict of emotions all I dare aver is that it has been my faithful study to collect my duty from a just appreciation of every circumstance by which it might be affected. All I dare hope is that if, in executing this task, I have been too much swayed by a grateful remembrance of former instances, or by an affectionate sensibility to this transcendent proof of the confidence of my fellow-citizens, and have thence too little consulted my incapacity as well as disinclination for the weighty and untried cares before me, my error will be palliated by the motives which mislead me, and its consequences be judged by my country with some share of the partiality in which they originated.

Such being the impressions under which I have, in obedience to the public summons, repaired to the present station, it would be peculiarly improper to omit in this first official act my fervent supplications to that Almighty Being who rules over the universe, who presides in the councils of nations, and whose providential aids can supply every

The 1889 painting by Ramon de Elorriaga entitled, "The Inauguration of George Washington"

human defect, that His benediction may consecrate to the liberties and happiness of the people of the United States a Government instituted by themselves for these essential purposes, and may enable every instrument employed in its administration to execute with success the functions allotted to his charge. In tendering this homage to the Great Author of every public and private good, I assure myself that it expresses your sentiments not less than my own, nor those of my fellow-citizens at large less than either. No people can be bound to acknowledge and adore the Invisible Hand which conducts the affairs of men more than those of the United States. Every step by which they have advanced to the character of an independent nation seems to have been distinguished by some token of providential agency; and in the important revolution just accomplished in the system of their united government the tranquil deliberations and voluntary consent of so many distinct communities from which the event has resulted can not be compared with the means by which most governments have been established without some return of pious gratitude, along with an humble anticipation of the future blessings which the past seem to presage. These reflections, arising out of the present crisis, have forced themselves too strongly on my mind to be suppressed. You will join with me, I trust, in thinking that there are none under the influence of which the proceedings of a new and free government can more auspiciously commence.

By the article establishing the executive department it is made the duty of the President "to recommend to your consideration such measures as he shall judge necessary and expedient." The circumstances under which I now meet you will acquit me from entering into that subject further than to refer to the great constitutional charter under which you are assembled, and which, in defining your powers, designates the objects to which your attention is to be given. It will be more consistent with those circumstances, and far more congenial with the feelings which actuate me, to substitute, in place of a recommendation of particular measures, the tribute that is due to the talents, the rectitude, and the patriotism which adorn the characters selected to devise and adopt them. In these honorable qualifications I behold the surest pledges that as on one side no local prejudices or attachments, no separate views nor party animosities, will misdirect the comprehensive and equal eye which ought to watch over this great assemblage of communities and interests, so, on another, that the foundation of our national policy will be laid in the pure and immutable principles of private morality, and the preeminence of free government be exemplified by all the attributes which can win the affections of its citizens and command the respect of the world. I dwell on this prospect with every satisfaction which an ardent love for my country can inspire, since there is no truth more thoroughly established than that there exists in the economy and course of nature an indissoluble union between virtue and happiness; between duty and advantage; between the genuine maxims of an honest and magnanimous policy and the solid rewards of public prosperity and felicity; since we ought to be no less persuaded that the propitious smiles of Heaven can never be expected on a nation that disregards the eternal rules of order and right which Heaven itself has ordained; and since the preservation of the sacred fire of liberty and the destiny of the republican model of government are justly considered, perhaps, as *deeply*, as *finally*, staked on the experiment entrusted to the hands of the American people.

> *"No people can be bound to acknowledge and adore the Invisible Hand which conducts the affairs of men more than those of the United States."*

Besides the ordinary objects submitted to your care, it will remain with your judgment to decide how far an exercise of the occasional power delegated by the fifth article of the Constitution is rendered expedient at the

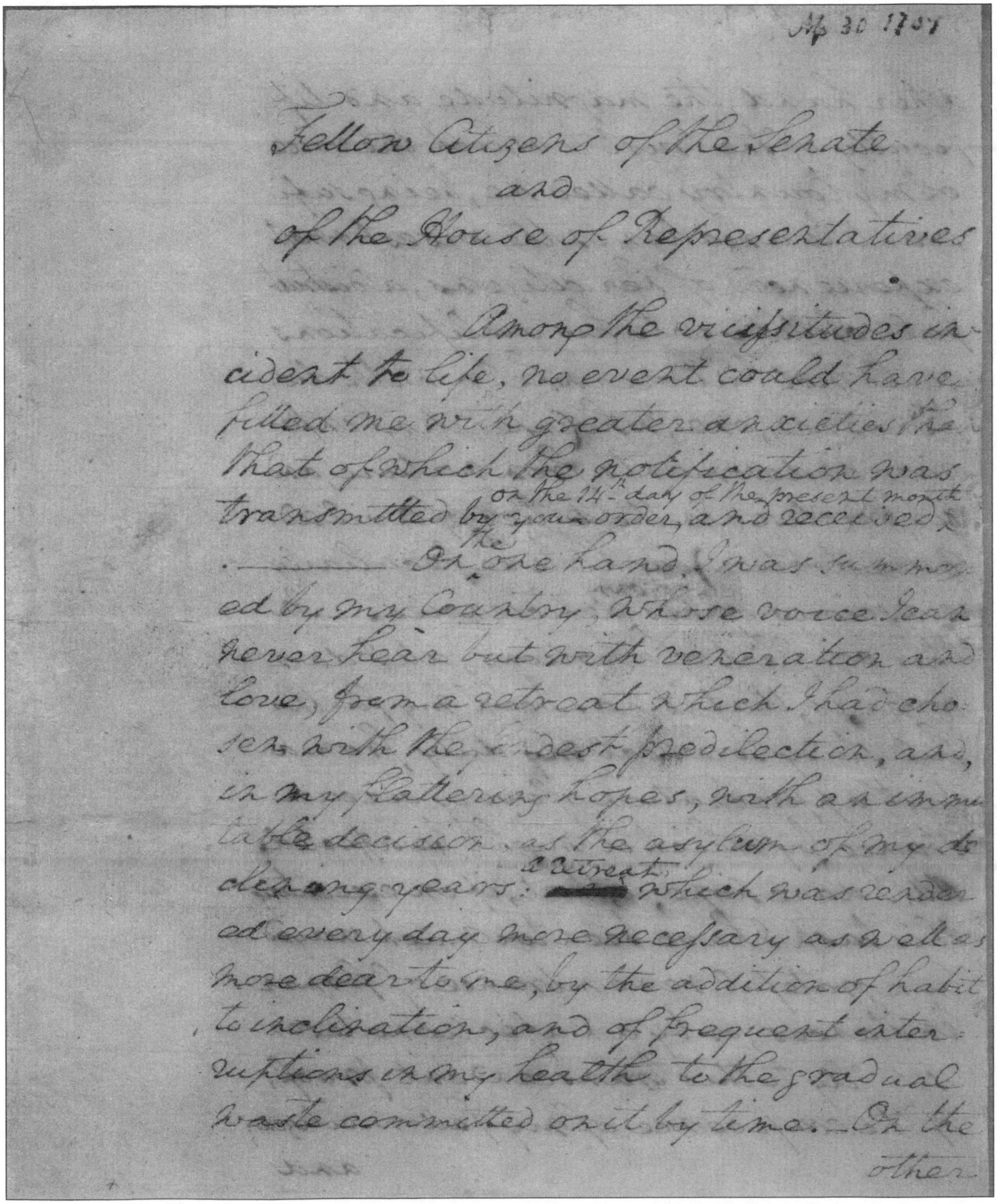

Ap 30 1789

Fellow Citizens of the Senate
and
of the House of Representatives

Among the vicissitudes incident to life, no event could have filled me with greater anxieties than that of which the notification was transmitted by your order, and received on the 14th day of the present month. On the one hand, I was summoned by my Country, whose voice I can never hear but with veneration and love, from a retreat which I had chosen with the fondest predilection, and, in my flattering hopes, with an immutable decision, as the asylum of my declining years: a retreat which was rendered every day more necessary as well as more dear to me, by the addition of habit to inclination, and of frequent interruptions in my health to the gradual waste committed on it by time. On the

other

Washington's handwritten draft of his first inaugural address present juncture by the nature of objections which have been urged against the system, or by the degree of inquietude which has given birth to them. Instead of undertaking particular recommendations on this subject, in which I could be guided by no lights derived from official opportunities, I shall again give way to my entire confidence in your discernment and pursuit of the public good; for I assure myself that whilst you carefully avoid every alteration which might endanger the benefits of an united and effective government, or which ought to await the future lessons of experience, a reverence for the characteristic rights of freemen and a regard for the public harmony will sufficiently influence your deliberations on the question how far the former can be impregnably fortified or the latter be safely and advantageously promoted.

To the foregoing observations I have one to add, which will be most properly addressed to the House of Representatives. It concerns myself, and will therefore be as brief as possible. When I was first honored with a call into the service of my country, then on the eve of an arduous struggle for its liberties, the light in which I contemplated my duty required that I should renounce every pecuniary compensation. From this resolution I have in no instance departed; and being still under the impressions which produced it, I must decline as inapplicable to myself any share in the personal emoluments which may be indispensably included in a permanent provision for the executive department, and

must accordingly pray that the pecuniary estimates for the station in which I am placed may during my continuance in it be limited to such actual expenditures as the public good may be thought to require.

Having thus imparted to you my sentiments as they have been awakened by the occasion which brings us together, I shall take my present leave; but not without resorting once more to the benign Parent of the Human Race in humble supplication that, since He has been pleased to favor the American people with opportunities for deliberating in perfect tranquillity, and dispositions for deciding with unparalleled unanimity on a form of government for the security of their union and the advancement of their happiness, so His divine blessing may be equally *conspicuous* in the enlarged views, the temperate consultations, and the wise measures on which the success of this Government must depend.

"You will join with me, I trust, in thinking that there are none under the influence of which the proceedings of a new and free government can more auspiciously commence."

2

"THESE COUNSELS OF AN OLD AND AFFECTIONATE FRIEND"

ON SEPTEMBER 19, 1796, in his seventh year in office, President George Washington rode from the capital in Philadelphia to his home at Mount Vernon. In the city he left behind, newspaper readers opened *Claypoole's American Daily Advertiser*. There, on page two, was a startling message addressed to "THE PEOPLE OF THE UNITED STATES"—not a speech, but a written address to the public. Within days, newspapers all across the country rushed it into print. One, in New Hampshire, dubbed it "Washington's Farewell Address." George Washington would not run for a third term.

Today, we take it for granted that leaders stay in office for an allotted time and then leave. Then, the idea was novel—an innovative contribution to democracy. In revolutions before and since, victorious strongmen clung to office until death. Kings passed on the throne to their heirs. King George III, hearing of an earlier decision by his adversary Washington to resign his army commission and decline the chance for ultimate power, is reported to have said, "If he does that, he will be the greatest man in the world."

As it happened, by the end of his second term, Washington was feeling rather bruised. He had mulled stepping aside after his first term, and had asked James Madison to draft a message explaining his reasons. Madison urged Washington not to go before Congress to deliver the address, but rather to aim it straight at the American people. As presidential historian Garry Wills has observed, it would have been the first use of the presidential "bully pulpit." Washington decided to run for reelection, but he kept Madison's draft in reserve.

Four years later, after a contentious second term, he was even more determined to decline a third term. The president wrote a bitter, self-pitying draft, defending his honor and denouncing his critics. He even included, in its entirety, Madison's draft from four years before, perhaps to show he had not cravenly sought power (and to show that one of his chief critics knew so). Washington sent his draft to Alexander Hamilton, the former secretary of the treasury, now living in New York, and asked him to edit it, worrying about its "egotism." Hamilton must have been aghast. In part, he was upset that Washington was working with Madison, a political rival. He stalled for weeks, made minor edits, and then ultimately wrote an entirely new version. It was lofty, visionary, and altogether different. When he saw this text, Washington realized Hamilton's version was much better. He used it as the basis of his Farewell Address.

Washington's address is remembered best for two things. The first is the denunciation of faction, accompanied by a call for national unity. As historian Joseph Ellis notes, Washington was addressing a nation that would have to fare without him, saying in effect: "Think of yourself as a single nation; subordinate your regional and political differences to your common identity as Americans; regard the federal government that represents your collective interest as an ally rather than as an enemy (as 'us,' if you will, rather than 'them')."

More influential was the discussion of foreign affairs. The new nation was being sucked, seemingly inexorably, into the ever-raging European wars—a small, powerless country that risked being caught up in the battles between European giants. The French Revolution had thrilled Thomas Jefferson's Republicans and horrified the Federalists. That split threatened the new American government. Washington's administration had enraged the Republicans by negotiating the Jay Treaty, which, by ending British aggression against American shipping with generous concessions, brought the United States closer to England. His purpose was not to tilt toward London, but neutrality. Washington believed the young nation could prosper only if it steered clear of "permanent alliances" with one side or the other. (He never referred to "entangling alliances," though many people wrongly think the phrase his. It belonged to Jefferson in his first inaugural.) In fact, Washington privately suggested the United States needed two decades of peace and isolation to build up strength enough to defend itself, a prophecy that was proven prescient in the war of 1812. His denunciation of faction was an early version of the later adage that "politics must stop at the water's edge."

The policy of isolationism set out in the Farewell Address was followed for over a century by presidents of all parties. Its doctrine was appealed to, frequently, by those opposing U.S. involvement in wars and foreign adventures.

Perhaps the most important thing about Washington's address was that it said "farewell." Biographer James Flexner has written, "Washington's desire to retire at the end of his second term was so climactic an act that the precedent he thus established was not violated for more than a century and then restored by a Constitutional amendment....He was demonstrating the principle essential to a free government that succession should be determined as a matter of course by the people rather than by Father Time's scythe. He had gone against the precedents of history, which made his act the more remarkable, the more endearing."

On March 4, 1797, his successor, John Adams, took the oath of office. As a gesture of esteem, Thomas Jefferson, the new vice president, signaled to Washington that he should go first as the three men left the stage. In full view of the crowd, Washington refused: he was now a private citizen. Republican government would live beyond its first president.

Alexander Hamilton wrote the first draft
of Washington's Farewell Address

George Washington's
FAREWELL ADDRESS

Published September 19, 1796

*hear....
disc 1
track 3

Friends and Fellow-Citizens:

The period for a new election of a citizen to administer the Executive Government of the United States being not far distant, and the time actually arrived when your thoughts must be employed in designating the person who is to be clothed with that important trust, it appears to me proper, especially as it may conduce to a more distinct expression of the public voice, that I should now apprise you of the resolution I have formed to decline being considered among the number of those out of whom a choice is to be made....

The acceptance of and continuance hitherto in the office to which your suffrages have twice called me have been a uniform sacrifice of inclination to the opinion of duty and to a deference for what appeared to be your desire. I constantly hoped that it would have been much earlier in my power, consistently with motives which I was not at liberty to disregard, to return to that retirement from which I had been reluctantly drawn. The strength of my inclination to do this previous to the last election had even led to the preparation of an address to declare it to you; but mature reflection on the then perplexed and critical posture of our affairs with foreign nations and the unanimous advice of persons entitled to my confidence impelled me to abandon the idea. I rejoice that the state of your concerns, external as well as internal, no longer renders the pursuit of inclination incompatible with the sentiment of duty or propriety, and am persuaded, whatever partiality may be retained for my services, that in the present circumstances of our country you will not disapprove my determination to retire....

Here, perhaps, I ought to stop. But a solicitude for your welfare which can not end but with my life, and the apprehension of danger natural to that solicitude, urge me on an occasion like the present to offer to your solemn contemplation and to recommend to your frequent review some sentiments which are the result of much reflection, of no inconsiderable observation, and which appear to me all important to the permanency of your felicity as a people. These will be offered to you with the more freedom as you can only see in them the disinterested warnings of a parting friend, who can possibly have no personal motive to bias his counsel....

> *"I should now apprise you of the resolution I have formed to decline being considered among the number of those out of whom a choice is to be made...."*

[The] common and continual mischiefs of the spirit of party are sufficient to make it the interest and duty of a wise people to discourage and restrain it.

It serves always to distract the public councils and enfeeble the public administration. It agitates the community with ill-founded jealousies and false alarms; kindles the animosity of one part against another; foments occasionally riot and insurrection. It opens the door to foreign influence and corruption, which find a facilitated access to the government itself through the channels of party passion. Thus the policy and the will of one country are subjected to the policy and will of another.

11

There is an opinion that parties in free countries are useful checks upon the administration of the government, and serve to keep alive the spirit of liberty. This within certain limits is probably true; and in governments of a monarchical cast patriotism may look with indulgence, if not with favor, upon the spirit of party. But in those of the popular character, in governments purely elective, it is a spirit not to be encouraged. From their natural tendency it is certain there will always be enough of that spirit for every salutary purpose; and there being constant danger of excess, the effort ought to be by force of public opinion to mitigate and assuage it. A fire not to be quenched, it demands a uniform vigilance to prevent its bursting into a flame, lest, instead of warming, it should consume.

It is important, likewise, that the habits of thinking in a free country should inspire caution in those intrusted with its administration to confine themselves within their respective constitutional spheres, avoiding in the exercise of the powers of one department to encroach upon another. The spirit of encroachment tends to consolidate the powers of all the departments in one, and thus to create, whatever the form of government, a real despotism. A just estimate of that love of power and proneness to abuse it which predominates in the human heart is sufficient to satisfy us of the truth of this position. The necessity of reciprocal checks in the exercise of political power, by dividing and distributing it into different depositories, and constituting each the guardian of the public weal against invasions by the others, has been evinced by experiments ancient and modern, some of them in our country and under our own eyes. To preserve them must be as necessary as to institute them. If in the opinion of the people the distribution or modification of the constitutional powers be in any particular wrong, let it be corrected by an amendment in the way which the Constitution designates. But let there be no change by usurpation; for though this in one instance may be the instrument of good, it is the customary weapon by which free governments are destroyed. The precedent must always greatly overbalance in permanent evil any partial or transient benefit which the use can at any time yield.

Of all the dispositions and habits which lead to political prosperity, religion and morality are indispensable supports. In vain would that man claim the tribute of patriotism who should labor to subvert these great pillars of human happiness—these firmest props of the duties of men and citizens. The mere politician, equally with the pious man, ought to respect and to cherish them. A volume could not trace all their connections with private and public felicity. Let it simply be asked, Where is the security for property, for reputation, for life, if the sense of religious obligation *desert* the oaths which are the instruments of investigation in courts of justice? And let us with caution indulge the supposition that morality can be maintained without religion. Whatever may be conceded to the influence of refined education on minds of peculiar structure, reason and experience both forbid us to expect that national morality can prevail in exclusion of religious principle.

> *"It is our true policy to steer clear of permanent alliances with any portion of the foreign world...."*

It is substantially true that virtue or morality is a necessary spring of popular government. The rule indeed extends with more or less force to every species of free government. Who that is a sincere friend to it can look with indifference upon attempts to shake the foundation of the fabric? Promote, then, as an object of primary importance, institutions for the general diffusion of knowledge. In proportion as the structure of a government gives force to public opinion, it is essential that public opinion should be enlightened.

As a very important source of strength and security, cherish public credit. One method of preserving it is to use it as sparingly as possible, avoiding occasions of expense by cultivating peace, but remembering also that timely disbursements to prepare for danger frequently prevent much greater disbursements to repel it; avoiding likewise the accumulation of debt, not only by shunning occasions of expense, but by vigorous exertions in time of peace to discharge the debts which unavoidable wars have occasioned, not ungenerously throwing upon posterity the burthen which we ourselves ought to bear. The execution of these maxims belongs to your representatives; but it is necessary that public opinion should cooperate. To facilitate to them the performance of their duty it is essential that you should practically bear in mind that toward the payment of debts there must be revenue; that to have revenue there must be taxes; that no taxes can be devised which are not more or less inconvenient and unpleasant; that the intrinsic embarrassment inseparable from the selection of the proper objects (which is always a choice of difficulties), ought to be a decisive motive for a candid construction of the conduct of the Government in making it, and for a spirit of acquiescence in the measures for obtaining revenue which the public exigencies may at any time dictate.

Observe good faith and justice toward all nations. Cultivate peace and harmony with all. Religion and morality enjoin this conduct. And can it be that good policy does not equally enjoin it? It will be worthy of a free, enlightened, and at no distant period a great nation to give to mankind the magnanimous and too novel example of a people always guided by an exalted justice and benevolence. Who can doubt that in the course of time and things the fruits of such a plan would richly repay any temporary advantages which might be lost by a steady adherence to it? Can it be that Providence has not connected the permanent felicity of a nation with its virtue? The experiment, at least, is recommended by every sentiment which ennobles human nature. Alas! is it rendered impossible by its vices?

In the execution of such a plan nothing is more essential than that permanent, inveterate antipathies against particular nations and passionate attachments for others should be excluded, and that in place of them just and amicable feelings toward all should be cultivated. The nation which indulges toward another an habitual hatred or an habitual fondness is in some degree a slave. It is a slave to its animosity or to its affection, either of which is sufficient to lead it astray from its duty and its interest. Antipathy in one nation against another disposes each more readily to offer insult and injury, to lay hold of slight causes of umbrage, and to be haughty and intractable when accidental or trifling occasions of dispute occur....

As avenues to foreign influence in innumerable ways, such attachments are particularly alarming to the truly enlightened and independent patriot. How many opportunities do they afford to tamper with domestic factions, to practice the arts of seduction, to mislead public opinion, to influence or awe the public councils! Such an attachment of a small or weak toward a great and powerful nation dooms the former to be the satellite of the latter. Against the insidious wiles of foreign influence (I conjure you to believe me, fellow-citizens) the jealousy of a free people ought to be *constantly* awake, since history and experience prove that foreign influence is one of the most baneful foes of republican government. But that jealousy, to be useful, must be impartial, else it becomes the instrument of the very influence to be avoided, instead of a defense against it. Excessive partiality for one foreign nation and excessive dislike of another cause those whom they actuate to see danger only on one side, and serve to veil and even second the arts of influence on the other. Real patriots who may resist the intrigues of the favorite are liable to become suspected and odious, while its tools and dupes usurp the applause and confidence of the people to surrender their interests.

The great rule of conduct for us in regard to foreign nations is, in extending our commercial relations to have with them as little *political* connection as possible. So far as we have already formed engagements let them be fulfilled with perfect good faith. Here let us stop.

Europe has a set of primary interests which to us have none or a very remote relation. Hence she must be engaged in frequent controversies, the causes of which are essentially foreign to our concerns. Hence, therefore, it must be unwise in us to implicate ourselves by artificial ties in the ordinary vicissitudes of her politics or the ordinary combinations and collisions of her friendships or enmities.

Our detached and distant situation invites and enables us to pursue a different course. If we remain one people, under an efficient government, the period is not far off when we may defy material injury from external annoyance; when we may take such an attitude as will cause the neutrality we may at any time resolve upon to be scrupulously respected; when belligerent nations, under the impossibility of making acquisitions upon us, will not lightly hazard the giving us provocation; when we may choose peace or war, as our interest, guided by justice, shall counsel.

Why forego the advantages of so peculiar a situation? Why quit our own to stand upon foreign ground? Why, by interweaving our destiny with that of any part of Europe, entangle our peace and prosperity in the toils of European ambition, rivalship, interest, humor, or caprice?

"I hold the maxim no less applicable to public than to private affairs that honesty is always the best policy."

It is our true policy to steer clear of permanent alliances with any portion of the foreign world, so far, I mean, as we are now at liberty to do it; for let me not be understood as capable of patronizing infidelity to existing engagements. I hold the maxim no less applicable to public than to private affairs that honesty is always the best policy. I repeat, therefore, let those engagements be observed in their genuine sense. But in my opinion it is unnecessary and would be unwise to extend them.

Taking care always to keep ourselves by suitable establishments on a respectable defensive posture, we may safely trust to temporary alliances for extraordinary emergencies....

In offering to you, my countrymen, these counsels of an old and affectionate friend I dare not hope they will make the strong and lasting impression I could wish—that they will control the usual current of the passions or prevent our nation from running the course which has hitherto marked the destiny of nations. But if I may even flatter myself that they may be productive of some partial benefit, some occasional good—that they may now and then recur to moderate the fury of party spirit, to warn against the mischiefs of foreign intrigue, to guard against the impostures of pretended patriotism—this hope will be a full recompense for the solicitude for your welfare by which they have been dictated.

How far in the discharge of my official duties I have been guided by the principles which have been delineated the public records and other evidences of my conduct must witness to you and to the world. To myself, the assurance of my own conscience is that I have at least believed myself to be guided by them....

Though in reviewing the incidents of my Administration I am unconscious of intentional error, I am nevertheless too sensible of my defects not to think it probable that I may have committed many errors. Whatever they may be, I fervently beseech the Almighty to avert or mitigate the evils to which they may tend. I shall also carry with me the hope that my country will never cease to view them with indulgence, and that, after forty-five years of my life dedicated to its service with an upright zeal, the faults of incompetent abilities will be consigned to oblivion, as myself must soon be to the mansions of rest.

Relying on its kindness in this as in other things, and actuated by that fervent love toward it which is so natural to a man who views in it the native soil of himself and his progenitors for several generations, I anticipate with pleasing expectation that retreat in which I promise myself to realize without alloy the sweet enjoyment of partaking in the midst of my fellow-citizens the benign influence of good laws under a free government—the ever-favorite object of my heart, and the happy reward, as I trust, of our mutual cares, labors, and dangers.

Thomas
JEFFERSON

3ᴿᴰ PRESIDENT: 1801–1809

Born: April 13, 1743, in Albermarle County, Virginia

Died: July 4, 1826, in Monticello in Virginia

Disc 1, Track 4

SPEECH

OF

THOMAS JEFFERSON, PRESIDENT OF THE UNITED STATES,

DELIVERED

AT HIS INSTALMENT,

MARCH 4, 1801,

AT THE CITY OF WASHINGTON.

FRIENDS, AND FELLOW-CITIZENS,

CALLED upon to undertake the duties of the first executive office of our country, I avail myself of the presence of that portion of my fellow-citizens, which is here assembled, to express my grateful thanks, for the favour with which they have been pleased to look towards me; to declare a sincere consciousness, that the task is above my talents; and that I approach it with those anxious and awful presentiments, which the greatness of the charge, and the weakness of my powers, so justly inspire. A rising nation, spread over a wide and fruitful land....traversing all the seas with the rich productions of their industry....engaged in commerce with nations who feel power and forget right....advancing rapidly to destinies beyond the reach of mortal eye....when I contemplate these transcendent objects, and see the honour, the happiness, and the hopes of this beloved country, committed to the issue and the auspices of this day, I shrink from the contemplation, and humble myself before the magnitude of the undertaking. Utterly, indeed, should I despair, did not the presence of many, whom I here see, remind me, that, in the other high authorities, provided by our constitution, I shall find resources of wisdom, of virtue, and of zeal, on which to rely under all difficulties. To you, then, gentlemen, who are charged with the sovereign functions of legislation, and to those associated with you, I look with encouragement for that guidance and support, which may enable us to steer, with safety, the vessel in which we are all embarked, amidst the conflicting elements of a troubled world.

During the contest of opinion, through which we have past, the animation of discussions and of exertions, has sometimes worn an aspect which might impose on strangers, unused to think freely, and to speak and to write what they think: but this being now decided by the voice of the nation, announced according to the rules of the constitution, all will, of course, arrange themselves under the will of the law, and unite in common efforts, for the common good. All, too, will bear in mind this sacred principle.... that though the will of the majority is, in all cases, to prevail, that will, to be rightful, must be reasonable....that the minority possess their equal rights, which equal laws must protect, and to violate would be oppression. Let us then, fellow-citizens, unite with one heart, and one mind. Let us restore to social intercourse, that harmony and affection, without which, liberty, and even life itself, are but dreary things. And let us reflect, that, having banished from our land, that religious intolerance, under which mankind so long bled and suffered, we have yet gained little, if we countenance a political intolerance, as despotic, as wicked, and capable of as bitter and bloody persecutions.

During the throes and convulsions of the ancient world....during the agonizing spasms of infuriated man, seeking, through blood and slaughter, his long-lost liberty ....it was not wonderful that the agitation of the billows should reach even this distant and peaceful shore....that this should be more felt and feared by some, and less by others....and should divide opinions, as to measures of safety. But every difference of opinion is not a difference of principle. We have called by different names, brethren of the same principle. WE ARE ALL REPUBLICANS; WE ARE ALL FEDERALISTS. If there

be any among us, who would wish to dissolve this union, or to change its republican form, let them stand undisturbed, as monuments of the safety with which error of opinion may be tolerated, where reason is left free to combat it. I know, indeed, that some honest men fear that a republican government cannot be strong.... that this government is not strong enough. But would the honest patriot, in the full tide of successful experiment, abandon a government which has so far kept us free and firm, on the theoretic and visionary fear, that this government, the world's best hope, may, by possibility, want energy to preserve itself?....I trust not....I believe this, on the contrary, the strongest government on earth....I believe it the only one, where every man, at the call of the law, would fly to the standard of the law, and would meet invasions of the public order as his own personal concern. Sometimes it is said, that man cannot be trusted with the government of himself. Can he then be trusted with the government of others? Or have we found angels, in the form of kings, to govern him? Let history answer this question.

Let us, then, with courage and confidence, pursue our own federal and republican principles....our attachment to union and representative government. Kindly separated, by nature and a wide ocean, from the exterminating havoc of one quarter of the globe....too high-minded to endure the degradations of the others....possessing a chosen country, with room enough for our descendents to the thousandth and thousandth generation....entertaining a due sense of our equal right to the use of our own faculties....to the acquisitions of our own industry....to honour and confidence from our fellow-citizens; resulting not from birth, but from our actions, and their sense of them....enlightened by a benign religion, professed, indeed, and practised in various forms, yet all of them inculcating honesty, truth, temperance, gratitude, and the love of man....acknowledging and adoring an over-ruling Providence, which, by all its dispensations, proves that it delights in the happiness of man here, and his greater happiness hereafter....with all these blessings, what more is necessary to make us a happy and a prosperous people?....Still one thing more, fellow-citizens, a wise and frugal government, which shall restrain men from injuring one another; shall leave them otherwise free to regulate their own pursuits of industry and improvement; and shall not take from the mouth of labor the bread it has earned. This is the sum of good government; and this is necessary to close the circle of our felicities.

About to enter, fellow-citizens, on the exercise of duties, which comprehend every thing dear and valuable to you, it is proper you should understand what I deem the essential principles of our government, and consequently those which ought to shape its administration. I will compress them within the narrowest compass they will bear, stating the general principle, but not all its limitations. Equal and exact justice to all men, of whatever state or persuasion, religious or political....peace, commerce, and honest friendship with all nations....entangling alliances with none....the support of the state governments in all their rights, as the most competent administrations for our domestic concerns, and the surest bulwarks against anti-republican tendencies....the preservation of the general

government in its whole constitutional vigor, as the sheet anchor of our peace at home, and safety abroad....a jealous care of the right of election by the people....a mild and safe corrective of abuses, which are lopped by the sword of revolution, where peaceable remedies are unprovided.... absolute acquiescence in the decisions of the majority, the vital principle of republics, from which is no appeal but to force, the vital principle and immediate parent of despotism....a well-disciplined militia, our best reliance in peace, and for the first moment of war, till regulars may relieve them....the supremacy of the civil over the military authority....economy in the public expence, that labor may be lightly burdened....the honest payment of our debts, and sacred preservation of public faith....encouragement of agriculture, and of commerce, as its handmaid....the diffusion of information, and arraignment of all abuses at the bar of the public reason....freedom of religion....freedom of the press....and freedom of person, under the protection of the habeas corpus, and trial by juries impartially selected. These principles form the bright constellation, which has gone before us, and guided our steps through an age of revolution and reformation. The wisdom of our sages, and blood of our heroes, have been devoted to their attainment. They should be the creed of our political faith....the text of civic instruction....the touchstone by which to try the services of those we trust: and should we wander from them, in moments of error or alarm, let us hasten to retrace our steps, and to regain the road which alone leads to peace, liberty, and safety.

I repair, then, fellow citizens, to the post you have assigned me. With experience enough in subordinate offices, to have seen the difficulties of this, the greatest of all, I have learned to expect, that it will rarely fall to the lot of imperfect man, to retire from this station, with the reputation, and the favor, which bring him into it. Without pretensions to that high confidence you reposed in our first and greatest revolutionary character, whose pre-eminent services had entitled him to the first place in his country's love, and destined for him the fairest page in the volume of faithful history, I ask so much confidence only, as may give firmness and effect to the legal administration of your affairs. I shall often go wrong, through defect of judgment. When right, I shall often be thought wrong, by those whose positions will not command a view of the whole ground. I ask your indulgence for my own errors, which will never be intentional; and your support against the errors of others, who may condemn what they would not, if seen in all its parts. The approbation implied by your suffrage, is a great consolation to me for the past; and my future solicitude will be, to retain the good opinion of those who have bestowed it in advance, to conciliate that of others by doing them all the good in my power, and to be instrumental to the happiness and freedom of all.

Relying, then, on the patronage of your good will I advance with obedience to the work, ready to retire from it whenever you become sensible how much better choices it is in your power to make. And may that infinite Power, which rules the destinies of the universe, lead our councils to what is best, and give them a favorable issue, for our peace and prosperity.

THOMAS JEFFERSON.

THIRD EDITION.

PHILADELPHIA, PUBLISHED BY MATHEW CAREY.

H. MAXWELL, PRINTER.

3

"WE ARE ALL REPUBLICANS, WE ARE ALL FEDERALISTS"

WHEN THOMAS JEFFERSON defeated President John Adams—"the revolution of 1800," the victor later called it—it was the nation's first transfer of power, and perhaps its most tumultuous election.

Divisions that began in Washington's term had burst into partisan warfare under Adams. Suspicious to the point of paranoia, Adams signed the Alien and Sedition Acts, which made it a crime to criticize the government. Jefferson and James Madison mobilized the new Republican Party (today's Democratic Party) to oust Adams' Federalists. In Jefferson's day, the people did not vote for presidential candidates. State legislatures chose members of the electoral college, and in the end, the Virginian won a narrow victory. But a constitutional fluke nearly let his foes derail the choice. Jefferson and his vice president–elect, Aaron Burr, though running as a ticket, had an equal number of electoral votes. Under the Constitution as then in effect, a tie vote threw the election into the Federalist-controlled House of Representatives. For weeks, it seemed bitter Federalists might tilt to Burr or seek to annul the election altogether. Finally, just eighteen days before Inauguration Day, on the thirty-sixth ballot, the House cast its lot with the dreaded Jefferson over the unprincipled Burr. (Alexander Hamilton helped undermine Burr. Four years later, Burr would kill Hamilton in a duel.) Adams left town by coach at four A.M. rather than attend his successor's swearing-in. Conspicuously dressed in common clothes, Jefferson walked two blocks from his boarding house to the partly built Capitol. He handed his inaugural address to a loyal newspaper publisher, who printed it in "Extra" editions sold on the streets outside by the time the ceremony was over. In this atmosphere of barely suppressed rancor,

Jefferson spoke so quietly that the hundreds crammed into the Senate chamber could hardly hear him.

His platform presence may have been wanting, but his inaugural address remains a classic. With eloquence and a sure political touch, he soothed still raw wounds. He urged his fellow citizens to "unite with one heart and one mind, to restore to social intercourse that harmony and affection without which liberty and even life itself are but dreary things." In the speech's most quoted lines, he reached to his political foes. "[E]very difference of opinion is not a difference of principle. We have called by different names brethren of the same principle. We are all Republicans, we are all Federalists." In his original handwritten text, those party names were not capitalized; editors who reprinted it altered the case. But surely Jefferson intended both meanings: all Americans, he seemed to say, supported both republican government and a strong federal presence. "With infinite tact the leader of the Republicans was carrying out his design of wooing the more moderate Federalists through appeals to reason and national unity," one historian noted. National survival required political tolerance.

Still, Jefferson couldn't resist swiping at the High Federalists, who sought a powerful central government for the United States. He privately derided them as "Monocrats" with little faith in democracy. "Sometimes it is said that man can not be trusted with the government of himself," he declared. "Can he, then, be trusted with the government of others? Or have we found angels in the forms of kings to govern him? Let history answer this question." The speech is remembered, too, for its articulation of general principles of sound government. "Equal and exact justice to all men, of whatever state or persuasion, religious or political," he said; "peace, commerce, and honest friendship with all nations, entangling alliances with none."

Jefferson took a distinctly restrained view of the presidency. Washington and Adams had gone before Congress to deliver the State of the Union message required by the Constitution; Jefferson thought this presumptuous, even kingly, and sent his messages in writing. (Presidents would follow this practice for more than a century.) Yet in office, he took numerous steps that enlarged the office and strengthened the government. In 1803, he agreed to the Louisiana Purchase from France, more than doubling the land mass of the United States, without prior congressional authorization. He waged undeclared war against France and the Barbary pirates as well. And he struggled with the courts, led by Chief Justice John Marshall, over proper powers of the branches of government.

We remember Jefferson's soothing tone as a moment when presidential eloquence helped defuse a tense time. George W. Bush cited his stance the night he prevailed in the contested presidential recount in 2000, decided by a 5–4 vote of the U.S. Supreme Court. And Bill Clinton quoted it in his farewell address from office.

Draft of Thomas Jefferson's first inaugural speech

Thomas Jefferson's
FIRST INAUGURAL ADDRESS

Washington, D.C. • March 4, 1801

*hear
disc 1
track 4

Friends and Fellow-Citizens:

Called upon to undertake the duties of the first executive office of our country, I avail myself of the presence of that portion of my fellow-citizens which is here assembled to express my grateful thanks for the favor with which they have been pleased to look toward me, to declare a sincere consciousness that the task is above my talents, and that I approach it with those anxious and awful presentiments which the greatness of the charge and the weakness of my powers so justly inspire. A rising nation, spread over a wide and fruitful land, traversing all the seas with the rich productions of their industry, engaged in commerce with nations who feel power and forget right, advancing rapidly to destinies beyond the reach of mortal eye—when I contemplate these transcendent objects, and see the honor, the happiness, and the hopes of this beloved country committed to the issue and the auspices of this day, I shrink from the contemplation, and humble myself before the magnitude of the undertaking. Utterly, indeed, should I despair did not the presence of many whom I here see remind me that in the other high authorities provided by our Constitution I shall find resources of wisdom, of virtue, and of zeal on which to rely under all difficulties. To you, then, gentlemen, who are charged with the sovereign functions of legislation, and to those associated with you, I look with encouragement for that guidance and support which may enable us to steer with safety the vessel in which we are all embarked amidst the conflicting elements of a troubled world.

During the contest of opinion through which we have passed the animation of discussions and of exertions has sometimes worn an aspect which might impose on strangers unused to think freely and to speak and to write what they think; but this being now decided by the voice of the nation, announced according to the rules of the Constitution, all will, of course, arrange themselves under the will of the law, and unite in common efforts for the common good. All, too, will bear in mind this sacred principle, that though the will of the majority is in all cases to prevail, that will to be rightful must be reasonable; that the minority possess their equal rights, which equal law must protect, and to violate would be oppression. Let us, then, fellow-citizens, unite with one heart and one mind. Let us restore to social intercourse that harmony and affection without which liberty and even life itself are but dreary things. And let us reflect that, having banished from our land that religious intolerance under which mankind so long bled and suffered, we have yet gained little if we countenance a political intolerance as despotic, as wicked, and capable of as bitter and bloody persecutions. During the throes and convulsions of the ancient world, during the agonizing spasms of infuriated man, seeking through blood and slaughter his long-lost liberty, it was not wonderful that the agitation of the billows should reach even this distant and peaceful shore; that this should be more felt and feared by some and less by others, and should divide opinions as to measures of safety. But

> *"The task is above my talents, and I approach it with those anxious and awful presentiments which the greatness of the charge and the weakness of my powers so justly inspire."*

every difference of opinion is not a difference of principle. We have called by different names brethren of the same principle. We are all Republicans, we are all Federalists. If there be any among us who would wish to dissolve this Union or to change its republican form, let them stand undisturbed as monuments of the safety with which error of opinion may be tolerated where reason is left free to combat it. I know, indeed, that some honest men fear that a republican government can not be strong, that this Government is not strong enough; but would the honest patriot, in the full tide of successful experiment, abandon a government which has so far kept us free and firm on the theoretic and visionary fear that this Government, the world's best hope, may by possibility want energy to preserve itself? I trust not. I believe this, on the contrary, the strongest Government on earth. I believe it the only one where every man, at the call of the law, would fly to the standard of the law, and would meet invasions of the public order as his own personal concern. Sometimes it is said that man can not be trusted with the government of himself. Can he, then, be trusted with the government of others? Or have we found angels in the forms of kings to govern him? Let history answer this question.

Let us, then, with courage and confidence pursue our own Federal and Republican principles, our attachment to union and representative government. Kindly separated by nature and a wide ocean from the exterminating havoc of one quarter of the globe; too high-minded to endure the degradations of the others; possessing a chosen country, with room enough for our descendants to the thousandth and thousandth generation; entertaining a due sense of our

"Let us restore to social intercourse that harmony and affection without which liberty and even life itself are but dreary things."

equal right to the use of our own faculties, to the acquisitions of our own industry, to honor and confidence from our fellow-citizens, resulting not from birth, but from our actions and their sense of them; enlightened by a benign religion, professed, indeed, and practiced in various forms, yet all of them inculcating honesty, truth, temperance, gratitude, and the love of man; acknowledging and adoring an overruling Providence, which by all its dispensations proves that it delights in the happiness of man here and his greater happiness hereafter—with all these blessings, what more is necessary to make us a happy and prosperous people? Still one thing more, fellow-citizens—a wise and frugal Government, which shall restrain men from injuring one another, shall leave them otherwise free to regulate their own pursuits of industry and improvement, and shall not take from the mouth of labor the bread it has earned. This is the sum of good government, and this is necessary to close the circle of our felicities.

About to enter, fellow-citizens, on the exercise of duties which comprehend everything dear and valuable to you, it is proper you should understand what I deem the essential principles of our Government, and consequently those which ought to shape its Administration. I will compress them within the narrowest compass they will bear, stating the general principle, but not all its limitations. Equal and exact justice to all men, of whatever state or persuasion, religious or political; peace, commerce, and honest friendship with all nations, entangling alliances with none; the support of the State governments in all their rights, as the most competent administrations for our domestic concerns and the surest bulwarks against antirepublican tendencies; the preservation of the General Government in its whole constitutional vigor, as the sheet anchor of our peace at home and safety abroad; a jealous care of the right of election by the people—a mild and safe corrective of abuses which are lopped by the sword of revolution where peaceable remedies are unprovided; absolute acquiescence in the decisions of the majority, the vital principle of republics, from which is no appeal but to force, the vital principle and immediate parent of despotism; a well disciplined militia, our best reliance in peace and for the first moments of war, till regulars may relieve them; the supremacy of the civil over the military authority; economy in the public expense, that labor may be lightly burthened; the honest payment of our debts and sacred preservation of the public faith; encouragement of agriculture, and of commerce as its hand-maid; the diffusion of information and arraignment of all abuses at the bar of the public reason; freedom of religion; freedom of the press, and freedom of person under the protection of the habeas corpus, and trial by juries impartially selected. These principles form the bright constellation which has gone before us and guided our steps through an age of revolution and reformation. The wisdom of our sages and blood of our heroes have been devoted to their attainment. They should be the creed of our political faith, the text of civic instruction, the touchstone by which to try the services of those we trust; and should we wander from them in moments of error or of alarm, let us hasten to retrace our steps and to regain the road which alone leads to peace, liberty, and safety.

I repair, then, fellow-citizens, to the post you have assigned me. With experience enough in subordinate offices to have seen the difficulties of this the greatest of all, I have learnt to expect that it will rarely fall to the lot of imperfect man to retire from this station with the reputation and the favor which bring him into it. Without pretensions to that high confidence you reposed in our first and greatest revolutionary character, whose preeminent services had entitled him to the first place in his country's love and destined for him the fairest page in the volume of faithful history, I

ask so much confidence only as may give firmness and effect to the legal administration of your affairs. I shall often go wrong through defect of judgment. When right, I shall often be thought wrong by those whose positions will not command a view of the whole ground. I ask your indulgence for my own errors, which will never be intentional, and your support against the errors of others, who may condemn what they would not if seen in all its parts. The approbation implied by your suffrage is a great consolation to me for the past, and my future solicitude will be to retain the good opinion of those who have bestowed it in advance, to conciliate that of others by doing them all the good in my power, and to be instrumental to the happiness and freedom of all.

Relying, then, on the patronage of your good will, I advance with obedience to the work, ready to retire from it whenever you become sensible how much better choice it is in your power to make. And may that Infinite Power which rules the destinies of the universe lead our councils to what is best, and give them a favorable issue for your peace and prosperity.

"Sometimes it is said that man can not be trusted with the government of himself. Can he, then, be trusted with the government of others?"

Andrew
JACKSON

7ᵀᴴ PRESIDENT: 1829–1837

Born: March 15, 1767, in Waxhaw, South Carolina

Died: June 8, 1845, at the Hermitage near Nashville, Tennessee

Disc 1, Tracks 5–6

4

"THE RICH AND POWERFUL TOO OFTEN BEND THE ACTS OF GOVERNMENT TO THEIR SELFISH PURPOSES"

IN THE NINETEENTH CENTURY, presidents rarely dominated government, and even less often appealed directly to voters for support. Andrew Jackson's two terms proved a significant exception. Jackson, a war hero and Indian fighter, brought enormous personal popularity to the office, and led the first modern political party—the Republican-Democrats, soon renamed the Democrats—with a Jeffersonian battle cry, "Equal rights for all, special privilege for none." Jackson was ahead of his time in seeing the latent power of a popular presidency. As states opened the rolls of voters to those without property (albeit only to white men), voter turnout doubled the year he was elected compared to four years before.

Jackson summoned that popular support in the grand political battle of his two terms, the "War Against the Bank." The Second Bank of the United States, successor to the bank founded by Alexander Hamilton and symbol of the nation's financial elite, served as a sort of privately owned central bank, chartered by the government. (Among other things, it printed the nation's paper money.) Its president, Nicholas Biddle, decided to force the issue of its role by seeking a recharter from Congress years ahead of schedule, in 1832. By threatening economic upheaval in an election year, Biddle sought to give Jackson no choice but to agree. Jackson believed the bank threatened the emerging democratic order, hoarding too much economic power in too few hands. He called it "The Monster."

With its financial capital, the bank had amassed enormous political capital. It won a new charter from Congress by comfortable margins. At first, it seemed Jackson might have no choice but to assent. Martin Van Buren, a key advisor, found the aged general resting on a couch in the White House. "The bank, Mr. Van Buren, is trying to kill me," Jackson said. "*But I will kill it.*" He decided to risk the political backlash and veto the bill. His cabinet wanted Jackson to leave room for compromise in the veto message, but Jackson did not want to reform the Bank; he wanted to finish it off. So he turned to a group of mostly unofficial advisors to draft the message, including Roger Taney, later chief justice of the United States. Jackson was no writer, but he understood well the virtues of vituperation. "What the president wanted was a message that had force and logic and strength to carry it across the nation and convince the people of its fundamental truth," historian Robert V. Remini explained. "Naturally he needed a closely reasoned paper, but he also desired one that would stir men and reach their minds and hearts, one that could later serve as a propaganda document during the election." An otherwise admiring Arthur M. Schlesinger Jr. calls the language "demagogic."

Later, a president seeking to sway public opinion might make an Oval Office television address or launch a speaking tour. In 1832, Jackson used the new machinery of party politics to distribute the message and amplify his ringing words. Local party newspapers reprinted the veto; it was read aloud to mass meetings; and Democratic clubs passed resolutions and staged parades.

The veto message had several themes. Jackson believed the Bank charter violated the Constitution. The U.S. Supreme Court had already ruled otherwise, in the case of *McCullough v. Maryland*. But Jackson asserted that the president and Congress each have a duty to conclude whether a law is constitutional, too. He also asserted the Bank encroached on the authority of the executive. But Jackson's arguments went beyond that. Previous presidents had issued only nine vetoes, all on constitutional grounds. Jackson for the first time explicitly vetoed a bill because he thought it was bad policy. The arguments that rang loudest were those designed to sway public opinion. Jackson simply ignored the substantial benefits to a growing economy of a strong central bank—a point that would seem obvious to later generations. Rather, he focused on the anti-democratic import of such a concentration of capital. The concluding paragraphs were widely reprinted. "It is to be regretted that the rich and powerful too often bend the acts of government to their selfish purposes," Jackson thundered. Government cannot legislate equality in result, but it can secure equal opportunity. Jackson appealed to "the humble members of society—the farmers, mechanics, and laborers" who watch as "the rich get richer." His words stirred issues of class and economic power that would only grow more potent with industrialization.

The veto message caused a sensation. Congress debated fiercely but could not muster the two-thirds vote required

to override it. Thus the issue, in effect, was put to the voters: the great Senator Henry Clay of Kentucky, a leading friend of the bank, ran against Jackson. The Bank poured huge funds into the effort to defeat the president. When Jackson easily won reelection, he prepared to shut down the Bank—still running under its old charter—altogether. The next year, he announced the national government would withdraw its funds from the Bank of the United States and place them in various state banks (dubbed "pet banks"). Biddle responded by cutting off loans made by the bank, causing a swift economic crash, unmistakably pressuring the president to relent. The Senate censured Jackson for his action. But public opinion turned against the Bank, and by 1834, it closed. Over years the lack of a central monetary authority threw the economy into repeated recession, a connection little understood at the time. Well recognized were the political consequences of Jackson's strong words: more than any other early president, Jackson spoke as more than just the "Chief Magistrate" who supervised the executive branch, but the voice of the people in Washington. His two terms served as the model for strong and vocal presidents in later years.

Jackson holding the "Order for the Removal of the Public Money deposited in the United States Bank"

Andrew Jackson's
VETO OF THE BANK OF THE UNITED STATES

Published July 10, 1832

To the Senate:

The bill "to modify and continue" the act entitled "An act to incorporate the subscribers to the Bank of the United States" was presented to me on the 4th July instant. Having considered it with that solemn regard to the principles of the Constitution which the day was calculated to inspire, and come to the conclusion that it ought not to become a law, I herewith return it to the Senate, in which it originated, with my objections....

[*Jackson goes through the provisions of the bill with which he disagrees. He focuses on the fact that much of the bank's stock is owned by foreign investors.*]

Should the stock of the bank principally pass into the hands of the subjects of a foreign country, and we should unfortunately become involved in a war with that country, what would be our condition? Of the course which would be pursued by a bank almost wholly owned by the subjects of a foreign power, and managed by those whose interests, if not affections, would run in the same direction there can be no doubt. All its operations within would be in aid of the hostile fleets and armies without. Controlling our currency, receiving our public moneys, and holding thousands of our citizens in dependence, it would be more formidable and dangerous than the naval and military power of the enemy.

If we must have a bank with private stockholders, every consideration of sound policy and every impulse of American feeling admonishes that it should be *purely American*. Its stockholders should be composed exclusively of our own citizens, who at least ought to be friendly to our Government and willing to support it in times of difficulty and danger....

It is maintained by the advocates of the bank that its constitutionality in all its features ought to be considered as settled by precedent and by the decision of the Supreme Court. To this conclusion I can not assent....

[*Then Jackson argues that the Supreme Court is not the only judge of constitutionality.*]

> *"It ought not to become a law, I herewith return it to the Senate, in which it originated, with my objections...."*

If the opinion of the Supreme Court covered the whole ground of this act, it ought not to control the coordinate authorities of this Government. The Congress, the Executive, and the Court must each for itself be guided by its own opinion of the Constitution. Each public officer who takes an oath to support the Constitution swears that he will support it as he understands it, and not as it is understood by others. It is as much the duty of the House of Representatives, of the Senate, and of the President to decide upon the constitutionality of any bill or resolution which may be presented to them for passage or approval as it is of the supreme judges when it may be brought before them for judicial decision. The opinion of the judges has no more authority over Congress than the opinion of Congress has over the judges, and on that point the President is independent of both. The authority of the Supreme Court must not, therefore, be permitted to control the Congress or the Executive when acting in their legislative capacities, but to have only such influence as the force of their reasoning may deserve....

[*Jackson then explains his view that the law granting a monopoly charter to the bank was an unconstitutional assertion of power by the Congress.*]

Under such circumstances the bank comes forward and asks a renewal of its charter for a term of fifteen years upon conditions which not only operate as a gratuity to the stockholders of many millions of dollars, but will sanction any abuses and legalize any encroachments.

Suspicions are entertained and charges are made of gross abuse and violation of its charter. An investigation unwillingly conceded and so restricted in time as necessarily to make it incomplete and unsatisfactory discloses enough to excite suspicion and alarm. In the practices of the principal bank partially unveiled, in the absence of important witnesses, and in numerous charges confidently made and as yet wholly uninvestigated there was enough to induce a majority of the committee of investigation—a committee which was selected from the most able and honorable members of the House of Representatives—to recommend a suspension of further action upon the bill and a prosecution of the inquiry. As the charter had yet four years to run, and as a renewal now was not necessary to the successful prosecution of its business, it was to have been expected that the bank itself, conscious of its purity and proud of its character, would have withdrawn its application for the present, and demanded the severest scrutiny into all its transactions. In their declining to do so there seems to be an additional reason why the functionaries of the Government should proceed with less haste and more caution in the renewal of their monopoly.

The bank is professedly established as an agent of the executive branch of the Government, and its constitutionality is maintained on that ground. Neither upon the propriety of present action nor upon the provisions of this act was the Executive consulted. It has had no opportunity to say that it neither needs nor wants an agent clothed with such powers and favored by such exemptions. There is nothing in its legitimate functions which makes it necessary or proper. Whatever interest or influence, whether public or private, has given birth to this act, it can not be found either in the wishes or necessities of the executive department, by which present action is deemed premature, and the powers conferred upon its agent not only unnecessary, but dangerous to the Government and country.

> *"It is as much the duty of the House of Representatives, of the Senate, and of the President to decide upon the constitutionality of any bill or resolution as it is of the supreme judges."*

It is to be regretted that the rich and powerful too often bend the acts of government to their selfish purposes. Distinctions in society will always exist under every just government. Equality of talents, of education, or of wealth can not be produced by human institutions. In the full enjoyment of the gifts of Heaven and the fruits of superior industry, economy, and virtue, every man is equally entitled to protection by law; but when the laws undertake to add to these natural and just advantages artificial distinctions, to grant titles, gratuities, and exclusive privileges, to make the rich richer and the potent more powerful, the humble members of society—the farmers, mechanics, and laborers—who have neither the time nor the means of securing like favors to themselves, have a right to complain of the injustice of their Government. There are no necessary evils in government. Its evils exist only in its abuses. If it would confine itself to equal protection, and, as Heaven does its rains, shower its favors alike on the high and the low, the rich and the poor, it would be an unqualified blessing. In the act before me there seems to be a wide and unnecessary departure from these just principles.

Nor is our Government to be maintained or our Union preserved by invasions of the rights and powers of the several States. In thus attempting to make our General Government strong we make it weak. Its true strength consists in leaving individuals and States as much as possible to themselves—in making itself felt, not in its power, but in its beneficence; not in its control, but in its protection; not in binding the States more closely to the center, but leaving each to move unobstructed in its proper orbit.

Experience should teach us wisdom. Most of the difficulties our Government now encounters and most of the dangers which impend over our Union have sprung from an abandonment of the legitimate objects of Government by our national legislation, and the adoption of such principles as are embodied in this act. Many of our rich men have not been content with equal protection and equal benefits, but have besought us to make them richer by act of Congress. By attempting to gratify their desires we have in the results of our legislation arrayed section against section, interest against interest, and man against man, in a fearful commotion which threatens to shake the foundations of our Union. It is time to pause in our career to review our principles, and if possible revive that devoted patriotism and spirit of compromise which distinguished the sages of the Revolution and the fathers of our Union. If we can not at once, in justice to interests vested under improvident legislation, make our Government what it ought to be, we can at least take a stand against all new grants of monopolies and exclusive privileges, against any prostitution of our Government to the advancement of the few at the expense of the many, and in favor of compromise and gradual reform in our code of laws and system of political economy.

I have now done my duty to my country. If sustained by my fellow-citizens, I shall be grateful and happy; if not, I shall find in the motives which impel me ample grounds for contentment and peace. In the difficulties which surround us and the dangers which threaten our institutions there is cause for neither dismay nor alarm. For relief and deliverance let us firmly rely on that kind Providence which I am sure watches with peculiar care over the destinies of our Republic, and on the intelligence and wisdom of our countrymen. Through *His* abundant goodness and *their* patriotic devotion our liberty and Union will be preserved.

"There are no necessary evils in government. Its evils exist only in its abuses."

5

"DISUNION BY ARMED FORCE IS TREASON"

THROUGH ITS FIRST DECADES, the United States felt the pull of disunion—facing questions about the nature of the nation not finally answered until the Civil War. John C. Calhoun of South Carolina, Andrew Jackson's vice president, was the chief proponent of a dramatic and destabilizing constitutional doctrine: nullification. Each state, Calhoun asserted, could decide for itself whether a federal law would be enforced within its borders. Behind the theory, southerners feared the national government might someday interfere with slavery. Though a slave owner, Jackson made his position clear in his toast at a large Democratic Party banquet in 1830. "Our Union," he declared, "*it must be preserved.*" Calhoun glared and replied: "The Union, next to our liberty, the most dear."

Two years later, nullification moved from dangerous doctrine to threatening crisis. The issue was not slavery, but the tariff. Northern states wanted a high tariff on imported goods to protect domestic industry. Southern states wanted low tariffs. South Carolina, especially, rebelled against the tax. Prodded by Calhoun, the state legislature moved toward putting the theory into effect. If nullification held, within a short time the United States might descend into anarchy.

Jackson trod carefully, seeking to crush the movement without alienating other southerners. He proposed a modified tariff, but that was not enough for the South Carolina nullifiers. The state's legislature appointed a convention to take action. Jackson mobilized the military and rushed the navy to Charleston. On November 29, 1832, South Carolina enacted an Ordinance of Nullification, declaring the federal government's tariffs void in the state. The next month, Calhoun resigned the vice presidency to take a seat

in the U.S. Senate so he could defend his home state. Jackson knew he could not simply send troops. "The union…will now be tested by the support I get by the people," he wrote privately. "I will die with the union." He wanted to stir dissent within South Carolina, too, so that anti-nullification forces would prepare to take arms. As

Andrew Jackson, published by Nathaniel Currier

30

with the Bank veto, he recognized that his message must be more a persuasive political paper than a dry legal document.

Jackson gave the job of drafting to Secretary of State Edward Livingston, but was unhappy with the work of Livingston and his aides. The old general urgently rewrote, pressed for arguments to be sharpened, hardened the angry language—aware of the historic import, he wrote a date and time on each revision. The document is a monument of constitutional argument. He denounced the nullifiers, in language he ordered the printer to italicize: "I consider, then, the power to annul a law of the United States, assumed by one State, *incompatible with the existence of the Union, contradicted expressly by the letter of the Constitution, unauthorized by its spirit, inconsistent with every principle on which it was founded and destructive of the great object for which it was formed.*" He systematically demolished the nullifiers' arguments. The Union, he said, predated the states and the Constitution; the people, not the states, created the government. The Union is perpetual. Then his tone shifts. He closed with an emotional appeal to the people of the rebellious state, asking them if they really wanted to discard "the very name of Americans." And then a threat: if they continued to act, he would crush them, and civil war would result.

Mass meetings and patriotic ceremonies around the country cheered the message, and several state legislatures, including some in the South, passed resolutions of agreement. South Carolina prepared for war, organizing an army. Congress passed a force bill, requested by Jackson, to authorize military action—but at the same time lowered the tariff. South Carolina retreated. Americans averted bloodshed—for a time. Many of the same issues arose again less than thirty years later. As a young lawyer, Abraham Lincoln carefully studied Jackson's nullification proclamation, and he relied heavily on its arguments in his first inaugural address on the eve of the Civil War.

Andrew Jackson's
PROCLAMATION ON NULLIFICATION

Published December 10, 1832

*hear....

disc 1
track 6

... I consider, then, the power to annul a law of the United States, assumed by one State, *incompatible with the existence of the Union, contradicted expressly by the letter of the Constitution, unauthorized by its spirit, inconsistent with every principle on which it was founded, and destructive of the great object for which it was formed.*

...The people of the United States formed the Constitution, acting through the State legislatures in making the compact, to meet and discuss its provisions, and acting in separate conventions when they ratified those provisions; but the terms used in its construction show it to be a Government in which the people of all the States, collectively, are represented. We are *one people* in the choice of President and Vice-President....

The Constitution of the United States, then, forms a *government*, not a league; and whether it be formed by compact between the States or in any other manner, its character is the same.

> *"Look on this picture of happiness and honor and say,* We too are citizens of America."

...The unity of our political character (as has been shown for another purpose) commenced with its very existence. Under the royal Government we had no separate character; our opposition to its oppression began as *united colonies*. We were the *United States* under the Confederation, and the name was perpetuated and the Union rendered more perfect by the Federal Constitution. In none of these stages did we consider ourselves in any other light than as forming one nation. Treaties and alliances were made in the name of all. Troops were raised for the joint defense. How, then, with all these proofs that under all changes of our position we had, for designated purposes and with defined powers, created national governments, how is it that the most perfect of these several modes of union should now be considered as a mere league that may be dissolved at pleasure?...

So obvious are the reasons which forbid this secession that it is necessary only to allude to them. The Union was formed for the benefit of all. It was produced by mutual sacrifices of interests and opinions. Can those sacrifices be recalled? Can the States who magnanimously surrendered their title to the territories of the West recall the grant? Will the inhabitants of the inland States agree to pay the duties that may be imposed without their assent by those on the Atlantic or the Gulf for their own benefit? Shall there be a free port in one State and onerous duties in another? No one believes that any right exists in a single State to involve all the others in these and countless other evils contrary to engagements solemnly made. Everyone must see that the other States, in self-defense, must oppose it at all hazards....

[It] is the intent of this instrument to *proclaim*, not only that the duty imposed on me by the Constitution, "to take care that the laws be faithfully executed," shall be performed to the extent of the powers already vested in me by law, or of such others as the wisdom of Congress shall devise and intrust to me for that purpose, but to warn the citizens of South Carolina who have been deluded into an opposition to the laws of the danger they will incur by obedience to the illegal and disorganizing ordinance of the convention; to exhort those who have refused to support it to persevere in their determination to uphold the Constitution and laws of their country; and to point out to all the perilous situation into which the good people of that State have been led, and that the course they are urged to pursue is one of ruin and disgrace to the very State whose rights they affect to support.

"Do our neighboring republics, every day suffering some new revolution or contending with some new insurrection—do they excite your envy?"

Fellow-citizens of my native State, let me not only admonish you, as the First Magistrate of our common country, not to incur the penalty of its laws, but use the influence that a father would over his children whom he saw rushing to certain ruin. In that paternal language, with that paternal feeling, let me tell you, my countrymen, that you are deluded by men who are either deceived themselves or wish to deceive you. Mark under what pretenses you have been led on to the brink of insurrection and treason on which you stand. First a diminution of the value of your staple commodity, lowered by overproduction in other quarters, and the consequent diminution in the value of your lands were the sole effect of the tariff laws. The effect of those laws was confessedly injurious, but the evil was greatly exaggerated by the unfounded theory you were taught to believe—that its burthens were in proportion to your exports, not to your consumption of imported articles. Your pride was roused by the assertion that a submission to those laws was a state of vassalage and that resistance to them was equal in patriotic merit to the opposition our fathers offered to the oppressive laws of Great Britain. You were told that this opposition might be peaceably, might be constitutionally, made; that you might enjoy all the advantages of the Union and bear none of its burthens. Eloquent appeals to your passions, to your State pride, to your native courage, to your sense of real injury, were used to prepare you for the period when the mask which concealed the hideous features of *disunion* should be taken off. It fell, and you were made to look with complacency on objects which not long since you would have regarded with horror....

I have urged you to look back to the means that were used to hurry you on to the position you have now assumed and forward to the consequences it will produce. Something more is necessary. Contemplate the condition of that country of which you still form an important part. Consider its Government, uniting in one bond of common interest and general protection so many different States, giving to all their inhabitants the proud title of *American citizen*, protecting their commerce, securing their literature and their arts, facilitating their intercommunication, defending their frontiers, and making their name respected in the remotest parts of the earth. Consider the extent of its territory, its increasing and happy population, its advance in arts which render life agreeable, and the sciences which elevate the mind! See education spreading the lights of religion, morality, and general information into every cottage in this wide extent of our Territories and States. Behold it as the asylum where the wretched and the oppressed find a refuge and support. Look on this picture of happiness and honor and say, *We too are citizens of America.* Carolina is one of these proud States; her arms have defended, her best blood has cemented, this happy Union. And then add, if you can, without horror and remorse, This happy Union we will dissolve; this picture of peace and prosperity we will deface; this free intercourse we will interrupt; these fertile fields we will deluge with blood; the protection of that glorious flag we renounce; the very name of Americans we discard. And for what, mistaken men? For what do you throw away these inestimable blessings? For what would you exchange your share in the advantages and honor of the Union? For the dream of a separate independence—a dream interrupted by bloody conflicts with your neighbors and a vile dependence on a foreign power. If your leaders could succeed in establishing a separation, what would be your situation? Are you united at home? Are you free from the apprehension of civil discord, with all its fearful consequences? Do our neighboring republics, every day suffering some new revolution or contending with some new insurrection, do they excite your envy? But the dictates of a high duty oblige me solemnly to announce that you cannot succeed. The laws of the United States must be executed. I have no discretionary power on the subject; my duty is emphatically pronounced in the Constitution. Those who told you that you might peaceably prevent their execution deceived you; they could not have been deceived themselves. They know that a forcible opposition could alone prevent the execution of the laws, and they know that such opposition must be repelled. Their object is disunion. But be not deceived by names. Disunion, by armed force, is *treason*. Are you really ready to incur its guilt? If you are, on the head of the instigators of the act be the dreadful consequences; on their heads be the dishonor, but on yours may fall the punishment. On your unhappy State will inevitably fall all the evils of the conflict you force upon the Government of your country. It cannot accede to the mad project of disunion, of which you would be the first victims. Its First Magistrate can not, if he would, avoid the performance of his duty. The consequence must be fearful for you, distressing to your fellow-citizens here and to the friends of good government throughout the world. Its enemies have beheld our prosperity with a vexation they could not conceal; it was a standing refutation of their slavish doctrines, and they will point to our discord with the triumph of malignant joy. It is yet in your power to disappoint them....

Fellow-citizens, the momentous case is before you. On your undivided support of your Government depends the decision of the great question it involves—whether your sacred Union will be preserved and the blessing it secures to us as one people shall be perpetuated. No one can doubt that the unanimity with which that decision will be expressed will be such as to inspire new confidence in republican institutions, and that the prudence, the wisdom, and the courage which it will bring to their defense will transmit

> ## *"Their object is disunion, but be not deceived by names; disunion, by armed force, is* treason."

them unimpaired and invigorated to our children.

May the Great Ruler of Nations grant that the signal blessings with which He has favored ours may not, by the madness of party or personal ambition, be disregarded and lost; and may His wise providence bring those who have produced this crisis to see the folly before they feel the misery of civil strife, and inspire a returning veneration for that Union which, if we may dare to penetrate His designs, He has chosen as the only means of attaining the high destinies to which we may reasonably aspire.

In testimony whereof I have caused the seal of the United States to be hereunto affixed, having signed the same with my hand.

Done at the city of Washington, this 10th day of December, A.D. 1832, and of the Independence of the United States the fifty-seventh.

Abraham
LINCOLN

16ᵀᴴ PRESIDENT: 1861–1865

Born: February 12, 1809, near Hodgenville, Hardin County, Kentucky

Died: April 15, 1865, assassinated in Washington, D.C.

Disc 1, Tracks 7–10

6

"A HOUSE DIVIDED AGAINST ITSELF CANNOT STAND"

ABRAHAM LINCOLN RAPIDLY rose to power in the tumult of controversy over slavery. He prevailed, ultimately, by force of arms in a brutal civil war. But he is remembered for the muscular beauty of his words.

For half a century, slavery festered, threatening to split the country as it reminded of the unfinished work of the Revolution. In 1820, the Missouri Compromise contained slavery in the South: northern territories would be free soil. But in the 1850s, instead of shriveling, slavery seemed to strengthen. In 1854, the Kansas-Nebraska Act gave new states the power to choose whether to be slave or free. Three years later, the U.S. Supreme Court made matters worse. In the *Dred Scott* decision, the Court ruled that Congress had no power at all to prohibit slavery in the territories. Kansas was torn by a violent struggle, as a rump faction of settlers sought admission for the state to the Union with a proslavery constitution. A bitter, agitating debate roiled the country.

Senator Stephen Douglas of Illinois was a leading Democrat and likely presidential candidate. The "Little Giant" broke with other party leaders and opposed Kansas's slave constitution. Douglas also argued that each new state should be able to decide for itself whether to be slave or free. This was good enough for some East Coast leaders of the new Republican Party, who wanted the Illinois chapter to back Douglas for reelection to the Senate. But Douglas's local foes refused.

Republican delegates gathered in the legislative chambers in Springfield to back a candidate for senate, and their choice was unanimous. Abraham Lincoln was a prosperous but little-known trial lawyer, who made his living riding from town to town in the judicial circuit to argue cases for railroads and other clients. He had served one term in Congress a decade before (when he opposed the Mexican-American War). But he was deft and known for eloquence. At eight in the evening on the night of June 16, from memory, he declaimed a speech accepting the nomination for Senate.

Lincoln long had been critical of slavery in the South; now he saw it as a threat to the North as well. His strident speech seemed to prophecy civil war. His political advisors warned him that the speech was "radical" and "dangerous." It also sliced through Douglas' arguments. Lincoln had carefully studied the Bible, Shakespeare, and the classic speeches of the great American orators—Clay, Calhoun, and Daniel Webster. He was already developing a lean style, shorn of ornamentation. His rapt listeners would hear the echo of the opening lines of a famous speech delivered by Webster in a debate with Robert Hayne on the floor of the U.S. Senate, but in a new, stripped-down style.

At the heart of the speech, Lincoln chose a scriptural metaphor: "A house divided against itself cannot stand." The poet Carl Sandburg wrote of this opening, "This was so plain that two farmers fixing fences on a rainy morning could talk it over." The passage was found in two of the Gospels. Lincoln had used the image as early as 1843 in a political speech, and Bible-reading audiences of Illinois knew it well.

Lincoln repeatedly charged there was a conspiracy to extend slavery to the entire nation, a conspiracy that included President James Buchanan and the reactionary Supreme Court. Douglas had contributed to that conspiracy. Therefore, he must be defeated. "The three sections...

had the inevitability of a syllogism," David Herbert Donald noted in his Pulitzer Prize–winning biography, *Lincoln*. His goal was to polarize opinion, "to elicit a clear-cut decision" on slavery. In fact, there was no actual plot to nationalize slavery, though Lincoln believed there was. By implying that slavery would be eradicated from the Union, the speech was heard as a call to arms—probably far more than Lincoln actually felt, or was able to say at the time.

The "House Divided" speech began the pyrotechnics in one of the most fabled campaigns ever. A month later, Lincoln attended a speech given by Douglas, and then the next day offered a reply. He began to follow the better-known incumbent across Illinois, and then challenged him to debate. They met in a series of seven debates across the state, shouting out their speeches to crowds as large as twelve thousand.

In the end, Douglas won. (Senators then were not elected by the public, but by state legislators.) Lincoln told visitors, "I feel like the boy who stubbed his toe. I am too big to cry and too badly hurt to laugh." But now he was a national figure. The issue of slavery had been joined. And civil war approached.

Abraham Lincoln's

ADDRESS TO THE STATE REPUBLICAN CONVENTION

Springfield, Illinois • June 16, 1858

*hear....

disc 1
track 7

Mr. President, and Gentlemen of the Convention:

If we could first know *where* we are, and *whither* we are tending, we could better judge *what* to do, and *how* to do it.

We are now far into the fifth year since a policy was initiated with the avowed object and confident promise of putting an end to slavery agitation.

Under the operation of that policy, that agitation has, not only not ceased, but has constantly augmented.

In my opinion, it will not cease until a crisis shall have been reached and passed.

"A house divided against itself cannot stand."

I believe this government cannot endure permanently half slave and half free.

I do not expect the Union to be dissolved—I do not expect the house to fall—but I do expect it will cease to be divided.

It will become all one thing or all the other.

Either the opponents of slavery will arrest the further spread of it, and place it where the public mind shall rest in the belief that it is in the course of ultimate extinction; or its advocates will push it forward, till it shall become alike lawful in all the States, old as well as new—North as well as South.

Have we no tendency to the latter condition?

"A *house divided against itself cannot stand.*"

Let any one who doubts carefully contemplate that now almost complete legal combination—piece of machinery, so as to speak—compounded of the Nebraska doctrine and the *Dred Scott* decision. Let him consider not only what work the machinery is adapted to do, and how well adapted, but also let him study the history of its construction, and trace, if he can, or rather fail, if he can, to trace the evidence of design and concert of action among its chief bosses, from the beginning.

[*Lincoln then, at length, traces the workings of what he charged was a conspiracy to extend slavery, beginning with the Kansas-Nebraska Act. He charges that President*

James Buchanan and other Democrats pushed the question of slavery into the Supreme Court, knowing it would rule as it did. Douglas and Buchanan, Lincoln said, were engaging in a "squabble" over a "mere question of fact," whether the pro-slavery constitution in Kansas actually represented the will of the people there. Douglas said he didn't care whether the state was in fact slave or free—and that helped prepare the North for its eventual expansion.]

> *"We shall lie down pleasantly dreaming that the people of Missouri are on the verge of making their State free, and we shall awake to the reality instead, that the Supreme Court has made Illinois a slave State."*

It will throw additional light on the latter, to go back, and run the mind over the string of historical facts already stated. Several things will now appear less dark and mysterious than they did when they were transpiring. The people were to be left "perfectly free," "subject only to the Constitution." What the Constitution had to do with it, outsiders could not then see. Plainly enough now, it was an exactly fitted niche, for the *Dred Scott* decision to afterward come in, and declare the perfect freedom of the people, to be just no freedom at all.

Why was the amendment, expressly declaring the right of the people, voted down? Plainly enough now: the adoption of it would have spoiled the niche for the *Dred Scott* decision.

Why was the court decision held up? Why even a Senator's individual opinion withheld, till after the presidential election? Plainly enough now, the speaking out then would have damaged the perfectly free argument upon which the election was to be carried.

Why the outgoing President's felicitation on the indorsement? Why the delay of a re-argument? Why the incoming President's advance exhortation in favor of the decision?

These things look like the cautious patting and petting of a spirited horse, preparatory to mounting him, when it is dreaded that he may give the rider a fall.

And why the hasty after-indorsement of the decision by the President and others?

We cannot absolutely know that all these exact adaptations are the result of preconcert. But when we see a lot of framed timbers, different portions of which we know have been gotten out at different times and places, and by different workmen—Stephen, Franklin, Roger, and James, for instance—and when we see these timbers joined together, and see they exactly matte the frame of a house or a mill, all the tenons and mortices exactly fitting, and all the lengths and proportions of the different pieces exactly adapted to their respective places, and not a piece too many or too few,—not omitting even scaffolding or, if a single piece be lacking, we see the place in the frame exactly fitted and prepared yet to bring such piece in—in such a case we find it impossible not to believe that Stephen and Franklin and Roger and James all understood one another from the beginning and all worked upon a common plan or draft drawn up before the first blow was struck.

It should not be overlooked that, by the Nebraska Bill, the people of a State, as well as a Territory, were to be left "perfectly free," "subject only to the Constitution."

Why mention a State? They were legislating for territories, and not for or about States. Certainly the people of a State are and ought to be subject to the Constitution of the United States; but why is mention of this lugged into this merely Territorial law? Why are the people of a Territory and the people of a State therein lumped together, and their relation to the Constitution therein treated as being precisely the same?

While the opinion of the court, by Chief-Justice Taney, in the *Dred Scott* case and the separate opinions of all the concurring judges, expressly declare that the Constitution of the United States neither permits Congress nor a Territorial legislature to exclude slavery from any United States Territory, they all omit to declare whether or not the same Constitution permits a State, or the people of a State, to exclude it.

Possibly this is a mere omission; but who can be quite sure, if McLean or Curtis had sought to get into the opinion a declaration of unlimited power in the people of a State to exclude slavery from their limits, just as Chase and Mace sought to get such declaration, in behalf of the people of a Territory, into the Nebraska Bill—I ask, who can be quite sure that it would not have been voted down in the one case as it had been in the other?

The nearest approach to the point of declaring the power of a State over slavery is made by Judge Nelson. He approaches it more than once, using the precise idea, and almost the language, too, of the Nebraska Act. On one occasion, his exact language is, "except in cases where the power is restrained by the Constitution of the United States the law of the State is supreme over the subject of slavery within its jurisdiction."

In what cases the power of the States is so restrained by the United States Constitution is left an open question, precisely as the same question, as to the restraint on the power of the Territories, was left open in the Nebraska Act. Put this and that together, and we have another nice little niche which we may ere long see filled with another Supreme Court decision declaring that the Constitution of the United States does not permit a State to exclude slavery from its limits.

And this may especially be expected if the doctrine of "care not whether slavery be voted down or voted up," shall gain upon the public mind sufficiently to give promise that such a decision can be maintained when made.

Such a decision is all that slavery now lacks of being alike lawful in all the States.

Welcome or unwelcome, such decision is probably coming, and will soon be upon us, unless the power of the present political dynasty shall be met and overthrown.

> *"Judge Douglas, if not a dead lion, for this work, is at least a caged and toothless one. How can he oppose the advances of slavery? He does not care anything about it.... For years he has labored to prove it a sacred right of white men to take negro slaves into the new Territories."*

We shall lie down pleasantly dreaming that the people of Missouri are on the verge of making their State free, and we shall awake to the reality instead, that the Supreme Court has made Illinois a slave State.

To meet and overthrow the power of that dynasty is the work now before all those who would prevent that consummation.

This is what we have to do.

But how can we best do it?

There are those who denounce us openly to their own friends and yet whisper us softly, that Senator Douglas is the aptest instrument there is with which to effect that object. They wish us to infer all from the fact that he now has a little quarrel with the present head of the dynasty; and that he has regularly voted with us on a single point, upon which he and we have never differed.

They remind us that he is a great man, and that the largest of us are very small ones. Let this be granted. But "a living dog is better than a dead lion." Judge Douglas, if not a dead lion, for this work, is at least a caged and toothless one. How can he oppose the advances of slavery? He does not care anything about it. His avowed mission is impressing the "public heart" to care nothing about it.

A leading Douglas Democratic newspaper thinks Douglas's superior talent will be needed to resist the revival of the African slave trade.

Does Douglas believe an effort to revive that trade is approaching? He has not said so. Does he really think so? But if it is, how can he resist it? For years he has labored to prove it a sacred right of white men to take negro slaves into the new Territories. Can he possibly show that it is less a sacred right to buy them where they can be bought cheapest? And unquestionably they can be bought cheaper in Africa than in Virginia.

He has done all in his power to reduce the whole question of slavery to one of a mere right of property; and as such, how can he oppose the foreign slave trade—how can he refuse that trade in that "property" shall be "perfectly free"—unless he does it as a protection to the home production? And as the home producers will probably not ask the protection, he will be wholly without a ground of opposition.

Senator Douglas holds, we know, that a man may rightfully be wiser today than he was yesterday—that he may rightfully change when he finds himself wrong.

But can we, for that reason, run ahead, and infer that he will make any particular change, of which he, himself, has given no intimation? Can we safely base our action upon any such vague inference?

Now, as ever, I wish not to misrepresent Judge Douglas's position, question his motives, or do aught that can be personally offensive to him.

Whenever, if ever, he and we can come together on principle so that our cause may have assistance from his great ability, I hope to have interposed no adventitious obstacle.

But clearly, he is not now with us—he does not pretend to be—he does not promise ever to be.

Our cause, then, must be intrusted to, and conducted by, its own undoubted friends—those whose hands are free, whose hearts are in the work—who do care for the result.

Two years ago the Republicans of the nation mustered over thirteen hundred thousand strong.

We did this under the single impulse of resistance to a common danger, with every external circumstance against us.

Of strange, discordant, and even hostile elements, we gathered from the four winds, and formed and fought the battle through, under the constant hot fire of a disciplined, proud, and pampered enemy.

Did we brave all them to falter now?—now, when that same enemy is wavering, dissevered, and belligerent?

The result is not doubtful. We shall not fail—if we stand firm, we shall not fail.

Wise councils may accelerate, or mistakes delay it, but, sooner or later, the victory is sure to come.

7

ABRAHAM LINCOLN

"THE BETTER ANGELS OF OUR NATURE"

AT DAWN ON FEBRUARY 23, 1861, a train pulled into Washington, D.C. A curious man, bent over, in a poorly fitting overcoat with a hat pulled down to conceal his face, slipped onto the platform. Abraham Lincoln, threatened with assassination as he passed through Baltimore, had gone ahead of his official presidential train. With southern states already in open rebellion, Lincoln arrived for his swearing in like no other president.

Lincoln rose swiftly after nearly defeating Douglas. In January of 1860, New York City Republicans invited the intriguing new figure from the West to visit. Interest was so great that the speech moved to the Cooper Union, where fifteen hundred people crowded the Great Hall. In a densely argued speech, Lincoln sought to prove that the founders had given Congress the power to regulate slavery and even to prohibit it from new territories. Lincoln impressed the sophisticated audience. "The taste is in my mouth," he confided to a friend. He was far from the best-known candidate. But William Seward of New York, Salmon Chase of Ohio, Simon Cameron of Pennsylvania, all men with large reputations and egos, had fleets of enemies; Lincoln had few. The Republican nomination was his.

The election of 1860 split the parties and the country with almost geometric precision. Four candidates contended. Lincoln, representing a party that did not exist eight years before, won a majority of the electoral votes. His victory was a polarizing, electrifying event. To the South, it marked the worst imaginable outcome: someone they saw as an opponent of their "peculiar Institution," who had vowed "a house divided would not stand," was now president. Lincoln himself believed that eventually the South would agree, however grudgingly, to his tenure.

Instead, the Union began to break apart. Republicans struggled to persuade border states to stay, offering concessions, convening a peace conference, even proposing a constitutional amendment to protect slavery in the South. Meantime, in what he called "a dingy, dusty, and neglected back room" above a store in Springfield, Lincoln wrote his

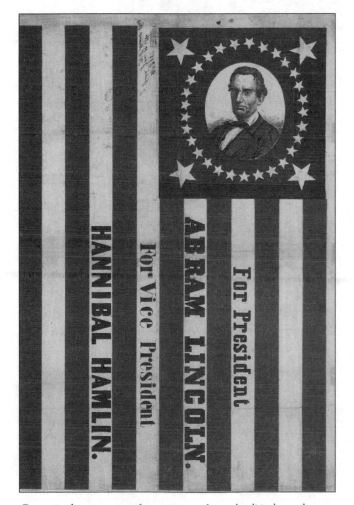

Campaign banner meant for use in parades and political speeches

The flag banner text: HANNIBAL HAMLIN. / For Vice President / ABRAM LINCOLN. / For President

I will venture to add that, to me, the
Convention mode seems preferable, in that it allows amendments to originate with the people themselves,
selves, instead of *only permitting* them ~~merely~~ to take,
or reject, propositions, originated by others, not especially
cially chosen for the purpose, and which might not
be precisely such, as they would wish to either accept or refuse.

which amendment, however, I have not seen,
I understand a proposed amendment to the constitution,
has passed ~~the House of Representatives~~ *Congress*, to the effect
that the federal government, shall never inter-
fere with the domestic institutions of the States, including that of persons held to service— To avoid
misconstruction of what I have said, I depart from
my purpose not to speak of particular amendments,
ments, so far as to say that, holding such a
provision to now be implied Constitutional law,
I have no objection to its being made express,
and irrevocable—

laws of your own framing under it; while the new administration will have no immediate power, if it would, to change either. If it were admitted that you who are
dissatisfied, hold the right side in the dispute, there still is no single good reason for
precipitate action. Intelligence, patriotism, Christianity, and a firm reliance on Him,
who has never yet forsaken this favored land, are still competent to adjust, in the best
way, all our present difficulty.

7744   In *your* hands, my dissatisfied fellow countrymen, and not in *mine*, is the momentous issue of civil war. The government will not assail *you*. ▬▬▬▬
You can have no conflict, without being yourselves the aggressors. You have no oath
registered in Heaven to destroy the government, while *I* shall have the most solemn one
to "preserve, protect and defend" it. ▬▬▬▬▬▬▬▬▬▬▬
▬▬▬▬▬▬▬▬ I am loth to close. We are not enemies,
but friends— We must not be enemies. Though passion may
have strained, it must not break our bonds of affection.
The mystic chords of memory, stretching from every battlefield and patriot grave, to every living heart and hearthstone, all over this broad land, will yet swell the chorus of the Union, when again touched, as surely they will
be, by the better angels of our nature.

Lincoln had his first inaugural printed up, and then continued to revise it by hand before delivering it inaugural address. While Lincoln journeyed to Washington, Jefferson Davis was sworn in as provisional president of the Confederate States of America. By the day Lincoln arrived, seven southern states had voted to secede.

Standing before the Capitol, its dome half built, Lincoln made one last attempt to keep the Union whole. Even today, we can feel him struggling almost palpably to hold the nation together. He sought to reassure the South that he was not a radical—would not seek to free their slaves—would not seek to impose abolitionism at bayonet point. But he did not waver on the basic legal premise: the Union must be preserved. He would enforce the law, he said; he made no pledge to withdraw troops from the South. Instead, he put the onus for the breakup on the rebels. "In your hands, my dissatisfied fellow countrymen, and not in mine, is the momentous issue of civil war. The government will not assail you," he said. "You can have no conflict without being yourselves the aggressors." The document, at times, has a logical legal tone—as if Lincoln were arguing before a judge against secession.

At first, the draft concluded with a question for the South: "Shall it be peace or sword?" After Lincoln arrived in Washington, his incoming secretary of state, William Seward, urged him to end with a more tempered emotional

Banner used in Lincoln's 1860 campaign

plea. Lincoln's reaction to this suggestion from his condescending rival is lost to history. But he rewrote Seward's paragraph, penning the peroration for which the speech is best remembered: "by the better angels of our nature."

Those "better angels" would not be heard from soon. On April 12, 1861, Confederate artillery began to shell a U.S. military outpost off the coast of South Carolina, Fort Sumter. The Civil War had begun.

SEWARD:
I close.

We are not, we must not be, aliens or enemies, but fellow countrymen and brethren. Although passion has strained our bonds of affection too hardly, they must not, I am sure they will not, be broken.

The mystic chords which, proceeding from so many battlefields and so many patriotic graves, pass through all the hearts and all hearths in this broad continent of ours, will yet again harmonize in their ancient music when breathed upon by the guardian angel of the nation.

LINCOLN:
I am loath to close.

We are not enemies, but friends. We must not be enemies. Though passion may have strained, it must not break our bonds of affection.

The mystic chords of memory, stretching from every battlefield and every patriot grave to every living heart and hearthstone all over this broad land, will yet swell the chorus of the Union when again touched as surely they will be, by the better angels of our nature.

Abraham Lincoln's
FIRST INAUGURAL ADDRESS

*hear...
disc 1
track 8

Washington, D.C. • March 4, 1861

Fellow-Citizens of the United States:

In compliance with a custom as old as the Government itself, I appear before you to address you briefly and to take in your presence the oath prescribed by the Constitution of the United States to be taken by the President "before he enters on the execution of this office."

I do not consider it necessary at present for me to discuss those matters of administration about which there is no special anxiety or excitement.

Apprehension seems to exist among the people of the Southern States that by the accession of a Republican Administration their property and their peace and personal security are to be endangered. There has never been any reasonable cause for such apprehension. Indeed, the most ample evidence to the contrary has all the while existed and been open to their inspection. It is found in nearly all the published speeches of him who now addresses you. I do but quote from one of those speeches when I declare that—

> I have no purpose, directly or indirectly, to interfere with the institution of slavery in the States where it exists. I believe I have no lawful right to do so, and I have no inclination to do so.

Those who nominated and elected me did so with full knowledge that I had made this and many similar declarations and had never recanted them; and more than this, they placed in the platform for my acceptance, and as a law to themselves and to me, the clear and emphatic resolution which I now read:

> *Resolved*, That the maintenance inviolate of the rights of the States, and especially the right of each State to

order and control its own domestic institutions according to its own judgment exclusively, is essential to that balance of power on which the perfection and endurance of our political fabric depend; and we denounce the lawless invasion by armed force of the soil of any State or Territory, no matter what pretext, as among the gravest of crimes.

I now reiterate these sentiments, and in doing so I only press upon the public attention the most conclusive evidence of which the case is susceptible that the property, peace, and security of no section are to be in any wise endangered by the now incoming Administration. I add, too, that all the protection which, consistently with the Constitution and the laws, can be given will be cheerfully given to all the States when lawfully demanded, for whatever cause—as cheerfully to one section as to another....

> ## *"I now enter upon the same task for the brief constitutional term of four years under great and peculiar difficulty."*

I take the official oath to-day with no mental reservations and with no purpose to construe the Constitution or laws by any hypercritical rules; and while I do not choose now to specify particular acts of Congress as proper to be enforced, I do suggest that it will be much safer for all, both in official and private stations, to conform to and abide by all those acts which stand unrepealed than to violate any of

Lincoln giving his first inaugural address on the steps of the partially finished Capitol

them trusting to find impunity in having them held to be unconstitutional.

It is seventy-two years since the first inauguration of a President under our National Constitution. During that period fifteen different and greatly distinguished citizens have in succession administered the executive branch of the Government. They have conducted it through many perils, and generally with great success. Yet, with all this scope of precedent, I now enter upon the same task for the brief constitutional term of four years under great and peculiar difficulty. A disruption of the Federal Union, heretofore only menaced, is now formidably attempted.

I hold that in contemplation of universal law and of the Constitution the Union of these States is perpetual.

Perpetuity is implied, if not expressed, in the fundamental law of all national governments. It is safe to assert that no government proper ever had a provision in its organic law for its own termination. Continue to execute all the express provisions of our National Constitution, and the Union will endure forever, it being impossible to destroy it except by some action not provided for in the instrument itself.

Again: If the United States be not a government proper, but an association of States in the nature of contract merely, can it, as a contract, be peaceably unmade by less than all the parties who made it? One party to a contract may violate it—break it, so to speak—but does it not require all to lawfully rescind it?

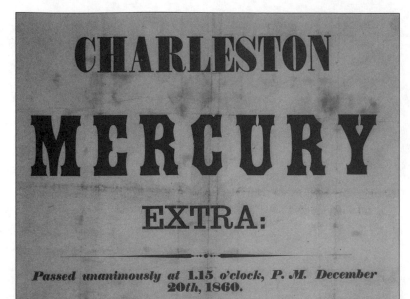

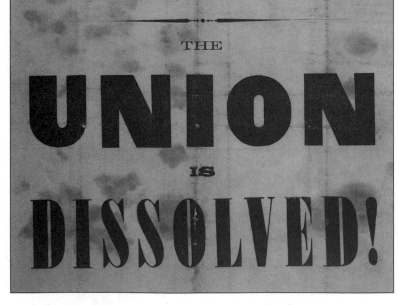

CHARLESTON

MERCURY

EXTRA:

Passed unanimously at 1.15 o'clock, P. M. December 20th, 1860.

AN ORDINANCE

To dissolve the Union between the State of South Carolina and other States united with her under the compact entitled "The Constitution of the United States of America."

We, the People of the State of South Carolina, in Convention assembled, do declare and ordain, and it is hereby declared and ordained,

That the Ordinance adopted by us in Convention, on the twenty-third day of May, in the year of our Lord one thousand seven hundred and eighty-eight, whereby the Constitution of the United States of America was ratified, and also, all Acts and parts of Acts of the General Assembly of this State, ratifying amendments of the said Constitution, are hereby repealed; and that the union now subsisting between South Carolina and other States, under the name of "The United States of America," is hereby dissolved.

THE

UNION

IS

DISSOLVED!

A Charlestonian newspaper announcing the secession of South Carolina within minutes following the vote to secede

Descending from these general principles, we find the proposition that in legal contemplation the Union is perpetual confirmed by the history of the Union itself. The Union is much older than the Constitution. It was formed, in fact, by the Articles of Association in 1774. It was matured and continued by the Declaration of Independence in 1776. It was further matured, and the faith of all the then thirteen States expressly plighted and engaged that it should be perpetual, by the Articles of Confederation in 1778. And finally, in 1787, one of the declared objects for ordaining and establishing the Constitution was "*to form a more perfect Union.*"

But if destruction of the Union by one or by a part only of the States be lawfully possible, the Union is *less* perfect than before the Constitution, having lost the vital element of perpetuity.

It follows from these views that no State upon its own mere motion can lawfully get out of the Union; that *resolves* and *ordinances* to that effect are legally void, and that acts of violence within any State or States against the authority of the United States are insurrectionary or revolutionary, according to circumstances.

"The Union is much older than the Constitution."

I therefore consider that in view of the Constitution and the laws the Union is unbroken, and to the extent of my ability, I shall take care, as the Constitution itself expressly enjoins upon me, that the laws of the Union be faithfully executed in all the States. Doing this I deem to be only a simple duty on my part, and I shall perform it so far as practicable unless my rightful masters, the American people, shall withhold the requisite means or in some authoritative manner direct the contrary. I trust this will not be regarded as a menace, but only as the declared purpose of the Union that it *will* constitutionally defend and maintain itself.

In doing this there needs to be no bloodshed or violence, and there shall be none unless it be forced upon the national authority....

Page 6

Line 1 Strike out "rule" and insert "practice",

Line 1 Strike out "But" and insert At the same time
~~~ the candid citizen must confess that

Line 3 After the word Court, strike out the words "it is plain
that" and insert "made in the ordinary course of litiga-
tion between "parties in personal actions"

                                    "having"
Lines 4 & 5 After the word ~~become~~ strike out the rest of the
                                              renower
sentence and write , practically ~~confided~~ their
government ~~~ into the hands of that eminent
tribunal "

Lines 9. 10. 11 Strike out the whole paragraph

Line 12 After the word "section" insert "of our country

Line 15 After the word "enforced" insert perhaps "

Line 16 Strike out the words "is against" and insert "are
perfectly supported

L~~~ ~~ ~~ word "be" insert ultimately "

Line 16 Strike out the whole sentence and insert
While so great a diversity of opinion exists on the question
what amendments if indeed any should be
effective in restoring peace and safety. it would only
tend to aggravate the dispute if I were to attempt
to give direction to the public mind in that respect

A draft of Lincoln's first inaugural

That there are persons in one section or another who seek to destroy the Union at all events and are glad of any pretext to do it I will neither affirm nor deny; but if there be such, I need address no word to them. To those, however, who really love the Union may I not speak?

"There needs to be no bloodshed or violence, and there shall be none unless it be forced upon the national authority...."

Before entering upon so grave a matter as the destruction of our national fabric, with all its benefits, its memories, and its hopes, would it not be wise to ascertain precisely why we do it? Will you hazard so desperate a step while there is any possibility that any portion of the ills you fly from have no real existence? Will you, while the certain ills you fly to are greater than all the real ones you fly from, will you risk the commission of so fearful a mistake?

All profess to be content in the Union if all constitutional rights can be maintained. Is it true, then, that any right plainly written in the Constitution has been denied? I think not. Happily, the human mind is so constituted that no party can reach to the audacity of doing this. Think, if you can, of a single instance in which a plainly written provision of the Constitution has ever been denied. If by the mere force of numbers a majority should deprive a minority of any clearly written constitutional right, it might in a moral point of view justify revolution; certainly would if such right were a vital one. But such is not our case. All the vital rights of minorities and of individuals are so plainly assured to them by affirmations and negations, guarantees and prohibitions, in the Constitution that controversies never arise concerning them. But no organic law can ever be framed with a provision specifically applicable to every question which may occur in practical administration. No foresight can anticipate nor any document of reasonable length contain express provisions for all possible questions. Shall fugitives from labor be surrendered by national or by State authority? The Constitution does not expressly say. *May* Congress prohibit slavery in the Territories? The Constitution does not expressly say. *Must* Congress protect slavery in the Territories? The Constitution does not expressly say.

From questions of this class spring all our constitutional controversies, and we divide upon them into majorities and minorities. If the minority will not acquiesce, the majority must, or the Government must cease. There is no other alternative, for continuing the Government is acquiescence on one side or the other. If a minority in such case will secede rather than acquiesce, they make a precedent which in turn will divide and ruin them, for a minority of their own will secede from them whenever a majority refuses to be controlled by such minority. For instance, why may not any portion of a new confederacy a year or two hence arbitrarily secede again, precisely as portions of the present Union now claim to secede from it? All who cherish disunion sentiments are now being educated to the exact temper of doing this.

Is there such perfect identity of interests among the States to compose a new union as to produce harmony only and prevent renewed secession?

Plainly the central idea of secession is the essence of anarchy. A majority held in restraint by constitutional checks and limitations, and always changing easily with deliberate changes of popular opinions and sentiments, is the only true sovereign of a free people. Whoever rejects it does of necessity fly to anarchy or to despotism. Unanimity is impossible. The rule of a minority, as a permanent arrangement, is wholly inadmissible; so that, rejecting the majority principle, anarchy or despotism in some form is all that is left....

This country, with its institutions, belongs to the people who inhabit it. Whenever they shall grow weary of the existing Government, they can exercise their *constitutional* right of amending it or their *revolutionary* right to dismember or overthrow it. I can not be ignorant of the fact that many worthy and patriotic citizens are desirous of having the National Constitution amended. While I make no recommendation of amendments, I fully recognize the rightful authority of the

Diary entry (in shorthand) for March 4, 1861: "Inauguration of President Lincoln at the U.S. Capitol" people over the whole subject, to be exercised in either of the modes prescribed in the instrument itself; and I should, under existing circumstances, favor rather than oppose a fair opportunity being afforded the people to act upon it. I will venture to add that to me the convention mode seems preferable, in that it allows amendments to originate with the people themselves, instead of only permitting them to take or reject propositions originated by others, not especially chosen for the purpose, and which might not be precisely such as they would wish to either accept or refuse. I understand a proposed amendment to the Constitution—which amendment, however, I have not seen—has passed Congress, to the effect that the Federal Government shall never interfere with the domestic institutions of the States, including that of persons held to service. To avoid misconstruction of what I have said, I depart from my purpose not to speak of particular amendments so far as to say that, holding such a provision to now be implied constitutional law, I have no objection to its being made express and irrevocable.

> ## *"The mystic chords of memory will yet swell the chorus of the Union, when again touched, as surely they will be, by the better angels of our nature."*

The Chief Magistrate derives all his authority from the people, and they have referred none upon him to fix terms for the separation of the States. The people themselves can do this if also they choose, but the Executive as such has nothing to do with it. His duty is to administer the present Government as it came to his hands and to transmit it unimpaired by him to his successor.

Why should there not be a patient confidence in the ultimate justice of the people? Is there any better or equal hope in the world? In our present differences, is either party without faith of being in the right? If the Almighty Ruler of Nations, with His eternal truth and justice, be on your side of the North, or on yours of the South, that truth and that justice will surely prevail by the judgment of this great tribunal of the American people.

By the frame of the Government under which we live this same people have wisely given their public servants but little power for mischief, and have with equal wisdom provided for the return of that little to their own hands at very short intervals. While the people retain their virtue and vigilance no Administration by any extreme of wickedness or folly can very seriously injure the Government in the short space of four years.

My countrymen, one and all, think calmly and *well* upon this whole subject. Nothing valuable can be lost by taking time. If there be an object to *hurry* any of you in hot haste to a step which you would never take *deliberately*, that object will be frustrated by taking time; but no good object can be frustrated by it. Such of you as are now dissatisfied still have the old Constitution unimpaired, and, on the sensitive point, the laws of your own framing under it; while the new Administration will have no immediate power, if it would, to change either. If it were admitted that you who are dissatisfied hold the right side in the dispute, there still is no single good reason for precipitate action. Intelligence, patriotism, Christianity, and a firm reliance on Him who has never yet forsaken this favored land are still competent to adjust in the best way all our present difficulty.

In *your* hands, my dissatisfied fellow-countrymen, and not in *mine*, is the momentous issue of civil war. The Government will not assail *you*. You can have no conflict without being yourselves the aggressors. *You* have no oath registered in heaven to destroy the Government, while I shall have the most solemn one to "preserve, protect, and defend it."

I am loath to close. We are not enemies, but friends. We must not be enemies. Though passion may have strained it must not break our bonds of affection. The mystic chords of memory, stretching from every battlefield and patriot grave to every living heart and hearthstone all over this broad land, will yet swell the chorus of the Union, when again touched, as surely they will be, by the better angels of our nature.

8

ABRAHAM LINCOLN

"A NEW BIRTH OF FREEDOM"

THE GETTYSBURG ADDRESS is the most important speech delivered by an American president. A concise masterpiece of prose and thought, it changed how Americans saw themselves—and even how they talked about their nation.

By late 1862, the Civil War had raged far more destructively than any had predicted. Tens of thousands were killed. European nations mulled granting diplomatic recognition to the Confederacy. The staggered Union army urgently needed men, especially from the ranks of freed slaves. Lincoln long had opposed slavery, but had held back from ending it. Once, he had said he would keep the slaves if it meant saving the union; now he realized that the key to saving the union was to free the slaves. In September 1862, he announced that in states still in rebellion at midnight on New Year's Eve, all slaves would be freed. On January 1, 1863, the Emancipation Proclamation took effect in the rebellious states.

Now the war to save the union had become a war for freedom. Still, Lincoln had not articulated this lofty rationale in public. His chance came in late 1863. At Gettysburg, Pennsylvania, over three days, the Union Army repulsed confederate troops at the cost of at least fifty-one thousand dead, wounded, or missing in perhaps the decisive battle of the war. A cemetery was to be dedicated on the battlefield. Former Senator and Harvard University President Edward Everett prepared a two-hour address on the battle and its significance, a length considered appropriate by audiences of the day. Lincoln was invited to give "a few appropriate remarks" to dedicate the field. He composed his words carefully, not on the back of an envelope, as legend has it. He was determined to attend the ceremony, even though his son was ill (his other son had recently died).

Lincoln visits the Union camp at Sharpsburg a few weeks after the Battle of Antietam

"Four score and seven years ago." These words, echoing scripture, carry a profound political import. They date the country's birth not to the Constitution of 1787, with its acceptance of slavery, as the audience might have expected. Rather, they reach back to the Declaration of Independence in 1776, with its proclamation that "all men

53

A casualty in a trench at Gettysburg

are created equal." (In its first draft, the Declaration actually denounced slavery; the Continental Congress removed any mention from the final version.) Born that day was "a new nation"—a nation, in other words, that precedes the legal document of the Constitution, moreover one dedicated to a purpose. The point of the Civil War was to test whether a nation committed to such notions of equality and democracy could survive. This was a strikingly abstract approach for a wartime leader to take— think of how Lincoln could have talked of victory, or of crushing aggression, or even of the wrongs done to the slaves. He concluded by asking how to carry on the work

of the soldiers still being buried at the cemetery. As Garry Wills notes, Lincoln followed conventions of classic Greek funeral oratory, by laying out a task for the audience to follow in memory of the dead—we dedicate ourselves to their cause by carrying on their work.

This speech worked a revolution of style as well. It was short, without bombast. It used simple words. Lincoln was ostentatiously humble, claiming his words would not be "long remembered." The address tapped deep wells of religious and patriotic sentiment: filled with language of birth ("conceived," "brought forth"), death, and resurrection ("a new birth of freedom"), the story of America is sanctified.

In his brilliant book, *Lincoln at Gettysburg*, Wills pointed out that before this speech, Americans spoke of the "Union"—the United States as a collection of governments: "the United States *are*." After this speech and the war it defined, the United States was a nation: the United States *is*. Since Gettysburg, we have tested ourselves by our fealty to Jefferson's defining vision. A century later, in the greatest American oration of the next century, Martin Luther King Jr. would stand "in the symbolic shadow" of Lincoln—"five score years ago," he began. His first dream was the same articulated by Lincoln—"that some day this nation will rise up and live out the true meaning of its creed that 'all men are created equal.'" No doubt some future speaker will add one more link in the chain, from Jefferson to Lincoln to King and beyond.

Historical legend holds that Lincoln was despondent after the talk. "That speech won't scour," he moaned to a friend, using the farming term for a plow that cut through the soil. In fact, supporters reprinted it widely and asked him to copy it out by hand several times. He was determined that the words would be heard, and they are well noted, and "long remembered."

Lincoln (circled) preparing to speak at Gettysburg, in a photograph unearthed in 1952

Abraham Lincoln's

GETTYSBURG ADDRESS

disc 1
track 9

Gettysburg, Pennsylvania • November 19, 1863

SEAL OF THE PRESIDENT OF THE UNITED STATES · E PLURIBUS UNUM

Four score and seven years ago our fathers brought forth on this continent, a new nation, conceived in Liberty, and dedicated to the proposition that all men are created equal.

Now we are engaged in a great civil war, testing whether that nation, or any nation so conceived and so dedicated, can long endure. We are met on a great battle-field of that war. We have come to dedicate a portion of that field, as a final resting place for those who here gave their lives that that nation might live. It is altogether fitting and proper that we should do this.

But, in a larger sense, we can not dedicate—we can not consecrate—we can not hallow—this ground. The brave men, living and dead, who struggled here, have consecrated it, far above our poor power to add or detract. The world will little note, nor long remember what we say here, but it can never forget what they did here. It is for us the living, rather, to be dedicated here to the unfinished work which they who fought here have thus far so nobly advanced. It is rather for us to be here dedicated to the great task remaining before us—that from these honored dead we take increased devotion to that cause for which they gave the last full measure of devotion—that we here highly resolve that these dead shall not have died in vain—that this nation, under God, shall have a new birth of freedom—and that government of the people, by the people, for the people, shall not perish from the earth.

A phrase familiar to Americans today begins this handwritten draft of the Gettysburg address

> *"The world will little note, nor long remember what we say here, but it can never forget what they did here."*

Executive Mansion,

Washington,   , 186 .

Four score and seven years ago our fathers brought forth, upon this continent, a new nation, conceived in liberty, and dedicated to the proposition that "all men are created equal"

Now we are engaged in a great civil war, testing whether that nation, or any nation so conceived, and so dedicated, can long endure. We are met on a great battle field of that war. We have come to dedicate a portion of it, as a final resting place for those who died here, that the nation might live. This we may, in all propriety do. But, in a larger sense, we can not dedicate—we can not consecrate—we can not hallow, this ground—The brave men, living and dead, who struggled here, have hallowed it, far above our poor power to add or detract. The world will little note, nor long remember what we say here; while it can never forget what they did here.

It is rather for us, the living, to stand here,

9

ABRAHAM LINCOLN

"WITH MALICE TOWARD NONE"

VISITORS TO THE Lincoln Memorial on the Mall see two speeches carved in full: the Gettysburg Address and the second inaugural. Lincoln himself considered the latter to be his best. It is a document of astonishing literary power. More than that: it was a supremely political document, and a surprising one at that.

Lincoln took the oath in front of the still-unfinished Capitol dome. Andrew Johnson, the new vice president, was sworn in earlier—and made a fool of himself, sloppy drunk. Lincoln's audience listened intently. He spoke, after all, as the North ground out the last embers of Southern rebellion. Four years before, in his first inaugural, Lincoln had made a lawyer's constitutional argument to hold the Union together. Now he faced questions even more agonizing. What would the policy be toward the South? Was it a conquered nation, or were its leaders criminals? After the death of more than 620,000 men, how could the United States be rewoven? Should the national government be harsh or forgiving? With this speech, Lincoln would give his answer.

His talk no doubt surprised and perhaps even disconcerted his expectant audience. He offered a sermon—a lyrical meditation on the war and God's will, by far the most explicitly religious of his major speeches. Listeners heard no declaration of triumph: "The Almighty has His own purposes." He did not even give a full

"Long Abe a Little Longer," reelection cartoon from 1864

accounting of the progress of the battle, saying the audience knew as much as he did.

Instead, he described the war as God's punishment of both South and North for the sin of slavery. "If God wills that it continue until all the wealth piled by the bondsman's two hundred and fifty years of unrequited toil shall be sunk," he said, using a bookkeepers' term for "depleted," "and until every drop of blood drawn with the lash shall be paid by another drawn with the sword, as was said three thousand years ago, so still it must be said 'the judgments of the Lord are true and righteous altogether.'" Today some citizens seek a presidential apology for slavery; in fact, Lincoln a century and a half ago proffered one, in the starkest of terms.

Despite the judgment implicit in his damnation of slavery, Lincoln's approach to the South was ultimately conciliatory. He concluded with the famous peroration—"with malice toward none, with charity for all"—and pledged to bind up the nation's wounds. As Garry Wills notes, Lincoln's approach to the South embodied both the harsh judgments of the Torah and the forgiveness of the New Testament.

Lincoln's writing is masterly. He uses alliteration (fondly, fervently) and rhyme (pray/pass away). As Ronald White observes in his book *Lincoln's Greatest Speech*, 505 of the 703 words in the speech are one syllable long. He reverses normal sentence structure for emphasis (not "we

57

pray fervently" but "fervently do we pray"). He alternates a long sentence of twenty-eight words, detailing the run up to the war, with the grim concluding clause, "and the war came." He quotes liberally from scripture.

The address drew mixed reaction. A puzzled writer for the *New York Herald* reported, "It was not strictly an inaugural address….It was more like a valedictory…." On the other hand, Frederick Douglass, the great abolitionist and former slave, told Lincoln afterwards at a White House reception that it had been a "sacred effort."

Looking ahead to hard years of reunification, Lincoln intended to be flexible, to be carried along from event to event, hoping to cool passions and absorb tension. He would try to steer a middle course between the radicals of his own party, who were intent on punishing the South and giving maximum power to the freed slaves, and border-state Democrats such as Andrew Johnson. As his own vision widened, he would find a way to seek full citizenship to the former slaves while remaining sensitive to the former slave owners. Lincoln would not live to carry out his plans. Visible in a photograph of the ceremony, several rows behind the president, the actor John Wilkes Booth lurked. Within a month, Booth would kill Lincoln, and Johnson would be president. Soon the radical Republicans would be in open rebellion in the Congress, eventually seeking to remove Johnson. Harsh Reconstruction lasted until 1877, but when troops left the sullen South, former slave owners instituted segregation and vicious racial laws that lasted until the civil rights movement nearly a century later.

PRESIDENT BILL CLINTON ON LINCOLN'S SECOND INAUGURAL

My favorite Lincoln speech was his second inaugural. A historian, Ronald White, wrote a book about it, arguing it was Lincoln's greatest speech—greater than the Gettysburg Address—and I agree. To me, it was the greatest of all inaugural addresses, as well, because it speaks so powerfully about reconciliation. Even though Lincoln delivered it while the Civil War was still going on, it's so different from the attitude that too often governs politics now, which stresses division over unity.

This was a very politically powerful speech, too. At the time, a large number of people in the North wanted to kick the South hard. Their attitude was, "We won, and we want to send our enemies straight to hell." Lincoln reminded people that both sides "read the same Bible and pray to the same God, and each invokes His aid against the other….The prayers of both could not be answered." He had a wonderful way of giving his adversaries their due, of seeing their point of view, of treating them with respect—which was enormously effective in bringing people together and finding a way to move forward after conflict. It is a tremendous example of leadership.

The writing is also brilliant. Lincoln had a great way of compressing the language. Thomas Jefferson once said, "If I had more time I could write shorter letters." Lincoln could say more in fewer words than anyone. He summed up the cause of the Civil War in one single sentence, which ends with, "and the war came." He marked the history of that moment for his countrymen.

All the while, his opponents were calling him everything from a "fool" to a "baboon." But Lincoln's response provides a vital lesson for anyone interested in public life. No matter how tough he had to be, he never lost his humanity or his generosity of spirit.

Abraham Lincoln's
SECOND INAUGURAL ADDRESS

Washington, D.C. • March 4, 1865

hear...
disc 1
track 10

Fellow-countrymen:

At this second appearing to take the oath of the Presidential office there is less occasion for an extended address than there was at the first. Then a statement somewhat in detail of a course to be pursued seemed fitting and proper. Now, at the expiration of four years, during which public declarations have been constantly called forth on every point and phase of the great contest which still absorbs the attention and engrosses the energies of the nation, little that is new could be presented. The progress of our arms, upon which all else chiefly depends, is as well known to the public as to myself, and it is, I trust, reasonably satisfactory and encouraging to all. With high hope for the future, no prediction in regard to it is ventured.

> *"Both parties deprecated war, but one of them would make war rather than let the nation survive, and the other would accept war rather than let it perish."*

On the occasion corresponding to this four years ago all thoughts were anxiously directed to an impending civil war. All dreaded it, all sought to avert it. While the inaugural address was being delivered from this place, devoted altogether to *saving* the Union without war, urgent agents were in the city seeking to *destroy* it without war—seeking to dissolve the Union and divide effects by negotiation. Both parties deprecated war, but one of them would *make* war rather than let the nation survive, and the other would *accept* war rather than let it perish, and the war came.

> *"Let us strive on to finish the work we are in, to bind up the nation's wounds."*

One-eighth of the whole population were colored slaves, not distributed generally over the Union, but localized in the southern part of it. These slaves constituted a peculiar and powerful interest. All knew that this interest was somehow the cause of the war. To strengthen, perpetuate, and extend this interest was the object for which the insurgents would rend the Union even by war, while the Government claimed no right to do more than to restrict the territorial enlargement of it. Neither party expected for the war the magnitude or the duration which it has already attained. Neither anticipated that the *cause* of the conflict might cease with or even before the conflict itself should cease. Each looked for an easier triumph, and a result less fundamental and astounding. Both read the same Bible and pray to the same God, and each invokes His aid against the other. It may seem strange that any men should dare to ask a just God's assistance in wringing their bread from the sweat of other men's faces, but let us judge not, that we be not judged. The prayers of both could not be answered. That of neither has been answered fully. The Almighty has His own purposes. "Woe unto the world because of offenses; for it must needs be that offenses come, but woe to that man by whom the offense cometh." If we shall suppose that Ameri-

Lincoln's second inauguration, Washington, D.C., six weeks before his assassination—to the right and behind an iron railing stands John Wilkes Booth

can slavery is one of those offenses which, in the providence of God, must needs come, but which, having continued through His appointed time, He now wills to remove, and that He gives to both North and South this terrible war as the woe due to those by whom the offense came, shall we discern therein any departure from those divine attributes which the believers in a living God always ascribe to Him? Fondly do we hope, fervently do we pray, that this mighty scourge of war may speedily pass away. Yet, if God wills that it continue until all the wealth piled by the bondsman's two hundred and fifty years of unrequited toil shall be sunk, and until every drop of blood drawn with the lash shall be paid by another drawn with the sword, as was said three thousand years ago, so still it must be said "the judgments of the Lord are true and righteous altogether."

With malice toward none, with charity for all, with firmness in the right as God gives us to see the right, let us strive on to finish the work we are in, to bind up the nation's wounds, to care for him who shall have borne the battle and for his widow and his orphan, to do all which may achieve and cherish a just and lasting peace among ourselves and with all nations.

Theodore
ROOSEVELT

26TH PRESIDENT: 1901–1909

Born: October 27, 1858, in New York, New York

Died: January 6, 1919, in Oyster Bay, New York

Disc 1, Tracks 12–13

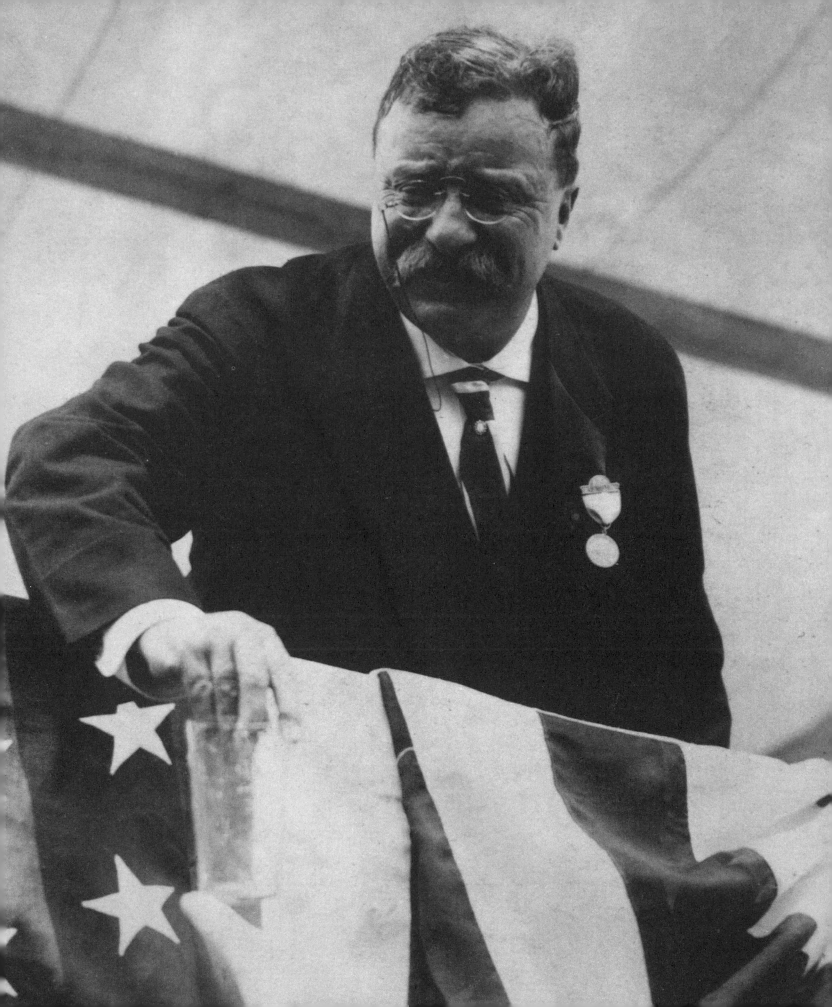

10

"THE MAN WITH THE MUCK-RAKE"

WHEN THE REPUBLICAN party chose Theodore Roosevelt as its candidate for vice president in 1900, party leader Mark Hanna exclaimed, "Don't any of you realize that there's only one life between that madman and the Presidency?" Roosevelt remains the most vivid character to serve as chief executive. Only forty-two years old when William McKinley was assassinated in 1901, he had been a state legislator, a police commissioner, a rancher, a civil service commissioner, the leader of the Rough Riders in Cuba, the governor of New York, and vice president of the United States. He was a prolific author, writing over a dozen books of history, biology, naturalism, and public policy. Commented his son, "Father always wanted to be the bride at every wedding and the corpse at every funeral."

Roosevelt's zest for public communication was a source of great power. He dubbed the presidency the "bully pulpit" ("bully" was his all-purpose word of praise), and he used that platform to harangue his enemies and sermonize on social ills. As political scientist Jeffrey Tulis notes, Roosevelt still felt constrained by earlier norms; for example, he held back from giving public speeches urging passage of a key bill during the weeks it was being considered by Congress. Still, by force of personality, Theodore Roosevelt launched the larger-than-life, twentieth-century presidency.

He governed at a time of great ferment. During the Industrial Revolution of the late nineteenth century, millions of Americans moved from farms to cities, living in squalor in an economy increasingly dominated by a few large businesses. The response came in the Progressive Era: an intense and broad focus on social reform. Roosevelt fed the energy of the reformers, and was himself changed by them. When he took office his views were orthodox. But his administration soon brought the first major antitrust prosecution, blocking a merger that had been engineered by financier J.P. Morgan. Soon he was denouncing "malefactors of great wealth" and giving dozens of speeches on the need to control corporations. He benefited from the rise of new media, especially the profusion of popular, nationally marketed newspapers and magazines; so did the reformers. Ida M. Tarbell wrote scathingly about John D. Rockefeller in *McClure's Magazine*. Upton Sinclair exposed the meat-packing industry in *The Jungle*, which led to pure food and drug laws. Jacob Riis, Roosevelt's friend, wrote about tenement life.

But Roosevelt was not yet comfortable in the radical camp. Anti-business sentiment reached a peak in March 1906, when William Randolph Hearst's *Cosmopolitan* magazine published a series entitled "The Treason of the Senate," an attack on the "Millionaires Club" of the upper chamber. (Senators then were chosen not directly by voters, but by notoriously corrupt state legislatures.) Roosevelt was seeking to pass the Pure Food and Drug Act and was being frustrated by conservative opposition. He took the moment to lash out not at those blocking him, but those urging him on. The scene was a dinner of the Gridiron Club. This is a peculiar Washington institution—which still meets annually—in which lawmakers, captains of industry, and reporters gather in white tie and tails to give speeches and roast one another. Roosevelt chose to make a serious talk, scolding the excesses of investigative journalists. He gave the same speech again two weeks later at an even more pointed public locale: the dedication of

the new House of Representatives office building (the structure now known as the Cannon Office Building).

Roosevelt took his metaphor from John Bunyan's classic allegory *The Pilgrim's Progress*. "You may recall," he said "the Man with the Muck-rake, the man who could look no way but downward, with the muck-rake in his hand." The text was a long poem written by a seventeenth-century Calvinist clergyman frequently jailed by the English crown—ironically, a muckraker for his time, one invested with the same moralistic fervor Roosevelt brought to public conflict. This speech by Roosevelt left our language the term "muckraker," used to describe a crusading investigative journalist. (It has become a term of praise, at least in some circles.)

Roosevelt was ambivalent about the crusaders: they "are often indispensable to the well being of society; but only if they know when to stop raking the muck, and to look upward to the celestial crown above them, to the crown of worthy endeavor." That tension long has bedeviled movements of left and right—creating workable reform necessarily involves compromise and illogic, both anathema to the moralizing reformer. A signal quality of this speech is its literary and intellectual heft. Roosevelt could draw on a deep knowledge of classic literature—and assume such knowledge on the part of his audience—in a way that could be matched by few politicians of later years. Few writers can brag of having coined a new phrase, let alone one as widely used as the one left us by Roosevelt.

Theodore Roosevelt's
DEDICATION OF THE HOUSE OFFICE BUILDING

Washington, D.C. • April 15, 1906

✱hear...
disc 1
track 12

Over a century ago Washington laid the cornerstone of the Capitol in what was then little more than a tract of wooded wilderness here beside the Potomac. We now find it necessary to provide by great additional buildings for the business of the Government. This growth in the need for the housing of the Government is but a proof and example of the way in which the Nation has grown and the sphere of action of the National Government has grown. We now administer the affairs of a nation in which the extraordinary growth of population has been outstripped by the growth of wealth and the growth in complex interests. The material problems that face us to-day are not such as they were in Washington's time, but the underlying facts of human nature are the same now as they were then. Under altered external form we war with the same tendencies toward evil that were evident in Washington's time, and are helped by the same tendencies for good. It is about some of these that I wish to say a word to-day.

In Bunyan's "Pilgrim's Progress" you may recall the description of the Man with the Muck-rake, the man who could look no way but downward, with the muck-rake in his hand; who was offered a celestial crown for his muck-rake, but who would neither look up nor regard the crown he was offered, but continue to rake to himself the filth of the floor.

In "Pilgrim's Progress" the Man with the Muck-rake is set forth as the example of him whose vision is fixed on carnal instead of spiritual things. Yet he also typifies the man who in this life consistently refuses to see aught that is lofty, and fixes his eyes with solemn intentness only on that which is vile and debasing. Now, it is very necessary that we should not flinch from seeing what is vile and debasing. There is filth on the floor, and it must be scraped up with the muck-rake; and there are times and places where this service is the most needed of all the services that can be performed. But the man who never does anything else, who never thinks or speaks or writes, save of his feats with the muck-rake, speedily becomes, not a help to society, not an incitement to good, but one of the most potent forces for evil.

There are, in the body politic, economic and social, many and grave evils, and there is urgent necessity for the sternest war upon them. There should be relentless exposure of and attack upon every evil man whether politician or business man, every evil practice, whether in politics, in business, or in social life. I hail as a benefactor every writer or speaker, every man who, on the platform, or in book, magazine, or newspaper, with merciless severity makes such attack, provided always that he in his turn remembers that the attack is of use only if it is absolutely truthful. The liar is no whit better than the thief, and if his mendacity takes the form of slander, he may be worse than most thieves. It puts a premium upon knavery untruthfully to attack an honest man, or even with hysterical exaggeration to assail a bad man with untruth. An epidemic of indiscriminate assault upon character does not good, but very great harm. The soul of every scoundrel is gladdened whenever an honest man is assailed, or even when a scoundrel is untruthfully assailed.

> ## *"In Bunyan's 'Pilgrim's Progress' you may recall the description of the Man with the Muck-rake..."*

Now, it is easy to twist out of shape what I have just said, easy to affect to misunderstand it, and, if it is slurred over in repetition, not difficult really to misunderstand it. Some persons are sincerely incapable of understanding that to denounce mud slinging does not mean the endorsement of whitewashing; and both the interested individuals who need whitewashing, and those others who practice mud slinging, like to encourage such confusion of ideas. One of the chief counts against those who make indiscriminate assault upon men in business or men in public life, is that they invite a reaction which is sure to tell powerfully in favor of the unscrupulous scoundrel who really ought to be attacked, who ought to be exposed, who ought, if possible, to be put in the penitentiary. If Aristides is praised overmuch as just, people get tired of hearing it; and overcensure of the unjust finally and from similar reasons results in their favor....

It is because I feel that there should be no rest in the endless war against the forces of evil that I ask that the war be conducted with sanity as well as with resolution. The men with the muck-rakes are often indispensable to the wellbeing of society; but only if they know when to stop raking the muck, and to look upward to the celestial crown above them, to the crown of worthy endeavor. There are beautiful things above and round about them; and if they gradually grow to feel that the whole world is nothing but muck, their power of usefulness is gone. If the whole picture is painted black there remains no hue whereby to single out the rascals for distinction from their fellows. Such painting finally induces a kind of moral color-blindness; and people affected by it come to the conclusion that no man is really black, and no man really white, but they are all gray. In other words, they neither believe in the truth of the attack, nor in the honesty of the man who is attacked; they grow as suspicious of the accusation as of the offense; it becomes wellnigh hopeless to stir them either to wrath against wrong-doing or to enthusiasm for what is right; and such a mental attitude in the public gives hope to every knave, and is the despair of honest men.

To assail the great and admitted evils of our political and industrial life with such crude and sweeping generalizations as to include decent men in the general condemnation means the searing of the public conscience. There results a general attitude either of cynical belief in and indifference to public corruption or else of a distrustful inability to discriminate between the good and the bad. Either attitude is fraught with untold damage to the country as a whole....

At this moment we are passing through a period of great unrest—social, political, and industrial unrest. It is of the utmost importance for our future that this should prove to be not the unrest of mere rebelliousness against life, of mere dissatisfaction with the inevitable inequality of conditions, but the unrest of a resolute and eager ambition to secure the betterment of the individual and the nation. So far as this movement of agitation throughout the country takes the form of a fierce discontent with evil, of a determination to punish the authors of evil, whether in industry or politics, the feeling is to be heartily welcomed as a sign of healthy life.

> *"Some persons are incapable of understanding that to denounce mud slinging does not mean the endorsement of whitewashing."*

If, on the other hand, it turns into a mere crusade of appetite against appetite, of a contest between the brutal greed of the "have-nots" and the brutal greed of the "haves," then it has no significance for good, but only for evil. If it seeks to establish a line of cleavage, not along the line which divides good men from bad, but along that other line, running at right angles thereto, which divides those who are well off from those who are less well off, then it will be fraught with immeasurable harm to the body politic.

We can no more and no less afford to condone evil in the man of capital than evil in the man of no capital. The wealthy man who exults because there is a failure of justice in the effort to bring some trust magnate to an account for his misdeeds is as bad as, and no worse than, the so-called labor leader who clamorously strives to excite a foul class feeling on behalf of some other labor leader who is implicated in murder. One attitude is as bad as the other, and no worse; in each case the accused is entitled to exact justice; and in neither case is there need of action by others which can be construed into an expression of sympathy for crime....

The eighth commandment reads, "Thou shalt not steal." It does not read, "Thou shalt not steal from the rich man." It does not read, "Thou shalt not steal from the poor man." It reads simply and plainly, "Thou shalt not steal." No good whatever will come from that warped and mock morality which denounces the misdeeds of men of wealth and forgets the misdeeds practiced at their expense; which denounces bribery, but blinds itself to blackmail; which foams with rage if a corporation secures favors by improper methods, and merely leers with hideous mirth if the corporation is itself wronged. The only public servant who can be trusted honestly to protect the rights of the public against the misdeed of a corporation is that public man who will just as surely protect the corporation itself from wrongful aggression. If a public man is willing to yield to popular clamor and do wrong to the men of wealth or to rich corporations, it may be set down as certain that if the opportunity comes he will secretly and furtively do wrong to the public in the interest of a corporation.

But, in addition to honesty, we need sanity. No honesty will make a public man useful if that man is timid or foolish, if he is a hot-headed zealot or an impracticable visionary. As we strive for reform we find that it is not at all merely the case of a long uphill pull. On the contrary, there is almost as much of breeching work as of collar work; to depend only on traces means that there will soon be a runaway and an upset. The men of wealth who to-day are trying to prevent the regulation and control of their business in the interest of the public by the proper Government authorities will not succeed, in my judgment, in checking the progress of the movement. But if they did succeed they would find that they had sown the wind and would surely reap the whirlwind, for they would ultimately provoke the violent excesses which accompany a reform coming by convulsion instead of by steady and natural growth.

On the other hand, the wild preachers of unrest and discontent, the wild agitators against the entire existing order, the men who act crookedly, whether because of sinister design or from mere puzzleheadedness, the men who preach destruction without proposing any substitute for what they intend to destroy, or who propose a substitute which would be far worse than the existing evils—all these men are the most dangerous opponents of real reform. If they get their way they will lead the people into a deeper pit than any into which they could fall under the present system. If they fail to get their way they will still do incalculable harm by provoking the kind of reaction which, in its revolt against the senseless evil of their teaching, would enthrone more securely than ever the evils which their misguided followers believe they are attacking.

More important than aught else is the development of the broadest sympathy of man for man. The welfare of the wage-worker, the welfare of the tiller of the soil, upon these depend the welfare of the entire country; their good is not to be sought in pulling down others; but their good must be the prime object of all our statesmanship.

Materially we must strive to secure a broader economic opportunity for all men, so that each shall have a better chance to show the stuff of which he is made. Spiritually and ethically we must strive to bring about clean living and right thinking. We appreciate that the things of the body are important; but we appreciate also that the things of the soul are immeasurably more important. The foundation-stone of national life is, and ever must be, the high individual character of the average citizen.

II

"THE NEW NATIONALISM"

READERS WHO HAVE occasionally griped about lackluster candidates in presidential elections ("the evil of two lessers" as James Reston called Carter and Reagan; "Gush and Bore," as the candidates of 2000 were mocked) might wish to avert their gaze from the 1912 election: you'll feel worse. That year, former President Theodore Roosevelt, running as a third-party Progressive candidate, squared off against Democrat Woodrow Wilson and incumbent Republican William Howard Taft. Rounding out the quartet was Socialist candidate Eugene V. Debs, one of America's great radical leaders. The campaign was an extended debate over how government could grapple with economic change.

Ironically, Roosevelt's most succinct summation of his political creed came not during his presidency but soon after. He left office at age fifty in 1909 hoping his successor would continue progressive policies. Roosevelt left for a world tour, and made headlines shooting rhinoceroses and posing with European royalty. When he returned, he realized that the Taft administration was moving in a far more conservative direction than he had hoped. At the same time, he was able to shed the political pragmatism and caution that marked his presidency—and which had sometimes warred with his impulsive nature. Roosevelt began a barnstorming tour ostensibly on behalf of Republican candidates for Congress in the 1910 election, but actually for his brand of progressive politics. "I am in the prophet business," he commented wryly of his post-presidential career.

He gave his most important speech at Osawatomie, Kansas. The small town was renowned as the home of John Brown, whose 1859 revolt against slavery in Harper's Ferry, Virginia, helped spark the Civil War and who was revered by generations of Republicans afterward. Roosevelt's thinking

had come far since he became president. He shed the idea that a return to small business was feasible. Now he argued for a muscular, centralized state to control the conduct of large corporations. "The citizens of the United States must effectively control the mighty commercial forces which they have themselves called into being," he declared.

A book heavily influenced Roosevelt: *The Promise of American Life*, published the previous year by Herbert Croly, who would cofound *The New Republic* magazine. Croly distinguished between the tradition of Jefferson, who extolled yeoman farmers, and Alexander Hamilton, who sought to build a commercial economy. America, Croly argued, needed to achieve Jefferson's egalitarian ends with Hamilton's big-government means. Roosevelt set out a breathtaking array of proposals in the New Nationalism: a minimum wage, campaign finance reform, workers' compensation schemes, government regulation of corporations. He contrasted his approach with an earlier nationalism, which was corrupted by special interests: "The New Nationalism puts the national need before sectional or personal advantage."

Roosevelt and Croly were at odds not only with the laissez-faire conservatism of many Republicans, but of the brand of Progressivism set out by Woodrow Wilson in the 1912 campaign. Wilson's economic guru was Louis Brandeis, the "People's Lawyer" from Boston. They focused on trust-busting as the key issue for Democrats in that campaign, arguing that large corporate monopolies should be broken up, not controlled.

This high intellectual jousting fed one of the most dramatic presidential races ever. Roosevelt openly challenged Taft at the Republican convention in 1912. "My hat is in the ring," he proclaimed (coining yet another phrase), saying he was "fit as a bull moose." The ex-president was the clear favorite of the party rank and file, and would have been elected had he won the party nomination. But Taft controlled the convention, and Roosevelt's delegates stalked out. Roosevelt addressed a frenzied convention of a newly formed Progressive Party seven weeks later in a speech titled "A Confession of Faith": "The old parties are husks, with no real soul within either, divided on artificial lines, boss-ridden and privilege-controlled, each a jumble of incongruous elements, and neither daring to speak out wisely and fearlessly what should be said on the vital issues of the day…." He concluded, "We stand at Armageddon, and we battle for the Lord!"

On October 14, in Milwaukee, the former president was standing in an open car, on his way to deliver a speech. An anti-third-term fanatic fired a pistol at him; Roosevelt's glasses and a thick reading copy of his text saved his life by blunting the bullet before it wounded him. He coughed, saw no blood, and told his secretary, "Get me to that speech. It may be the last I shall deliver, but I am going to deliver this one."

"Friends, I shall ask you to be as quiet as possible," he stilled the crowd. "I don't know whether you fully understand that I have just been shot; but it takes more than that to kill a bull moose." Milking the moment, the candidate spoke for over an hour.

In the end, Wilson won, with Roosevelt second and Taft a distant third. The two progressive candidates had gained an overwhelming majority. Wilson enacted much of Roosevelt's agenda in his first term, creating the Federal Trade Commission to fight monopoly and the Federal Reserve to stabilize the banking system. Much of Roosevelt's plan remained unrealized—and would stay so until the term of his cousin, Franklin.

A typical Roosevelt oratorial pose

Theodore Roosevelt's
SPEECH AT
OSAWATOMIE, KANSAS

Osawatomie, Kansas • August 31, 1910

★hear...
disc 1
track 13

We come here to-day to commemorate one of the epoch-making events of the long struggle for the rights of man—the long struggle for the uplift of humanity. Our country—this great republic—means nothing unless it means the triumph of a real democracy, the triumph of popular government, and, in the long run, of an economic system under which each man shall be guaranteed the opportunity to show the best that there is in him. That is why the history of America is now the central feature of the history of the world; for the world has set its face hopefully toward our democracy; and, O my fellow citizens, each one of you carries on your shoulders not only the burden of doing well for the sake of your own country, but the burden of doing well and of seeing that this nation does well for the sake of mankind.

There have been two great crises in our country's history: first, when it was formed, and then, again, when it was perpetuated; and, in the second of these great crises—in the time of stress and strain which culminated in the Civil War, on the outcome of which depended the justification of what had been done earlier, you men of the Grand Army, you men who fought through the Civil War, not only did you justify your generation, not only did you render life worth living for our generation, but you justified the wisdom of Washington and Washington's colleagues. If this republic had been founded by them only to be split asunder into fragments when the strain came, then the judgment of the world would have been that Washington's work was not worth doing. It was you who crowned Washington's work, as you carried to achievement the high purpose of Abraham Lincoln.

Now, with this second period of our history the name of John Brown will be forever associated; and Kansas was the theater upon which the first act of the second of our great national life dramas was played. It was the result of the struggle in Kansas which determined that our country should be in deed as well as in name devoted to both union and freedom; that the great experiment of democratic government on a national scale should succeed and not fail. In name we had the Declaration of Independence in 1776; but we gave the lie by our acts to the words of the Declaration of Independence until 1865; and words count for nothing except in so far as they represent acts. This is true everywhere; but, O my friends, it should be truest of all in political life. A broken promise is bad enough in private life. It is worse in the field of politics. No man is worth his salt in public life who makes on the stump a pledge which he does not keep after election; and, if he makes such a pledge and does not keep it, hunt him out of public life. I care for the great deeds of the past chiefly as spurs to drive us onward in the present. I speak of the men of the past partly that they may be honored by our praise of them, but more that they may serve as examples for the future....

"The history of America is now the central feature of the history of the world."

As for the veterans of the Grand Army of the Republic, they deserve honor and recognition such as is paid to no other citizens of the republic; for to them the republic owes its all; for to them it owes its very existence. It is because of what you and your comrades did in the dark years that we of to-day walk, each of us, head erect, and proud that we belong, not to one of a dozen little squabbling contemptible commonwealths, but to the mightiest nation upon which the sun shines.

"No man is worth his salt in public life who makes on the stump a pledge which he does not keep after election."

I do not speak of this struggle of the past merely from the historic standpoint. Our interest is primarily in the application to-day of the lessons taught by the contest of half a century ago. It is of little use for us to pay lip loyalty to the mighty men of the past unless we sincerely endeavor to apply to the problems of the present precisely the qualities which in other crises enabled the men of that day to meet those crises. It is half melancholy and half amusing to see the way in which well-meaning people gather to do honor to the men who, in company with John Brown, and under the lead of Abraham Lincoln, faced and solved the great problems of the nineteenth century, while, at the same time, these same good people nervously shrink from, or frantically denounce, those who are trying to meet the problems of the twentieth century in the spirit which was accountable for the successful solution of the problems of Lincoln's time.

Of that generation of men to whom we owe so much, the man to whom we owe most is, of course, Lincoln. Part of our debt to him is because he forecast our present struggle and saw the way out. He said:

I hold that while man exists it is his duty to improve not only his own condition, but to assist in ameliorating mankind.

And again:

Labor is prior to, and independent of, capital. Capital is only the fruit of labor, and could never have existed if labor had not first existed. Labor is the superior of capital, and deserves much the higher consideration.

If that remark was original with me, I should be even more strongly denounced as a communist agitator than I shall be anyhow. It is Lincoln's. I am only quoting it; and that is one side; that is the side the capitalist should hear. Now, let the workingman hear his side.

Capital has its rights, which are as worthy of protection as any other rights....Nor should this lead to a war upon the owners of property. Property is the fruit of labor;... property is desirable; is a positive good in the world.

And then comes a thoroughly Lincolnlike sentence:

Let not him who is houseless pull down the house of another, but let him work diligently and build one for himself, thus by example assuring that his own shall be safe from violence when built.

It seems to me that, in these words, Lincoln took substantially the attitude that we ought to take; he showed the proper sense of proportion in his relative estimates of capital and labor, of human rights and property rights. Above all, in this speech, as in many others, he taught a lesson in wise kindliness and charity; an indispensable lesson to us of today. But this wise kindliness and charity never weakened his arm or numbed his heart. We cannot afford weakly to blind ourselves to the actual conflict which faces us to-day. The issue is joined, and we must fight or fail.

In every wise struggle for human betterment one of the main objects, and often the only object, has been to achieve in large measure equality of opportunity. In the struggle for this great end, nations rise from barbarism to civilization, and through it people press forward from one stage of enlightenment to the next. One of the chief factors in progress is the destruction of special privilege. The essence of any struggle for healthy liberty has always been, and must always be, to take from some one man or class of men the right to enjoy power, or wealth, or position, or immunity, which has not been earned by service to his or their fellows. That is what you fought for in the Civil War, and that is what we strive for now.

At many stages in the advance of humanity, this conflict between the men who possess more than they have earned and the men who have earned more than they possess is the central condition of progress. In our day it appears as the struggle of free men to gain and hold the right of self-government as against the special interests, who twist the methods of free government into machinery for defeating the popular will. At every stage, and under all circumstances, the essence of the struggle is to equalize opportunity, destroy privilege, and give to the life and citizenship of every individual the highest possible value both to himself and to the commonwealth. That is nothing new. All I ask in civil life is what you fought for in the Civil War....

I stand for the square deal. But when I say that I am for the square deal, I mean not merely that I stand for fair play under the present rules of the games, but that I stand for having those rules changed so as to work for a more substantial equality of opportunity and of reward for equally good service. One word of warning, which, I think, is hardly necessary in Kansas. When I say I want a square deal for the poor man, I do not mean that I want a square deal for the man who remains poor because he has not got the energy to work for himself. If a man who has had a chance will not make good, then he has got to quit. And you men of the Grand Army, you want justice for the brave man who fought, and punishment for the coward who shirked his work. Is not that so?

Now, this means that our government, national and state, must be freed from the sinister influence or control of special interests. Exactly as the special interests of cotton and slavery threatened our political integrity before the Civil War, so now the great special business interests too often control and corrupt the men and methods of government for their own profit. We must drive the special interests out of politics. That is one of our tasks to-day. Every special interest is entitled to justice—full, fair, and complete,—and, now, mind you, if there were any attempt by mob violence to plunder and work harm to the special interest, whatever it may be, that I most dislike, and the wealthy man, whomsoever he may be, for whom I have the greatest contempt, I would fight for him, and you would if you were worth your salt. He should have justice. For every special interest is entitled to justice, but not one is entitled to a vote in Congress, to a voice on the bench, or to representation in any public office. The Constitution guarantees protection to property, and we must make that promise good. But it does not give the right of suffrage to any corporation.

The true friend of property, the true conservative, is he who insists that property shall be the servant and not the master of the commonwealth; who insists that the creature of man's making shall be the servant and not the master of the man who made it. The citizens of the United States must effectively control the mighty commercial forces which they have themselves called into being.

There can be no effective control of corporations while their political activity remains. To put an end to it will be neither a short nor an easy task, but it can be done.

We must have complete and effective publicity of corporate affairs, so that people may know beyond peradventure whether the corporations obey the law and whether their management entitles them to the confidence of the public. It is necessary that laws should be passed to prohibit the use of corporate funds directly or indirectly for political purposes; it is still more necessary that such laws should be thoroughly enforced. Corporate expenditures for political purposes, and especially such expenditures by public service corporations, have supplied one of the principal sources of corruption in our political affairs.

It has become entirely clear that we must have government supervision of the capitalization, not only of public service corporations, including, particularly, railways, but of all corporations doing an interstate business....

> "The Constitution guarantees protections to property, and we must make that promise good. But it does not give the right of suffrage to any corporation."

"*I believe that the officers, and, especially, the directors, of corporations should be held personally responsible when any corporation breaks the law.*"

I believe that the officers, and, especially, the directors, of corporations should be held personally responsible when any corporation breaks the law.

Combinations in industry are the result of an imperative economic law which cannot be repealed by political legislation. The effort at prohibiting all combination has substantially failed. The way out lies, not in attempting to prevent such combinations, but in completely controlling them in the interest of the public welfare....

The absence of effective state, and, especially, national, restraint upon unfair money getting has tended to create a small class of enormously wealthy and economically powerful men, whose chief object is to hold and increase their power. The prime need is to change the conditions which enable these men to accumulate power which is not for the general welfare that they should hold or exercise. We grudge no man a fortune which represents his own power and sagacity, when exercised with entire regard to the welfare of his fellows. Again, comrades over there, take the lesson from your own experience. Not only did you not grudge, but you gloried in the promotion of the great generals who gained their promotion by leading the army to victory. So it is with us. We grudge no man a fortune in civil life if it is honorably obtained and well used. It is not even enough that it should have been gained without doing damage to the community. We should permit it to be gained only so long as the gaining represents benefit to the community. This, I know, implies a policy of a far more active governmental interference with social and economic conditions in this country than we have yet had, but I think we have got to face the fact that such an increase in governmental control is now necessary.

No man should receive a dollar unless that dollar has been fairly earned. Every dollar received should represent a dollar's worth of service rendered—not gambling in stocks, but service rendered. The really big fortune, the swollen fortune, by the mere fact of its size acquires qualities which differentiate it in kind as well as in degree from what is possessed by men of relatively small means. Therefore, I believe in a graduated income tax on big fortunes, and in another tax which is far more easily collected and far more effective—a graduated inheritance tax on big fortunes, properly safeguarded against evasion and increasing rapidly in amount with the size of the estate.

The people of the United States suffer from periodical financial panics to a degree substantially unknown among the other nations which approach us in financial strength. There is no reason why we should suffer what they escape. It is of profound importance that our financial system should be promptly investigated, and so thoroughly and effectively revised as to make it certain that hereafter our currency will no longer fail at critical times to meet our needs....

Of conservation I shall speak more at length elsewhere. Conservation means development as much as it does protection. I recognize the right and duty of this generation to develop and use the natural resources of our land; but I do not recognize the right to waste them, or to rob, by wasteful use, the generations that come after us. I ask nothing of the nation except that it so behave as each farmer here behaves with reference to his own children. That farmer is a poor creature who skins the land and leaves it worthless to his children. The farmer is a good farmer who, having enabled the land to support himself and to provide for the education of his children, leaves it to them a little better than he found it himself. I believe the same thing of a nation.

Moreover, I believe that the natural resources must be used for the benefit of all our people, and not monopolized for the benefit of the few, and here again is another case in which

I am accused of taking a revolutionary attitude. People forget now that one hundred years ago there were public men of good character who advocated the nation selling its public lands in great quantities, so that the nation could get the most money out of it, and giving it to the men who could cultivate it for their own uses. We took the proper democratic ground that the land should be granted in small sections to the men who were actually to till it and live on it. Now, with the water power, with the forests, with the mines, we are brought face to face with the fact that there are many people who will go with us in conserving the resources only if they are to be allowed to exploit them for their benefit. That is one of the fundamental reasons why the special interests should be driven out of politics. Of all the questions which can come before this nation, short of the actual preservation of its existence in a great war, there is none which compares in importance with the great central task of leaving this land even a better land for our descendants than it is for us, and training them into a better race to inhabit the land and pass it on. Conservation is a great moral issue, for it involves the patriotic duty of insuring the safety and continuance of the nation. Let me add that the health and vitality of our people are at least as well worth conserving as their forests, waters, lands, and minerals, and in this great work the national government must bear a most important part....

The right to regulate the use of wealth in the public interest is universally admitted. Let us admit also the right to regulate the terms and conditions of labor, which is the chief element of wealth, directly in the interest of the common good. The fundamental thing to do for every man is to give him a chance to reach a place in which he will make the greatest possible contribution to the public welfare. Understand what I say there. Give him a chance, not push him up if he will not be pushed....No man can be a good citizen unless he has a wage more than sufficient to cover the bare cost of living, and hours of labor short enough so that after his day's work is done he will have time and energy to bear his share in the management of the community, to help in carrying the general load. We keep countless men from being good citizens by the conditions of life with which we surround them. We need comprehensive workmen's compensation acts, both state and national laws to regulate child labor and work for women, and, especially, we need in our common schools not merely education in book learning, but also practical training for daily life and work. We need to enforce better sanitary conditions for our workers and to extend the use of safety appliances for our workers in industry and commerce, both within and between the states. Also, friends, in the interest of the workingman himself we need to set our faces like flint against mob violence just as against corporate greed; against violence and injustice and lawlessness by wage workers just as much as against lawless cunning and greed and selfish arrogance of employers....

National efficiency has many factors. It is a necessary result of the principle of conservation widely applied. In the end it will determine our failure or success as a nation. National efficiency has to do, not only with natural resources and with men, but it is equally concerned with institutions. The state must be made efficient for the work which concerns only the people of the state; and the nation for that which concerns all the people. There must remain no neutral ground to serve as a refuge for lawbreakers, and especially for lawbreakers of great wealth, who can hire the vulpine legal cunning which will teach them how to avoid both jurisdictions. It is a misfortune when the national legislature fails to do its duty in providing a national remedy, so that the only national activity is the purely negative activity of the judiciary in forbidding the state to exercise power in the premises.

I do not ask for overcentralization; but I do ask that we work in a spirit of broad and far-reaching nationalism when we work for what concerns our people as a whole. We are all Americans. Our common interests are as broad as the continent. I speak to you here in Kansas exactly as I would speak in New York or Georgia, for the most vital problems are those which affect us all alike. The national government belongs to the whole American people, and where the whole American people are interested, that interest can be guarded effectively only by the national government. The betterment which we seek must be accomplished, I believe, mainly through the national government.

"*The New Nationalism puts the national need before the sectional or personal advantage.*"

The American people are right in demanding that New Nationalism, without which we cannot hope to deal with new problems. The New Nationalism puts the national need before sectional or personal advantage. It is impatient of the utter confusion that results from local legislatures attempting to treat national issues as local issues. It is still more impatient of the impotence which springs from overdivision of governmental powers, the impotence which makes it possible for local selfishness or for legal cunning, hired by wealthy special interests, to bring national activities to a deadlock. This New Nationalism regards the executive power as the steward of the public welfare. It demands of the judiciary that it shall be interested primarily in human welfare rather than in property, just as it demands that the representative body shall represent all the people rather than any one class or section of the people....

If our political institutions were perfect, they would absolutely prevent the political domination of money in any part of our affairs. We need to make our political representatives more quickly and sensitively responsive to the people whose servants they are. More direct action by the people in their own affairs under proper safeguards is vitally necessary. The direct primary is a step in this direction, if it is associated with a corrupt practices act effective to prevent the advantage of the man willing recklessly and unscrupulously to spend money over his more honest competitor. It is particularly important that all moneys received or expended for campaign purposes should be publicly accounted for, not only after election, but before election as well. Political action must be made simpler, easier, and freer from confusion for every citizen....

The object of government is the welfare of the people. The material progress and prosperity of a nation are desirable chiefly so far as they lead to the moral and material welfare of all good citizens. Just in proportion as the average man and woman are honest, capable of sound judgment and high ideals, active in public affairs,—but, first of all, sound in their home life, and the father and mother of healthy children whom they bring up well,—just so far, and no farther, we may count our civilization a success. We must have—I believe we have already—a genuine and permanent moral awakening, without which no wisdom of legislation or administration really means anything; and, on the other hand, we must try to secure the social and economic legislation without which any improvement due to purely moral agitation is necessarily evanescent. Let me again illustrate by a reference to the Grand Army. You could not have won simply as a disorderly and disorganized mob. You needed generals; you needed careful administration of the most advanced type; and a good commissary—the cracker line. You well remember that success was necessary in many different lines in order to bring about general success. You had to have the administration at Washington good, just as you had to have the administration in the field; and you had to have the work of the generals good. You could not have triumphed without that administration and leadership; but it would all have been worthless if the average soldier had not had the right stuff in him. He had to have the right stuff in him, or you could not get it out of him. In the last analysis, therefore, vitally necessary though it was to have the right kind of organization and the right kind of generalship, it was even more vitally necessary that the average soldier should have the fighting edge, the right character. So it is in our civil life. No matter how honest and decent we are in our private lives, if we do not have the right kind of law and the right kind of administration of the law, we cannot go forward as a nation. That is imperative; but it must be an addition to, and not a substitution for, the qualities that make us good citizens. In the last analysis, the most important elements in any man's career must be the sum of those qualities which, in the aggregate, we speak of as character. If he has not got it, then no law that the wit of man can devise, no administration of the law by the boldest and strongest executive, will avail to help him. We must have the right kind of character—character that makes a man, first of all, a good man in the home, a good father, a good husband—that makes a man a good neighbor. You must have that, and, then, in addition, you must have the kind of law and the kind of administration of the law which will give to those qualities in the private citizen the best possible chance for development. The prime problem of our nation is to get the right type of good citizenship, and, to get it, we must have progress, and our public men must be genuinely progressive.

Woodrow
WILSON

28TH PRESIDENT: 1913–1921

Born: December 28, 1856, in Staunton, Virginia
Died: February 3, 1924, in Washington, D.C.

Disc 1, Tracks 14-15

12

"THE WORLD MUST BE MADE SAFE FOR DEMOCRACY"

IN 1885, PROFESSOR WOODROW WILSON published a classic book, *Congressional Government*, decrying the weak presidents of his day. After watching Theodore Roosevelt in action, though, Wilson came to believe that the president should be a strong, public presence. "The nation as a whole has chosen him," he wrote, "and is conscious that it has no other political spokesman. His is the only national voice in affairs. Let him once win the admiration and confidence of the country, and no other single force can withstand him, no combination of forces will easily overpower him." When the reed-thin, bespectacled Wilson became president after serving as governor of New Jersey, he put his theories into effect. He broke a century of precedent by addressing a joint session of Congress to propose cuts in the tariff. Wilson wanted the lawmakers to see he was a real person, he said, "not a mere department of the Government hailing Congress from some isolated island of jealous power." (Riding back to the White House, his wife told him that "going to the Hill" was just what Theodore Roosevelt would have done, "if only he had thought of it." "Yes," Wilson exulted, "I think I put one over on Teddy.")

He used that "national voice" in a decisive moment of war and peace. World War I (then known as the Great War) broke out in August 1914, pitting Germany and its allies against Great Britain, France, and Russia. For two tense years, as millions of young men struggled in trench warfare, the United States remained neutral. Wilson sought reelection in 1916 on the slogan, "He Kept Us Out of War." He declared, "There is such a thing as a man being too proud to fight. There is such a thing as a nation being so right that it does not need to convince others by force that it is right."

Just months later, the situation changed. In February 1917, Wilson told Congress we would stay neutral unless Germany attacked our ships, which would be armed as a precaution. The next month, the Kaiser's submarines sunk three U.S. civilian ships. Former President Theodore Roosevelt demanded a declaration of war, and thousands rallied at New York's Madison Square Garden to denounce Germany. Wilson's cabinet unanimously urged him to cease neutrality. He kept silent. Then the president announced he would call Congress into special emergency session twelve days later. What would he do—and what would he say? Public debate worked to a frenzy. Wilson told his secretary of state the way to face criticism is "not by words, but by some action which has met with the approval of the major part of the country." For a week, he played golf and tried to relax. Then he locked himself in his study and mulled his options and his words.

Wilson spoke in a night of high drama. He began without emotion, but soon his words rose and fell, with the carefully crafted speech reaching several crescendos and punctuated by cheers. More in sorrow than in anger, "with a profound sense of the solemn and even tragical character of the step I am taking," Wilson asked for a declaration of war. Amid what already seemed a pointless bloodbath, he tried to lift not only America but humanity to a higher level. We "fight thus for the ultimate peace of the world and for the liberation of its peoples, the German peoples included; for the rights of nations great and small and the privilege of men everywhere to choose their way of life and of obedience. The world must be made safe for democracy."

Wilson's biographer August Heckscher writes that the speech's peroration "lives in the anthology of American

Wilson requests a declaration of war from Congress, April 2, 1917

political prose along with a few of the utterances of Lincoln, engaged in an earlier war and in an earlier contradiction of ends and means." Like so many of the best wartime speeches of American presidents, it is not triumphal, jingoistic, or bellicose. The war is necessary, but "it is a fearful thing to lead this great peaceful people into war, into the most terrible and disastrous of all wars." America entered global power politics with a distinct, if ill-defined, strain of idealism.

Citizens were electrified. The famed political columnist Walter Lippmann wrote, "Only a statesman who will be called great could have made America's intervention mean so much to the generous forces of the world, could have lifted the inevitable horror of war into a deed so full of meaning." Within two days, Congress overwhelmingly voted for a declaration of war against Germany. Public opinion had swung toward U.S. involvement. For the first time, we would join a general war well beyond our borders.

hear...
disc 1
track 14

Gentlemen of the Congress:

I have called the Congress into extraordinary session because there are serious, very serious, choices of policy to be made, and made immediately which it was neither right nor constitutionally permissible that I should assume the responsibility of making.

On the third of February last, I officially laid before you the extraordinary announcement of the Imperial German Government that on and after the first day of February it was its purpose to put aside all restraints of law or of humanity and use its submarines to sink every vessel that sought to approach either the ports of Great Britain and Ireland or the western coast of Europe or any of the ports controlled by the enemies of Germany within the Mediterranean. That had seemed to be the object of the German submarine warfare earlier in the war; but since April of last year the Imperial Government had somewhat restrained the commanders of its undersea craft, in conformity with its promise then given to us that passenger boats should not be sunk, and that due warning would be given to all other vessels which its submarines might seek to destroy, when no resistance was offered or escape attempted, and care taken that their crews were given at least a fair chance to save their lives in their open boats. The precautions taken were meager and haphazard enough, as was proved in distressing instance after instance in the progress of the cruel and unmanly business, but a certain degree of restraint was observed.

The new policy has swept every restriction aside. Vessels of every kind, whatever their flag, their character, their cargo, their destination, their errand, have been ruthlessly sent to the bottom without warning and without thought of help or mercy for those on board—the vessels of friendly neutrals along with those of belligerents. Even hospital ships and ships carrying relief to the sorely bereaved and stricken people of Belgium, though the latter were provided with safe conduct through the proscribed areas by the German Government itself, and were distinguished by unmistakable marks of identity, have been sunk with the same reckless lack of compassion or of principle.

I was for a little while unable to believe that such things would in fact be done by any government that had hitherto subscribed to the humane practices of civilized nations. International law had its origin in the attempt to set up some law which would be respected and observed upon the seas, where no nation had right of dominion and where lay the free highways of the world. By painful stage after stage has that law been built up, with meager enough results, indeed, after all was accomplished that could be accomplished, but always with a clear view, at least, of what the heart and conscience of mankind demanded.

> ## *"The present German submarine warfare against commerce is a warfare against mankind."*

This minimum of right the German Government has swept aside under the plea of retaliation and necessity, and because it had no weapons which it could use at sea except these which it is impossible to employ as it is employing them without throwing to the winds all scruples of humanity or of respect for the understandings that were supposed to underlie the intercourse of the world.

I am not now thinking of the loss of property involved, immense and serious as that is, but only of the wanton and wholesale destruction of the lives of noncombatants, men, women and children, engaged in pursuits which have always, even in the darkest period of modern history, been deemed innocent and legitimate. Property can be paid for; the lives of peaceful and innocent people cannot be.

The present German submarine warfare against commerce is a warfare against mankind. It is a war against all nations. American ships have been sunk, American lives taken in ways which it has stirred us very deeply to learn of, but the ships and people of other neutral and friendly nations have been sunk and overwhelmed in the waters in the same way. There has been no discrimination. The challenge is to all mankind. Each nation must decide for itself how it will meet it. The choice we make for ourselves must be made with a moderation of counsel and a temperateness of judgment befitting our character and our motives as a nation.

Over four million copies of this poster were printed between 1917 and 1918, as the U.S. entered World War I

We must put excited feeling away. Our motive will not be revenge or the victorious assertion of the physical might of the nation, but only the vindication of right, of human right, of which we are only a single champion.

"Armed neutrality, it now appears, is impracticable."

When I addressed the Congress on the 26th of February last, I thought that it would suffice to assert our neutral right with arms; our right to use the sea against unlawful interference; our right to keep our people safe against unlawful violence. But armed neutrality, it now appears, is impracticable. Because submarines are in effect outlaws when used as the German submarines have been used against merchant shipping, it is impossible to defend ships against their attacks as the law of nations has assumed that merchantmen would defend themselves against privateers or cruisers, visible craft giving chase upon the open sea. It is common prudence in such circumstances, grim necessity indeed, to endeavor to destroy them before they have shown their own intention. They must be dealt with upon sight, if dealt with at all.

The German Government denies the right of neutrals to use arms at all within the areas of the sea which it has prescribed, even in the defense of rights which no modern publicist has ever before questioned their right to defend. The intimation is conveyed that the armed guards which we have placed on our merchant ships will be treated as beyond the pale of law and subject to be dealt with as pirates would be. Armed neutrality is ineffectual enough at best; in such circumstances and in the face of such pretensions, it is worse than ineffectual: it is likely only to produce what it was meant to prevent; it is practically certain to draw us into the war without either the rights or the effectiveness of belligerents.

There is one choice we cannot make, we are incapable of making—we will not choose the path of submission and suffer the most sacred rights of our nation and our people to be ignored or violated. The wrongs against which we now array ourselves are no common wrongs; they cut to the very roots of human life.

With a profound sense of the solemn and even tragical character of the step I am taking and of the grave responsibilities which it involves, but in unhesitating obedience to what I deem my constitutional duty, I advise that the Congress declare the recent course of the Imperial German Government to be, in fact, nothing less than war against the Government and people of the United States; that it formally accept the status of belligerent which has thus been thrust upon it; and that it take immediate steps not only to put the country in a more thorough state of defense, but also to exert all its power and employ all its resources to bring the Government of the German Empire to terms and end the war.

What this will involve is clear. It will involve the utmost practicable co-operation in counsel and action with the governments now at war with Germany; and, as incident to that, the extension to those governments of the most liberal financial credits, in order that our resources may, so far as possible, be added to theirs. It will involve the organization and mobilization of all the material resources of the country to supply the materials of war and serve the incidental needs of the nation in the most abundant and yet the most economical and efficient way possible. It will involve the immediate full equipment of the navy in all respects, but particularly in supplying it with the best means of dealing with the enemy's submarines. It will involve the immediate addition to the armed forces of the United States already provided for by law in case of war at least 500,000 men, who should, in my opinion, be chosen upon the principle of universal liability to service, and also the authorization of subsequent additional increments of equal force so soon as they may be needed and can be handled in training.

It will involve also, of course, the granting of adequate credits to the Government, sustained, I hope, so far as they can equitably be sustained by the present generation, by well-conceived taxation. I say sustained so far as may be equitable by taxation because it seems to me that it would be most unwise to base the credits which will now be necessary

entirely on money borrowed. It is our duty, I most respectfully urge, to protect our people so far as we may against the very serious hardships and evils which would be likely to arise out of the inflation which would be produced by vast loans.

In carrying out the measures by which these things are to be accomplished, we should keep constantly in mind the wisdom of interfering as little as possible in our own preparation and in the equipment of our own military forces with the duty—for it will be a very practical duty—of supplying the nations already at war with Germany with the materials which they can obtain only from us or by our assistance. They are in the field, and we should help them in every way to be effective there.

> *"There is one choice we cannot make, we are incapable of making—we will not choose the path of submission."*

I shall take the liberty of suggesting, through the several executive departments of the Government, for the consideration of your committees, measures for the accomplishment of the several objects I have mentioned. I hope that it will be your pleasure to deal with them as having been framed after very careful thought by the branch of the Government upon which the responsibility of conducting the war and safeguarding the nation will most directly fall.

While we do these things, these deeply momentous things, let us be very clear, and make very clear to all the world what our motives and our objects are. My own thought has not been driven from its habitual and normal course by the unhappy events of the last two months, and I do not believe that the thought of the nation has been altered or clouded by them.

I have exactly the same things in mind now that I had in mind when I addressed the Senate on the 22nd of January last; the same that I had in mind when I addressed the Congress on the 3rd of February and on the 26th of February.

Our object now, as then, is to vindicate the principles of peace and justice in the life of the world as against selfish and autocratic power and to set up among the really free and self-governed peoples of the world such a concert of purpose and of action as will henceforth insure the observance of those principles.

Neutrality is no longer feasible or desirable where the peace of the world is involved and the freedom of its peoples, and the menace to that peace and freedom lies in the existence of autocratic governments backed by organized force which is controlled wholly by their will, not by the will of their people. We have seen the last of neutrality in such circumstances.

We are at the beginning of an age where it will be insisted that the same standards of conduct and of responsibility for wrong done shall be observed among nations and their governments that are observed among the individual citizens of civilized states.

"I advise that the Congress declare the recent course of the Imperial German Government to be, in fact, nothing less than war."

We have no quarrel with the German people. We have no feeling toward them but one of sympathy and friendship. It was not upon their impulse that their Government acted in entering this war. It was not with their previous knowledge or approval. It was a war determined upon as wars used to be determined upon in the old, unhappy days when peoples were nowhere consulted by their rulers and wars were provoked and waged in the interest of dynasties or of little groups of ambitious men who were accustomed to use their fellow-men as pawns and tools.

Self-governed nations do not fill their neighbor states with spies or set the course of intrigue to bring about some critical posture of affairs which will give them an opportu-

nity to strike and make conquest. Such designs can be successfully worked out only under cover and where no one has the right to ask questions.

Cunningly contrived plans of deception or aggression, carried, it may be, from generation to generation, can be worked out and kept from the light only within the privacy of courts or behind the carefully guarded confidences of a narrow and privileged class. They are happily impossible where public opinion commands and insists upon full information concerning all the nation's affairs.

A steadfast concert for peace can never be maintained except by a partnership of democratic nations. No autocratic government could be trusted to keep faith within it or observe its covenants. It must be a league of honor, a partnership of opinion. Intrigue would eat its vitals away; the plottings of inner circles who could plan what they would and render account to no one would be a corruption seated at its very heart. Only free peoples can hold their purpose and their honor steady to a common end and prefer the interests of mankind to any narrow interest of their own.

Does not every American feel that assurance has been added to our hope for the future peace of the world by the wonderful and heartening things that have been happening within the last few weeks in Russia?

Russia was known by those who knew her best to have been always in fact democratic at heart, in all the vital habits of her thought, in all the intimate relationships of her people that spoke their natural instinct, their habitual attitude toward life.

The autocracy that crowned the summit of her political structure, long as it had stood and terrible as was the reality of its power, was not in fact Russian in origin, character, or purpose; and now it has been shaken off and the great generous Russian people have been added in all their native majesty and might to the forces that are fighting for a freedom in the world, for justice and for peace. Here is a fit partner for a league of honor.

One of the things that has served to convince us that the Prussian autocracy was not and could never be our friend is that from the very outset of the present war it has filled our unsuspecting communities and even our offices of government with spies and set criminal intrigues everywhere afoot against our national unity of council, our peace within and without, our industries and our commerce.

Indeed it is now evident that its spies were here even before the war began; and it unhappily is not a matter of conjecture, but a fact proved in our courts of justice, that the intrigues which have more than once come perilously near to disturbing the peace and dislocating the industries of the country have been carried on at the instigation, with the support, and even under the personal direction of official agents of the Imperial Government accredited to the Government of the United States.

"We have no quarrel with the German people."

Even in checking these things and trying to extirpate them we have sought to put the most generous interpretation possible upon them, because we knew that their source lay, not in any hostile feeling or purpose of the German people toward us (who were, no doubt, as ignorant of them as we ourselves were), but only in the selfish designs of a government that did what it pleased and told its people nothing. But they have played their part in serving to convince us at last that that government entertains no real friendship for us and means to act against our peace and security at its convenience. That it means to stir up enemies against us at our very doors, the intercepted note to the German Minister at Mexico City is eloquent evidence.

We are accepting this challenge of hostile purpose because we know that in such a government, following such methods, we can never have a friend; and that in the presence of its organized power always lying in wait to accomplish we know not what purpose, there can be no assured security for the democratic governments of the world. We are now about to accept gauge of battle with this natural foe to liberty and shall, if necessary, spend the whole force of the nation to check and nullify its pretensions and end its power. We are glad, now that we see the facts with

no veil of false pretense about them, to fight thus for the ultimate peace of the world and for the liberation of its peoples, the German peoples included; for the rights of nations great and small and the privilege of men everywhere to choose their way of life and of obedience. The world must be made safe for democracy. Its peace must be planted upon the tested foundations of political liberty.

We have no selfish ends to serve. We desire no conquest, no dominion. We seek no indemnities for ourselves, no material compensation for the sacrifices we shall freely make. We are but one of the champions of the rights of mankind. We shall be satisfied when those rights have been made as secure as the faith and the freedom of the nations can make them.

Just because we fight without rancor and without selfish object, seeking nothing for ourselves but what we shall wish to share with all free peoples, we shall, I feel confident, conduct our operations as belligerents without passion and ourselves observe with proud punctilio the principles of right and of fair play we profess to be fighting for.

I have said nothing of the Governments allied with the Imperial Government of Germany because they have not made war upon us or challenged us to defend our right and our honor. The Austro-Hungarian Government has, indeed, avowed its unqualified indorsement and acceptance of the reckless and lawless submarine warfare adopted now without disguise by the Imperial German Government, and it has therefore not been possible for this Government to receive Count Tarnowski, the Ambassador recently accredited to this Government by the Imperial and Royal Government of Austria-Hungary; but that Government has not actually engaged in warfare against citizens of the United States on the seas, and I take the liberty, for the present at least, of postponing a discussion of our relations with the authorities at Vienna. We enter this war only where we are clearly forced into it because there are no other means of defending our rights.

It will be all the easier for us to conduct ourselves as belligerents in a high spirit of right and fairness because we act without animus, not in enmity toward a people nor with the desire to bring any injury or disadvantage upon them, but only in armed opposition to an irresponsible Government which has thrown aside all considerations of humanity and of right and is running amuck.

We are, let me say again, the sincere friends of the German people, and shall desire nothing so much as the early re-establishment of intimate relations of mutual advantage between us—however hard it may be for them, for the time being, to believe that this is spoken from our hearts. We have borne with their present Government through all these bitter months because of that friendship—exercising a patience and forbearance which would otherwise have been impossible. We shall, happily, still have an opportunity to prove that friendship in our daily attitude and actions toward the millions of men and women of German birth and native sympathy who live among us and share our life, and we shall be proud to prove it toward all who are in fact loyal to their neighbors and to the Government in the hour of test. They are, most of them, as true and loyal Americans as if they had never known any other fealty or allegiance. They will be prompt to stand with us in rebuking and restraining the few who may be of a different mind and purpose.

> *"It is a fearful thing to lead this great peaceful people into war, into the most terrible and disastrous of all wars, civilization itself seeming to be in the balance."*

If there should be disloyalty, it will be dealt with with a firm hand of stern repression; but if it lifts its head at all, it will lift it only here and there and without countenance, except from a lawless and malignant few.

It is a distressing and oppressive duty, gentlemen of the Congress, which I have performed in thus addressing you.

There are, it may be, many months of fiery trial and sacrifice ahead of us. It is a fearful thing to lead this great peaceful people into war, into the most terrible and disastrous of all wars, civilization itself seeming to be in the balance.

But the right is more precious than peace, and we shall fight for the things which we have always carried nearest our hearts—for democracy, for the right of those who submit to authority to have a voice in their own governments, for the rights and liberties of small nations, for a universal domination of right by such a concert of free peoples as shall bring peace and safety to all nations and make the world itself at last free. To such a task we can dedicate our lives and our fortunes, everything that we are and everything that we have, with the pride of those who know that the day has come when America is privileged to spend her blood and her might for the principles that gave her birth and happiness and the peace which she has treasured. God helping her, she can do no other.

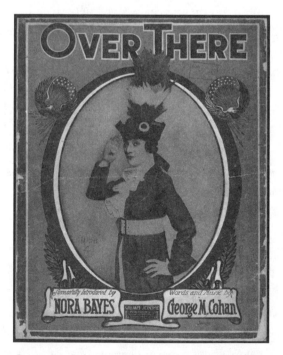

George M. Cohan was awarded the Congressional Gold Medal of Honor for his patriotic "Over There"

13

"THE FOURTEEN POINTS"

WHEN THE BOLSHEVIKS seized power in Russia in 1917, they revealed to the world the secret treaties that bound many of the allies. Americans may have been carried into war by Wilson's idealistic words, but other nations craved the lands of their foes. The secret treaties, historian Ronald Steel writes, were "a calamity for Wilson."

Angered by the pacts, sensing the moral authority for the war was slipping away, and wanting to set the terms of peace, Wilson took an audacious step: he drew up a plan for a just settlement. Few in the U.S. government knew about the effort. Colonel Edward House, Wilson's closest advisor, led a team of social scientists, mapmakers, geologists, and lawyers known as "the Inquiry," working out of sight in New York. The group labored without rest for weeks, studying Europe and tracing out a possible resolution. Walter Lippmann, the very journalist who had so lavishly praised Wilson's war speech of 1917, directed the Inquiry's daily work. His job, he recalled, was to "take the secret treaties, analyze the parts which were tolerable, and separate them from those which we regarded as intolerable, and then develop an American position which conceded as much to the Allies as it could, but took away the poison."

Wilson relished surprise, believing that long silence from a chief executive forced audiences to focus on the words when they were finally spoken. Laden with maps and carrying a memo drafted by Lippmann setting out peace points, Colonel House visited the White House where he and Wilson worked through a weekend. When the president finally summoned a joint session of Congress, the capital was so startled that much of the cabinet and diplomatic corps were out of town.

British Prime Minister Lloyd George, French Premier Georges Clemenceau, and Wilson in Paris during negotiations for the Treaty of Versailles

Earlier, before the U.S. entered the war, Wilson called for "peace without victory." Even now, he made clear he did not see Germany, or at least its people, as an enemy. Wilson drafted the first five points himself, setting out general principles for a postwar world—and in his text he declared they "must" be done. They convey a vision of democracy, free trade, and self-determination among

Wilson addresses Congress on January 8, 1918

nations. The first bluntly warns the other combatants: no more secret treaties. Two of the territorial points, drafted by the Inquiry, were deemed imperative too—including the insistence that foreign troops leave Russia, now embroiled in revolution. Most "points," however, plainly were open to negotiation. Point Fourteen, also added by Wilson, called for an international organization to guarantee secure borders and keep the peace, what soon became the League of Nations. Historian John Morton Blum concludes, "The Fourteen Points gave a global application to Wilson's moral principles."

Just as Wilson had learned to appeal to the American public over the heads of members of Congress, he hoped to pressure European governments by swaying their constituents. This speech kindled intense hope across the Continent. "It would almost be superfluous to remark upon the impact and importance of the Fourteen Points Address," writes Arthur Link, the editor of Wilson's papers. "It immediately became the moral standard [around the world]." The very leaders who had signed secret treaties were far more cynical about the Fourteen Points. Georges Clemenceau, prime minister of France, reportedly commented acidly, "God Himself only had ten commandments."

Immediate hope for peace was dashed when Russia's new rulers pulled out of the war, giving Germany land and emboldening it to fight on. War raged for nearly another year. But when Germany sued for an armistice peace ten months after the speech, it based its appeal on Wilson's plan. The American president traveled to Europe for six months to negotiate the new map of the world. Hundreds of thousands of supporters greeted him on the streets of Paris. But the Fourteen Points did not truly frame the Versailles Treaty, which left Germany impoverished and set the stage for the Second World War two decades later. The Senate resisted Wilson's plea for the United States to join the League of Nations. He set out on a cross-country speaking tour hoping to once again stir public opinion. Midway through, however, he suffered a massive stroke and was a spent force for the remainder of his term. He never spoke in public again.

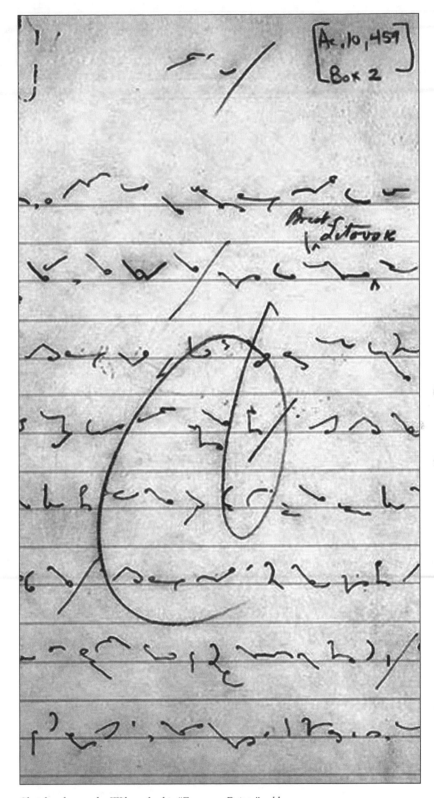

Shorthand notes by Wilson for his "Fourteen Points" address

disc 1
track 15

Gentlemen of the Congress:

[In the first part of the speech, Wilson discusses negotiations between Russia and Germany. Then he turns to his broader purpose.]

But whatever the results of the parleys at Brest-Litovsk [between Russia and Germany], whatever the confusions of counsel and of purpose in the utterances of the spokesmen of the Central Empires, they have again attempted to acquaint the world with their objects in the war and have again challenged their adversaries to say what their objects are and what sort of settlement they would deem just and satisfactory. There is no good reason why that challenge should not be responded to, and responded to with the utmost candor....No statesman who has the least conception of his responsibility ought for a moment to permit himself to continue this tragical and appalling outpouring of blood and treasure unless he is sure beyond a peradventure that the objects of the vital sacrifice are part and parcel of the very life of society and that the people for whom he speaks think them right and imperative as he does....

It will be our wish and purpose that the processes of peace, when they are begun, shall be absolutely open, and that they shall involve and permit henceforth no secret understandings of any kind. The day of conquest and aggrandizement is gone by; so is also the day of secret covenants entered into in the interest of particular governments and likely at some unlooked-for moment to upset the peace of the world. It is this happy fact, now clear to the view of every public man whose thoughts do not still linger in an age that is dead and gone, which makes it possible for every nation whose purposes are consistent with justice and the peace of the world to avow now or at any other time the objects it has in view.

> *"It will be our wish and purpose that the processes of peace shall be absolutely open and that they shall involve and permit henceforth no secret understandings of any kind."*

We entered this war because violations of right had occurred which touched us to the quick and made the life of our own people impossible unless they were corrected and the world secured once for all against their recurrence. What we demand in this war, therefore, is nothing peculiar to ourselves. It is that the world be made fit and safe to live in; and particularly that it be made safe for every peace-loving nation which, like our own, wishes to live its own life, determine its own institutions, be assured of justice and fair dealings by the other peoples of the world, as against force and selfish aggression. All the peoples of the world are in effect partners in this interest, and for our own part we see very clearly that unless justice be done to others it will not be done to us.

The program of the world's peace, therefore, is our program, and that program, the only possible program, as we see it, is this:

I. Open covenants of peace, openly arrived at, after which there shall be no private international understandings of any kind, but diplomacy shall proceed always frankly and in the public view.

II. Absolute freedom of navigation upon the seas, outside territorial waters, alike in peace and in war, except as the seas may be closed in whole or in part by international action for the enforcement of international covenants.

III. The removal, so far as possible, of all economic barriers and the establishment of an equality of trade conditions among all the nations consenting to the peace and associating themselves for its maintenance.

IV. Adequate guarantees given and taken that national armaments will be reduced to the lowest point consistent with domestic safety.

V. Free, open-minded, and absolutely impartial adjustment of all colonial claims, based upon a strict observance of the principle that in determining all such questions of sovereignty the interests of the population concerned must have equal weight with the equitable claims of the Government whose title is to be determined.

VI. The evacuation of all Russian territory and such a settlement of all questions affecting Russia as will secure the best and freest cooperation of the other nations of the world in obtaining for her an unhampered and unembarrassed opportunity for the independent determination of her own political development and national policy, and assure her of a sincere welcome into the society of free nations under institutions of her own choosing; and, more than a welcome, assistance also of every kind that she may need and may herself desire. The treatment accorded Russia by her sister nations in the months to come will be the acid test of their good-will, of their comprehension of her needs as distinguished from their own interests, and of their intelligent and unselfish sympathy.

VII. Belgium, the whole world will agree, must be evacuated and restored, without any attempt to limit the sovereignty which she enjoys in common with all other free nations. No other single act will serve as this will serve to restore confidence among the nations in the laws which they have themselves set

and determined for the government of their relations with one another. Without this healing act the whole structure and validity of international law is forever impaired.

VIII. All French territory should be freed and the invaded portions restored, and the wrong done to France by Prussia in 1871 in the matter of Alsace-Lorraine, which has unsettled the peace of the world for nearly fifty years, should be righted, in order that peace may once more be made secure in the interest of all.

IX. A readjustment of the frontiers of Italy should be effected along clearly recognizable lines of nationality.

X. The peoples of Austria-Hungary, whose place among the nations we wish to see safeguarded and assured, should be accorded the freest opportunity of autonomous development.

XI. Rumania, Serbia, and Montenegro should be evacuated; occupied territories restored; Serbia accorded free and secure access to the sea; and the relations of the several Balkan states to one another determined by friendly counsel along historically established lines of allegiance and nationality; and international guarantees of the political and economic independence and territorial integrity of the several Balkan states should be entered into.

XII. The Turkish portions of the present Ottoman Empire should be assured a secure sovereignty, but the other nationalities which are now under Turkish rule should be assured an undoubted security of life and an absolutely unmolested opportunity of autonomous development, and the Dardanelles should be permanently opened as a free passage to the ships and commerce of all nations under international guarantees.

XIII. An independent Polish state should be erected which should include the territories inhabited by indisputably Polish populations, which should be assured a free and secure access to the sea, and whose political and economic independence and territorial integrity should be guaranteed by international covenant.

XIV. A general association of nations must be formed under specific covenants for the purpose of affording mutual guarantees of political independence and territorial integrity to great and small states alike.

In regard to these essential rectifications of wrong and assertions of right, we feel ourselves to be intimate partners of all the governments and peoples associated together against the imperialists. We cannot be separated in interest or divided in purpose. We stand together until the end.

"The treatment accorded Russia by her sister nations in the months to come will be the acid test of their good will."

For such arrangements and covenants we are willing to fight and to continue to fight until they are achieved; but only because we wish the right to prevail and desire a just and stable peace, such as can be secured only by removing the chief provocations to war, which this program does remove. We have no jealousy of German greatness, and there is nothing in this program that impairs it. We grudge her no achievement or distinction of learning or of pacific enterprise such as have made her record very bright and very enviable. We do not wish to injure her or to block in any way her legitimate influence or power. We do not wish to fight her either with arms or with hostile arrangements of trade, if she is willing to associate herself with us and the other peace-loving nations of the world in covenants of justice and law and fair dealing. We wish her only to accept a place of equality among the peoples of the world—the new world in which we now live—instead of a place of mastery.

"The wrong done to France by Prussia in 1871 in matter of Alsace-Lorraine should be righted."

Neither do we presume to suggest to her any alteration or modification of her institutions. But it is necessary, we must frankly say, and necessary as a preliminary to any intelligent dealings with her on our part, that we should know whom her spokesmen speak for when they speak to us, whether for the Reichstag majority or for the military party and the men whose creed is imperial domination.

We have spoken now, surely, in terms too concrete to admit of any further doubt or question. An evident principle runs through the whole program I have outlined. It is the principle of justice to all peoples and nationalities, and their right to live on equal terms of liberty and safety with one another, whether they be strong or weak. Unless this principle be made its foundation no part of the structure of international justice can stand. The people of the United States could act upon no other principle; and to the vindication of this principle they are ready to devote their lives, their honor, and everything that they possess. The moral climax of this the culminating and final war for human liberty has come, and they are ready to put their own strength, their own highest purpose, their own integrity and devotion to the test.

Franklin Delano
ROOSEVELT

32ND PRESIDENT: 1933–1945

Born: January 30, 1882, in Hyde Park, New York

Died: April 12, 1945, in Warm Springs, Georgia

Disc 1, Tracks 17-21

14

FRANKLIN DELANO ROOSEVELT

"THE ONLY THING WE HAVE TO FEAR IS FEAR ITSELF"

THE GREAT DEPRESSION was the darkest crisis of spirit since the Civil War. In the three years following the stock market crash of 1929, thirteen million Americans—one-third of the workforce—became unemployed. Farm income dropped by more than two-thirds. Six hundred thousand homeowners lost their homes. Ragged men and women in the great cities lived in "Hoovervilles," mocking President Herbert Hoover and his pledge that "prosperity is just around the corner."

Franklin Delano Roosevelt, Democratic governor of New York, easily beat Hoover in 1932. FDR's policies were vague, but he made clear his intent to act. He shed the tradition by which presidential nominees waited at home to be notified of their nomination, and flew to Chicago to accept the nomination in person (a striking move when air travel was still seen as risky, just five years after Charles Lindbergh flew across the Atlantic). Roosevelt told the convention it would be his party's task "to break foolish traditions," concluding, "I pledge you, I pledge myself to a New Deal for the American people." Earlier, the governor had expressed his instincts at Oglethorpe University. "The country demands bold, persistent experimentation," he said. "It is common sense to take a method and try it: if it fails, admit it frankly and try another. But above all, try something."

Under the Constitution as then in effect, four months stretched between the election and the oath taking. Each day, it seemed, things got worse. In February, an assassin fired into Roosevelt's car in Miami, killing the mayor of Chicago, Anton Cermak, and narrowly missing the president-elect. That month, a bank panic began in Michigan and spread throughout the country. Depositors had seen thousands of banks fail already, taking the savings of

Depression-era homeless in New York seek shelter

millions with them. Now they rushed to withdraw their own funds. By inauguration day, nearly all the nation's banks were closed. Hoover, bitter over his loss, begged Roosevelt to agree to emergency measures and to endorse the outgoing regime's economic plans, but the president-elect would not act until he was sworn in. The night before the inauguration, Hoover called Roosevelt at 10:30 and again at 1:00 A.M., to no avail. "We are at the end of our string," he groaned. The next day, the outgoing president looked stricken while the two rode to the Capitol.

"This is a day of national consecration," Roosevelt began his address, in a line he added while sitting in the capitol rotunda before the ceremony. He pledged action to end the Depression, which, he said with bravado, affected "only material things." Roosevelt had a simple but intense religious faith, and the speech is suffused with biblical imagery ("the money changers have been driven from the temple"). It was strong, plain, and, above all, confident. "This great nation will endure as it has endured, will revive and will prosper," he declared. "So, first of all, let me assert my firm belief that the only thing we have to fear is fear itself—nameless, unreasoning, unjustified terror which paralyzes needed efforts to convert retreat into advance." The image was especially powerful since Roosevelt himself could not walk.

Who wrote the speech? Though earlier presidents had help writing their addresses—think of Hamilton drafting Washington's farewell—Roosevelt began the modern practice of using increasingly visible speechwriters for major addresses. Columbia University professor Raymond Moley probably penned the first draft; FDR then copied it in longhand at his home in Hyde Park, New York, and made substantial revisions. "Fear itself" was added in later drafts. First Lady Eleanor Roosevelt told longtime aide Samuel Rosenman that a friend had given the governor a book by Henry David Thoreau, which contained the line, "Nothing is so much to be feared as fear." According to later historians, however, Roosevelt's political advisor Louis Howe added the line, claiming to have seen it in an advertisement. (Even the immortals "spin.")

As Roosevelt spoke, the audience stood rapt, silent. It cheered loudly only once: when he vowed to take drastic steps if necessary. Weeks before, columnist Walter Lippmann had privately implored, "The situation is critical, Franklin. You may have no alternative but to assume dictatorial power." Now, Roosevelt warned that if Congress failed to act, he would ask for "broad Executive power to wage a war against the emergency, as great as the power that would be given to me if we were in fact invaded by a foreign foe."

"It was very, very solemn, and a little terrifying," Eleanor Roosevelt told a reporter friend afterward. "The crowds were so tremendous, and you felt that they would do anything—if only someone would tell them what to do."

The next day, Roosevelt proclaimed a national bank holiday, convened leading financiers, and called the Congress into emergency session. Five days later, after just forty minutes of debate in the House, Congress passed an emergency banking bill, and Roosevelt signed it into law that night. On Sunday, March 12, Roosevelt gave his first radio speech (what became known as a "fireside chat"). He explained the workings of the banking system, assuring listeners "that it is safer to keep your money in a reopened bank than under the mattress." The next morning, the bank panic was over. The steps taken were far from radical, and had in fact been drafted largely by Hoover's Treasury Department; they sought not to

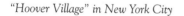
"Hoover Village" in New York City

revolutionize finance but to stabilize the system. Raymond Moley said simply, "Capitalism was saved in eight days."

"It would be difficult to exaggerate the extent of the change in national mood which took place in Franklin Roosevelt's first thirty-six hours in the White House," concludes historian Kenneth Davis. The inaugural transformed the relationship between the people and the president. In that first week, some four hundred fifty thousand letters and telegrams flooded the White House. (Hoover had employed one man in the mailroom; Roosevelt had to hire seventy.) In its first one hundred days, the New Deal created an "alphabet soup" of new agencies. The Federal Deposit Insurance Corporation (FDIC) regulated banks and insured deposits; the Securities and Exchange Commission (SEC) monitored the stock market; the National Recovery Administration (NRA) was established to try to set prices and wages; the Agriculture Adjustment Administration (AAA) began to boost farm prices. The Depression would in fact continue for years. But a period of reform and renewal had begun.

FDR himself later explained: "The widespread unemployment which accompanied the collapse had created a general feeling of utter helplessness. I sought principally in the…inaugural address to banish, so far as possible, the fear of the present and of the future which held the American people and the American spirit in its grasp."

PRESIDENT BILL CLINTON ON FRANKLIN D. ROOSEVELT

I quoted Franklin Roosevelt's 1932 Commonwealth Club address in a speech I gave soon after I declared my candidacy for president. I look back to FDR's speech because it discussed the need to experiment in government.

I look at it in part from the perspective of our party. Democrats believe in certain basic things that are different from what Republicans believe—we believe that government has a central role in bringing the nation together and making it a "more perfect union," as the Constitution put it. I think our basic fundamental values don't change. But too often, back when I was running, many Democrats seemed to feel that political correctness meant you had to adhere to the same policy means that had been used throughout history. If you changed the means, they felt, you were being unfaithful to the party's philosophy. In his Commonwealth Club speech in San Francisco, Roosevelt made very clear that political parties and government have to change with new circumstances and new times. That was what being true to the spirit of the New Deal meant, not sticking with every last bit of the old policies—including the ones whose time had passed. I found that very wise and very useful.

Excerpt from FDR's September 23, 1932 speech:

Faith in America, faith in our tradition of personal responsibility, faith in our institutions, faith in ourselves demands the we recognize the new terms of the old social contract.

We shall fulfill them, as we fulfilled the obligation of the apparent utopia which Jefferson imagined for us in 1776 and which Jefferson, [Theodore] Roosevelt, and Wilson sought to bring to realization. We must do so, lest a rising tide of misery, engendered by our common failure engulf us all. But failure is not an American habit, and in the strength of great hope we must all shoulder our common load.

Franklin Delano Roosevelt's
FIRST INAUGURAL ADDRESS

Washington, D.C. • March 4, 1933

President Hoover, Mr. Chief Justice, my friends:

This is a day of national consecration.

I am certain that my fellow Americans expect that on my induction into the Presidency I will address them with a candor and a decision which the present situation of our nation impels. This is preeminently the time to speak the truth, the whole truth, frankly and boldly. Nor need we shrink from honestly facing conditions in our country today. This great Nation will endure as it has endured, will revive and will prosper. So, first of all, let me assert my firm belief that the only thing we have to fear is fear itself—nameless, unreasoning, unjustified terror which paralyzes needed efforts to convert retreat into advance. In every dark hour of our national life a leadership of frankness and vigor has met with that understanding and support of the people themselves which is essential to victory. I am convinced that you will again give that support to leadership in these critical days.

In such a spirit on my part and on yours we face our common difficulties. They concern, thank God, only material things. Values have shrunken to fantastic levels; taxes have risen; our ability to pay has fallen; government of all kinds is faced by serious curtailment of income; the means of exchange are frozen in the currents of trade; the withered leaves of industrial enterprise lie on every side; farmers find no markets for their produce; the savings of many years in thousands of families are gone.

More important, a host of unemployed citizens face the grim problem of existence, and an equally great number toil with little return. Only a foolish optimist can deny the dark realities of the moment.

Yet our distress comes from no failure of substance. We are stricken by no plague of locusts. Compared with the perils which our forefathers conquered because they believed and were not afraid, we have still much to be thankful for. Nature still offers her bounty and human efforts have multiplied it. Plenty is at our doorstep, but a generous use of it languishes in the very sight of the supply. Primarily, this is because rulers of the exchange of mankind's goods have failed through their own stubbornness and their own incompetence, have admitted their failure, and have abdicated. Practices of the unscrupulous money changers stand indicted in the court of public opinion, rejected by the hearts and minds of men.

"*The only thing we have to fear is fear itself.*"

True they have tried, but their efforts have been cast in the pattern of an outworn tradition. Faced by failure of credit they have proposed only the lending of more money. Stripped of the lure of profit by which to induce our people to follow their false leadership, they have resorted to exhortations, pleading tearfully for restored confidence. They know only the rules of a generation of self-seekers. They have no vision, and when there is no vision the people perish.

The money changers have fled from their high seats in the temple of our civilization. We may now restore that temple to the ancient truths. The measure of the restoration lies in the extent to which we apply social values more noble than mere monetary profit.

Happiness lies not in the mere possession of money; it lies in the joy of achievement, in the thrill of creative effort. The joy and moral stimulation of work no longer must be forgotten in the mad chase of evanescent profits. These dark days will be worth all they cost us if they teach us that our

Roosevelt's inaugural address

true destiny is not to be ministered unto but to minister to ourselves and to our fellow men.

Recognition of the falsity of material wealth as the standard of success goes hand in hand with the abandonment of the false belief that public office and high political position are to be valued only by the standards of pride of place and personal profit; and there must be an end to a conduct in banking and in business which too often has given to a sacred trust the likeness of callous and selfish wrongdoing. Small wonder that confidence languishes, for it thrives only on honesty, on honor, on the sacredness of obligations, on faithful protection, on unselfish performance; without them it cannot live.

Restoration calls, however, not for changes in ethics alone. This Nation asks for action, and action now.

Our greatest primary task is to put people to work. This is no unsolvable problem if we face it wisely and courageously. It can be accomplished in part by direct recruiting

by the Government itself, treating the task as we would treat the emergency of a war, but at the same time, through this employment, accomplishing greatly needed projects to stimulate and reorganize the use of our natural resources.

"The rulers of the exchange of mankind's goods have failed through their own stubbornness and their own incompetence."

Hand in hand with this we must frankly recognize the overbalance of population in our industrial centers and, by engaging on a national scale in a redistribution, endeavor to provide a better use of the land for those best fitted for the land. The task can be helped by definite efforts to raise the values of agricultural products and with this the power to purchase the output of our cities. It can be helped by preventing realistically the tragedy of the growing loss through foreclosure of our small homes and our farms. It can be helped by insistence that the Federal, State and local governments act forthwith on the demand that their cost be drastically reduced. It can be helped by the unifying of relief activities which today are often scattered, uneconomical, and unequal. It can be helped by national planning for and supervision of all forms of transportation and of communications and other utilities which have a definitely public character. There are many ways in which it can be helped, but it can never be helped merely by talking about it. We must act and act quickly.

"Practices of the unscrupulous money changers stand indicted in the court of public opinion, rejected by the hearts and minds of men."

Finally, in our progress toward a resumption of work we require two safeguards against a return of the evils of the old order: there must be a strict supervision of all banking and credits and investments, so that there will be an end to speculation with other people's money; and there must be provision for an adequate but sound currency.

These are the lines of attack. I shall presently urge upon a new Congress, in special session, detailed measure for their fulfillment, and I shall seek the immediate assistance of the several States.

Through this program of action we address ourselves to putting our own national house in order and making income balance outgo. Our international trade relations, though vastly important, are in point of time and necessity secondary to the establishment of a sound national economy. I favor as a practical policy the putting of first things first. I shall spare no effort to restore world trade by international

economic readjustment, but the emergency at home cannot wait on that accomplishment.

The basic thought that guides these specific means of national recovery is not narrowly nationalistic. It is the insistence, as a first consideration, upon the interdependence of the various elements in and parts of the United States—a recognition of the old and permanently important manifestation of the American spirit of the pioneer. It is the way to recovery. It is the immediate way. It is the strongest assurance that the recovery will endure.

In the field of world policy I would dedicate this Nation to the policy of the good neighbor—the neighbor who resolutely respects himself and, because he does so, respects the rights of others—the neighbor who respects his obligations and respects the sanctity of his agreements in and with a world of neighbors.

If I read the temper of our people correctly, we now realize as we have never realized before our interdependence on each other; that we cannot merely take but we must give as well; that if we are to go forward, we must move as a trained and loyal army willing to sacrifice for the good of a common discipline, because without such discipline no progress is made, no leadership becomes effective. We are, I know, ready and willing to submit our lives and property to such discipline, because it makes possible a leadership which aims at a larger good. This I propose to offer, pledging that the larger purposes will bind upon us all as a sacred obligation with a unity of duty hitherto evoked only in time of armed strife.

"They have no vision, and when there is no vision the people perish."

With this pledge taken, I assume unhesitatingly the leadership of this great army of our people dedicated to a disciplined attack upon our common problems.

Action in this image and to this end is feasible under the form of government which we have inherited from our ancestors. Our Constitution is so simple and practical that it is possible always to meet extraordinary needs by changes in emphasis and arrangement without loss of essential form. That is why our constitutional system has proved itself the most superbly enduring political mechanism the modern world has produced. It has met every stress of vast expansion of territory, of foreign wars, of bitter internal strife, of world relations.

It is to be hoped that the normal balance of Executive and legislative authority may be wholly adequate to meet the unprecedented task before us. But it may be that an

"The nation asks for action, and action now."

unprecedented demand and need for undelayed action may call for temporary departure from that normal balance of public procedure.

I am prepared under my constitutional duty to recommend the measures that a stricken Nation in the midst of a stricken world may require.

These measures, or such other measures as the Congress may build out of its experience and wisdom, I shall seek, within my constitutional authority, to bring to speedy adoption.

But in the event that the Congress shall fail to take one of these two courses, and in the event that the national emergency is still critical, I shall not evade the clear course of duty that will then confront me. I shall ask the Congress for the one remaining instrument to meet the crisis—broad Executive power to wage a war against the emergency, as great as the power that would be given to me if we were in fact invaded by a foreign foe.

For the trust reposed in me I will return the courage and the devotion that befit the time. I can do no less.

We face the arduous days that lie before us in the warm courage of national unity; with the clear consciousness of seeking old and precious moral values; with the clean satisfaction that comes from the stern performance of duty by old and young alike. We aim at the assurance of a rounded and permanent national life.

We do not distrust the future of essential democracy. The people of the United States have not failed. In their need they have registered a mandate that they want direct, vigorous action. They have asked for discipline and direction under leadership. They have made me the present instrument of their wishes. In the spirit of the gift I take it.

In this dedication of a Nation we humbly ask the blessing of God. May He protect each and every one of us. May He guide me in the days to come.

I5

"A RENDEZVOUS WITH DESTINY"

DURING THE NEW Deal, the government took unprecedented steps to help ordinary citizens: Social Security benefits for the elderly, the National Labor Relations Act to guarantee the right to organize labor unions, securities laws to protect investors. New laws created the minimum wage, broke up power utilities, and authorized massive spending for public works and conservation. The modern social welfare state was created in the span of a few years. Thus the 1936 election would be a historic contest over the newly assertive central government. The Supreme Court had begun to strike down New Deal laws as unconstitutional. The Republican platform argued that "political liberty…for the first time…is threatened by Government itself."

Roosevelt responded with one of history's most memorable campaign speeches, delivered at the Democratic Convention in Philadelphia. At first, he was unsure how hard to press. He asked Raymond Moley and key aide, Thomas Corcoran to write a conciliatory draft. At the same time, without telling the first two writers, he asked Samuel Rosenman and a Protestant clergyman named Stanley High to write what Rosenman remembered as a "militant, bare-fisted statement." The night before he was nominated, FDR invited the two rival teams of speechwriters to dinner. "That night, in the small family dining room, for the first and only time in my life, I saw the President forget himself as a gentleman," Rosenman wrote. "He began twitting Moley about his new conservatism and about the influence of his 'new, rich friends' on his recent writings, which had been very critical of the Administration. Moley responded with what I thought was justifiable heat. The President grew angry, and the exchanges between them became very bitter." Roosevelt asked that the two dissonant drafts be combined, then redictated the speech himself, further smoothing the approaches.

For Roosevelt's appearance, one hundred thousand people convened outdoors at Franklin Field. His open car pulled up to the podium, and as an orchestra conducted by Leopold Stokowski played "Hail to the Chief," the president in heavy metal braces "walked" toward the podium, swinging stiff-legged on the arm of his son. As the crowd roared, the elderly poet William Markham grasped Roosevelt's hand, then tumbled into him, sending the president sprawling. The pages of the text scattered into the crowd. Arthur M. Schlesinger Jr. describes the scene: "Roosevelt was pale and shaken as [his guards] raised him to his feet. 'Clean me up,' he ordered; then, thinking of his speech, told those around him to keep their feet off 'those damned sheets.'" "It was the most frightful few minutes of my life," he said that night. But a moment later, Roosevelt stood on the platform, composed, beaming and waving at the crowd.

In the speech, Roosevelt sought to defend the New Deal not as a threat to freedom but as the latest incarnation of it. FDR often invoked Thomas Jefferson, insisting on building the Jefferson Memorial (and angering Eleanor by cutting down cherry trees to do it). Now, like Lincoln at Gettysburg, Roosevelt sought to justify a new and potentially radical policy on the grounds that it embodied the ideals of the Declaration of Independence. "This is a good city in which to write history," he declared. In 1776, the colonists had declared revolution against the King; now he faced "economic royalists" (suggested by High). The success of the effort to modernize democracy mattered not only to Americans, but also to the world. Americans had "a rendezvous with destiny" (a felicitous phrase penned by Corcoran).

Roosevelt on his way to lay the cornerstone of the Jersey City Medical Center, October 2, 1936

Roosevelt grew more militant as election day drew near. "I should like to have it said of my first administration that in it the forces of selfishness and lust for power met their *match*," he declared at New York's Madison Square Garden. "I should like to have it said of my second administration that in it these forces met their *master*." Roosevelt was outspent by his opponents, opposed by most newspapers, and public opinion polls (then in their infancy) suggested he might lose. In the end, he won overwhelmingly, carrying all but two states. It seemed as if reform was at its high mark. In his second inaugural address, he said the problems of the Depression were not over: "I see one third of a nation ill-housed, ill-clad, ill-nourished." But two days later, he proposed a plan to expand the Supreme Court and "pack" it with pro–New Deal justices. In a bitter fight, Congress rejected the plan, though the justices quickly began to uphold New Deal measures. The age of domestic reform would soon be over. Americans turned their attention to the threat of war overseas.

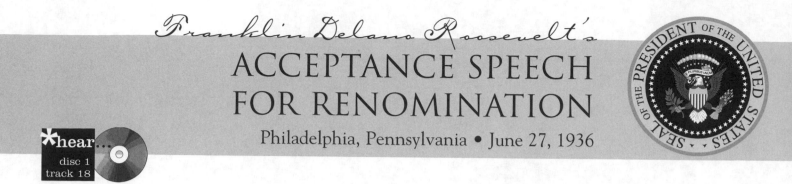

Franklin Delano Roosevelt's
ACCEPTANCE SPEECH FOR RENOMINATION

Philadelphia, Pennsylvania • June 27, 1936

*hear...
disc 1
track 18

Senator Robinson, Members of the Democratic Convention, my friends:

Here, and in every community throughout the land, we are met at a time of great moment to the future of the Nation. It is an occasion to be dedicated to the simple and sincere expression of an attitude toward problems, the determination of which will profoundly affect America.

I come not only as a leader of a party, not only as a candidate for high office, but as one upon whom many critical hours have imposed and still impose a grave responsibility.

For the sympathy, help and confidence with which Americans have sustained me in my task I am grateful. For their loyalty I salute the members of our great party, in and out of political life in every part of the Union. I salute those of other parties, especially those in the Congress of the United States who on so many occasions have put partisanship aside. I thank the Governors of the several States, their Legislatures, their State and local officials who participated unselfishly and regardless of party in our efforts to achieve recovery and destroy abuses. Above all I thank the millions of Americans who have borne disaster bravely and have dared to smile through the storm.

America will not forget these recent years, will not forget that the rescue was not a mere party task. It was the concern of all of us. In our strength we rose together, rallied our energies together, applied the old rules of common sense, and together survived.

In those days we feared fear. That was why we fought fear. And today, my friends, we have won against the most dangerous of our foes. We have conquered fear.

But I cannot, with candor, tell you that all is well with the world. Clouds of suspicion, tides of ill-will and intolerance gather darkly in many places. In our own land we enjoy indeed a fullness of life greater than that of most Nations. But the rush of modern civilization itself has raised for us new difficulties, new problems which must be solved if we are to preserve to the United States the political and economic freedom for which Washington and Jefferson planned and fought.

> *"In those days we feared fear.... And today, my friends, we have won against the most dangerous of our foes. We have conquered fear."*

Philadelphia is a good city in which to write American history. This is fitting ground on which to reaffirm the faith of our fathers; to pledge ourselves to restore to the people a wider freedom; to give to 1936 as the founders gave to 1776—an American way of life.

That very word freedom, in itself and of necessity, suggests freedom from some restraining power. In 1776 we sought freedom from the tyranny of a political autocracy—from the eighteenth century royalists who held special privileges from the crown. It was to perpetuate their privilege that they governed without the consent of the governed; that they denied the right of free assembly and free speech; that they restricted the worship of God; that they put the average man's property and the average man's life in pawn to the mercenaries of dynastic power; that they regimented the people.

Franklin Delano Roosevelt

And so it was to win freedom from the tyranny of political autocracy that the American Revolution was fought. That victory gave the business of governing into the hands of the average man, who won the right with his neighbors to make and order his own destiny through his own Government. Political tyranny was wiped out at Philadelphia on July 4, 1776.

Since that struggle, however, man's inventive genius released new forces in our land which reordered the lives of our people. The age of machinery, of railroads; of steam and electricity; the telegraph and the radio; mass production, mass distribution—all of these combined to bring forward a new civilization and with it a new problem for those who sought to remain free.

For out of this modern civilization economic royalists carved new dynasties. New kingdoms were built upon concentration of control over material things. Through new uses of corporations, banks and securities, new machinery of industry and agriculture, of labor and capital—all

A demonstration in support of Roosevelt in Convention Hall, at the Democratic National Convention in Philadelphia

undreamed of by the fathers—the whole structure of modern life was impressed into this royal service.

There was no place among this royalty for our many thousands of small business men and merchants who sought to make a worthy use of the American system of initiative and profit. They were no more free than the worker or the farmer. Even honest and progressive-minded men of wealth, aware of their obligation to their generation, could never know just where they fitted into this dynastic scheme of things.

"Philadelphia is a good city in which to write American history."

It was natural and perhaps human that the privileged princes of these new economic dynasties, thirsting for power, reached out for control over Government itself. They created a new despotism and wrapped it in the robes of legal sanction. In its service new mercenaries sought to regiment the people, their labor, and their property. And as a result the average man once more confronts the problem that faced the Minute Man.

The hours men and women worked, the wages they received, the conditions of their labor—these had passed beyond the control of the people, and were imposed by this new industrial dictatorship. The savings of the average family, the capital of the small business man, the investments set aside for old age—other people's money—these were tools which the new economic royalty used to dig itself in.

Those who tilled the soil no longer reaped the rewards which were their right. The small measure of their gains was decreed by men in distant cities.

Throughout the Nation, opportunity was limited by monopoly. Individual initiative was crushed in the cogs of a great machine. The field open for free business was more and more restricted. Private enterprise, indeed, became too private. It became privileged enterprise, not free enterprise.

An old English judge once said: "Necessitous men are not free men." Liberty requires opportunity to make a living—a living decent according to the standard of the time, a living which gives man not only enough to live by, but something to live for.

For too many of us the political equality we once had won was meaningless in the face of economic inequality. A small group had concentrated into their own hands an almost complete control over other people's property, other people's money, other people's labor—other people's lives. For too many of us life was no longer free; liberty no longer real; men could no longer follow the pursuit of happiness.

Against economic tyranny such as this, the American citizen could appeal only to the organized power of Government. The collapse of 1929 showed up the despotism for what it was. The election of 1932 was the people's mandate to end it. Under that mandate it is being ended.

The royalists of the economic order have conceded that political freedom was the business of the Government, but they have maintained that economic slavery was nobody's business. They granted that the Government could protect the citizen in his right to vote, but they denied that the Government could do anything to protect the citizen in his right to work and his right to live.

Today we stand committed to the proposition that freedom is no half-and-half affair. If the average citizen is guaranteed equal opportunity in the polling place, he must have equal opportunity in the market place.

"Out of this modern civilization economic royalists carved new dynasties."

These economic royalists complain that we seek to overthrow the institutions of America. What they really complain of is that we seek to take away their power. Our allegiance to American institutions requires the overthrow of this kind of power. In vain they seek to hide behind the Flag and the Constitution. In their blindness they forget what the Flag and the Constitution stand for. Now, as always, they stand for democracy, not tyranny; for free-

Roosevelt declares a "Rendezvous with Destiny" and accepts the Democratic nomination for president at Franklin Field, Philadelphia, June 27, 1936

dom, not subjection; and against a dictatorship by mob rule and the overprivileged alike.

The brave and clear platform adopted by this Convention, to which I heartily subscribe, sets forth that Government in a modern civilization has certain inescapable obligations to its citizens, among which are protection of the family and the home, the establishment of a democracy of opportunity, and aid to those overtaken by disaster.

But the resolute enemy within our gates is ever ready to beat down our words unless in greater courage we will fight for them.

For more than three years we have fought for them. This Convention, in every word and deed, has pledged that that fight will go on.

The defeats and victories of these years have given to us as a people a new understanding of our Government and of ourselves. Never since the early days of the New England town meeting have the affairs of Government been so widely discussed and so clearly appreciated. It has been brought home to us that the only effective guide for the safety of this most worldly of worlds, the greatest guide of all, is moral principle.

"Freedom is no half-and-half affair. If the average citizen is guaranteed equal opportunity in the polling place, he must have equal opportunity in the market place."

We do not see faith, hope and charity as unattainable ideals, but we use them as stout supports of a Nation fighting the fight for freedom in a modern civilization.

Faith—in the soundness of democracy in the midst of dictatorships.

Hope—renewed because we know so well the progress we have made.

Charity—in the true spirit of that grand old word. For charity literally translated from the original means love, the love that understands, that does not merely share the wealth of the giver, but in true sympathy and wisdom helps men to help themselves.

We seek not merely to make Government a mechanical implement, but to give it the vibrant personal character that is the very embodiment of human charity.

We are poor indeed if this Nation cannot afford to lift from every recess of American life the dread fear of the unemployed that they are not needed in the world. We cannot afford to accumulate a deficit in the books of human fortitude.

In the place of the palace of privilege we seek to build a temple out of faith and hope and charity.

It is a sobering thing, my friends, to be a servant of this great cause. We try in our daily work to remember that the cause belongs not to us, but to the people. The standard is not in the hands of you and me alone. It is carried by America.

We seek daily to profit from experience, to learn to do better as our task proceeds.

Governments can err, Presidents do make mistakes, but the immortal Dante tells us that divine justice weighs the sins of the cold-blooded and the sins of the warm-hearted in different scales.

Better the occasional faults of a Government that lives in a spirit of charity than the consistent omissions of a Government frozen in the ice of its own indifference.

There is a mysterious cycle in human events. To some generations much is given. Of other generations much is expected. This generation of Americans has a rendezvous with destiny.

In this world of ours in other lands, there are some people, who, in times past, have lived and fought for freedom, and seem to have grown too weary to carry on the fight. They have sold their heritage of freedom for the illusion of a living. They have yielded their democracy.

I believe in my heart that only our success can stir their ancient hope. They begin to know that here in America we are waging a great and successful war. It is not alone a war against want and destitution and economic demoralization. It is more than that; it is a war for the survival of democracy. We are fighting to save a great and precious form of government for ourselves and for the world.

I accept the commission you have tendered me. I join with you. I am enlisted for the duration of the war.

"To some generations much is given. Of other generations much is expected. This generation of Americans has a rendezvous with destiny."

16

"THE FOUR FREEDOMS"

IN 1940, WAR raged in Europe. Adolf Hitler's Germany ruled Europe from Poland to the Atlantic, and Britain stood alone. In a speech rebroadcast in the United States, Prime Minister Winston Churchill vowed that the battle would be Britain's "finest hour."

It was not America's finest hour. Franklin Roosevelt was mired in what historian David Kennedy called "the agony of neutrality." Domestic sentiment was strongly isolationist, and American military leaders implored Roosevelt to save all weapons for the U.S.'s own weak forces. Indeed, running for reelection for an unprecedented third term, Roosevelt himself declared, "I have said this before, but I shall say it again and again and again: your boys are not going to be sent into any foreign wars." In fact, Roosevelt believed the U.S. had to help England, and ultimately, that we would have to enter the war. Heroically, through a series of speeches and executive actions, mixed with caution and outright guile, he prepared America for war, tugging a reluctant nation toward its duty in the world.

The immediate threat, spelled out in an impassioned letter from Churchill in November 1940, was that Britain soon could not pay for arms shipments. Congress would not support a loan. What to do? Roosevelt had a brainstorm while on a cruise—what his labor secretary Frances Perkins called a "flash of almost clairvoyant knowledge and understanding." The United States would not *sell* Britain the weapons it needed; it would *lend* them, a program known as "Lend-Lease." The day after he returned to Washington, on December 17, he explained the rationale for Lend-Lease in a press conference, using a homey metaphor. "Well, let me give you an illustration: suppose my neighbor's home catches on fire, and I have a length of garden hose four or five hundred feet away. If he can take my garden hose and connect it up with his hydrant, I may help to put out his fire....I don't want $15—I want my garden hose back after the fire is over." (Isolationist Senator Robert Taft replied that lending military equipment is more like chewing gum: "You don't want it back.")

Over the next two weeks, he made two major speeches in support of Lend-Lease. The first was a fireside chat. Roosevelt made these radio talks only rarely, believing that he could wear out the public's attention if he spoke more, and one poll showed this particular chat was heard by nearly six out of ten Americans. He argued that arming Britain would keep the United States out of the war. We could not appease Germany; "No man can tame a tiger into a kitten by stroking it." If the "unholy alliance" of Germany, Japan, and Italy were allowed to continue, then "all of us in the Americas would be living at the point of a gun." The United States must vastly increase its arms production, he declared. "We must be the great arsenal of democracy. For us this is an emergency as serious as war itself." The phrase "arsenal of democracy" was first suggested by French diplomat Jean Monnet; some officials worried that the phrase would preclude aid to the Soviet Union, but it stayed in the speech.

Eight days later, Roosevelt went before Congress to deliver his annual message (the kind of speech known in later years as a State of the Union address). It amounted to an extended alarum and a case for Lend-Lease. But he raised the argument to a far higher plane. Even though the United States had not yet entered the war, he set out ambitious and visionary aims. We would support nations that fought for "four essential human freedoms": freedom of speech, freedom of religion, freedom from want, freedom from fear. Along with the Economic Bill of Rights spelled out in the speech, he sought to extend the New Deal's social vision worldwide. ("Freedom from fear" evokes Roosevelt's inaugural warning against "fear itself.") The commitment of the United States to universal human rights, first articulated in the preamble of the Declaration of Independence, now had been given a global cast.

Roosevelt dictated the famous peroration in a session with his speechwriters Samuel Rosenman, Robert Sherwood (the Pulitzer Prize–winning playwright), and top aide Harry Hopkins. Hopkins worried about the universality of the phrase "everywhere in the world." "That covers an awful lot of territory, Mr. President. I don't know how

interested Americans are going to be in the people of Java." "I'm afraid they'll have to be some day, Harry," Roosevelt replied.

Lend-Lease passed later that month. Soon the Four Freedoms were central to Allied war propaganda. Norman Rockwell's paintings illustrating them appeared in the *Saturday Evening Post* in April 1943, and were widely reproduced as posters. The canvasses toured the country, and toured again in 2002. The goals formed the basis of the Atlantic Charter signed with Churchill in 1941, and led to the Universal Declaration of Human Rights, passed by the United Nations in 1948. Half a century later, speechwriters for President George W. Bush studied the Four Freedoms as they prepared his remarks following the terrorist attacks in New York, Washington, D.C., and Pennsylvania.

Roosevelt delivers his annual message to Congress and requests a "swift and driving increase" in armaments for countries fighting aggressor nations

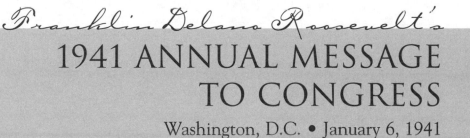

Franklin Delano Roosevelt's

1941 ANNUAL MESSAGE
TO CONGRESS

Washington, D.C. • January 6, 1941

Mr. President, Mr. Speaker, Members of the Seventy-seventh Congress:

I address you, the Members of the Seventy-seventh Congress, at a moment unprecedented in the history of the Union. I use the word "unprecedented," because at no previous time has American security been as seriously threatened from without as it is today.

Since the permanent formation of our Government under the Constitution, in 1789, most of the periods of crisis in our history have related to our domestic affairs. Fortunately, only one of these—the four-year War Between the States—ever threatened our national unity. Today, thank God, one hundred and thirty million Americans, in forty-eight States, have forgotten points of the compass in our national unity.

It is true that prior to 1914 the United States often had been disturbed by events in other Continents. We had even engaged in two wars with European nations and in a number of undeclared wars in the West Indies, in the Mediterranean and in the Pacific for the maintenance of American rights and for the principles of peaceful commerce. But in no case had a serious threat been raised against our national safety or our continued independence.

What I seek to convey is the historic truth that the United States as a nation has at all times maintained clear, definite opposition, to any attempt to lock us in behind an ancient Chinese wall while the procession of civilization went past. Today, thinking of our children and of their children, we oppose enforced isolation for ourselves or for any other part of the Americas.

That determination of ours, extending over all these years, was proved, for example, during the quarter century of wars following the French Revolution.

While the Napoleonic struggles did threaten interests of the United States because of the French foothold in the West Indies and in Louisiana, and while we engaged in the War of 1812 to vindicate our right to peaceful trade, it is nevertheless clear that neither France nor Great Britain, nor any other nation, was aiming at domination of the whole world.

"We may take pride in the fact that we are soft-hearted; but we cannot afford to be soft-headed."

In like fashion from 1815 to 1914—ninety-nine years—no single war in Europe or in Asia constituted a real threat against our future or against the future of any other American nation.

Except in the Maximilian interlude in Mexico, no foreign power sought to establish itself in this Hemisphere; and the strength of the British fleet in the Atlantic has been a friendly strength. It is still a friendly strength.

Even when the World War broke out in 1914, it seemed to contain only small threat of danger to our own American future. But, as time went on, the American people began to visualize what the downfall of democratic nations might mean to our own democracy.

We need not overemphasize imperfections in the Peace of Versailles. We need not harp on failure of the democracies to deal with problems of world reconstruction. We should remember that the Peace of 1919 was far less unjust than the kind of "pacification" which began even before Munich, and which is being carried on under the new order of tyranny that seeks to spread over every continent

111

Posters by Norman Rockwell illustrating two of the four freedoms extolled by FDR in his January 6, 1941 annual address to Congress

today. The American people have unalterably set their faces against that tyranny.

Every realist knows that the democratic way of life is at this moment being directly assailed in every part of the world—assailed either by arms, or by secret spreading of poisonous propaganda by those who seek to destroy unity and promote discord in nations that are still at peace.

During sixteen long months this assault has blotted out the whole pattern of democratic life in an appalling number of independent nations, great and small. The assailants are still on the march, threatening other nations, great and small.

Therefore, as your President, performing my constitutional duty to "give to the Congress information of the state of the Union," I find it, unhappily, necessary to report that the future and the safety of our country and of our democracy are overwhelmingly involved in events far beyond our borders.

Armed defense of democratic existence is now being gallantly waged in four continents. If that defense fails, all the population and all the resources of Europe, Asia, Africa and Australasia will be dominated by conquerors. Let us remember that the total of those populations and their resources in those four continents greatly exceeds the sum total of the population and the resources of the whole of the Western Hemisphere—many times over.

In times like these it is immature—and incidentally, untrue—for anybody to brag that an unprepared America, single-handed, and with one hand tied behind its back, can hold off the whole world.

No realistic American can expect from a dictator's peace international generosity, or return of true independence, or world disarmament, or freedom of expression, or freedom of religion—or even good business.

"We must especially beware of that small group of selfish men who would clip the wings of the American eagle in order to feather their own nests."

Such a peace would bring no security for us or for our neighbors. "Those, who would give up essential liberty to purchase a little temporary safety, deserve neither liberty nor safety."

As a nation, we may take pride in the fact that we are soft-hearted; but we cannot afford to be soft-headed.

We must always be wary of those who with sounding brass and a tinkling cymbal preach the "ism" of appeasement.

We must especially beware of that small group of selfish men who would clip the wings of the American eagle in order to feather their own nests.

I have recently pointed out how quickly the tempo of modern warfare could bring into our very midst the physical attack which we must eventually expect if the dictator nations win this war.

There is much loose talk of our immunity from immediate and direct invasion from across the seas. Obviously, as long as the British Navy retains its power, no such danger exists. Even if there were no British Navy, it is not probable that any enemy would be stupid enough to attack us by landing troops in the United States from across thousands of miles of ocean, until it had acquired strategic bases from which to operate.

But we learn much from the lessons of the past years in Europe—particularly the lesson of Norway, whose essential seaports were captured by treachery and surprise built up over a series of years.

The first phase of the invasion of this Hemisphere would not be the landing of regular troops. The necessary strategic points would be occupied by secret agents and their dupes—and great numbers of them are already here, and in Latin America.

As long as the aggressor nations maintain the offensive, they—not we—will choose the time and the place and the method of their attack.

That is why the future of all the American Republics is today in serious danger.

That is why this Annual Message to the Congress is unique in our history.

That is why every member of the Executive Branch of the Government and every member of the Congress faces great responsibility and great accountability.

The need of the moment is that our actions and our policy should be devoted primarily—almost exclusively—to meeting this foreign peril. For all our domestic problems are now a part of the great emergency.

Just as our national policy in internal affairs has been based upon a decent respect for the rights and the dignity of all our fellow men within our gates, so our national policy in foreign affairs has been based on a decent respect for the rights and the dignity of all nations, large and small. And the justice of morality must and will win in the end.

Our national policy is this:

"Enduring peace cannot be bought at the cost of other people's freedom."

First, by an impressive expression of the public will and without regard to partisanship, we are committed to all-inclusive national defense.

Second, by an impressive expression of the public will and without regard to partisanship, we are committed to full support of all those resolute peoples, everywhere, who are resisting aggression and are thereby keeping war away from our Hemisphere. By this support, we express our determination that the democratic cause shall prevail; and we strengthen the defense and the security of our own nation.

Third, by an impressive expression of the public will and without regard to partisanship, we are committed to the proposition that principles of morality and considerations for our own security will never permit us to acquiesce in a peace dictated by aggressors and sponsored by appeasers. We know that enduring peace cannot be bought at the cost of other people's freedom.

In the recent national election there was no substantial difference between the two great parties in respect to that national policy. No issue was fought out on this line before the American electorate. Today it is abundantly evident that American citizens everywhere are demanding and supporting speedy and complete action in recognition of obvious danger.

Therefore, the immediate need is a swift and driving increase in our armament production.

Leaders of industry and labor have responded to our summons. Goals of speed have been set. In some cases these goals are being reached ahead of time; in some cases we are on schedule; in other cases there are slight but not serious delays; and in some cases—and I am sorry to say very important cases—we are all concerned by the slowness of the accomplishment of our plans.

"We shall send you, in ever-increasing numbers, ships, planes, tanks, guns. This is our promise and our pledge."

The Army and Navy, however, have made substantial progress during the past year. Actual experience is improving and speeding up our methods of production with every passing day. And today's best is not good enough for tomorrow.

I am not satisfied with the progress thus far made. The men in charge of the program represent the best in training, in ability, and in patriotism. They are not satisfied with the progress thus far made. None of us will be satisfied until the job is done.

No matter whether the original goal was set too high or too low, our objective is quicker and better results.

To give you two illustrations:

We are behind schedule in turning out finished airplanes; we are working day and night to solve the innumerable problems and to catch up.

We are ahead of schedule in building warships but we are working to get even further ahead of that schedule.

To change a whole nation from a basis of peacetime production of implements of peace to a basis of wartime production of implements of war is no small task. And the greatest difficulty comes at the beginning of the program, when new tools, new plant facilities, new assembly lines, and new ship ways must first be constructed before the actual matériel begins to flow steadily and speedily from them.

The Congress, of course, must rightly keep itself informed at all times of the progress of the program. However, there is certain information, as the Congress itself will readily recognize, which, in the interests of our own security and those of the nations that we are supporting, must of needs be kept in confidence.

New circumstances are constantly begetting new needs for our safety. I shall ask this Congress for greatly increased new appropriations and authorizations to carry on what we have begun.

I also ask this Congress for authority and for funds sufficient to manufacture additional munitions and war supplies of many kinds, to be turned over to those nations which are now in actual war with aggressor nations.

Our most useful and immediate role is to act as an arsenal for them as well as for ourselves. They do not need man power, but they do need billions of dollars worth of the weapons of defense.

The time is near when they will not be able to pay for them all in ready cash. We cannot, and we will not, tell them that they must surrender, merely because of present inability to pay for the weapons which we know they must have.

I do not recommend that we make them a loan of dollars with which to pay for these weapons—a loan to be repaid in dollars.

I recommend that we make it possible for those nations to continue to obtain war materials in the United States, fitting their orders into our own program. Nearly all their matériel would, if the time ever came, be useful for our own defense.

Taking counsel of expert military and naval authorities, considering what is best for our own security, we are free to decide how much should be kept here and how much should be sent abroad to our friends who by their determined and heroic resistance are giving us time in which to make ready our own defense.

For what we send abroad, we shall be repaid within a reasonable time following the close of hostilities, in similar materials, or, at our option, in other goods of many kinds, which they can produce and which we need.

Let us say to the democracies: "We Americans are vitally concerned in your defense of freedom. We are putting forth our energies, our resources and our organizing powers to give you the strength to regain and maintain a free world.

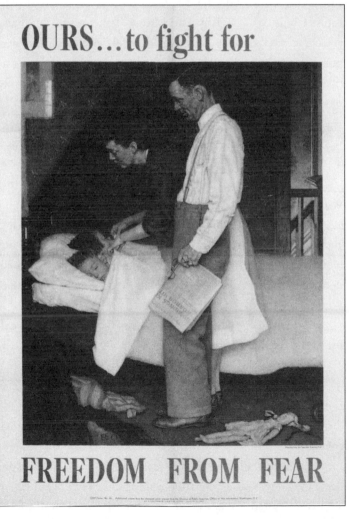

Posters by Norman Rockwell illustrating America's freedom from fear and want, described in FDR's January 6, 1941 address to Congress

We shall send you, in ever-increasing numbers, ships, planes, tanks, guns. This is our purpose and our pledge."

In fulfillment of this purpose we will not be intimidated by the threats of dictators that they will regard as a breach of international law or as an act of war our aid to the democracies which dare to resist their aggression. Such aid is not an act of war, even if a dictator should unilaterally proclaim it so to be.

When the dictators, if the dictators, are ready to make war upon us, they will not wait for an act of war on our part. They did not wait for Norway or Belgium or the Netherlands to commit an act of war.

Their only interest is in a new one-way international law, which lacks mutuality in its observance, and, therefore, becomes an instrument of oppression.

The happiness of future generations of Americans may well depend upon how effective and how immediate we can make our aid felt. No one can tell the exact character of the emergency situations that we may be called upon to meet. The Nation's hands must not be tied when the Nation's life is in danger.

We must all prepare to make the sacrifices that the emergency—almost as serious as war itself—demands. Whatever stands in the way of speed and efficiency in defense preparations must give way to the national need.

A free nation has the right to expect full cooperation from all groups. A free nation has the right to look to the leaders of business, of labor, and of agriculture to take the lead in stimulating effort, not among other groups but within their own groups.

The best way of dealing with the few slackers or trouble makers in our midst is, first, to shame them by patriotic example, and, if that fails, to use the sovereignty of Government to save Government.

As men do not live by bread alone, they do not fight by armaments alone. Those who man our defenses, and those behind them who build our defenses, must have the stamina and the courage which come from an unshakable belief in the manner of life which they are defending. The mighty action that we are calling for cannot be based on a disregard of all things worth fighting for.

"Our strength is our unity of purpose."

The Nation takes great satisfaction and much strength from the things which have been done to make its people conscious of their individual stake in the preservation of democratic life in America. Those things have toughened the fiber of our people, have renewed their faith and strengthened their devotion to the institutions we make ready to protect.

Certainly this is no time for any of us to stop thinking about the social and economic problems which are the root cause of the social revolution which is today a supreme factor in the world. For there is nothing mysterious about the foundations of a healthy and strong democracy. The basic things expected by our people of their political and economic systems are simple. They are :

Equality of opportunity for youth and for others.

Jobs for those who can work.

Security for those who need it.

The ending of special privilege for the few.

The preservation of civil liberties for all.

The enjoyment of the fruits of scientific progress in a wider and constantly rising standard of living.

These are the simple, basic things that must never be lost sight of in the turmoil and unbelievable complexity of our modern world. The inner and abiding strength of our economic and political systems is dependent upon the degree to which they fulfill these expectations.

Many subjects connected with our social economy call for immediate improvement.

As examples:

We should bring more citizens under the coverage of old-age pensions and unemployment insurance.

We should widen the opportunities for adequate medical care.

We should plan a better system by which persons deserving or needing gainful employment may obtain it.

I have called for personal sacrifice. I am assured of the willingness of almost all Americans to respond to that call.

A part of the sacrifice means the payment of more money in taxes. In my Budget Message I shall recommend that a greater portion of this great defense program be paid for from taxation than we are paying today. No person should try, or be allowed, to get rich out of this program; and the principle of tax payments in accordance with ability to pay should be constantly before our eyes to guide our legislation.

If the Congress maintains these principles, the voters, putting patriotism ahead of pocketbooks, will give you their applause.

In the future days, which we seek to make secure, we look forward to a world founded upon four essential human freedoms.

The first is freedom of speech and expression—everywhere in the world.

The second is freedom of every person to worship God in his own way—everywhere in the world.

The third is freedom from want—which, translated into world terms, means economic understandings which will secure to every nation a healthy peacetime life for its inhabitants—everywhere in the world.

The fourth is freedom from fear—which, translated into world terms, means a world-wide reduction of armaments to such a point and in such a thorough fashion that no nation will be in a position to commit an act of physical aggression against any neighbor—anywhere in the world.

That is no vision of a distant millennium. It is a definite basis for a kind of world attainable in our own time and generation. That kind of world is the very antithesis of the so-called new order of tyranny which the dictators seek to create with the crash of a bomb.

To that new order we oppose the greater conception—the moral order. A good society is able to face schemes of world domination and foreign revolutions alike without fear.

Since the beginning of our American history, we have been engaged in change—in a perpetual peaceful revolution—a revolution which goes on steadily, quietly adjusting itself to changing conditions—without the concentration camp or the quick-lime in the ditch. The world order which we seek is the cooperation of free countries, working together in a friendly, civilized society.

This nation has placed its destiny in the hands and heads and hearts of its millions of free men and women; and its faith in freedom under the guidance of God. Freedom means the supremacy of human rights everywhere. Our support goes to those who struggle to gain those rights or keep them. Our strength is our unity of purpose.

To that high concept there can be no end save victory.

17

"A DATE WHICH WILL LIVE IN INFAMY"

ALL AMERICANS ALIVE at the time remember where they were when they learned of the attack on Pearl Harbor. Franklin D. Roosevelt was in his study, chatting with aide Harry Hopkins and working with his stamp collection. Phones jangled with reports from Hawaii, each worse than the last. Japanese planes launched from an aircraft carrier had surprised the fleet at Pearl Harbor. The attack destroyed eight battleships and 180 airplanes, and killed 2,403 Americans. Roosevelt summoned incredulous congressional leaders to an angry meeting at the White House. "Where were our patrols?" demanded one senator. "They knew these negotiations [between the U.S. and Japan] were going on!" It was agreed that he would go before Congress the next day to ask for a declaration of war.

Samuel Rosenman and Robert Sherwood, the star speechwriters, were given the task of writing a radio address for delivery two days later—expected to be the more important talk, today largely forgotten. Roosevelt dictated the remarks to Congress himself, to his secretary Grace Tully. At the presidential library at Hyde Park, visitors can see Roosevelt's original draft. Originally, the first sentence referred to "a date which will live in world history"—with the last two words crossed out and "infamy" scrawled in. On the morning of the speech, new reports were added in: attacks on Hong Kong, Wake Island, Midway Island.

The speech has the terse urgency of a telegram. Its power comes not from grandiloquent phrasing but from the repetition of bad news. Roosevelt—like Winston Churchill—recognized that to mobilize public opinion, he could not sugar-coat the news from the battlefield. Successful leadership in a crisis requires, first, that the public understands the gravity of the situation, and trusts the leaders to tell the truth. Only then will citizens rally and believe the good news when it comes.

The surprise attack dissolved the bitter debate between isolationists and interventionists. Immediately after Roosevelt's speech, Congress voted to declare war against Japan, with only one dissent (by Jeannette Rankin, who had voted against World War I, too). Roosevelt's great aim was still the defeat of Nazi Germany, yet the first attack had come from Japan. Hitler could have worked mischief on the alliance. Instead, three days later, without new provocation, he declared Roosevelt "mad" and declared war against the United States. America was now at war on two continents.

USS Shaw exploding during the Japanese raid on Pearl Harbor, December 7, 1941

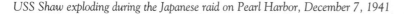

PROPOSED MESSAGE TO THE CONGRESS

Yesterday, December 7, 1941, a date which will live in ~~world history~~ *infamy* — *Japan*

the United States of America was ~~simultaneously~~ *suddenly* and deliberately attacked

by naval and air forces of the Empire of Japan. ~~without warning~~ .

The United States was at the moment at peace with that nation and was

still in

~~continuing the~~ conversation with its Government and its Emperor looking

toward the maintenance of peace in the Pacific. Indeed, one hour after

Oahu

Japanese air squadrons had commenced bombing in ~~Hawaii and in the Philippines~~

the Japanese Ambassador to the United States and his colleague delivered

recent American

to the Secretary of State a formal reply to a ~~recent~~ message, ~~from the~~

~~Secretary.~~ *While* This reply ~~contained a statement~~ *stated* *it seemed useless* that diplomatic negotiations *to continue the*

~~must be considered at an end, but~~ *it* contained no threat ~~and no~~ hint of ~~an~~ *or war or*

armed attack.

It will be recorded that the distance ~~of Hawaii, and especially~~ of

was

Hawaii from Japan makes it obvious that the attack ~~was~~ deliberately

or even weeks

planned many days ago. During the intervening time the Japanese Govern-

ment has deliberately sought to deceive the United States by false

statements and expressions of hope for continued peace.

FDR makes revisions to a typed draft of his address to Congress given on December 8, 1941

Franklin Delano Roosevelt's
REQUEST FOR DECLARATION
OF WAR AGAINST JAPAN

Washington, D.C. • December 8, 1941

hear....
disc 1
track 20

Mr. Vice President, and Mr. Speaker, and Members of the Senate and House of Representatives:

Yesterday, December 7, 1941—a date which will live in infamy—the United States of America was suddenly and deliberately attacked by naval and air forces of the Empire of Japan.

The United States was at peace with that Nation and, at the solicitation of Japan, was still in conversation with its Government and its Emperor looking toward the maintenance of peace in the Pacific. Indeed, one hour after Japanese air squadrons had commenced bombing in the American Island of Oahu, the Japanese Ambassador to the United States and his colleague delivered to our Secretary of State a formal reply to a recent American message. And while this reply stated that it seemed useless to continue the existing diplomatic negotiations, it contained no threat or hint of war or of armed attack.

It will be recorded that the distance of Hawaii from Japan makes it obvious that the attack was deliberately planned many days or even weeks ago. During the intervening time the Japanese Government has deliberately sought to deceive the United States by false statements and expressions of hope for continued peace.

The attack yesterday on the Hawaiian Islands has caused severe damage to American naval and military forces. I regret to tell you that very many American lives have been lost. In addition American ships have been reported torpedoed on the high seas between San Francisco and Honolulu.

Yesterday the Japanese Government also launched an attack against Malaya.

Last night Japanese forces attacked Hong Kong.

Last night Japanese forces attacked Guam.

Last night Japanese forces attacked the Philippine Islands.

Last night the Japanese attacked Wake Island.

And this morning the Japanese attacked Midway Island.

Japan has, therefore, undertaken a surprise offensive extending throughout the Pacific area. The facts of yesterday

"December 7, 1941—a date which will live in infamy."

Roosevelt asks a joint session of Congress for a declaration of war against the Empire of Japan

Cabinet members watch as President Franklin D. Roosevelt, wearing a black armband, signs the United States' declaration of war against Japan at 4:10 p.m. Washington time on December 8, 1941

and today speak for themselves. The people of the United States have already formed their opinions and well understand the implications to the very life and safety of our Nation.

As Commander in Chief of the Army and Navy I have directed that all measures be taken for our defense.

But always will our whole Nation remember the character of the onslaught against us.

No matter how long it may take us to overcome this premeditated invasion, the American people in their righteous might will win through to absolute victory.

I believe that I interpret the will of the Congress and of the people when I assert that we will not only defend ourselves to the uttermost but will make it very certain that this form of treachery shall never again endanger us.

"I regret to tell you that very many American lives have been lost."

"No matter how long it may take us to overcome this premeditated invasion, the American people in their righteous might will win through to absolute victory."

Hostilities exist. There is no blinking at the fact that our people, our territory, and our interests are in grave danger.

With confidence in our armed forces—with the unbounding determination of our people—we will gain the inevitable triumph—so help us God.

I ask that the Congress declare that since the unprovoked and dastardly attack by Japan on Sunday, December 7, 1941, a state of war has existed between the United States and the Japanese Empire.

18

FRANKLIN DELANO ROOSEVELT

"OUR SONS, PRIDE OF OUR NATION"

AT TEN O'CLOCK on the evening of June 5, 1944, President Roosevelt addressed the American people on radio. The Fifth Army had captured Rome. "The first of the Axis capitals is now in our hands," he said. "One up and two to go!" His tone was ebullient, but his mind was restless. He knew that at that moment, American, British, and Allied forces were steaming across the English Channel toward France. Indeed, paratroopers had already started to land. The D-Day invasion of Normandy had begun.

The invasion of western Europe by one million men stands as America's greatest military effort. Planning for a "second front" had taken years. The dictator of the Soviet Union, Joseph Stalin, insistently demanded action to relieve his besieged nation, while Britain's Churchill worried that a direct attack would bog down. At Teheran in 1943, the Big Three—Roosevelt, Stalin, Churchill—agreed on an assault on France for the spring of 1944. Fevered preparations took months, including elaborate efforts to trick the Germans to expect fighting in a different location. Then, on the eve of the planned invasion, June 4, sheets of rain drenched the region. General Dwight D. Eisenhower postponed the landings. The next day, as rain continued, weather forecasters came with news of a brief opening in the clouds. Eisenhower decided to send the troops: a gamble with potentially catastrophic consequences. If the storm resumed, boats would be scuttled and the invasion would fail.

That night, after his fireside chat on the fall of Rome, Roosevelt was in constant touch with the Pentagon (newly built headquarters of the military). At four in the morning, the first fragmentary and confusing reports came in: the

landings were underway. By mid-morning, 181 reporters crowded into the Oval Office for an ebullient press conference—as Roosevelt noted, they were "all smiles." "I'm a little sleepy," he confessed happily.

D-Day was marked across America by a solemn display, with churches crowded in prayer. Roosevelt's four sons were on active military duty. Eleanor wrote to a friend, "I feel as

Military staff at La Guardia Field in New York gather around a radio and listen intently as President Franklin D. Roosevelt prays for the Allied invaders of Normandy on D-Day, June 6, 1944

On D-Day, June 6, 1944, American soldiers wade to the Normandy shore fighting heavy machine-gun fire

though a sword were hanging over my head, dreading its fall and yet know it must fall to end the war." The tone of Roosevelt's talk was especially striking—"a far cry," as Samuel Rosenman noted, "from the kind of speech Hitler would have made if his troops were landing on the beaches of England." There is no talk of blood, of conquest, or of revenge. Roosevelt had decided to read a prayer the previous weekend while staying in Virginia, and he composed it with the aid of his daughter Anna, consulting with the Book of Common Prayer. The uncomplicated religious strain often evident in his writing now was fully to the fore.

If ever prayers were needed, it was now: boats were sent to the wrong beach, bombs missed their targets, men were cut down before reaching shore. But by midnight, 156,000 men had crowded onto the beaches of Northern France. The optimism of June proved premature. Paris fell three months later, but Germany continued to resist for nearly a year. A fierce counterattack at the Battle of the Bulge in December 1944 nearly halted the Allied offensive. Finally, in April 1945, American, British, and Soviet forces converged on Germany. Roosevelt was at his vacation cottage in Warm Springs, Georgia, working on a speech. On April 12, he suffered a cerebral hemorrhage and died. The last line of his undelivered text read: "The only limit to our realization of tomorrow will be our doubts of today. Let us move forward with strong and active faith."

My Fellow Americans:

Last night, when I spoke with you about the fall of Rome, I knew at that moment that troops of the United States and our Allies were crossing the Channel in another and greater operation. It has come to pass with success thus far.

And so, in this poignant hour, I ask you to join with me in prayer:

Almighty God: Our sons, pride of our nation, this day have set upon a mighty endeavor, a struggle to preserve our Republic, our religion, and our civilization, and to set free a suffering humanity.

Lead them straight and true; give strength to their arms, stoutness to their hearts, steadfastness in their faith.

They will need Thy blessings. Their road will be long and hard. For the enemy is strong. He may hurl back our forces. Success may not come with rushing speed, but we shall return again and again; and we know that by Thy grace, and by the righteousness of our cause, our sons will triumph.

They will be sore tried, by night and by day, without rest—until the victory is won. The darkness will be rent by noise and flame. Men's souls will be shaken with the violences of war.

"They will need Thy blessings. Their road will be long and hard. For the enemy is strong."

For these men are lately drawn from the ways of peace. They fight not for the lust of conquest. They fight to end conquest. They fight to liberate. They fight to let justice arise, and tolerance and goodwill among all Thy people. They yearn but for the end of battle, for their return to the haven of home.

"Men's souls will be shaken in the violences of war."

Some will never return. Embrace these, Father, and receive them, Thy heroic servants, into Thy kingdom.

And for us at home—fathers, mothers, children, wives, sisters, and brothers of brave men overseas, whose thoughts and prayers are ever with them—help us, Almighty God, to rededicate ourselves in renewed faith in Thee in this hour of great sacrifice.

"Some will never return. Embrace these, Father, and receive them, Thy heroic servants, into Thy kingdom."

Many people have urged that I call the nation into a single day of special prayer. But because the road is long and the desire is great, I ask that our people devote themselves in a continuance of prayer. As we rise to each new day, and again when each day is spent, let words of prayer be on our lips, invoking Thy help to our efforts.

Give us strength, too—strength in our daily tasks, to redouble the contributions we make in the physical and the material support of our armed forces.

"All the News That's Fit to Print"

The New York Times.

6 A. M. EXTRA
Partly cloudy and warmer today; moderate to fresh winds.
Temperatures Yesterday—Max., 67; Min., 51
Sunrise, 5:25 A. M.; Sunset, 8:26 P. M.

VOL. XCIII. No. 31,545. Entered as Second-Class Matter, Postoffice, New York, N. Y. NEW YORK, TUESDAY, JUNE 6, 1944. THREE CENTS NEW YORK CITY

ALLIED ARMIES LAND IN FRANCE IN THE HAVRE-CHERBOURG AREA; GREAT INVASION IS UNDER WAY

ROOSEVELT SPEAKS

Says Rome's Fall Marks 'One Up and Two to Go' Among Axis Capitals

WARNS WAY IS HARD

Asks World to Give the Italians a Chance for Recovery

The text of President Roosevelt's address is on Page 5.

By CHARLES HURD

Special to The New York Times.

WASHINGTON, June 5—President Roosevelt hailed tonight the capture of Rome, first of the three major Axis capitals to fall, as a great achievement on the road toward total conquest of the Axis. Rome, he said, marked "one up and two to go."

The President spoke for a quarter-hour on the radio, as had been announced yesterday, but his speech was notable for its lack of heroics. It was in no sense a speech of triumph, but rather a tribute to the United Nations forces and leadership that drove the Germans from Rome.

With this tribute he combined a solemn warning that much greater fighting lies ahead before the Axis is defeated, as well as high tributes to the Italian people, whom he again welcomed as a people into the family of nations opposed to the Axis.

"Italy should go on," Mr. Roosevelt said, "as a great mother nation, contributing to the culture and the progress and the good-will of mankind, developing her special talents in the arts, crafts, and sciences, and preserving her historic and cultural heritage for the benefit of all peoples.

"We want and expect the help of the future Italy toward lasting peace. All the other nations opposed to fascism and nazism ought to help to give Italy a chance."

Shrines Should Live, He Says

President Roosevelt saw considerable significance in the fact that Rome should be the first Axis capital to fall. He remarked its shrines, "visible symbols of the faith and determination of the early saints and martyrs that Christianity should live and become universal," and added that "it will be a source of deep satisfaction that the freedom of the Pope and of Vatican City is assured by the armies of the United Nations."

There is significance, too, he added, in the fact that Rome was liberated by a composite force of soldiers from many nations.

Reviewing the military picture, the President pointed out that "it would be unwise to inflate in our own minds the military importance of the capture of Rome." He cautioned his auditors that while the Germans have retreated "thousands of miles" across Africa and back through Italy "they have suffered heavy losses, but not great enough yet to cause collapse."

"Therefore," he added, "the victory still lies some distance ahead. That distance will be covered in due time—have no fear of that. But it will be tough and it will be costly."

Turning to the relief problem in the newly liberated portion of Italy, Mr. Roosevelt noted that some persons thought of the financial cost, but he maintained that the work would pay dividends "by eliminating fascism" and any future desire by Italians to "start another war of aggression." Relief has been planned, he added, but transport demands are so great that "improvement must be gradual."

He warned Italy that it "cannot grow in stature by seeking to build up a great militaristic empire,"

Continued on Page 5

Conferees Accept Cabaret Tax Cut

By The Associated Press.

WASHINGTON, June 5—A House-Senate conference committee agreed today to cut back the cabaret tax from 30 to 20 per cent, but eliminated a provision exempting service men and women from the levy.

The group decided to put the national debt limit at $260,000,000,000 as originally requested by the Administration.

The action is subject to House and Senate votes. The conferees met informally today, but members said that the decisions probably would stand as their final recommendation.

The House, at the insistence of a group of Republicans, passed a bill raising the debt ceiling only from $210,000,000,000 to $240,000,000,000. The Senate then put the figure at $260,000,000,000 and attached a rider reducing the cabaret tax from 30 to 20 per cent and exempting men and women in uniform from paying the tax on their checks.

Some tax experts argued that this exemption would make administration of the excise on night clubs impossible.

FEDERAL LAW HELD RULING INSURANCE

Supreme Court, 4-3, Decides Business Is Interstate and Subject to Trust Act

Special to The New York Times.

WASHINGTON, June 5—The Supreme Court, by a four-to-three decision today, held that the insurance companies of the country, with assets of $37,000,000,000 and annual premium collections in excess of $6,000,000,000, are in interstate commerce and thus subject to the Sherman Anti-Trust Law.

The decision upset precedents which began with a contrary decision by the court more than seventy-five years ago and have been reaffirmed repeatedly since the adoption of the anti-trust law in 1890.

The majority decision, written

Continued on Page 13

PURSUIT ON IN ITALY

Allies Pass Rome, Cross Tiber as Foe Quits Bank Below City

PLANES JOIN IN CHASE

1,200 Vehicles Wrecked —Eighth Army Battles Into More Towns

By The Associated Press.

ROME, June 5—The Allies' armor and motorized infantry roared through Rome today without pausing, crossed the Tiber River and proceeded with the grim task of destroying two battered German armies fleeing to the north.

Fighter-bombers spearheaded the pursuit, jamming the escape highways with burning enemy transport and littering the fields with dead and wounded Germans. The enemy was tired, disorganized and bewildered by the slashing assault, which in twenty-five days had inflicted a major catastrophe on the Germans and liberated Rome almost without damage.

Railway Yards Bombed

Five hundred American heavy bombers blasted railway yards at five points in northern Italy between Venice and Rimini along which the Germans might attempt to move reinforcements and equipment to bolster their beaten armies. Hour after hour, the Allies' planes swept down on highways leading northward and tore the fleeing enemy apart. Twelve hundred combat vehicles were destroyed from dawn to dark yesterday, and hundreds more today. Farther north, medium bombers smashed bridges and rail facilities.

[The Germans have abandoned the entire left bank of the Tiber from Ostia, at its mouth, to Rome, according to a Vichy broadcast quoted by The Associated Press.

[The Germans are already entrenched in mountain positions

Continued on Page 2

FIRST ALLIED LANDING MADE ON SHORES OF WESTERN EUROPE

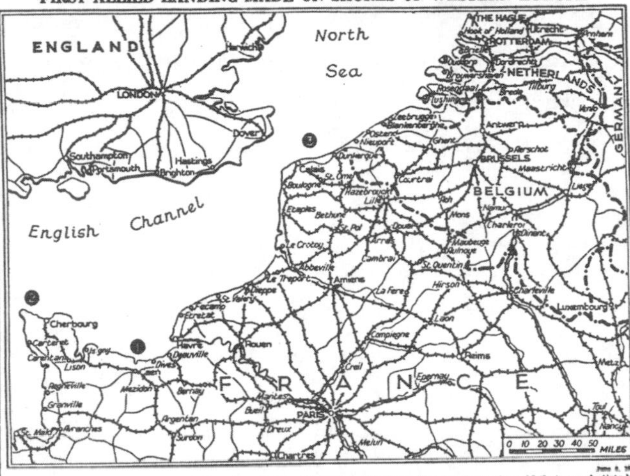

June 6, 1944

General Eisenhower's armies invaded northern France this morning. While the landing points were not specified, the Germans said that troops had gone ashore near Havre and that fighting raged at Caen (1). The enemy also said that parachutists had descended at the northern tip of the Normandy Peninsula (2) and heavy bombing had been visited on Calais and Dunkerque (3).

War News Summarized

TUESDAY, JUNE 6, 1944

The invasion of western Europe began this morning.

General Eisenhower, in his first communiqué from Supreme Headquarters, Allied Expeditionary Force, issued at 3:30 A. M., said that "Allied naval forces supported by strong air forces began landing Allied armies this morning on the northern coast of France."

The assault was made by British, American and Canadian troops who, under command of Gen. Sir Bernard L. Montgomery, landed in Normandy. London gave no further details but earlier Berlin had broadcast that parachute troops had landed on the Normandy Peninsula near Cherbourg and that invasion forces were pouring from landing craft under cover of warships near Havre. Dunkerque and Calais were being heavily bombed, the Germans said.

Later announcements from Berlin said that there was fighting between Caen and Trouville and that shock troops had swung into action to halt the invasion. [All the foregoing, 1:8.]

General Eisenhower, in an order of the day to each member of the "great crusade," told his men the enemy would fight savagely and added: "We will accept nothing less than full victory. Good luck." In a broadcast to the "Peoples of Western Europe," he said the day would come when he would need their full help. A special word to France added that Frenchmen would rule the country. [1:6-7.] Almost simultaneously it was announced that General de Gaulle had arrived in London. [6:2.]

The liberation of Rome in no way slowed the Allied pursuit of the tired and disorganized German armies in Italy yesterday. Armored and motorized units sped across the Tiber River to press hard upon the retreating enemy's heels. Five hundred heavy bombers joined with lighter aircraft to smash rail and road routes leading to northern Italy and to add to the foe's demoralization. The Eighth Army, despite heavy opposition, especially northeast of Valmontone, captured a number of strategic towns. [1:3; map P. 2.]

General Clark said that parts of the two German armies had been smashed. He doubted the ability of the German Fourteenth to put up effective opposition and declared that the Tenth had taken a bad beating. [3:1.]

King Victor Emmanuel fulfilled his promise and turned over all authority to his son, Crown Prince Humbert. [1:5-6.]

President Roosevelt warned the people of the United States in a radio talk last night not to over-emphasize the military significance of the liberation of Rome. "Germany has not yet been driven to surrender," he said. "Victory still lies some distance ahead. * * * It will be tough and it will be costly." The President appealed to the world to give Italy a chance to contribute her share to a lasting peace. [1:1.]

In the Pacific theatre Americans were converging on the Biak airfields. Allied planes sank one and damaged two Japanese destroyers and shot down at least eighteen aircraft. [8:1.]

POPE GIVES THANKS ROME WAS SPARED

Voices Appreciation to Both Belligerents in Message to Throng at St. Peter's

By Wireless to The New York Times.

VATICAN CITY, June 5—Pope Pius XII appeared on the balcony of St. Peter's at 6 P. M. today to thank God that Rome had been spared from the ravages of war while before him in the densely packed square of St. Peter's and the new broad Via Della Conciliazione tens of thousands of Romans cheered themselves hoarse.

It was the third time today that the Pontiff had showed himself to cheering crowds, as he had appeared twice at a window of his office this morning. But this was a solemn, sacred occasion and no one knowing anything about Pius XII can doubt the fervor of his thankfulness that Rome had been saved.

The Pontiff seemed strong and well and his voice carried far, though it was difficult to hear every word he said because of the crowd.

"We must give thanks to God for the favors we have received," said the Pope. "Rome has been spared. This day will go down in the annals of Rome."

He went on to say he hoped that Italians would be worthy of the grace shown them and put aside hatred and all personal vendettas. He then thanked both belligerents—the Allies and Germany—for having left Rome intact.

After a prayer of thankfulness to the Blessed Virgin and Saints Peter and Paul, guardians of Rome, the Pontiff gave his blessing, "urbe et orbis," as the immense crowd knelt before him.

[The Associated Press estimated the crowd was between 250,000 and 500,000.]

The world has changed for Rome but the Vatican goes on imperturbably as it has through so many other conquests in centuries gone by. It is neutral in fact and spirit. The Pope and all high officials went about their daily routine today as in the past. Except for the tanks and armored cars running along the street in front of St. Peter's one could never know what had happened today.

Continued on Page 5

Italy's Monarch Yields Rule To Son, but Retains Throne

By The Associated Press.

NAPLES, June 5—Victor Emmanuel III stepped aside as King of Italy today, as he previously had said he would do upon the liberation of Rome, and handed to his 39-year-old son, Crown Prince Humbert, all "royal prerogatives." Italian political pressure had been brought to bear against him since the occupation of Naples.

In a decree signed by himself and countersigned by Premier Pietro Badoglio, head of the Italian Liberation Government, the King named his son Lieutenant General of the Realm. The monarch, however, retained his title as head of the House of Savoy and remains as King without power.

[The first act of the Council of Ministers after the transfer of royal powers was a formal denunciation of the 1940 armistice treaty inflicted on France, The United Press said.]

Victor Emmanuel, who became King July 29, 1900, had announced last April 12 his "irrevocable" decision to withdraw from public life "on the day on which Allied troops enter Rome."

Little more than a figurehead since Benito Mussolini assumed the dictatorship of Italy, Victor Emmanuel had won a reputation in the first years of his reign as a sympathetic monarch, interested in his people and their problems.

Prince Humbert, tall and erect, opposed fascism in Italy at the start, but later made a truce with Mussolini. In effect, Humbert becomes the King's regent.

TEXT OF ROYAL DECREE

The King's withdrawal decree:

I, Victor Emmanuel III, by the grace of God and by the will of the nation King of Italy, in collaboration with the President of the Council of Ministers and with the agreement of the Council, have ordered and order as follows:

My beloved son, Humbert of Savoy, Prince of Piedmont, is nominated our Lieutenant General. In collaboration with responsible Ministers he will in our name superintend all matters of administration and exercise all royal prerogatives without exception, signing royal decrees which will be countersigned and authenticated in the usual way.

We order all concerned to observe this decree and to see that it is observed as the law of the State.

Given at Ravello June 5, 1944.
VICTOR EMMANUEL.
(Countersigned) PIETRO BADOGLIO.

The withdrawal was presented to

Continued on Page 4

ALLIED WARNING FLASHED TO COAST

People Told to Clear Area 22 Miles Inland as Soon as Instructions Are Given

By Cable to The New York Times.

LONDON, Tuesday, June 6—The British Broadcasting Corporation began its 8 A. M. news bulletin this morning with quotations from a Supreme Headquarters' "urgent warning" to inhabitants of the enemy-occupied countries living near the coast.

Gen. Dwight D. Eisenhower has directed that whenever possible in France a warning shall be given to towns in which certain targets will be intensively bombed.

This warning, the broadcast said,

Continued on Page B

PARADE OF PLANES CARRIES INVADERS

Witness Says First 'Chutists Met Only Light Fire When They Landed in France

The first eyewitness account of the Allies' invasion of Europe was given in a pool broadcast from London this morning by Wright Bryan of the National Broadcasting Company, who accompanied the airborne troops in their landings.

His account said the first spearhead of Allied forces landed by parachute in northern France in the first hour of D-day.

"In the navigator's dome in the flight deck of a C-47, I rode across the English Channel with the first group of planes from the United States Ninth Air Force Troop Carrier Command to take our fighting men into Europe," Mr. Bryan said.

He added that just before he left French soil for the return trip he saw seventeen American paratroopers, led by a lieutenant colonel, jump with their arms, ammunition and equipment into German-occupied France."

He declared that his group at the head of the leading wing was met with "only scattering small

Continued on Page B

Eisenhower Instructs Europeans; Gives Battle Order to His Armies

Following are the texts of a statement by Gen. Dwight D. Eisenhower broadcast to the people of western Europe and his Order of the Day to the Allied Expeditionary Force as recorded by The New York Times and the Columbia Broadcasting System:

People of western Europe! A landing was made this morning on the coast of France by troops of the Allied Expeditionary Force. This landing is part of the concerted United Nations plan for the liberation of Europe, made in conjunction with our great Russian Allies. I have this message for all of you. Although the initial assault may not have been made in your own country, the hour of your liberation is approaching.

All patriots, men and women, young and old, have a part to play in the achievement of final victory. To members of resistance movements, whether led by national or outside leaders, I say: "Follow the instructions you have received." To patriots who are not members of organized resistance groups I say, "continue your passive resistance, but do not needlessly endanger your lives until I give you the signal to rise and strike the enemy. The day will come when I shall need your united strength. Until that day, I call on you for the hard task of discipline and restraint."

Citizens of France! I am proud to have again under my command the gallant forces of France. Fighting beside their Allies, they will play a worthy part in the liberation of their

Continued on Page 3

EISENHOWER ACTS

U. S., British, Canadian Troops Backed by Sea, Air Forces

MONTGOMERY LEADS

Nazis Say Their Shock Units Are Battling Our Parachutists

Communique No. 1 On Allied Invasion

By Broadcast to The New York Times.

LONDON, Tuesday, June 6—The Supreme Headquarters of the Allied Expeditionary Force issued this communiqué this morning:

"Under the command of General Eisenhower, Allied naval forces, supported by strong air forces, began landing Allied armies this morning on the northern coast of France."

By RAYMOND DANIELL

By Cable to The New York Times.

SUPREME HEADQUARTERS ALLIED EXPEDITIONARY FORCES, Tuesday, June 6—The invasion of Europe from the west has begun.

In the gray light of a summer dawn Gen. Dwight D. Eisenhower threw his great Anglo-American force into action today for the liberation of the Continent. The spearhead of attack was an Army group commanded by Gen. Sir Bernard L. Montgomery and comprising troops of the United States, Britain and Canada.

General Eisenhower's first communiqué was terse and calculated to give little information to the enemy. It said merely that "Allied naval forces supported by strong air forces began landing Allied armies this morning on the northern coast of France."

After the first communiqué was released it was announced that the Allied landing was in Normandy.

Caen Battle Reported

German broadcasts, beginning at 6:30 A. M., London time, [12:30 A. M. Eastern war time] gave first word of the assault. [The Associated Press said General Eisenhower, for the sake of surprise, deliberately let the Germans have the "first word."]

The German DNB agency said the Allied invasion operations began with the landing of airborne troops in the area of the mouth of the Seine River.

[Berlin said the "center of gravity" of the fierce fighting was at Caen, thirty miles southwest of Havre and sixty-five miles southeast of Cherbourg, The Associated Press reported. Caen is ten miles inland from the sea, at the base of the seventy-five-mile-wide Normandy Peninsula, and fighting there might indicate the Allies' seizing of a beachhead.

[DNB said in a broadcast just before 10 A. M. (4 A. M. Eastern war time) that the Anglo-American troops had been reinforced at dawn at the mouth of the Seine River in the Havre area.]

[An Allied correspondent broadcasting from Supreme Headquarters, according to the Columbia Broadcasting System, said this morning that "German tanks are moving up

Continued on Page A Following Page 8

And let our hearts be stout, to wait out the long travail, to bear sorrows that may come, to impart our courage unto our sons wheresoever they may be.

"I ask that our people devote themselves in a continuance of prayer."

And, O Lord, give us faith. Give us faith in Thee; faith in our sons; faith in each other; faith in our united crusade. Let not the keenness of our spirit ever be dulled. Let not the impacts of temporary events, of temporal matters of but fleeting moment—let not these deter us in our unconquerable purpose.

With Thy blessing, we shall prevail over the unholy forces of our enemy. Help us to conquer the apostles of greed and racial arrogances. Lead us to the saving of our country, and with our sister nations into a world unity that will spell a sure peace—a peace invulnerable to the schemings of unworthy men. And a peace that will let all of men live in freedom, reaping the just rewards of their honest toil.

Thy will be done, Almighty God.

Amen.

33RD PRESIDENT: 1945–1953

Born: May 8, 1884, in Lamar, Missouri
Died: December 26, 1972, in Kansas City, Missouri

Disc 1, Tracks 22–23

19

"THE TRUMAN DOCTRINE"

ON FEBRUARY 21, 1947, the British ambassador brought an urgent message to the U.S. State Department: London was broke, and would cut off aid to Greece and Turkey in a month. That meant those two nations might fall to communism, giving the Soviet Union and its allies a toehold in the eastern Mediterranean. The note was stark: the United States must decide whether to take Britain's place, spending $400 million to save Greece and Turkey.

World War II had been won less than two years earlier, and most Americans pined for peacetime routine. But relations between the U.S. and its former ally in Moscow were worsening. In 1946, White House aide Clark Clifford and his associate George Elsey wrote a one hundred thousand–word, secret report claiming that the Soviet Union had broken its promises and that its expansionism threatened peace and American security. Still, tensions had eased lately, and isolationist habits died hard. The funds needed—though they seem small now—then were over one percent of the federal budget. President Harry Truman faced a decision: would he inject the U.S. into Europe, standing down the communist insurgency there? And how could he persuade isolationist lawmakers, who had already cut foreign aid spending, to act?

In a meeting at the White House, Senator Arthur Vandenberg made clear to Truman what it would take for Congress to consider aid to Greece and Turkey. "Mr. President, the only way you are ever going to get this is to make a speech," the Republican lawmaker said, "and scare the hell out of the country." Truman remembered, "I wanted no hedging....It had to be clear and free of hesitation or double talk." Drafting was begun by the State Department, but taken over by Clifford and Elsey: their job was to "Trumanize" the bland bureaucratic prose. (Truman remembered the original draft read like an "investment prospectus.")

The speech proclaimed a "fateful hour" in a great philosophical conflict with communism. "At the present moment in world history, nearly every nation must choose between alternate ways of life," Truman said. The most important passage set out a new activist role for America in the world. The State Department draft had read: "It is essential to our security that we assist free peoples to work out their own destiny in their own way and our help must be primarily in the form of that economic and financial aid which is essential to economic stability and orderly political processes." Now the final text declared: "I believe that it must be the policy of the United States to support free peoples who are resisting attempted subjugation by armed minorities or by outside pressures. I believe that we must assist free peoples to work out their own destinies in their own way. I believe that our help should be primarily through economic and financial aid which is essential to economic stability and orderly political processes." Truman claimed in his memoirs that he had penciled in the word "must." Clifford ruefully notes that the muscular assertion in fact came from Under Secretary of State Dean Acheson. Still, it was Truman's blunt sentiment, and it became known as the "Truman Doctrine." Coming after Washington's Farewell Address, with its avoidance of Europe, and the turn inward after Wilson's failures, this was a marked change in tone for U.S. presidents in peacetime.

Truman delivered the speech grimly to a near-silent audience in Congress. According to Acheson, the standing ovation at the end "was a tribute to a brave man rather than unanimous acceptance of his policy." The *New York*

Times compared it to the Monroe Doctrine (which held that the U.S. would block foreign interference in the Western Hemisphere). *Newsweek* commented, "If words could shape the future of nations, these unquestionably would. They had clearly put America into power politics to stay." Two months later, Congress approved the aid.

Historians still debate the speech and its import. Some argue that Truman's belligerent tone deepened the chance of conflict. Acheson himself admitted that the fire-alarm language and broad commitments used by the administration during these years were "clearer than truth." But the hot words were deliberate. Foreign policy scholar James Chace noted, "By using universalistic rhetoric to attain more modest ends, Acheson and Truman laid the groundwork for the belief, which would become ever more widely shared by government officials as well as the larger public,

that the United States saw little alternative but to embark on the global containment of communism." Clifford, at the end of his life, wrote: "The policy set forth by President Truman took over forty years to succeed, was controversial and expensive, and was at times misapplied—most notably in Vietnam. But a major war with the Soviet Union was avoided during a dangerous half century, and by 1989 it was clear that the Cold War was over. This was the direct, if long-delayed, result of the policies laid out in 1947 by Harry Truman and followed, despite all the political controversies at home, by every one of his successors."

With this speech, the United States made clear it would seek to block Soviet expansionism. The Marshall Plan, with its massive aid to rebuild Europe, and the creation of the NATO military alliance would soon follow. The Cold War had begun.

PRESIDENT GERALD R. FORD ON THE TRUMAN DOCTRINE

As a first-time candidate for Congress in 1948, I was impressed by the speeches of Harry S. Truman—especially his proposal for aid to Greece and Turkey, the "Truman Doctrine." I campaigned frankly as a Republican, challenging a Republican incumbent for the House—but I fully endorsed the Truman Doctrine speech and Marshall Plan. The incumbent I was running against that year had been in the House for ten years and was a senior member of the Committee on Foreign Affairs. He was a devout isolationist, totally supporting the line of the *Chicago Tribune*. In the primary, the basic issue was internationalism and foreign policy. I borrowed a lot of the arguments and recommendations made by Harry Truman in the speech calling for Greek-Turkish aid. I thought it was right then, and I think it was right in retrospect. Although I have always been a loyal Republican, I thought Harry Truman was a first-class president on foreign policy.

Truman was a down-to-earth, hard-nosed, Midwestern orator. He would not have won an oratorical contest, but his common sense was very persuasive. This approach turned around the 1948 election for Truman, whose victory was a shock to me—not as much as it was to the *Chicago Tribune*, but I still couldn't believe it.

Harry S. Truman's
ADDRESS TO CONGRESS ON GREECE AND TURKEY

Washington, D.C. • March 12, 1947

Mr. President, Mr. Speaker, Members of the Congress of the United States:

The gravity of the situation which confronts the world today necessitates my appearance before a joint session of the Congress.

The foreign policy and the national security of this country are involved.

One aspect of the present situation, which I present to you at this time for your consideration and decision, concerns Greece and Turkey.

The United States has received from the Greek Government an urgent appeal for financial and economic assistance. Preliminary reports from the American Economic Mission now in Greece and reports from the American Ambassador in Greece corroborate the statement of the Greek Government that assistance is imperative if Greece is to survive as a free nation.

I do not believe that the American people and the Congress wish to turn a deaf ear to the appeal of the Greek Government.

> ## *"Assistance is imperative if Greece is to survive as a free nation."*

Greece is not a rich country. Lack of sufficient natural resources has always forced the Greek people to work hard to make both ends meet. Since 1940, this industrious, peace loving country has suffered invasion, four years of cruel enemy occupation, and bitter internal strife.

When forces of liberation entered Greece they found that the retreating Germans had destroyed virtually all the railways, roads, port facilities, communications, and merchant marine. More than a thousand villages had been burned. Eighty-five percent of the children were tubercular. Livestock, poultry, and draft animals had almost disappeared. Inflation had wiped out practically all savings.

> ## *"If Turkey is to have the assistance it needs, the United States must supply it."*

As a result of these tragic conditions, a militant minority, exploiting human want and misery, was able to create political chaos which, until now, has made economic recovery impossible.

Greece is today without funds to finance the importation of those goods which are essential to bare subsistence. Under these circumstances the people of Greece cannot make progress in solving their problems of reconstruction. Greece is in desperate need of financial and economic assistance to enable it to resume purchases of food, clothing, fuel and seeds. These are indispensable for the subsistence of its people and are obtainable only from abroad. Greece must have help to import the goods necessary to restore internal order and security so essential for economic and political recovery.

The Greek Government has also asked for the assistance of experienced American administrators, economists and technicians to insure that the financial and other aid given to Greece shall be used effectively in creating a stable and self-sustaining economy and in improving its public administration.

The very existence of the Greek state is today threatened by the terrorist activities of several thousand armed men, led by Communists, who defy the government's authority at a number of points, particularly along the northern boundaries. A Commission appointed by the United Nations Security Council is at present investigating disturbed conditions in northern Greece and alleged border violations along the frontier between Greece on the one hand and Albania, Bulgaria, and Yugoslavia on the other.

Meanwhile, the Greek Government is unable to cope with the situation. The Greek army is small and poorly equipped. It needs supplies and equipment if it is to restore authority to the government throughout Greek territory.

Greece must have assistance if it is to become a self-supporting and self-respecting democracy.

The United States must supply this assistance. We have already extended to Greece certain types of relief and economic aid but these are inadequate.

There is no other country to which democratic Greece can turn.

> *"I believe that it must be the policy of the United States to support free peoples who are resisting attempted subjugation by armed minorities or by outside pressures."*

No other nation is willing and able to provide the necessary support for a democratic Greek government.

The British Government, which has been helping Greece, can give no further financial or economic aid after March 31. Great Britain finds itself under the necessity of reducing or liquidating its commitments in several parts of the world, including Greece.

We have considered how the United Nations might assist in this crisis. But the situation is an urgent one requiring immediate action, and the United Nations and its related organizations are not in a position to extend help of the kind that is required.

It is important to note that the Greek Government has asked for our aid in utilizing effectively the financial and other assistance we may give to Greece, and in improving its public administration. It is of the utmost importance that we supervise the use of any funds made available to Greece, in such a manner that each dollar spent will count toward making Greece self-supporting, and will help to build an economy in which a healthy democracy can flourish.

No government is perfect. One of the chief virtues of a democracy, however, is that its defects are always visible and under democratic processes can be pointed out and corrected. The government of Greece is not perfect. Nevertheless it represents 85 percent of the members of the Greek Parliament who were chosen in an election last year. Foreign observers, including 692 Americans, considered this election to be a fair expression of the views of the Greek people.

The Greek Government has been operating in an atmosphere of chaos and extremism. It has made mistakes. The extension of aid by this country does not mean that the United States condones everything that the Greek Government has done or will do. We have condemned in the past, and we condemn now, extremist measures of the right or the left. We have in the past advised tolerance, and we advise tolerance now.

Greece's neighbor, Turkey, also deserves our attention.

The future of Turkey as an independent and economically sound state is clearly no less important to the freedom-loving peoples of the world than the future of Greece. The circumstances in which Turkey finds itself today are considerably different from those of Greece. Turkey has been spared the disasters that have beset Greece. And during the war, the United States and Great Britain furnished Turkey with material aid.

Nevertheless, Turkey now needs our support.

President Harry Truman asks a joint session of Congress for $400 million and American military advisors for Greece and Turkey to make the Mediterranean countries bulwarks against the spread of Communism

Since the war Turkey has sought additional financial assistance from Great Britain and the United States for the purpose of effecting that modernization necessary for the maintenance of its national integrity.

That integrity is essential to the preservation of order in the Middle East.

The British Government has informed us that, owing to its own difficulties, it can no longer extend financial or economic aid to Turkey.

As in the case of Greece, if Turkey is to have the assistance it needs, the United States must supply it. We are the only country able to provide that help.

I am fully aware of the broad implications involved if the United States extends assistance to Greece and Turkey, and I shall discuss these implications with you at this time.

One of the primary objectives of the foreign policy of the United States is the creation of conditions in which we and other nations will be able to work out a way of life free from coercion. This was a fundamental issue in the war with Germany and Japan. Our victory was won over countries which sought to impose their will, and their way of life, upon other nations.

To ensure the peaceful development of nations, free from coercion, the United States has taken a leading part in

133

establishing the United Nations. The United Nations is designed to make possible lasting freedom and independence for all its members. We shall not realize our objectives, however, unless we are willing to help free peoples to maintain their free institutions and their national integrity against aggressive movements that seek to impose upon them totalitarian regimes. This is no more than a frank recognition that totalitarian regimes imposed upon free peoples, by direct or indirect aggression, undermine the foundations of international peace and hence the security of the United States.

The peoples of a number of countries of the world have recently had totalitarian regimes forced upon them against their will. The Government of the United States has made frequent protests against coercion and intimidation, in violation of the Yalta agreement, in Poland, Rumania, and Bulgaria. I must also state that in a number of other countries there have been similar developments.

"The seeds of totalitarian regimes are nurtured by misery and want."

At the present moment in world history nearly every nation must choose between alternative ways of life. The choice is too often not a free one.

One way of life is based upon the will of the majority, and is distinguished by free institutions, representative government, free elections, guarantees of individual liberty, freedom of speech and religion, and freedom from political oppression.

The second way of life is based upon the will of a minority forcibly imposed upon the majority. It relies upon terror and oppression, a controlled press and radio, fixed elections, and the suppression of personal freedoms.

I believe that it must be the policy of the United States to support free peoples who are resisting attempted subjugation by armed minorities or by outside pressures.

I believe that we must assist free peoples to work out their own destinies in their own way.

I believe that our help should be primarily through economic and financial aid which is essential to economic stability and orderly political processes.

The world is not static, and the *status quo* is not sacred. But we cannot allow changes in the *status quo* in violation of the Charter of the United Nations by such methods as coercion, or by such subterfuges as political infiltration. In helping free and independent nations to maintain their freedom, the United States will be giving effect to the principles of the Charter of the United Nations.

It is necessary only to glance at a map to realize that the survival and integrity of the Greek nation are of grave importance in a much wider situation. If Greece should fall under the control of an armed minority, the effect upon its neighbor, Turkey, would be immediate and serious. Confusion and disorder might well spread throughout the entire Middle East.

Moreover, the disappearance of Greece as an independent state would have a profound effect upon those countries in Europe whose peoples are struggling against great difficulties to maintain their freedoms and their independence while they repair the damages of war.

It would be an unspeakable tragedy if these countries, which have struggled so long against overwhelming odds, should lose that victory for which they sacrificed so much. Collapse of free institutions and loss of independence would be disastrous not only for them but for the world. Discouragement and possibly failure would quickly be the lot of neighboring peoples striving to maintain their freedom and independence.

Should we fail to aid Greece and Turkey in this fateful hour, the effect will be far reaching to the West as well as to the East.

We must take immediate and resolute action.

I therefore ask the Congress to provide authority for assistance to Greece and Turkey in the amount of $400,000,000 for the period ending June 30, 1948. In requesting these funds, I have taken into consideration the maximum amount of relief assistance which would be furnished to Greece out of the $350,000,000 which I recently requested that the Congress authorize for the prevention of starvation and suffering in countries devastated by the war.

"The free peoples of the world look to us for support in maintaining their freedoms."

In addition to funds, I ask the Congress to authorize the detail of American civilian and military personnel to Greece and Turkey, at the request of those countries, to assist in the tasks of reconstruction, and for the purpose of supervising the use of such financial and material assistance as may be furnished. I recommend that authority also be provided for the instruction and training of selected Greek and Turkish personnel.

Finally, I ask that the Congress provide authority which will permit the speediest and most effective use, in terms of needed commodities, supplies, and equipment, of such funds as may be authorized.

If further funds, or further authority, should be needed for the purposes indicated in this message, I shall not hesitate to bring the situation before the Congress. On this subject the Executive and Legislative branches of the Government must work together.

This is a serious course upon which we embark.

I would not recommend it except that the alternative is much more serious.

The United States contributed $341,000,000,000 toward winning World War II. This is an investment in world freedom and world peace.

The assistance that I am recommending for Greece and Turkey amounts to little more than 1/10 of 1 percent of this investment. It is only common sense that we should safeguard this investment and make sure that it was not in vain.

The seeds of totalitarian regimes are nurtured by misery and want. They spread and grow in the evil soil of poverty and strife. They reach their full growth when the hope of a people for a better life has died.

We must keep that hope alive.

The free peoples of the world look to us for support in maintaining their freedoms.

If we falter in our leadership, we may endanger the peace of the world—and we shall surely endanger the welfare of this Nation.

Great responsibilities have been placed upon us by the swift movement of events.

I am confident that the Congress will face these responsibilities squarely.

20

"DO-NOTHING CONGRESS"

IT IS AN IRRESISTIBLE morality tale—the plucky underdog, never giving up; the favorite oozing with confidence and self-regard; the people rallying to the side of the little guy. Think Rocky, the tortoise and the hare, the 1969 Mets. For mythic appeal, none surpasses Harry Truman's 1948 victory over Thomas E. Dewey.

When Eleanor Roosevelt told Truman of Franklin Roosevelt's death in 1945, Truman asked if he could do anything for her. "No, Harry," she replied, "is there anything I can do for *you*? For you are the one in trouble now." Truman's first years were nothing but trouble. Voters were weary of war and emergency. Next to Roosevelt, he seemed puny: "To err is Truman," was the gibe. With the slogan "Had Enough?" Republicans won control of both houses of Congress in 1946, and blocked efforts to extend the New Deal (while backing hard-line foreign policy). It seemed certain that Truman would be a less-than-one-term president.

Certainly, Dewey, the Republican nominee, was serenely confident of victory. He stuck to platitudes, declaring, "The future lies ahead" (a line Truman mocked mercilessly). A *Newsweek* survey of political writers found all fifty expecting a Dewey sweep. The Elmo Roper organization stopped polling because the outcome seemed so assured.

In fact, Truman was quietly forging the elements of an upset. He believed the key to victory was to reassemble the Roosevelt coalition and to constantly remind voters what they had gained from the New Deal. Still, Democrats split three ways at their convention. Former Vice President Henry Wallace formed a new leftist party, attacking Truman's foreign policy as too war-like. When convention delegates strongly endorsed civil rights for African-Americans, Southerners bolted and backed then-Democratic Governor

Strom Thurmond of South Carolina. When time came for his acceptance, Truman was delayed backstage, and did not speak until two A.M. He shook dispirited delegates awake with a feisty, combative oration. "[Running mate Alben] Barkley and I will win this election and make these Republicans like it—don't you forget that! We will do that because they are wrong and we are right, and I will prove it to you in just a few minutes." After years of Roosevelt's thespian sparkle, Truman jabbed at the lectern and spoke without a text (using just an outline). "Never in the world were the farmers of any republic or any kingdom or any other country as prosperous as the farmers of the United States; and if they don't do their duty by the Democratic Party, they are the most ungrateful people in the world!" The Republican platform, seeking to emulate the New Deal, had promised progressive measures. With relish, Truman announced he would

Senator Alben Barkley bids Truman good luck as Truman leaves Washington's Union Station on his trans-continental campaign trip

Truman, on his victorious return trip to Washington, D.C., laughs over an early edition of the Chicago Tribune *that jumped to an erroneous conclusion based on early election returns, November 4, 1948*

call Congress back into session on "Turnip Day," daring them to pass the very proposals set out in the GOP platform. Congress assembled and passed nothing, seeming to prove Truman's "do nothing" charge.

With two months to go before the election, Truman embarked on a nearly nonstop tour of the country by rail. Robert Taft, leader of the Senate Republicans, had complained Truman was "blackguarding Congress at whistle-stops all across the country." Democrats seized on the sneer. In the "whistle-stop" campaign, Truman crossed twenty-two thousand miles to give three hundred speeches in cities, towns, and villages. As he prepared to leave for the first leg of the trip, he declared to his running mate, "I'll mow 'em down, Alben, and I'll give 'em hell." Soon audience members were calling out, "Give 'em hell, Harry!" (Later he said, "I never gave anybody hell. I just told the truth, and they thought it was hell.")

The speech that follows, from the rear platform of a train in downtown Chariton, Iowa, at 5:36 in the afternoon, is a sample—one of dozens, some to tiny crowds in dusty rail junctions, others to throngs in big cities. They

are a rare bit of Americana. Truman was corny and cantankerous. Journalist Robert J. Donovan covered them, describing them as: "sharp speeches fairly criticizing Republican policy and defending New Deal liberalism, mixed with sophistries, bunkum piled higher than haystacks, and demagoguery tooting merrily down the track." In these speeches, Truman seldom attacked Dewey, but he never let up on the Congress and the "special interests." The eightieth Congress, he said repeatedly, had "stuck a pitchfork in the farmer's back." He was aided by a plunge in farm prices, and by effective organizing by labor unions in the Northern cities. The black vote, too, stuck with Truman (he made the first ever presidential campaign appearance in Harlem). Ironically, the defection of Wallace's leftists and Thurmond's racists freed Truman to campaign in the political center.

The story of election night has been told often. The head of the Secret Service stationed himself with Governor Dewey in New York; the mayor of Truman's home town had not thought to plan a victory celebration. Truman slipped away to a secluded hotel and went to sleep. He woke to hear famed radio commentator H.V. Kaltenborn announce that while the president was well ahead in the popular vote, he was surely beaten anyway. Truman went back to sleep, confident of victory. In the morning it was clear: not only had rural voters carried him to victory, but Democrats regained both houses of Congress.

Upon his return to Washington, two hundred thousand supporters greeted Truman. The photo of the victor holding aloft the *Chicago Tribune* front page with the premature headline "DEWEY DEFEATS TRUMAN" still brings a smile a half-century later.

PRESIDENT JIMMY CARTER ON HARRY S. TRUMAN

Among those who have served during my lifetime, Harry Truman is the president whom I've admired most. He was honest, modest, plainspoken, courageous, and bold in the face of crisis.

I was in the U.S. Navy when Franklin Roosevelt died and Truman became my commander-in-chief. I wept with disappointment over FDR's death, and a lack of confidence in Truman. My opinions changed quickly, as I learned to respect his judgment as my new leader. He first affected my personal life with his order to end racial discrimination within the military services—an unprecedented and unheralded decision.

Although I never met a Democratic president until Bill Clinton was inaugurated, I saw Harry Truman when he laid the keel of the first nuclear submarine in New London, Connecticut. (I was assigned to the second nuclear sub.)

Later, when I sought the presidency myself, I was heavily influenced by his human rights policies. The most notable was his benevolent decision to restore basic rights to our defeated enemies in Japan, Germany, and Italy, and to ensure that they would have democratic governments. This philosophy was well described in a speech he made on Independence Day—July 4, 1947—at the home of Thomas Jefferson.

Excerpt from Truman's July 4th speech:

The first requisite of peace among nations is common adherence to the principle that governments derive their just powers from the consent of the governed. There must be genuine effort to translate that principle into reality.…

A second requisite of peace among nations is common respect for basic human rights. Jefferson knew the relationship between respect for these rights and peaceful democracy. We see today with equal clarity the relationship between respect for these human rights and the maintenance of world peace. So long as the basic rights of men are denied in any substantial portion of the Earth, men everywhere must live in fear of their own rights and their own security.

We have learned much in the last fifteen years from Germany, Italy, and Japan about the intimate relationship of dictatorship, aggression, and the loss of human rights.…

No country has yet reached the absolute in protecting human rights. In all countries, certainly including our own, there is much to be accomplished. The maintenance of peace will depend to an important degree upon the progress that is made within nations and by the United Nations in protecting human rights.

Whistle Stop Speeches
1948 Campaign
Harry S. Truman

September 6, 1948

Grand Rapids, Michigan	9:10 a.m.
Lansing	11:05
Detroit	1:40 p.m.
Hamtramck	2:45
Pontiac	4:00
Flint	7:15
Toledo, Ohio	11:55

September 17

Pittsburg, Pennsylvania	6:25 p.m.
Crestline, Ohio	10:30

September 18

Rock Island, Illinois	5:45 a.m.
Davenport, Iowa	6:10
Iowa City	7:25
Oxford	8:50
Grinnell	8:55
Des Moines	10:20
Dexter	12:15 p.m. and 12:30
Des Moines	4:10
Melcher	5:08
Chariton	5:36
Trenton, Missouri	7:10
Polo	8:10

September 19

Junction City, Kansas	11:05

September 20

Denver, Colorado	11:17 a.m., 12 noon and 1:55 p.m.
Colorado Springs	4:26
Pueblo	6:07
Canon City	7:32
Salida	9:47

On the one hand, the Republicans are telling industrial workers

that the high cost of food in the cities is due to this

Government's farm price policy.   On the other hand,

the Republicans are telling farmers that the high cost of

manufactured goods on the farm is due to this Government's

labor policy.

That's plain hokum.   It's an old political trick.

"If you can't convince them, confuse them."

But this time it won 't work.

The farmer and the worker know that their troubles

have been coming from another source.

In 1932 under the Republicans we 12 to 15 million unemployed with average wages 45 cent — and we [illegible] 15 cent corn & [illegible]

539.

A page of Truman's speech, with his handwritten notes, given at Dexter, Iowa, one of the stops on the day he spoke in Chariton

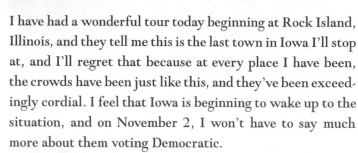

WHISTLE-STOP SPEECH

Chariton, Iowa • September 18, 1948

I have had a wonderful tour today beginning at Rock Island, Illinois, and they tell me this is the last town in Iowa I'll stop at, and I'll regret that because at every place I have been, the crowds have been just like this, and they've been exceedingly cordial. I feel that Iowa is beginning to wake up to the situation, and on November 2, I won't have to say much more about them voting Democratic.

You know, the reason for that is that the Democratic Party gave the farmers the price support program, soil conservation, rural electrification, crop insurance, and other progressive measures of this kind. They have led to the greatest prosperity for the farmer that the farmer has ever had in the history of the world.

In 1932, 123,000 farmers in the United States had lost their farms. In 1947, less than eight hundred farms were foreclosed. That's the greatest record in history.

In 1932, the farmers were hopelessly in debt. Their indebtedness has been reduced by more than 50 percent and they have $18 billion in assets. Think of that! Just think of that!

Now, there are people in the United States that would like to go back to that condition, when labor was receiving an average of forty-five cents an hour, and when the farmer was getting three cents for hogs and fifteen cents for corn and burning the corn because it wasn't worth the price. Those same people now have made an attempt to do away with the price-support program which is responsible for this immense production which we have had in the last seven years and which has kept millions of people in this world alive.

I'm asking you just to read history, to use your own judgment, and to decide whether you want to go forward with the Democratic Party or whether you want to turn the clock back to the horse-and-buggy days with such people that made up that "do-nothing" eightieth Congress.

That Congress tried its level best to take all the rights away from labor. That Congress tried its level best to put the farmer back to 1932. That Congress tried its level best to put small business out of business. For what purpose? To help the big interests which they represented.

Do you know that there were more and bigger lobbies in Washington than at any time in the history of the Congress of the United States? Sometime a little later on I'm going to tell you about those terrible lobbies: the Association of Manufacturers' and the speculators' lobbies and several others that I could name right now; and I've got the facts and figures on them. They spent more money lobbying for special privilege in this "do-nothing" eightieth Congress than has been spent in Washington in the whole history of the country.

Now, why did they do that? Because they wanted to take you to town. I'll tell you—you're going to get taken to town if you don't use your privilege on election day.

> *"I'm asking you…to decide whether you want to go forward with the Democratic Party or whether you want to turn the clock back to the horse-and-buggy days with such people that made up that 'do-nothing' eightieth Congress."*

The above text is a transcript of the speech as it was given in Chariton, Iowa.

You stayed at home in 1946 and you got the eightieth Congress, and you got just exactly what you deserved. You didn't exercise your God-given right to control this country. Now you're going to have another chance. If you let that chance slip, you won't have my sympathy.

If you don't let that chance slip, you'll do me a very great favor, for I'll live in the White House another four years.

"You stayed at home in 1946 and you got the eightieth Congress, and you got just exactly what you deserved."

It's been a very great pleasure to be in Iowa, and I appreciate it. I have had the privilege of riding with all your public officials today. It's been a very great pleasure to ride with your candidate for governor, who is a wonderful man, the Democratic candidate for governor. And I was with Guy Gillette, with whom I served in the Senate, and there never was a better senator in the Senate than Guy Gillette. I'm extremely fond of him, and I hope, for your own welfare and for the welfare of this great state, that you'll send Guy Gillette back to the Senate, and that you'll elect the Democratic candidate for governor and all the Democratic congressmen and public officials you possibly can. I like Democrats no matter what office they're running for.

I hope that everything will go well with you. I can't tell you how I appreciate this wonderful turnout, this wonderful reception. It's been just like this all day long. I have come to the conclusion that the people in Iowa like their president and appreciate what he's trying to do for the common people.

Dwight D. EISENHOWER

34TH PRESIDENT: 1953–1961

Born: October 14, 1890, in Denison, Texas

Died: March 28, 1969, in Washington, D.C.

Disc 1, Tracks 24–25

21

"ATOMS FOR PEACE"

GENERAL DWIGHT DAVID EISENHOWER had led the Allied armies to victory in western Europe during World War II, and had won the presidency with his broad grin amid chants of "We Like Ike." Comedians mocked his mangled syntax, and he sometimes seemed a placid golfing retiree. But appearances deceived. Ike garbled his words when he didn't want to be pinned down. He himself had served as chief speechwriter for one of the century's most colorful orators, General Douglas MacArthur. (Ike once asked one of his speechwriters, "Who do you think wrote all those speeches?" MacArthur, in turn, dismissed Eisenhower as "the best clerk I ever had.")

In a major speech before the United Nations early in his presidency, Eisenhower tried to forestall the nuclear arms race. Shortly before he took office, the U.S. exploded the first hydrogen bomb, almost a thousand times more powerful than the weapon used at Hiroshima. Eisenhower began to warn of the consequences two months into his term. To the American Society of Newspaper Editors (ASNE), he spoke of the danger and huge cost of an arms race. "This world in arms is not spending money alone," he said. "It is spending the sweat of its laborers, the genius of its scientists, the hopes of its children." Josef Stalin, the dictator of the Soviet Union, had just died. No one in the West knew what impact this would have on the course of Soviet conduct, but Eisenhower believed this was a chance to test a new Russian attitude.

In April 1953, he directed his special assistant in charge of nuclear weapons policy, C.D. Jackson, and a former *Time* magazine writer named Emmett Hughes, to write a major speech warning of the dangers to the U.S. from nuclear war. (Originally, the plan was to reveal the size of the U.S.

arsenal. This was known as "Operation Candor.") Eisenhower worked closely with them, but ultimately told the writers that their draft was too scary. (Apparently, it contained too much candor.) A second round of rewriting detailed the devastation nuclear war would bring the Soviet Union as well. Eisenhower rejected this draft, too, saying, "This leaves everybody dead on both sides, with no hope anywhere. Can't we find some hope here?" Through it all, the writers were opposed by Secretary of State John Foster Dulles, a hard-line anticommunist who did not want any steps that might lead toward disarmament. "Red lights blinking all over the place," Jackson worried to his diary after a meeting with Dulles.

The stakes were raised once more. In August, the Soviets exploded their own hydrogen bomb: a nuclear war between the two nations now could devastate life on Earth. Mulling the speech while on vacation, Eisenhower had the idea of inviting the nuclear powers to donate part of their stockpiles to common peaceful purposes. He summoned his aides to a breakfast meeting: now the project was called "Operation Wheaties." Officials continued to wrangle for months over what the policy should be and what the speech should say.

On December 3, Eisenhower decided, finally, to deliver "Atoms for Peace" at a United Nations General Assembly meeting. He flew the next day for a talk with British Prime Minister Winston Churchill and French Premier Joseph Laniel at Bermuda. Jackson worked on the seventh draft of "Wheaties" at a hotel. Eisenhower did not look at it again until the three-and-a-half-hour flight to New York. The drafting ended as the plane circled New York for thirty minutes, and then taxied slowly, as the starchy secretary of state joined frazzled presidential aides to print, collate and staple copies of the speech. Before delivering the speech, Eisenhower stopped at the UN's meditation room to pray.

At the UN, Eisenhower appealed to the world to ward off the coming arms race, which he warned could bankrupt all sides. He spoke with the authority of a warrior. "I feel impelled to speak today in a language that in a sense is new—one which I, who have spent so much of my life in the military profession, would have preferred never to use," he said. "That new language is the language of atomic warfare." He touched on the strange new calculus of nuclear deterrence: each side would threaten the other with destruction if attacked. "Surely no sane member of the human race could discover victory in such desolation," he said. (The speech has several prophetic touches. Eisenhower warned of the day when all nations will have access to nuclear weapons. Interestingly, in light of later debates over missile defense systems, he added, "No system of defense can guarantee absolute safety for the cities and the citizens of any nation.") Eisenhower proposed

that the U.S., its allies, and the Soviet Union pool some of their nuclear material to a new International Atomic Energy Agency, under the aegis of the UN, to work toward energy power, agriculture, and other peaceful uses. The speech dates itself by assuming that nuclear energy is non-controversial.

Eisenhower was greeted with strong applause by the diplomats, and enthusiastic praise by the press. The Soviet Union did not rise to the challenge, however. The East and West bickered over the plan for several years, and in the end, it produced no immediate treaty. No arms control pacts—or any other cooperative steps to reduce the tensions of the arms race—were negotiated during Eisenhower's term. Still, the speech set out the arguments used by proponents of disarmament for decades to come. Throughout his two terms, his soldierly ability to keep the U.S. from being stampeded into war was to prove useful, as when he refused to intervene in the Suez War in the Middle East or rescue the French as they lost their colonies in Vietnam.

PRESIDENT GERALD R. FORD ON DWIGHT D. EISENHOWER

I thought Eisenhower's forthright speeches on behalf of NATO were very impressive, and I agreed with his decisions and his approach. I recall vividly how he had to sell some of the hardline isolationists on the idea of working together with our European allies—that we shouldn't repeat the mistakes made at the end of World War I. We had to put together a coalition in defense of Western Europe and the United States. That ended up becoming the consensus view—and Ike's leadership was what did it.

Eisenhower was not very eloquent in the manner of a real arm-waving orator like Senator Everett Dirksen of Illinois. Dirksen could make a forty-five-minute speech, and everybody loved it. But you would ask, "What did he say?" and they couldn't remember. Ike was not that kind of an orator—he was persuasive because of his personality and his background. He wasn't a dramatic speaker, but his presence and his record spoke for themselves.

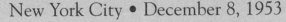

Dwight D. Eisenhower's
ADDRESS BEFORE THE
UN GENERAL ASSEMBLY

New York City • December 8, 1953

Madame President, Members of the General Assembly:

When Secretary General Hammarskjöld's invitation to address this General Assembly reached me in Bermuda, I was just beginning a series of conferences with the Prime Ministers and Foreign Ministers of Great Britain and of France. Our subject was some of the problems that beset our world.

During the remainder of the Bermuda Conference, I had constantly in mind that ahead of me lay a great honor. That honor is mine today as I stand here, privileged to address the General Assembly of the United Nations.

At the same time that I appreciate the distinction of addressing you, I have a sense of exhilaration as I look upon this Assembly.

Never before in history has so much hope for so many people been gathered together in a single organization. Your deliberations and decisions during these somber years have already realized part of those hopes.

"If a danger exists in the world, it is a danger shared by all."

But the great tests and the great accomplishments still lie ahead. And in the confident expectation of those accomplishments, I would use the office which, for the time being, I hold, to assure you that the Government of the United States will remain steadfast in its support of this body. This we shall do in the conviction that you will provide a great share of the wisdom, the courage, and the faith which can bring to this world lasting peace for all nations, and happiness and well-being for all men.

Clearly, it would not be fitting for me to take this occasion to present to you a unilateral American report on Bermuda. Nevertheless, I assure you that in our deliberations on that lovely island we sought to invoke those same great concepts of universal peace and human dignity which are so clearly etched in your Charter.

Neither would it be a measure of this great opportunity merely to recite, however hopefully, pious platitudes.

I therefore decided that this occasion warranted my saying to you some of the things that have been on the minds and hearts of my legislative and executive associates and on mine for a great many months—thoughts I had originally planned to say primarily to the American people.

I know that the American people share my deep belief that if a danger exists in the world, it is a danger shared by all—and equally, that if hope exists in the mind of one nation, that hope should be shared by all.

Finally, if there is to be advanced any proposal designed to ease even by the smallest measure the tensions of today's world, what more appropriate audience could there be than the members of the General Assembly of the United Nations?

I feel impelled to speak today in a language that in a sense is new—one which I, who have spent so much of my life in the military profession, would have preferred never to use.

That new language is the language of atomic warfare.

The atomic age has moved forward at such a pace that every citizen of the world should have some comprehension, at least in comparative terms, of the extent of this development of the utmost significance to every one of us. Clearly, if the peoples of the world are to conduct an intelligent search for peace, they must be armed with the significant facts of today's existence.

My recital of atomic danger and power is necessarily stated in United States terms, for these are the only incontrovertible facts that I know. I need hardly point out to this

Assembly, however, that this subject is global, not merely national in character.

On July 16, 1945, the United States set off the world's first atomic explosion. Since that date in 1945, the United States of America has conducted 42 test explosions.

"I feel impelled to speak today in a language that in a sense is new—the language of atomic warfare."

Atomic bombs today are more than twenty-five times as powerful as the weapons with which the atomic age dawned, while hydrogen weapons are in the ranges of millions of tons of TNT equivalent.

Today, the United States' stockpile of atomic weapons, which, of course, increases daily, exceeds by many times the explosive equivalent of the total of all bombs and all shells that came from every plane and every gun in every theatre of war in all of the years of World War II.

A single air group, whether afloat or land-based, can now deliver to any reachable target a destructive cargo exceeding in power all the bombs that fell on Britain in all of World War II.

In size and variety, the development of atomic weapons has been no less remarkable. The development has been such that atomic weapons have virtually achieved conventional status within our armed services. In the United States, the Army, the Navy, the Air Force, and the Marine Corps are all capable of putting this weapon to military use.

But the dread secret, and the fearful engines of atomic might, are not ours alone.

In the first place, the secret is possessed by our friends and allies, Great Britain and Canada, whose scientific genius made a tremendous contribution to our original discoveries, and the designs of atomic bombs.

The secret is also known by the Soviet Union.

The Soviet Union has informed us that, over recent years, it has devoted extensive resources to atomic weapons. During this period, the Soviet Union has exploded a series of atomic devices, including at least one involving thermonuclear reactions.

If at one time the United States possessed what might have been called a monopoly of atomic power, that monopoly ceased to exist several years ago. Therefore, although our earlier start has permitted us to accumulate what is today a great quantitative advantage, the atomic realities of today comprehend two facts of even greater significance.

First, the knowledge now possessed by several nations will eventually be shared by others—possibly all others.

Second, even a vast superiority in numbers of weapons, and a consequent capability of devastating retaliation, is no preventive, of itself, against the fearful material damage and toll of human lives that would be inflicted by surprise aggression.

The free world, at least dimly aware of these facts, has naturally embarked on a large program of warning and defense systems. That program will be accelerated and expanded.

"A single air group can now deliver to any reachable target a destructive cargo exceeding in power all the bombs that fell on Britain in all of World War II."

But let no one think that the expenditure of vast sums for weapons and systems of defense can guarantee absolute safety for the cities and citizens of any nation. The awful arithmetic of the atomic bomb does not permit of any such easy solution. Even against the most powerful defense, an aggressor in possession of the effective minimum number of atomic bombs for a surprise attack could probably place a

On December 8, 1953, President Eisenhower makes his address to the United Nations

sufficient number of his bombs on the chosen targets to cause hideous damage.

Should such an atomic attack be launched against the United States, our reactions would be swift and resolute. But for me to say that the defense capabilities of the United States are such that they could inflict terrible losses upon an aggressor—for me to say that the retaliation capabilities of the United States are so great that such an aggressor's land would be laid waste—all this, while fact, is not the true expression of the purpose and the hope of the United States.

To pause there would be to confirm the hopeless finality of a belief that two atomic colossi are doomed malevolently to eye each other indefinitely across a trembling world. To stop there would be to accept helplessly the probability of civilization destroyed—the annihilation of the irreplaceable heritage of mankind handed down to us generation from generation—and the condemnation of mankind to begin all over again the age-old struggle upward from savagery toward decency, and right, and justice.

Surely no sane member of the human race could discover victory in such desolation. Could anyone wish his name to be coupled by history with such human degradation and destruction.

Occasional pages of history do record the faces of the "Great Destroyers" but the whole book of history reveals mankind's never-ending quest for peace, and mankind's God-given capacity to build.

It is with the book of history, and not with isolated pages, that the United States will ever wish to be identified.

149

My country wants to be constructive, not destructive. It wants agreements, not wars, among nations. It wants itself to live in freedom, and in the confidence that the people of every other nation enjoy equally the right of choosing their own way of life.

"The dread secret, and the fearful engines of atomic might are not ours alone."

So my country's purpose is to help us move out of the dark chamber of horrors into the light, to find a way by which the minds of men, the hopes of men, the souls of men everywhere, can move forward toward peace and happiness and well-being.

In this quest, I know that we must not lack patience.

I know that in a world divided, such as ours today, salvation cannot be attained by one dramatic act.

I know that many steps will have to be taken over many months before the world can look at itself one day and truly realize that a new climate of mutually peaceful confidence is abroad in the world.

But I know, above all else, that we must start to take these steps—*now*.

The United States and its allies, Great Britain and France, have over the past months tried to take some of these steps. Let no one say that we shun the conference table.

On the record has long stood the request of the United States, Great Britain, and France to negotiate with the Soviet Union the problems of a divided Germany.

On that record has long stood the request of the same three nations to negotiate an Austrian Peace Treaty.

On the same record still stands the request of the United Nations to negotiate the problems of Korea.

Most recently, we have received from the Soviet Union what is in effect an expression of willingness to hold a Four Power Meeting. Along with our allies, Great Britain and France, we were pleased to see that this note did not contain the unacceptable preconditions previously put forward.

As you already know from our joint Bermuda communique, the United States, Great Britain, and France have agreed promptly to meet with the Soviet Union.

The Government of the United States approaches this conference with hopeful sincerity. We will bend every effort of our minds to the single purpose of emerging from that conference with tangible results toward peace—the only true way of lessening international tension.

We never have, we never will, propose or suggest that the Soviet Union surrender what is rightfully theirs.

We will never say that the peoples of Russia are an enemy with whom we have no desire ever to deal or mingle in friendly and fruitful relationship.

On the contrary, we hope that this coming Conference may initiate a relationship with the Soviet Union which will eventually bring about a free intermingling of the peoples of the East and of the West—the one sure, human way of developing the understanding required for confident and peaceful relations.

"The knowledge now possessed by several nations will eventually be shared by others—possibly all others."

Instead of the discontent which is now setting upon Eastern Germany, occupied Austria, and the countries of Eastern Europe, we seek a harmonious family of free European nations, with none a threat to the other, and least of all a threat to the peoples of Russia.

Beyond the turmoil and strife and misery of Asia, we seek peaceful opportunity for these peoples to develop their natural resources and to elevate their lives.

These are not idle words or shallow visions. Behind them lies a story of nations lately come to independence, not as a result of war, but through free grant or peaceful negotiation. There is a record, already written, of assistance gladly given by nations of the West to needy peoples, and to those suffering the temporary effects of famine, drought, and natural disaster.

These are deeds of peace. They speak more loudly than promises or protestations of peaceful intent.

But I do not wish to rest either upon the reiteration of past proposals or the restatement of past deeds. The gravity of the time is such that every new avenue of peace, no matter how dimly discernible, should be explored.

There is at least one new avenue of peace which has not yet been well explored—an avenue now laid out by the General Assembly of the United Nations.

In its resolution of November 18, 1953, this General Assembly suggested—and I quote—"that the Disarmament Commission study the desirability of establishing a sub-committee consisting of representatives of the Powers principally involved, which should seek in private an acceptable solution...and report such a solution to the General Assembly and to the Security Council not later than I September 1954."

The United States, heeding the suggestion of the General Assembly of the United Nations, is instantly prepared to meet privately with such other countries as may be "principally involved," to seek "an acceptable solution" to the atomic armaments race which overshadows not only the peace, but the very life, of the world.

We shall carry into these private or diplomatic talks a new conception.

The United States would seek more than the mere reduction or elimination of atomic materials for military purposes.

It is not enough to take this weapon out of the hands of the soldiers. It must be put into the hands of those who will know how to strip its military casing and adapt it to the arts of peace.

The United States knows that if the fearful trend of atomic military buildup can be reversed, this greatest of destructive forces can be developed into a great boon, for the benefit of all mankind.

The United States knows that peaceful power from atomic energy is no dream of the future. That capability, already proved, is here—now—today. Who can doubt, if the entire body of the world's scientists and engineers had adequate amounts of fissionable material with which to test and develop their ideas, that this capability would rapidly be transformed into universal, efficient, and economic usage.

"The United States would seek more than the mere reduction or elimination of atomic materials for military purposes."

To hasten the day when fear of the atom will begin to disappear from the minds of people, and the governments of the East and West, there are certain steps that can be taken now.

I therefore make the following proposals:

The Governments principally involved, to the extent permitted by elementary prudence, to begin now and continue to make joint contributions from their stockpiles of normal uranium and fissionable materials to an International Atomic Energy Agency. We would expect that such an agency would be set up under the aegis of the United Nations.

The ratios of contributions, the procedures and other details would properly be within the scope of the "private conversations" I have referred to earlier.

The United States is prepared to undertake these explorations in good faith. Any partner of the United States acting in the same good faith will find the United States a not unreasonable or ungenerous associate.

Undoubtedly initial and early contributions to this plan would be small in quantity. However, the proposal has the great virtue that it can be undertaken without the irritations and mutual suspicions incident to any attempt to set up a completely acceptable system of world-wide inspection and control.

The Atomic Energy Agency could be made responsible for the impounding, storage, and protection of the contributed fissionable and other materials. The ingenuity of our scientists will provide special safe conditions under which such a bank of fissionable material can be made essentially immune to surprise seizure.

> *"The United States does not wish merely to present strength, but also the desire and the hope for peace."*

The more important responsibility of this Atomic Energy Agency would be to devise methods whereby this fissionable material would be allocated to serve the peaceful pursuits of mankind. Experts would be mobilized to apply atomic energy to the needs of agriculture, medicine, and other peaceful activities. A special purpose would be to provide abundant electrical energy in the power-starved areas of the world. Thus the contributing powers would be dedicating some of their strength to serve the needs rather than the fears of mankind.

The United States would be more than willing—it would be proud to take up with others "principally involved" the development of plans whereby such peaceful use of atomic energy would be expedited.

Of those "principally involved" the Soviet Union must, of course, be one.

I would be prepared to submit to the Congress of the United States, and with every expectation of approval, any such plan that would:

First—encourage world-wide investigation into the most effective peacetime uses of fissionable material, and with the certainty that they had all the material needed for the conduct of all experiments that were appropriate;

Second—begin to diminish the potential destructive power of the world's atomic stockpiles;

Third—allow all peoples of all nations to see that, in this enlightened age, the great powers of the earth, both of the East and of the West, are interested in human aspirations first, rather than in building up the armaments of war;

Fourth—open up a new channel for peaceful discussion, and initiate at least a new approach to the many difficult problems that must be solved in both private and public conversations, if the world is to shake off the inertia imposed by fear, and is to make positive progress toward peace.

Against the dark background of the atomic bomb, the United States does not wish merely to present strength, but also the desire and the hope for peace.

The coming months will be fraught with fateful decisions. In this Assembly; in the capitals and military headquarters of the world; in the hearts of men everywhere, be they governors or governed, may they be the decisions which will lead this world out of fear and into peace.

To the making of these fateful decisions, the United States pledges before you—and therefore before the world—its determination to help solve the fearful atomic dilemma—to devote its entire heart and mind to find the way by which the miraculous inventiveness of man shall not be dedicated to his death, but consecrated to his life.

I again thank the delegates for the great honor they have done me, in inviting me to appear before them, and in listening to me so courteously. Thank you.

22

"THE MILITARY-INDUSTRIAL COMPLEX"

DWIGHT EISENHOWER, like George Washington, ended a long public career with a farewell address. Eisenhower, too, left his countrymen a warning—but with a twist. A president who spent nearly his entire career in the military and was backed by industrialists warned against the political power of both forces.

Eisenhower and his contemporaries were well aware of the parallel to the first president. Both were old and revered, entitled to speak as patriarchs. Both had said good-bye before, when leaving the military: Eisenhower, like Washington, issued a two-paragraph message "To the American Soldier" when he resigned his command in 1948. But the world situation was markedly different. Washington's farewell as president took note of "our detached and distant situation," but Eisenhower spoke in the middle of the Cold War.

Magazine editor Norman Cousins first urged Eisenhower to give a farewell talk. Eisenhower worked closely with Malcolm Moos, a political scientist and speechwriter on his staff, to draft it. The president's tone was fatherly, and his theme was "balance" (which matched his moderate political philosophy), especially "balance between cost and hoped for advantage." In that context, he issued his famous warning. The nation had needed arms manufacturing before, he said, but civilian producers had been able to convert to military need in times of crisis. Since World War II, however, for the first time, a distinct and large defense industry had grown up, employing hundreds of thousands and dominating the economies of many communities. This was necessary, Eisenhower said, but could easily become too powerful, taking on a political life of its own and distorting national priorities. "In the councils of government," he warned, "we must guard against the acquisition of unwarranted influence, whether sought or unsought, by the military-industrial complex. The potential for the disastrous rise of misplaced power exists and will persist." At first, Eisenhower wanted to decry a "military-industrial-congressional" complex, but backed off, feeling it inappropriate to lecture Congress.

Then Eisenhower issued a less-remembered caveat: the dangers to universities from reliance on government funds. "Partly because of the huge costs involved, a government contract becomes virtually a substitute for intellectual curiosity," he said.

There was a political subtext to Eisenhower's warning about the military-industrial complex. John F. Kennedy would succeed Eisenhower three days later. The Massachusetts Democrat had decried the "missile gap," our supposed lag behind the Soviets. Eisenhower knew that gap was fiction. He was worried that Kennedy would be too enamored of the military, unable to stand up to it, and too prone to hot rhetoric. Eisenhower's warning had little impact on the new administration. But it echoed in quarters he likely did not expect. A year later, the Port Huron Statement founding the Students for a Democratic Society quoted Eisenhower's speech as a rallying cry for the New Left.

Dwight D. Eisenhower's
FAREWELL ADDRESS

hear....
disc 1
track 25

Washington, D.C. • January 17, 1961

My fellow Americans:

Three days from now, after half a century of service of our country, I shall lay down the responsibilities of office as, in traditional and solemn ceremony, the authority of the Presidency is vested in my successor.

This evening I come to you with a message of leave-taking and farewell, and to share a few final thoughts with you, my countrymen.

Like every other citizen, I wish the new President, and all who will labor with him, Godspeed. I pray that the coming years will be blessed with peace and prosperity for all.

I.

Our people expect their President and the Congress to find essential agreement on issues of great moment, the wise resolution of which will better shape the future of the Nation.

My own relations with the Congress, which began on a remote and tenuous basis when, long ago, a member of the Senate appointed me to West Point, have since ranged to the intimate during the war and immediate post-war period, and, finally, to the mutually interdependent during these past eight years.

In this final relationship, the Congress and the Administration have, on most vital issues, cooperated well, to serve the national good rather than mere partisanship, and so have assured that the business of the Nation should go forward. So, my official relationship with the Congress ends in a feeling, on my part, of gratitude that we have been able to do so much together.

II.

We now stand ten years past the midpoint of a century that has witnessed four major wars among great nations. Three of these involved our own country. Despite these holocausts America is today the strongest, the most influential and most productive nation in the world. Understandably proud of this pre-eminence, we yet realize that America's leadership and prestige depend, not merely upon our unmatched material progress, riches and military strength, but on how we use our power in the interests of world peace and human betterment.

III.

Throughout America's adventure in free government, our basic purposes have been to keep the peace; to foster progress in human achievement, and to enhance liberty, dignity and integrity among people and among nations. To strive for less would be unworthy of a free and religious people. Any failure traceable to arrogance, or our lack of comprehension or readiness to sacrifice would inflict upon us grievous hurt both at home and abroad.

> *"We face a hostile ideology—global in scope, atheistic in character, ruthless in purpose, and insidious in method."*

Progress toward these noble goals is persistently threatened by the conflict now engulfing the world. It commands our whole attention, absorbs our very beings. We face a hostile ideology—global in scope, atheistic in character, ruthless in purpose, and insidious in method. Unhappily the danger it poses promises to be of indefinite duration. To meet it successfully, there is called for, not so much the emotional and transitory sacrifices of crisis, but rather

154

Eisenhower makes his nationally televised farewell speech, January 17, 1961

those which enable us to carry forward steadily, surely, and without complaint the burdens of a prolonged and complex struggle—with liberty the stake. Only thus shall we remain, despite every provocation, on our charted course toward permanent peace and human betterment.

Crises there will continue to be. In meeting them, whether foreign or domestic, great or small, there is a recurring temptation to feel that some spectacular and costly action could become the miraculous solution to all current difficulties. A huge increase in newer elements of our defense; development of unrealistic programs to cure every ill in agriculture; a dramatic expansion in basic and applied research—these and many other possibilities, each possibly promising in itself, may be suggested as the only way to the road we wish to travel.

But each proposal must be weighed in the light of a broader consideration: the need to maintain balance in and among national programs—balance between the private and the public economy, balance between cost and hoped for advantage—balance between the clearly necessary and the comfortably desirable; balance between our essential requirements as a nation and the duties imposed by the nation upon the individual; balance between the actions of the moment and the national welfare of the future. Good judgment seeks balance and progress; lack of it eventually finds imbalance and frustration.

The record of many decades stands as proof that our people and their government have, in the main, understood these truths and have responded to them well, in the face of stress and threat. But threats, new in kind or degree, constantly arise. I mention two only.

IV.

A vital element in keeping the peace is our military establishment. Our arms must be mighty, ready for instant action, so that no potential aggressor may be tempted to risk his own destruction.

Our military organization today bears little relation to that known by any of my predecessors in peacetime, or indeed by the fighting men of World War II or Korea.

Until the latest of our world conflicts, the United States had no armaments industry. American makers of plowshares could, with time and as required, make swords as well. But now we can no longer risk emergency improvisation of national defense; we have been compelled to create a permanent armaments industry of vast proportions. Added to this, three and a half million men and women are directly engaged in the defense establishment. We annually spend on military security more than the net income of all United States corporations.

This conjunction of an immense military establishment and a large arms industry is new in the American experience. The total influence—economic, political, even spiritual—is felt in every city, every State house, every office of the Federal government. We recognize the imperative need for this development. Yet we must not fail to comprehend its grave implications. Our toil, resources and livelihood are all involved; so is the very structure of our society.

In the councils of government, we must guard against the acquisition of unwarranted influence, whether sought or unsought, by the military-industrial complex. The potential for the disastrous rise of misplaced power exists and will persist.

> *"We must guard against the acquisition of unwarranted influence, whether sought or unsought, by the military-industrial complex."*

We must never let the weight of this combination endanger our liberties or democratic processes. We should take nothing for granted. Only an alert and knowledgeable citizenry can compel the proper meshing of the huge industrial and military machinery of defense with our peaceful methods and goals, so that security and liberty may prosper together.

Akin to, and largely responsible for the sweeping changes in our industrial-military posture, has been the technological revolution during recent decades.

In this revolution, research has become central; it also becomes more formalized, complex, and costly. A steadily increasing share is conducted for, by, or at the direction of, the Federal government.

Today, the solitary inventor, tinkering in his shop, has been overshadowed by task forces of scientists in laboratories and testing fields. In the same fashion, the free university, historically the fountainhead of free ideas and scientific discovery, has experienced a revolution in the conduct of research. Partly because of the huge costs involved, a government contract becomes virtually a substitute for intellectual curiosity. For every old blackboard there are now hundreds of new electronic computers.

The prospect of domination of the nation's scholars by Federal employment, project allocations, and the power of money is ever present—and is gravely to be regarded.

Yet, in holding scientific research and discovery in respect, as we should, we must also be alert to the equal and opposite danger that public policy could itself become the captive of a scientific-technological elite.

It is the task of statesmanship to mold, to balance, and to integrate these and other forces, new and old, within the principles of our democratic system—ever aiming toward the supreme goals of our free society.

V.

Another factor in maintaining balance involves the element of time. As we peer into society's future, we—you and I, and our government—must avoid the impulse to live only for today, plundering, for our own ease and convenience, the precious resources of tomorrow. We cannot mortgage the material assets of our grandchildren without risking the loss also of their political and spiritual heritage. We want democracy to survive for all generations to come, not to become the insolvent phantom of tomorrow.

VI.

Down the long lane of the history yet to be written America knows that this world of ours, ever growing smaller, must avoid becoming a community of dreadful fear and hate, and be, instead, a proud confederation of mutual trust and respect.

Such a confederation must be one of equals. The weakest must come to the conference table with the same confidence as do we, protected as we are by our moral, economic, and military strength. That table, though scarred by many past frustrations, cannot be abandoned for the certain agony of the battlefield.

Disarmament, with mutual honor and confidence, is a continuing imperative. Together we must learn how to compose differences, not with arms, but with intellect and decent purpose. Because this need is so sharp and apparent I confess that I lay down my official responsibilities in this field with a definite sense of disappointment. As one who has witnessed the horror and the lingering sadness of war—as one who knows that another war could utterly destroy this civilization which has been so slowly and painfully built over thousands of years—I wish I could say tonight that a lasting peace is in sight.

Happily, I can say that war has been avoided. Steady progress toward our ultimate goal has been made. But, so much remains to be done. As a private citizen, I shall never cease to do what little I can to help the world advance along that road.

VII.

So—in this my last good night to you as your President—I thank you for the many opportunities you have given me for public service in war and peace. I trust that in that service you find some things worthy; as for the rest of it, I know you will find ways to improve performance in the future.

You and I—my fellow citizens—need to be strong in our faith that all nations, under God, will reach the goal of peace with justice. May we be ever unswerving in devotion to principle, confident but humble with power, diligent in pursuit of the Nation's great goals.

"We pray that all peoples will come to live together in a peace guaranteed by the binding forces of mutual respect and love."

To all the peoples of the world, I once more give expression to America's prayerful and continuing aspiration:

We pray that peoples of all faiths, all races, all nations, may have their great human needs satisfied; that those now denied opportunity shall come to enjoy it to the full; that all who yearn for freedom may experience its spiritual blessings; that those who have freedom will understand, also, its heavy responsibilities; that all who are insensitive to the needs of others will learn charity; that the scourges of poverty, disease and ignorance will be made to disappear from the earth, and that, in the goodness of time, all peoples will come to live together in a peace guaranteed by the binding force of mutual respect and love.

John F. KENNEDY

35TH PRESIDENT: 1961–1963

Born: May 29, 1917, in Brookline, Massachusetts

Died: November 22, 1963, assassinated in Dallas, Texas

Disc 1, Track 26
Disc 2, Tracks 1–3

23

"ASK NOT WHAT YOUR COUNTRY CAN DO FOR YOU"

WHEN JOHN F. KENNEDY took the oath of office on a frigid day in January, the country's youngest elected leader, at forty-three, replaced its then-oldest president. Eisenhower had made his mordant farewell just three days before. Kennedy won his narrow election victory demanding, "Let's get this country moving again." Now he stood hatless in the cold (hurting the men's hat industry with his fashion effrontery), ready to address the nation.

Most presidential inaugural addresses are mediocre. Those that are better are remembered mostly because they summon dramatic times: Lincoln struggling to hold together the Union, Roosevelt addressing a nation in panic. Kennedy's inaugural address, nearly alone, stands out as a bracing, eloquent call to defend freedom. It is the only great inaugural remembered on its own merits, detached from some signal event.

Kennedy's address was largely drafted by Ted Sorensen, his intellectual alter ego. Sorensen remembered wryly that the impatient president-elect "asked me to study the secret of Lincoln's Gettysburg Address." ("My conclusion, which [the] inaugural applied, was that Lincoln never used a two- or three-syllable word where a one-syllable word would do, and never used two or three words where one word would do.") Friends and advisors, including journalist Walter Lippmann, Adlai Stevenson, and John Kenneth Galbraith added ideas. Sorensen was far more than a wordsmith. As Kennedy's legislative aide and policy advisor, he drafted the proposals Kennedy would advance, and had helped Kennedy with his book *Profiles in Courage*, which won the Pulitzer Prize.

They began to write the speech just a week before inauguration day. After days of work by the pool at his father's home in Palm Springs, Kennedy flew north. "The opening paragraphs were redictated by the president-elect to [his secretary] Evelyn Lincoln en route," Sorensen remembered in his book, *Kennedy*, "and he smilingly placed in the plane's desk drawer his handwritten notes from which he had dictated, saying, 'An early draft of Roosevelt's Inaugural was discovered the other day—and brought $200,000 at an auction.'"

Kennedy's speech is striking both for its bellicose urgency and its classical rhetoric. What humorist Calvin Trillin has dubbed Kennedy's "reversible raincoat sentences," known to the ancient Greeks as parallelisms, are studded throughout. Most famous, of course, is the "ask not" peroration, which summoned a generation to service and sacrifice. The president's advisor, historian Arthur M. Schlesinger Jr., noted Kennedy had toyed with such language for years. Departing from his script the previous autumn, Kennedy told a Detroit campaign rally, "The New Frontier is not what I promise I am going to do for you. The new frontier is what I ask you to do for your country." The formal, even archaic, structure of "ask not" is memorable and perilous to copy. Many presidents since have sought to mimic Kennedy's cadences, with mixed success. Richard Nixon declared, "In our own lives, let each of us ask—not just what will government do for me, but what can I do for myself?" Bill Clinton proclaimed, "There is nothing wrong with America that cannot be cured by what is right with America."

With the words, "a long twilight struggle," the speech lives as a stirring call to contest the Cold War. Kennedy mentioned no domestic issues. (The closest was a reference, added late, to human rights "at home.") He sought to reverse the mood of defeatism and worry bred by the Soviet Union's launch of the *Sputnik* satellite, by the victory of Fidel Castro in Cuba, and by the humiliation of the shooting down of a U-2 spy plane the previous year. His language has been challenged as over-promising. If there was no crisis when Kennedy spoke, soon there were many—impelled, perhaps, by his urgent words. How would we remember this speech had Kennedy not been murdered?

The peroration—"all this will not be accomplished in the first one thousand days"—sends chills: he would live only that long. There is no pedestrian second Kennedy inaugural to compare with the first. It is a sobering thought to consider that among the millions of Americans who heard his summons to "pay any price, bear any burden" were fifty-seven thousand young men who would die over the next fourteen years in Vietnam.

HOW KENNEDY'S INAUGURAL WAS DRAFTED

First Draft	Next-to-Last Draft	Final Text
We celebrate today not a victory of party but the sacrament of democracy.	We celebrate today not a victory of party but a convention of freedom.	We observe today not a victory of party but a celebration of freedom.
Each of us, whether we hold office or not, shares the responsibility for guiding this most difficult of all societies along the path of self-discipline and self-government.	In your hands, my fellow citizens, more than in mine, will be determined the success or failure of our course.	In your hands, my fellow citizens, more than in mine, will rest the final success or failure of our course.
Nor can two great and powerful nations forever continue on this reckless course, both overburdened by the staggering cost of modern weapons…	…neither can two great and powerful nations long endure their present reckless course, both overburdened by the staggering cost of modern weapons…	…neither can two great and powerful groups of nations take comfort from our present course—both sides over-burdened by the cost of modern weapons…
And if the fruits of cooperation prove sweeter than the dregs of suspicion, let both sides join ultimately in creating a true world order—neither a Pax Americana, nor a Pax Russiana, nor even a balance of power—but a community of power.	And if a beachhead of cooperation can be made in the jungles of suspicion, let both sides join some day in creating, not a new balance of power but a new world of law…	And if a beachhead of cooperation can push back the jungle of suspicion, let both sides join in creating a new endeavor, not a new balance of power, but a new world of law…

Used by permission of Theodore Sorensen, from his book, Kennedy

*hear...
disc 1
track 26

Vice President Johnson, Mr. Speaker, Mr. Chief Justice, President Eisenhower, Vice President Nixon, President Truman, Reverend Clergy, fellow citizens:

We observe today not a victory of party but a celebration of freedom—symbolizing an end as well as a beginning—signifying renewal as well as change. For I have sworn before you and Almighty God the same solemn oath our forebears prescribed nearly a century and three quarters ago.

> ## "We observe today not a victory of party but a celebration of freedom."

The world is very different now. For man holds in his mortal hands the power to abolish all forms of human poverty and all forms of human life. And yet the same revolutionary beliefs for which our forebears fought are still at issue around the globe—the belief that the rights of man come not from the generosity of the state but from the hand of God.

We dare not forget today that we are the heirs of that first revolution. Let the word go forth from this time and place, to friend and foe alike, that the torch has been passed to a new generation of Americans—born in this century, tempered by war, disciplined by a hard and bitter peace, proud of our ancient heritage—and unwilling to witness or permit the slow undoing of those human rights to which this nation has always been committed, and to which we are committed today at home and around the world.

Let every nation know, whether it wishes us well or ill, that we shall pay any price, bear any burden, meet any hardship, support any friend, oppose any foe to assure the survival and the success of liberty.

This much we pledge—and more.

To those old allies whose cultural and spiritual origins we share, we pledge the loyalty of faithful friends. United, there is little we cannot do in a host of cooperative ventures. Divided, there is little we can do—for we dare not meet a powerful challenge at odds and split asunder.

To those new states whom we welcome to the ranks of the free, we pledge our word that one form of colonial control shall not have passed away merely to be replaced by a far more iron tyranny. We shall not always expect to find them supporting our view. But we shall always hope to find them strongly supporting their own freedom—and to remember that, in the past, those who foolishly sought power by riding the back of the tiger ended up inside.

> ## "Let the word go forth from this time and place, to friend and foe alike, that the torch has been passed to a new generation of Americans."

To those people in the huts and villages of half the globe struggling to break the bonds of mass misery, we pledge our best efforts to help them help themselves, for whatever period is required—not because the communists may be doing it, not because we seek their votes, but because it is right. If a free society cannot help the many who are poor, it cannot save the few who are rich.

To our sister republics south of our border, we offer a special pledge—to convert our good words into good deeds—in a new alliance for progress—to assist free men and free governments in casting off the chains of poverty. But this peaceful revolution of hope cannot become the prey of hostile powers. Let all our neighbors know that we shall join with them to oppose aggression or subversion anywhere in the Americas. And let every other power know that this Hemisphere intends to remain the master of its own house.

To that world assembly of sovereign states, the United Nations, our last best hope in an age where the instruments of war have far outpaced the instruments of peace, we renew our pledge of support—to prevent it from becoming merely a forum for invective—to strengthen its shield of the new and the weak—and to enlarge the area in which its writ may run.

Finally, to those nations who would make themselves our adversary, we offer not a pledge but a request: that both sides begin anew the quest for peace, before the dark powers of destruction unleashed by science engulf all humanity in planned or accidental self-destruction.

We dare not tempt them with weakness. For only when our arms are sufficient beyond doubt can we be certain beyond doubt that they will never be employed.

But neither can two great and powerful groups of nations take comfort from our present course—both sides overburdened by the cost of modern weapons, both rightly alarmed by the steady spread of the deadly atom, yet both racing to alter that uncertain balance of terror that stays the hand of mankind's final war.

So let us begin anew—remembering on both sides that civility is not a sign of weakness, and sincerity is always

Kennedy's inaugural address, January 20, 1961

subject to proof. Let us never negotiate out of fear. But let us never fear to negotiate.

Let both sides explore what problems unite us instead of belaboring those problems which divide us.

Let both sides, for the first time, formulate serious and precise proposals for the inspection and control of arms—and bring the absolute power to destroy other nations under the absolute control of all nations.

Let both sides seek to invoke the wonders of science instead of its terrors. Together let us explore the stars, conquer the deserts, eradicate disease, tap the ocean depths and encourage the arts and commerce.

> *"Together let us explore the stars, conquer the deserts, eradicate disease, tap the ocean depths and encourage the arts and commerce."*

Let both sides unite to heed in all corners of the earth the command of Isaiah—to "undo the heavy burdens...(and) let the oppressed go free."

And if a beachhead of cooperation may push back the jungle of suspicion, let both sides join in creating a new endeavor, not a new balance of power, but a new world of law, where the strong are just and the weak secure and the peace preserved.

All this will not be finished in the first one hundred days. Nor will it be finished in the first one thousand days, nor in the life of this Administration, nor even perhaps in our lifetime on this planet. But let us begin.

In your hands, my fellow citizens, more than mine, will rest the final success or failure of our course. Since this country was founded, each generation of Americans has been summoned to give testimony to its national loyalty. The graves of young Americans who answered the call to service surround the globe.

Now the trumpet summons us again—not as a call to bear arms, though arms we need—not as a call to battle, though embattled we are—but a call to bear the burden of a long twilight struggle, year in and year out, "rejoicing in hope, patient in tribulation"—a struggle against the common enemies of man: tyranny, poverty, disease and war itself.

Can we forge against these enemies a grand and global alliance, North and South, East and West, that can assure a more fruitful life for all mankind? Will you join in that historic effort?

In the long history of the world, only a few generations have been granted the role of defending freedom in its hour of maximum danger. I do not shrink from this responsibility—I welcome it. I do not believe that any of us would exchange places with any other people or any other generation. The energy, the faith, the devotion which we bring to this endeavor will light our country and all who serve it—and the glow from that fire can truly light the world.

And so, my fellow Americans: ask not what your country can do for you—ask what you can do for your country.

My fellow citizens of the world: ask not what America will do for you, but what together we can do for the freedom of man.

Finally, whether you are citizens of America or citizens of the world, ask of us here the same high standards of strength and sacrifice which we ask of you. With a good conscience our only sure reward, with history the final judge of our deeds, let us go forth to lead the land we love, asking His blessing and His help, but knowing that here on earth God's work must truly be our own.

> *"Ask not what your country can do for you—ask what you can do for your country."*

24

"MISSILES IN CUBA"

THE THIRTEEN DAYS of the Cuban Missile Crisis were the most terrifying of the Cold War. The United States and the Soviet Union, for the only time, directly confronted each other with the threat of nuclear devastation. Here, the drafting of a major presidential speech helped shape the policy and ultimately set the stage for the end of the crisis.

On October 16, the CIA told John F. Kennedy it had proof the Soviet Union was within days of installing medium-range nuclear missiles in Cuba. A month before, Kennedy had warned Moscow that such a move would directly imperil U.S. security (even though, in fact, Soviet long-range missiles had threatened for years). Now he secretly convened his top advisors (dubbed the Executive Committee of the National Security Council, or the "Ex Comm") in a series of free-wheeling sessions. Kennedy himself sometimes stayed away, to encourage his men to speak freely. Ted Sorensen, preparing for an eventual speech, took notes of the sessions, and often that was how Kennedy kept pace with the deliberations. Among many possible approaches, debate soon narrowed to two: bomb the missiles, as the military urged, or blockade Cuba, as Defense Secretary Robert McNamara and, eventually, Attorney General Robert Kennedy recommended. (UN ambassador Adlai Stevenson proposed making a deal, but others denounced him as weak.) Before he left for a campaign trip—canceling would have signaled crisis—Kennedy told Sorensen to prepare two drafts of a speech to the nation, one explaining each approach.

Sorensen began the draft announcing a blockade. But as historian Carol Gelderman recalls, he needed answers to several questions: "When the Ex Comm reconvened...

Sorensen offered them questions instead of a speech draft. 'As the concrete answers were provided in our discussion,' Sorensen said, 'the final shape of the president's policy began to take shape.'" As the writer worked late, eventually producing five drafts, the policy was formed and honed. Kennedy chose the blockade, not bombing. Kennedy sought to find a way for Soviet leader Nikita Khrushchev to step back, to avoid war. (He decided to call the blockade a less war-like "quarantine," borrowing from Franklin Roosevelt's 1937 call to "quarantine the aggressors." Sorensen also read Roosevelt's "Day of Infamy" speech for guidance.) Sorensen remembers that he never could bring himself to write an "invasion" speech, although one of unknown authorship recently turned up in Kennedy administration archives.

At noon on Monday, October 22, the White House asked the television networks for airtime seven hours later—Kennedy would announce the crisis and make his demands of Khrushchev all at once. The text was sent to U.S. embassies throughout the world, and as editing continued throughout the afternoon, the revisions were transmitted, too. "A Day of Mystery in D.C.!" declared the *San Francisco Examiner*.

Kennedy took the air, thin and grim, for what historian Michael Beschloss has called "perhaps the most important address of the Cold War." He opened by revealing the presence of the missiles in Cuba, and declared that they were unacceptable to the U.S. He justified his outrage with reference to treaties, history, and public lies by the Russians, while minimizing his own earlier warnings. He then declared his "*initial*" steps, a word his official text italicized. The hint of nuclear war still hung heavy. Sorensen's first draft had ended, "I tell you, therefore, that these missiles now in Cuba will someday go—and no others will take their place." By Monday night, Kennedy now said more tentatively, "Our goal is not the victory of might, but the vindication of right....God willing, that goal will be achieved." After seventeen minutes, the speech was over. Kennedy said, "Well, that's it, unless the son of a bitch fouls it up."

For eight days more, the two superpowers edged toward war—the famous confrontations between ships at sea; frantic negotiations with spies, journalists, and the president's brother acting as go-betweens; the decision to respond to one of Khrushchev's conciliatory letters while ignoring his

most warlike. In the end, though it was not revealed to the public until years later, after the Soviet Union withdrew its missiles from Cuba, Kennedy did withdraw our obsolete missiles in Turkey—the very linkage that led Robert Kennedy to brand Adlai Stevenson an appeaser.

The wisdom of restraint was also underscored later: it turned out there were at least twenty-two thousand Soviet military personnel in Cuba, and that local commanders may have had battlefield nuclear weapons to repel American invaders. As close as the world knew we came to nuclear war, in fact we likely came closer.

Kennedy proclaims in a televised speech on October 22, 1962, that Cuba has become an offensive Soviet base

ADDRESS TO THE NATION ON THE CUBAN MISSILE CRISIS

Washington, D.C. • October 22, 1962

hear...
disc 2
track 1

Good evening, my fellow citizens:

This Government, as promised, has maintained the closest surveillance of the Soviet military buildup on the island of Cuba. Within the past week, unmistakable evidence has established the fact that a series of offensive missile sites is now in preparation on that imprisoned island. The purpose of these bases can be none other than to provide a nuclear strike capability against the Western Hemisphere.

Upon receiving the first preliminary hard information of this nature last Tuesday morning at 9 a.m., I directed that our surveillance be stepped up. And having now confirmed and completed our evaluation of the evidence and our decision on a course of action, this Government feels obliged to report this new crisis to you in fullest detail.

The characteristics of these new missile sites indicate two distinct types of installations. Several of them include medium range ballistic missiles, capable of carrying a nuclear warhead for a distance of more than 1,000 nautical miles. Each of these missiles, in short, is capable of striking Washington, D.C., the Panama Canal, Cape Canaveral, Mexico City, or any other city in the southeastern part of the United States, in Central America, or in the Caribbean area.

> *"Each of these missiles...is capable of striking Washington, D.C., the Panama Canal, Cape Canaveral, Mexico City, or any other city in the southeastern part of the United States."*

Additional sites not yet completed appear to be designed for intermediate range ballistic missiles—capable of traveling more than twice as far—and thus capable of striking most of the major cities in the Western Hemisphere, ranging as far north as Hudson Bay, Canada, and as far south as Lima, Peru. In addition, jet bombers, capable of carrying nuclear weapons, are now being uncrated and assembled in Cuba, while the necessary air bases are being prepared.

This urgent transformation of Cuba into an important strategic base—by the presence of these large, long-range, and clearly offensive weapons of sudden mass destruction—constitutes an explicit threat to the peace and security of all the Americas, in flagrant and deliberate defiance of the Rio Pact of 1947, the traditions of this Nation and hemisphere, the joint resolution of the 87th Congress, the Charter of the United Nations, and my own public warnings to the Soviets on September 4 and 13. This action also contradicts the repeated assurances of Soviet spokesmen, both publicly and privately delivered, that the arms buildup in Cuba would retain its original defensive character, and that the Soviet Union had no need or desire to station strategic missiles on the territory of any other nation.

The size of this undertaking makes clear that it has been planned for some months. Yet only last month, after I had made clear the distinction between any introduction of ground-to-ground missiles and the existence of defensive anti-aircraft missiles, the Soviet Government publicly stated on September 11 that, and I quote, "the armaments and military equipment sent to Cuba are designed exclusively for defensive purposes," that, and I quote the Soviet Government, "there is no need for the Soviet Government to shift its weapons...for a retaliatory blow to any other country, for instance Cuba," and that, and I quote their government, "the Soviet Union

168

has so powerful rockets to carry these nuclear warheads that there is no need to search for sites for them beyond the boundaries of the Soviet Union." That statement was false.

"Jet bombers, capable of carrying nuclear weapons, are now being uncrated and assembled in Cuba."

Only last Thursday, as evidence of this rapid offensive buildup was already in my hand, Soviet Foreign Minister Gromyko told me in my office that he was instructed to make it clear once again, as he said his government had already done, that Soviet assistance to Cuba, and I quote,

"pursued solely the purpose of contributing to the defense capabilities of Cuba," that, and I quote him, "training by Soviet specialists of Cuban nationals in handling defensive armaments was by no means offensive, and if it were otherwise," Mr. Gromyko went on, "the Soviet Government would never become involved in rendering such assistance." That statement also was false.

Neither the United States of America nor the world community of nations can tolerate deliberate deception and offensive threats on the part of any nation, large or small. We no longer live in a world where only the actual firing of weapons represents a sufficient challenge to a nation's security to constitute maximum peril. Nuclear weapons are so destructive and ballistic missiles are so swift, that any substantially increased possibility of their use or any sudden change in their deployment may well be regarded as a definite threat to peace.

A Cuban refugee listens to Kennedy's televised October 22, 1962, address in which the president explained the U.S. position on the Cuban situation

For many years, both the Soviet Union and the United States, recognizing this fact, have deployed strategic nuclear weapons with great care, never upsetting the precarious status quo which insured that these weapons would not be used in the absence of some vital challenge. Our own strategic missiles have never been transferred to the territory of any other nation under a cloak of secrecy and deception; and our history—unlike that of the Soviets since the end of World War II—demonstrates that we have no desire to dominate or conquer any other nation or impose our system upon its people. Nevertheless, American citizens have become adjusted to living daily on the bull's-eye of Soviet missiles located inside the U.S.S.R. or in submarines.

> ## "We will not prematurely or unnecessarily risk the costs of worldwide nuclear war in which even the fruits of victory would be ashes in our mouth."

In that sense, missiles in Cuba add to an already clear and present danger—although it should be noted the nations of Latin America have never previously been subjected to a potential nuclear threat.

But this secret, swift, and extraordinary buildup of Communist missiles—in an area well known to have a special and historical relationship to the United States and the nations of the Western Hemisphere, in violation of Soviet assurances, and in defiance of American and hemispheric policy—this sudden, clandestine decision to station strategic weapons for the first time outside of Soviet soil—is a deliberately provocative and unjustified change in the status quo which cannot be accepted by this country, if our courage and our commitments are ever to be trusted again by either friend or foe.

The 1930's taught us a clear lesson: aggressive conduct, if allowed to go unchecked and unchallenged, ultimately leads to war. This nation is opposed to war. We are also true to our word. Our unswerving objective, therefore, must be to prevent the use of these missiles against this or any other country, and to secure their withdrawal or elimination from the Western Hemisphere.

Our policy has been one of patience and restraint, as befits a peaceful and powerful nation, which leads a worldwide alliance. We have been determined not to be diverted from our central concerns by mere irritants and fanatics. But now further action is required—and it is under way; and these actions may only be the beginning. We will not prematurely or unnecessarily risk the costs of worldwide nuclear war in which even the fruits of victory would be ashes in our mouth—but neither will we shrink from that risk at any time it must be faced.

Acting, therefore, in the defense of our own security and of the entire Western Hemisphere, and under the authority entrusted to me by the Constitution as endorsed by the resolution of the Congress, I have directed that the following *initial* steps be taken immediately:

First: To halt this offensive buildup, a strict quarantine on all offensive military equipment under shipment to Cuba is being initiated. All ships of any kind bound for Cuba from whatever nation or port will, if found to contain cargoes of offensive weapons, be turned back. This quarantine will be extended, if needed, to other types of cargo and carriers. We are not at this time, however, denying the necessities of life as the Soviets attempted to do in their Berlin blockade of 1948.

> ## "It shall be the policy of this Nation to regard any nuclear missile launched from Cuba against any nation in the Western Hemisphere as an attack by the Soviet Union on the United States."

Second: I have directed the continued and increased close surveillance of Cuba and its military buildup. The foreign ministers of the OAS, in their communique of October 6, rejected secrecy on such matters in this hemisphere. Should these offensive military preparations continue, thus increasing the threat to the hemisphere, further action will be justified. I have directed the Armed Forces to prepare for any eventualities; and I trust that in the interest of both the Cuban people and the Soviet technicians at the sites, the hazards to all concerned of continuing this threat will be recognized.

Third: It shall be the policy of this Nation to regard any nuclear missile launched from Cuba against any nation in the Western Hemisphere as an attack by the Soviet Union on the United States, requiring a full retaliatory response upon the Soviet Union.

An aerial reconnaissance photo taken over San Cristobal in Cuba in late October 1962

Fourth: As a necessary military precaution, I have reinforced our base at Guantanamo, evacuated today the dependents of our personnel there, and ordered additional military units to be on a standby alert basis.

Fifth: We are calling tonight for an immediate meeting of the Organ of Consultation under the Organization of American States, to consider this threat to hemispheric security and to invoke articles 6 and 8 of the Rio Treaty in support of all necessary action. The United Nations Charter allows for regional security arrangements—and the nations of this hemisphere decided long ago against the military presence of outside powers. Our other allies around the world have also been alerted.

Sixth: Under the Charter of the United Nations, we are asking tonight that an emergency meeting of the Security Council be convoked without delay to take action against this latest Soviet threat to world peace. Our resolution will call for the prompt dismantling and withdrawal of all offensive weapons in Cuba, under the supervision of UN observers, before the quarantine can be lifted.

Seventh and finally: I call upon Chairman Khrushchev to halt and eliminate this clandestine, reckless, and provocative threat to world peace and to stable relations between our two nations. I call upon him further to abandon this course of world domination, and to join in an historic effort to end the perilous arms race and to transform the history of man. He has an opportunity now to move the world back from the abyss of destruction—by returning to his government's own words that it had no need to station missiles outside its own territory, and withdrawing these weapons from Cuba—by refraining from any action which will widen or deepen the present crisis—and then by participating in a search for peaceful and permanent solutions.

This Nation is prepared to present its case against the Soviet threat to peace, and our own proposals for a peaceful world, at any time and in any forum—in the OAS, in the United Nations, or in any other meeting that could be useful—without limiting our freedom of action. We have in the past made strenuous efforts to limit the spread of nuclear weapons. We have proposed the elimination of all arms and

military bases in a fair and effective disarmament treaty. We are prepared to discuss new proposals for the removal of tensions on both sides—including the possibilities of a genuinely independent Cuba, free to determine its own destiny. We have no wish to war with the Soviet Union—for we are a peaceful people who desire to live in peace with all other peoples.

"*The greatest danger of all would be to do nothing.*"

But it is difficult to settle or even discuss these problems in an atmosphere of intimidation. That is why this latest Soviet threat—or any other threat which is made either independently or in response to our actions this week—must and will be met with determination. Any hostile move anywhere in the world against the safety and freedom of peoples to whom we are committed—including in particular the brave people of West Berlin—will be met by whatever action is needed.

Finally, I want to say a few words to the captive people of Cuba, to whom this speech is being directly carried by special radio facilities. I speak to you as a friend, as one who knows of your deep attachment to your fatherland, as one who shares your aspirations for liberty and justice for all. And I have watched and the American people have watched with deep sorrow how your nationalist revolution was betrayed—and how your fatherland fell under foreign domination. Now your leaders are no longer Cuban leaders inspired by Cuban ideals. They are puppets and agents of an international conspiracy which has turned Cuba against your friends and neighbors in the Americas—and turned it into the first Latin American country to become a target for nuclear war—the first Latin American country to have these weapons on its soil.

These new weapons are not in your interest. They contribute nothing to your peace and well-being. They can only undermine it. But this country has no wish to cause you to suffer or to impose any system upon you. We know that your

TCS - 10/20/62
1st Draft

Good evening, my fellow citizens:

Within the last week, unmistakable evidence has ~~been gathered by this~~

~~Government~~ establishing the fact that a series of offensive nuclear missile

bases is now under intensive preparation on ~~the communist island, of Cuba.~~

Three of these ~~missile~~ sites, contain launchers, ~~who a site, to be loaded~~ with

Medium Range Ballistic Missiles, two for each launcher, ~~for a total of 24.~~

Each of these missiles is capable of carrying a 3000 pound nuclear warhead

of ~~up to~~ 2 megatons in yield 100 times as destructive as the bomb which

destroyed Hiroshima -- for a distance of more than 1000 nautical miles.

Each of these missiles, in short, is capable of wiping out Washington, D.C.,

the Panama Canal, Cape Canaveral, Florida, Mexico City, or any other city

in the Southeastern part of the United States, Central America or the

Caribbean. ~~Twelve~~ other launch pads now under construction designed

for Intermediate Range Ballistic Missiles -- capable of travelling more than

twice as far and causing several times as much destruction -- and thus

capable of devastating most of the United States mainland, most of Latin

America and most of Canada. In addition, large numbers of medium range

jet bombers, capable of carrying nuclear weapons, are now being uncrated

on Cuba, while appropriate air bases are being prepared.

~~The presence in~~ Cuba of these large, long-range and clearly offensive

weapons of sudden destruction constitutes a threat to the peace and security

of ~~this Hemisphere~~ -- in naked and deliberate defiance of the Rio Pact of 1947,

*Draft of Kennedy's October 22, 1962, speech announcing a
"quarantine" of Cuba (above)*

*A recently discovered alternate draft (right), probably written
by the State Department, announcing an invasion of Cuba,
which could have led to World War III*

PRESIDENT'S SPEECH
— AIR ATTACK —

My fellow Americans:

With a heavy heart, and in necessary fulfillment of

my oath of office, I have ordered -- and the United

States Air Force has now carried out -- military operations,

with conventional weapons only, to remove a major nuclear

weapons build-up from the soil of Cuba. This action has

been taken under Article 51 of the Charter of the United

Nations and in fulfillment of the requirements of the

national safety. Further military action has been

authorized to ensure that this threat is fully removed

and not restored.

~~Let me first tell you what has been going on. What~~

~~it is that we have had to attack?~~ In sum there have been unconfirmed

rumors of offensive installations in Cuba for some weeks,

but it is only within the last week that we have had unmistakable

and certain evidence of the character and magnitude of the

Communist offensive deployment. What this evidence

established beyond doubt is that in a rapid, secret and

frequently denied military operation, the Communists were

attempting to establish a series of offensive nuclear

lives and land are being used as pawns by those who deny your freedom.

Many times in the past, the Cuban people have risen to throw out tyrants who destroyed their liberty. And I have no doubt that most Cubans today look forward to the time when they will be truly free—free from foreign domination, free to choose their own leaders, free to select their own system, free to own their own land, free to speak and write and worship without fear or degradation. And then shall Cuba be welcomed back to the society of free nations and to the associations of this hemisphere.

My fellow citizens: let no one doubt that this is a difficult and dangerous effort on which we have set out. No one can foresee precisely what course it will take or what costs or casualties will be incurred. Many months of sacrifice and self-discipline lie ahead—months in which both our patience and our will will be tested—months in which many threats and denunciations will keep us aware of our dangers. But the greatest danger of all would be to do nothing.

The path we have chosen for the present is full of hazards, as all paths are—but it is the one most consistent with our character and courage as a nation and our commitments around the world. The cost of freedom is always high—but Americans have always paid it. And one path we shall never choose, and that is the path of surrender or submission.

Our goal is not the victory of might, but the vindication of right—not peace at the expense of freedom, but both peace *and* freedom, here in this hemisphere, and, we hope, around the world. God willing, that goal will be achieved.

Thank you and good night.

Kennedy with aide Ted Sorensen, March 12, 1963

25

JOHN F. KENNEDY

"LET US REEXAMINE OUR ATTITUDE TOWARD THE COLD WAR"

"WE HAVE TO remember that no one who went through the missile crisis came out the same as they went in," Secretary of State Dean Rusk observed to President Kennedy in the spring of 1963. The standoff had frightened the public, but the two superpowers still were locked in an ever-escalating arms race without ever having reached arms control agreements. That would soon change. In June 1963, Kennedy gave a speech that marked a major shift in the Cold War—an easing of tone and reduction of rhetoric that was to prove as significant as the treaties that followed.

The immediate issue was a hoped-for treaty to ban atmospheric nuclear tests. The tests were scattering fallout; strontium 90 had been found in the milk of American schoolchildren. As historian Richard Reeves observes, the number one book was *Fail-Safe*, in which an error sends a U.S. bomber to destroy Moscow; to avoid retaliation, a president seemingly modeled on Kennedy must destroy New York as well. Less than two years after Kennedy's militant inaugural address, the public now was ready for a turn from confrontation. But talks between the U.S., its allies, and the Soviet Union had broken down. Soviet premier Nikita Khrushchev angrily rejected overtures from the West, claiming he had been double-crossed on issues such as the number of inspections required to verify compliance with the treaty.

Norman Cousins, the magazine editor who had suggested Eisenhower's farewell address, had just met with Khrushchev, and wrote to Kennedy with a last-ditch idea to save the talks. "You ought to beat Mr. K to the punch," calling for peace before Khrushchev himself was to address a major Communist Party meeting. "The moment is now at hand for the most important speech of your presidency…in its breathtaking proposals for genuine peace, in its tone of friendliness for the Soviet people and its understanding of their ordeal during the last war." Kennedy decided it was worth a try.

In preparing the speech, Kennedy's aides showed how the modern White House can override the wishes and sensitivities of Cabinet departments. Speechwriter Ted Sorensen and National Security Advisor McGeorge Bundy worked on it in secret. Only on June 7—just three days before delivery—did they show the text to the secretaries

Kennedy speaking at commencement exercises at American University in Washington, D.C., June 10, 1963

of state and defense—by which time it was too late for them to lobby for a more confrontational speech. Kennedy himself worked on the text as he flew back to Washington from a trip to Hawaii. He arrived at the White House, changed his shirt, and drove straight to American University to address the graduates.

Kennedy spoke first of peace and the dangers of war, eloquently but unremarkably. Then he went further: "We must reexamine our own attitude—as individuals and as a nation—for our attitude is as essential as theirs [the Soviets]." After years of blistering Cold War rhetoric, this was something new from a president. He warned his fellow citizens not to "fall into the same trap as the Soviets, not to see only a distorted and desperate view of the other side, not to see conflict as inevitable, accommodation as impossible, and communication as nothing more than an exchange of threats." Arthur M. Schlesinger Jr. wrote in A Thousand Days, "Its central substantive proposal was a moratorium on atmospheric testing; but its effect was to redefine the whole national attitude toward the Cold War." Historian Jeff Shesol notes, "Kennedy sought to reclaim peace for the pragmatists, from the idealists. Repeatedly he spoke of peace as a 'rational end of rational men'—as 'practical, attainable,' not the result of messianic fervor. In a direct response to Woodrow Wilson, he says, 'at least we can help make the world safe for diversity.'"

Moscow reacted swiftly. *Isvestia*, the official newspaper, printed the text in full. The jammers that normally blocked Western radio broadcasts were turned off so average Russians could hear the speech.

The two superpowers quickly negotiated a nuclear test ban treaty, which the U.S. Senate approved on September 24, 1963. The pact was the first arms control agreement of any kind between the two Cold War rivals.

John F. Kennedy's
COMMENCEMENT ADDRESS, AMERICAN UNIVERSITY

Washington, D.C. • June 10, 1963

disc 2
track 2

President Anderson, members of the faculty, board of trustees, distinguished guests, my old colleague, Senator Bob Byrd, who has earned his degree through many years of attending night law school, while I am earning mine in the next 30 minutes, ladies and gentlemen:

[*Kennedy begins by speaking briefly on the history of American University and of the value of higher education.*]

[I have] chosen this time and this place to discuss a topic on which ignorance too often abounds and the truth is too rarely perceived—yet it is the most important topic on earth: world peace.

What kind of peace do I mean? What kind of peace do we seek? Not a Pax Americana enforced on the world by American weapons of war. Not the peace of the grave or the security of the slave. I am talking about genuine peace, the kind of peace that makes life on earth worth living, the kind that enables men and nations to grow and to hope and to build a better life for their children—not merely peace for Americans but peace for all men and women—not merely peace in our time but peace for all time.

"What kind of peace do we seek?"

I speak of peace because of the new face of war. Total war makes no sense in an age when great powers can maintain large and relatively invulnerable nuclear forces and refuse to surrender without resort to those forces. It makes no sense in an age when a single nuclear weapon contains almost ten times the explosive force delivered by all of the allied air forces in the Second World War. It makes no sense in an age when the deadly poisons produced by a nuclear exchange would be carried by wind and water and soil and seed to the far corners of the globe and to generations yet unborn.

Today the expenditure of billions of dollars every year on weapons acquired for the purpose of making sure we never need to use them is essential to keeping the peace. But surely the acquisition of such idle stockpiles—which can only destroy and never create—is not the only, much less the most efficient, means of assuring peace.

"I speak of peace because of the new face of war."

I speak of peace, therefore, as the necessary rational end of rational men. I realize that the pursuit of peace is not as dramatic as the pursuit of war—and frequently the words of the pursuer fall on deaf ears. But we have no more urgent task.

Some say that it is useless to speak of world peace or world law or world disarmament—and that it will be useless until the leaders of the Soviet Union adopt a more enlightened attitude. I hope they do. I believe we can help them do it. But I also believe that we must reexamine our own attitude—as individuals and as a Nation—for our attitude is as essential as theirs. And every graduate of this school, every thoughtful citizen who despairs of war and wishes to bring peace, should begin by looking inward—by examining his own attitude toward the possibilities of peace, toward the Soviet Union, toward the course of the cold war and toward freedom and peace here at home.

First: Let us examine our attitude toward peace itself. Too many of us think it is impossible. Too many think it unreal. But that is a dangerous, defeatist belief. It leads to the conclusion that war is inevitable—that mankind is doomed—that we are gripped by forces we cannot control.

We need not accept that view. Our problems are man-made—therefore, they can be solved by man. And man can be as big as he wants. No problem of human destiny is beyond human beings. Man's reason and spirit have often solved the seemingly unsolvable—and we believe they can do it again.

"I speak of peace… as the necessary rational end of rational men."

I am not referring to the absolute, infinite concept of universal peace and good will of which some fantasies and fanatics dream. I do not deny the value of hopes and dreams but we merely invite discouragement and incredulity by making that our only and immediate goal.

Let us focus instead on a more practical, more attainable peace—based not on a sudden revolution in human nature but on a gradual evolution in human institutions—on a series of concrete actions and effective agreements which are in the interest of all concerned. There is no single, simple key to this peace—no grand or magic formula to be adopted by one or two powers. Genuine peace must be the product of many nations, the sum of many acts. It must be dynamic, not static, changing to meet the challenge of each new generation. For peace is a process—a way of solving problems.

With such a peace, there will still be quarrels and conflicting interests, as there are within families and nations. World peace, like community peace, does not require that each man love his neighbor—it requires only that they live together in mutual tolerance, submitting their disputes to a just and peaceful settlement. And history teaches us that enmities between nations, as between individuals, do not last forever. However fixed our likes and dislikes may seem, the tide of time and events will often bring surprising changes in the relations between nations and neighbors.

So let us persevere. Peace need not be impracticable, and war need not be inevitable. By defining our goal more clearly, by making it seem more manageable and less remote, we can help all peoples to see it, to draw hope from it, and to move irresistibly toward it.

Second: Let us reexamine our attitude toward the Soviet Union. It is discouraging to think that their leaders may actually believe what their propagandists write. It is discouraging to read a recent authoritative Soviet text on *Military Strategy* and find, on page after page, wholly baseless and incredible claims—such as the allegation that "American imperialist circles are preparing to unleash different types of wars…that there is a very real threat of a preventive war being unleashed by American imperialists against the Soviet Union…[and that] the political aims of the American imperialists are to enslave economically and politically the European and other capitalist countries…[and] to achieve world domination…by means of aggressive wars."

Truly, as it was written long ago: "The wicked flee when no man pursueth." Yet it is sad to read these Soviet statements—to realize the extent of the gulf between us. But it is also a warning—a warning to the American people not to fall into the same trap as the Soviets, not to see only a distorted and desperate view of the other side, not to see conflict as inevitable, accommodation as impossible, and communication as nothing more than an exchange of threats.

"We must reexamine our own attitude…for our attitude is as essential as theirs."

No government or social system is so evil that its people must be considered as lacking in virtue. As Americans, we find communism profoundly repugnant as a negation of personal freedom and dignity. But we can still hail the Russian people for their many achievements—in science and space, in economic and industrial growth, in culture and in acts of courage.

Among the many traits the peoples of our two countries have in common, none is stronger than our mutual abhorrence of war. Almost unique, among the major world powers, we have never been at war with each other. And no nation in the history of battle ever suffered more than the Soviet Union suffered in the course of the Second World War. At least 20 million lost their lives. Countless millions of homes and farms were burned or sacked. A third of the nation's territory, including nearly two thirds of its industrial base, was turned into a wasteland—a loss equivalent to the devastation of this country east of Chicago.

"It is also a warning— a warning to the American people not to fall into the same trap as the Soviets, not to see only a distorted and desperate view of the other side, not to see conflict as inevitable."

Today, should total war ever break out again—no matter how—our two countries would become the primary targets. It is an ironic but accurate fact that the two strongest powers are the two in the most danger of devastation. All we have built, all we have worked for, would be destroyed in the first 24 hours. And even in the cold war, which brings burdens and dangers to so many countries, including this Nation's closest allies—our two countries bear the heaviest burdens. For we are both devoting massive sums of money to weapons that could be better devoted to combating ignorance, poverty, and disease. We are both caught up in a vicious and dangerous cycle in which suspicion on one side breeds suspicion on the other, and new weapons beget counterweapons.

In short, both the United States and its allies, and the Soviet Union and its allies, have a mutually deep interest in a just and genuine peace and in halting the arms race. Agreements to this end are in the interests of the Soviet Union as well as ours—and even the most hostile nations can be relied upon to accept and keep those treaty obligations, and only those treaty obligations, which are in their own interest.

So, let us not be blind to our differences—but let us also direct attention to our common interests and to the means by which those differences can be resolved. And if we cannot end now our differences, at least we can help make the world safe for diversity. For, in the final analysis, our most basic common link is that we all inhabit this small planet. We all breathe the same air. We all cherish our children's future. And we are all mortal.

Third: Let us reexamine our attitude toward the cold war, remembering that we are not engaged in a debate, seeking to pile up debating points. We are not here distributing blame or pointing the finger of judgment. We must deal with the world as it is, and not as it might have been had the history of the last 18 years been different.

We must, therefore, persevere in the search for peace in the hope that constructive changes within the Communist bloc might bring within reach solutions which now seem beyond us. We must conduct our affairs in such a way that it becomes in the Communists' interest to agree on a genuine peace. Above all, while defending our own vital interests, nuclear powers must avert those confrontations which bring an adversary to a choice of either a humiliating retreat or a nuclear war. To adopt that kind of course in the nuclear age would be evidence only of the bankruptcy of our policy—or of a collective death-wish for the world.

"If we cannot end now our differences, at least we can help make the world safe for diversity."

To secure these ends, America's weapons are non-provocative, carefully controlled, designed to deter, and capable of selective use. Our military forces are committed to peace and disciplined in self-restraint. Our diplomats are instructed to avoid unnecessary irritants and purely rhetorical hostility.

For we can seek a relaxation of tensions without relaxing our guard. And, for our part, we do not need to use threats to prove that we are resolute. We do not need to jam foreign broadcasts out of fear our faith will be eroded. We are unwilling to impose our system on any unwilling people—but we are willing and able to engage in peaceful competition with any people on earth....

[*Kennedy discusses America's role with respect to the UN and its commitments to other non-communist nations. He proposes a direct line of communication between Washington and Moscow, and then begins to talk about the first steps to arms control.*]

The pursuit of disarmament has been an effort of this Government since the 1920's. It has been urgently sought by the past three administrations. And however dim the prospects may be today, we intend to continue this effort—to continue it in order that all countries, including our own, can better grasp what the problems and possibilities of disarmament are.

The one major area of these negotiations where the end is in sight, yet where a fresh start is badly needed, is in a treaty to outlaw nuclear tests. The conclusion of such a treaty, so near and yet so far, would check the spiraling arms race in one of its most dangerous areas. It would place the nuclear powers in a position to deal more effectively with one of the greatest hazards which man faces in 1963, the further spread of nuclear arms. It would increase our security—it would decrease the prospects of war. Surely this goal is sufficiently important to require

our steady pursuit, yielding neither to the temptation to give up the whole effort nor the temptation to give up our insistence on vital and responsible safeguards.

I am taking this opportunity, therefore, to announce two important decisions in this regard.

First: Chairman Khrushchev, Prime Minister Macmillan, and I have agreed that high-level discussions will shortly begin in Moscow looking toward early agreement on a comprehensive test ban treaty. Our hopes must be tempered with the caution of history—but with our hopes go the hopes of all mankind.

Second: To make clear our good faith and solemn convictions on the matter, I now declare that the United States does not propose to conduct nuclear tests in the atmosphere so long as other states do not do so. We will not be the first to resume. Such a declaration is no substitute for a formal binding treaty, but I hope it will help us achieve one. Nor would such a treaty be a substitute for disarmament, but I hope it will help us achieve it....

"*The United States, as the world knows, will never start a war.*"

The United States, as the world knows, will never start a war. We do not want a war. We do not now expect a war. This generation of Americans has already had enough—more than enough—of war and hate and oppression. We shall be prepared if others wish it. We shall be alert to try to stop it. But we shall also do our part to build a world of peace where the weak are safe and the strong are just. We are not helpless before that task or hopeless of its success. Confident and unafraid, we labor on—not toward a strategy of annihilation but toward a strategy of peace.

26

"ICH BIN EIN BERLINER"

BERLIN WAS THE FLASHPOINT of the Cold War: a place where a shot fired in anger or by accident could set off a consuming crisis, the place where World War III, if it were to happen, would likely begin. After 1945, the German city was divided into Russian and Western Zones. West Berlin—a democratic enclave surrounded by grim East Germany—was a constant irritant to Moscow and a lure for those fleeing communism. With yet another "Berlin Crisis" simmering in 1961, the Soviets finally acted. They built a concrete and barbed wire wall that divided the city and dammed the flow of refugees. The immediate crisis passed. Many Germans were angry at Kennedy for letting it happen.

Two weeks after the American University "peace speech," Kennedy went to Berlin. His trip had little formal business but was freighted with symbolism. For four hours, he drove through the streets of Berlin—several million of the city's population cheered him on. He mounted guard platforms and for the first time saw the ugly wall. The communists tried to block the view of their city. A few East Berliners waved from their windows, and Kennedy realized they had put their lives in danger. Kennedy climbed down angry and shaken. He decided his speech draft was "terrible." In Washington, Robert Kennedy had suggested his brother speak some words of German. On Air Force One,

Kennedy pledges support against Communist threats before a huge crowd in West Berlin on June 26, 1963

Kennedy had asked an aide, "What was the proud boast of the Romans?…Send [McGeorge] Bundy up here. He'll know how to translate it into German." He would improvise his speech.

Now at city hall, hundreds of thousands, perhaps a million Berliners screamed for the young American president. Kennedy distrusted mass emotion, shunning the florid politics of his grandfather, the mayor of Boston—but for once he was carried by the crowd's passion and his own. "Two thousand years ago, the proudest boast was '*civis Romanus sum*,'" he declaimed. "Today, in the world of freedom, the proudest boast is—'*Ich bin ein Berliner.*'" Listeners shrieked, realizing that with those visceral words Kennedy had effectively declared an attack on their city to be an attack on America. (It is true that *berliner* is also the name of a pastry, but few in the crowd thought Kennedy was saying, "I am a jelly doughnut." The crowd's roar was not from hunger.) Kennedy's rhetoric built momentum—what historian Michael Beschloss called "rhythmic, precisely delineated phrases that turned his words into a kind of angry poetry." In fact, he went too far. "There are some who say in Europe and elsewhere, 'we can work with the Communists,'" he concluded. "Let them come to Berlin!" But that was exactly what he himself had said two weeks before, and, as Ted Sorensen recounted with understatement, "the ad lib caused some consternation," a point presidential aides made on the drive to the next stop. So to the next audience, he tried to explain and cushion his words, saying he was merely referring to including Communists in government. (In this case, reversing roles from the Missile Crisis, it was Khrushchev who chose to believe the more conciliatory speech.)

The fierce adulation exhilarated and unnerved Kennedy and those around him. "Could this mean Germany could have another Hitler," asked the chancellor of West Germany, elderly Konrad Adenauer. Kennedy mused that if he had commanded, "March to the wall—tear it down," the throng would have done it. As he ended his trip, Kennedy joked that he would leave an envelope for his successor, "to be opened at a time of some discouragement." The note inside would read: "Go to Germany."

PRESIDENT BILL CLINTON ON KENNEDY'S BERLIN SPEECH

My favorite line from John F. Kennedy was from the Berlin speech—a speech most people only remember for, "*Ich bin ein Berliner.*" The part I remember is this: "Freedom has many difficulties and democracy is not perfect, but we have never had to put a wall up to keep our people in." I thought that was one of the most thrilling lines I had ever heard. It gave me a lot of hope in America when I heard it. I came across it again during the early 1970s, during a very dark time in the country, and again, reading it and thinking about it gave me hope that things would get better. It served as a reminder of who we really were.

There is a sense that, during a time of crisis, people want to be told, "Don't worry, don't pay attention, we'll take care of you." In fact, this is exactly when they need the most time to think—and leaders should challenge them to do that. I think Kennedy did that with this speech, particularly with that one line.

I was in high school when Kennedy visited Berlin, and I watched that speech on television—and I remember that incredible crowd. When I went back to Berlin in 1994, I was the first American president to speak on the East side—at the Brandenberg Gate. It was very moving—and as I looked around, I kept thinking of Kennedy and his words.

John F. Kennedy's
SPEECH AT THE BERLIN WALL

West Berlin, Germany • June 26, 1963

*hear....
disc 2
track 3

I am proud to come to this city as the guest of your distinguished Mayor, who has symbolized throughout the world the fighting spirit of West Berlin. And I am proud to visit the Federal Republic with your distinguished Chancellor who for so many years has committed Germany to democracy and freedom and progress, and to come here in the company of my fellow American, General Clay, who has been in this city during its great moments of crisis and will come again if ever needed.

Two thousand years ago the proudest boast was "*civis Romanus sum*." Today, in the world of freedom, the proudest boast is "*Ich bin ein Berliner*."

I appreciate my interpreter translating my German!

There are many people in the world who really don't understand, or say they don't, what is the great issue between the free world and the Communist world. Let them come to Berlin. There are some who say that communism is the wave of the future. Let them come to Berlin. And there are some who say in Europe and elsewhere we can work with the Communists. Let them come to Berlin. And there are even a few who say that it is true that communism is an

"All free men, wherever they may live, are citizens of Berlin."

Kennedy on a platform overlooking the Berlin Wall, June 26, 1963

evil system, but it permits us to make economic progress. *Laßt sie nach Berlin kommen*. Let them come to Berlin.

Freedom has many difficulties and democracy is not perfect, but we have never had to put a wall up to keep our people in, to prevent them from leaving us. I want to say, on behalf of my countrymen, who live many miles away on the other side of the Atlantic, who are far distant from you, that they take the greatest pride that they have been able to share with you, even from a distance, the story of the last 18 years. I know of no town, no city, that has been besieged for 18 years that still lives with the vitality and the force, and the hope and the determination of the city of West Berlin. While the wall is the most obvious and vivid demonstration of the failures of the Communist system, for all the world to see, we take no satisfaction in it, for it is, as your Mayor has said, an offense not only against history but an offense against humanity, separating families, dividing husbands and wives and brothers and sisters, and dividing a people who wish to be joined together.

What is true of this city is true of Germany—real, lasting peace in Europe can never be assured as long as one German out of four is denied the elementary right of free men, and that is to make a free choice. In 18 years of peace and good faith, this generation of Germans has earned the right to be free, including the right to unite their families and their nation in lasting peace, with good will to all people. You live in a defended island of freedom, but your life is part of the main. So let me ask you as I close, to lift your eyes beyond the dangers of today, to the hopes of tomorrow, beyond the freedom merely of this city of Berlin, or your country of Germany, to the advance of freedom everywhere, beyond the wall to the day of peace with justice, beyond yourselves and ourselves to all mankind.

"Today, in the world of freedom, the proudest boast is 'Ich bin ein Berliner.'"

Freedom is indivisible, and when one man is enslaved, all are not free. When all are free, then we can look forward to that day when this city will be joined as one and this country and this great Continent of Europe in a peaceful and hopeful globe. When that day finally comes, as it will, the people of West Berlin can take sober satisfaction in the fact that they were in the front lines for almost two decades.

All free men, wherever they may live, are citizens of Berlin, and, therefore, as a free man, I take pride in the words "*Ich bin ein Berliner*."

One of President Kennedy's speech cards carrying his famous remark "Ich bin ein Berliner," spelled phonetically

Lyndon B. JOHNSON

36TH PRESIDENT: 1963–1969

Born: August 27, 1908, near Stonewall, Texas

Died: January 22, 1973, in Johnson City, Texas

Disc 2, Tracks 4–6

27

LYNDON B. JOHNSON

"LET US CONTINUE"

ON NOVEMBER 22, 1963, less than two hours after John F. Kennedy was murdered, Lyndon Johnson took the oath of office on Air Force One. Jacqueline Kennedy stood by, dazed and caked in blood. Later that night, for less than a minute in the dark at Andrews Air Force Base, the new president spoke to the nation. "I will do my best," he concluded. "That is all I can do. I ask for your help—and God's."

Johnson, perhaps the most complex man ever to occupy the presidency, had now reached his lifetime goal—but faced an excruciating test of leadership. The country was in shock.

Nobody knew whether the murder was a lone act or conspiracy. Johnson feared being seen as illegitimate. He worried that his White House, full of New Frontiersmen, would fracture. He knew that the public—still swooning over the Boston glamour of Kennedy—now would see an older, less educated, ungainly man with a thick Texas accent.

"Everything was in chaos," Johnson later told his biographer, Doris Kearns Goodwin. "We were all spinning around and around, trying to come to grips with what had happened, but the more we tried to understand it, the more

confused we got. We were like a bunch of cattle caught in the swamp, unable to move in either direction, simply circling 'round and 'round. I understood that; I knew what had to be done. There is but one way to get the cattle out of the swamp. And that is for the man on the horse to take the lead, to assume command, to provide direction. In the period of confusion after the assassination, I was that man."

As Senate majority leader in the 1950s, Johnson was one of the most powerful congressional chiefs of the twentieth century, but as vice president he had languished. Now his awesome political skill reemerged. He greeted a stream of foreign dignitaries and reassured the world. He let the Kennedy family grieve, and slept at his suburban home while Jacqueline Kennedy continued to live in the White House. The country's shock was redoubled when the accused assassin, Lee Harvey Oswald, was murdered live on national television in the basement of a Dallas jail. Johnson remained publicly silent until the achingly formal funeral, and the burial of John F. Kennedy in Arlington National Cemetery.

His first speech would be delivered to the Congress, returning to the well of his power. To draft it, he turned to Kennedy's staff. Managing their shattered sensitivities and egos tested his skill. On secretly recorded tapes, Johnson talked to Kennedy aide Ted Sorensen about a draft submitted by economist John Kenneth Galbraith. Johnson seemed to think the way to please Sorensen was to praise his fellow liberal.

"Well, anyway, you liked Galbraith," Sorensen asked.

"Yes, sir, I did," Johnson replied.

"Well, you see, I didn't," Sorensen laughed.

Johnson realized he had to backpedal quickly. "I didn't think it was any ball of *fire*. I thought it was something you could *improve* on," he concluded. "I think a much better speech could be written. I'm expecting you to write one."

The draft—written by Sorensen and Galbraith, with input from Johnson allies Bill Moyers and Abe Fortas—found perfect pitch. "All I have I would have given gladly not to be standing here today," Johnson began. Kennedy in his inaugural had said, "Let us begin." Now Johnson

declared, "Let us continue." Throughout the speech he invoked the late president's name as the source of legitimacy and energy. "First, no memorial oration or eulogy could more eloquently honor President Kennedy's memory than the earliest possible passage of the civil rights bill for which he fought so long." Of course, Johnson knew that his predecessor's domestic record was skimpy. "For thirty-two years Capitol Hill has been my home," Johnson wrote in pencil on the final draft. He knew the members of Congress—knew their secrets, their weaknesses, their vanities, their political allegiances. Now he intended to use that knowledge.

Doris Kearns Goodwin wrote, "If at the beginning of his address one missed the clipped delivery of John Kennedy, by the end one was grateful for the measured steadiness of Lyndon Johnson." Perhaps. What is undeniable is that for all the later swings of this complex man—the vaulting ambition of the Great Society, the agony of Vietnam—at this moment he found a way to soothe a traumatized country.

Robert Kennedy listening to President Johnson's address to a joint session of Congress, November 27, 1963

Mr. Speaker, Mr. President, Members of the House, Members of the Senate, my fellow Americans:

All I have I would have given gladly not to be standing here today.

The greatest leader of our time has been struck down by the foulest deed of our time. Today John Fitzgerald Kennedy lives on in the immortal words and works that he left behind. He lives on in the mind and memories of mankind. He lives on in the hearts of his countrymen.

No words are sad enough to express our sense of loss. No words are strong enough to express our determination to continue the forward thrust of America that he began.

The dream of conquering the vastness of space—the dream of partnership across the Atlantic—and across the Pacific as well—the dream of a Peace Corps in less developed nations—the dream of education for all of our children—the dream of jobs for all who seek them and need them—the dream of care for our elderly—the dream of an all-out attack on mental illness—and above all, the dream of equal rights for all Americans, whatever their race or color—these and other American dreams have been vitalized by his drive and by his dedication.

"All I have I would have given gladly not to be standing here today."

And now the ideas and the ideals which he so nobly represented must and will be translated into effective action.

Under John Kennedy's leadership, this Nation has demonstrated that it has the courage to seek peace, and it has the fortitude to risk war. We have proved that we are a good and reliable friend to those who seek peace and freedom. We have shown that we can also be a formidable foe to those who reject the path of peace and those who seek to impose upon us or our allies the yoke of tyranny.

This Nation will keep its commitments from South Viet-Nam to West Berlin. We will be unceasing in the search for peace; resourceful in our pursuit of areas of agreement even with those with whom we differ; and generous and loyal to those who join with us in common cause.

"No words are sad enough to express our sense of loss."

In this age when there can be no losers in peace and no victors in war, we must recognize the obligation to match national strength with national restraint. We must be prepared at one and the same time for both the confrontation of power and the limitation of power. We must be ready to defend the national interest and to negotiate the common interest. This is the path that we shall continue to pursue. Those who test our courage will find it strong, and those who seek our friendship will find it honorable. We will demonstrate anew that the strong can be just in the use of strength; and the just can be strong in the defense of justice.

And let all know we will extend no special privilege and impose no persecution. We will carry on the fight against poverty and misery, and disease and ignorance, in other lands and in our own.

We will serve all the Nation, not one section or one sector, or one group, but all Americans. These are the United States—a united people with a united purpose.

Johnson addresses Congress, November 27, 1963, with the text of his speech before him on the podium

Our American unity does not depend upon unanimity. We have differences; but now, as in the past, we can derive from those differences strength, not weakness, wisdom, not despair. Both as a people and a government, we can unite upon a program, a program which is wise and just, enlightened and constructive.

For 32 years Capitol Hill has been my home. I have shared many moments of pride with you, pride in the ability of the Congress of the United States to act, to meet any crisis, to distill from our differences strong programs of national action.

An assassin's bullet has thrust upon me the awesome burden of the Presidency. I am here today to say I need your help; I cannot bear this burden alone. I need the help of all Americans, and all America. This Nation has experienced a profound shock, and in this critical moment, it is our duty, yours and mine, as the Government of the United States, to do away with uncertainty and doubt and delay, and to show that we are capable of decisive action; that from the brutal loss of our leader we will derive not weakness, but strength; that we can and will act and act now.

"This Nation will keep its commitments from South Viet-Nam to West Berlin."

190

From this chamber of representative government, let all the world know and none misunderstand that I rededicate this Government to the unswerving support of the United Nations, to the honorable and determined execution of our commitments to our allies, to the maintenance of military strength second to none, to the defense of the strength and the stability of the dollar, to the expansion of our foreign trade, to the reinforcement of our programs of mutual assistance and cooperation in Asia and Africa, and to our Alliance for Progress in this hemisphere.

"For 32 years Capitol Hill has been my home."

On the 20th day of January, in 1961, John F. Kennedy told his countrymen that our national work would not be finished "in the first thousand days, nor in the life of this administration, nor even perhaps in our lifetime on this planet. But," he said, "let us begin."

Today, in this moment of new resolve, I would say to all my fellow Americans, let us continue.

This is our challenge—not to hesitate, not to pause, not to turn about and linger over this evil moment, but to continue on our course so that we may fulfill the destiny that history has set for us. Our most immediate tasks are here on this Hill.

"An assassin's bullet has thrust upon me the awesome burden of the Presidency."

First, no memorial oration or eulogy could more eloquently honor President Kennedy's memory than the earliest possible passage of the civil rights bill for which he fought so long. We have talked long enough in this country about equal rights. We have talked for one hundred years or more. It is time now to write the next chapter, and to write it in the books of law.

I urge you again, as I did in 1957 and again in 1960, to enact a civil rights law so that we can move forward to eliminate from this Nation every trace of discrimination and oppression that is based upon race or color. There could be no greater source of strength to this Nation both at home and abroad.

And second, no act of ours could more fittingly continue the work of President Kennedy than the early passage of the tax bill for which he fought all this long year. This is a bill designed to increase our national income and Federal revenues, and to provide insurance against recession. That bill, if passed without delay, means more security for those now working, more jobs for those now without them, and more incentive for our economy.

"Let us continue."

In short, this is no time for delay. It is a time for action—strong, forward-looking action on the pending education bills to help bring the light of learning to every home and hamlet in America—strong, forward-looking action on youth employment opportunities; strong, forward-looking action on the pending foreign aid bill, making clear that we are not forfeiting our responsibilities to this hemisphere or to the world, nor erasing Executive flexibility in the conduct of our foreign affairs—and strong, prompt, and forward-looking action on the remaining appropriation bills.

In this new spirit of action, the Congress can expect the full cooperation and support of the executive branch. And in particular, I pledge that the expenditures of your Government will be administered with the utmost thrift and frugality. I will insist that the Government get a dollar's value for a dollar spent. The Government will set an example of prudence and economy. This does not mean that we will not meet out unfilled needs or that we will not honor our commitments. We will do both.

As one who has long served in both Houses of the Congress, I firmly believe in the independence and the integrity of the legislative branch. And I promise you that I shall always respect this. It is deep in the marrow of my bones. With equal firmness, I believe in the capacity and I believe in the ability of the Congress, despite the divisions of opinions which characterize our Nation, to act—to act wisely, to act vigorously, to act speedily when the need arises.

"Let us here highly resolve that John Fitzgerald Kennedy did not live—or die—in vain."

The need is here. The need is now. I ask your help.

We meet in grief, but let us also meet in renewed dedication and renewed vigor. Let us meet in action, in tolerance, and in mutual understanding. John Kennedy's death commands what his life conveyed—that America must move forward. The time has come for Americans of all races and creeds and political beliefs to understand and to respect one another. So let us put an end to the teaching and the preaching of hate and evil and violence. Let us turn away from the fanatics of the far left and the far right, from the apostles of bitterness and bigotry, from those defiant of law, and those who pour venom into our Nation's bloodstream.

I profoundly hope that the tragedy and the torment of these terrible days will bind us together in new fellowship, making us one people in our hour of sorrow. So let us here highly resolve that John Fitzgerald Kennedy did not live—or die—in vain. And on this Thanksgiving eve, as we gather together to ask the Lord's blessing, and give Him our thanks, let us unite in those familiar and cherished words:

America, America,
God shed His grace on thee,
And crown thy good
With brotherhood
From sea to shining sea.

192

28

"WE SHALL OVERCOME"

ON MARCH 7, 1965, a line of civil rights marchers approached the Edmund Pettus Bridge in Selma, Alabama, slowly singing the anthem of protest, "We Shall Overcome." Inspired by Reverend Dr. Martin Luther King Jr., they were walking to the state capitol in Birmingham demanding the right to vote. Police assaulted the marchers, flailing with billy clubs. The ugly scene flashed around the country on television.

An eruption of nationwide horror gave Lyndon Johnson his chance. In 1964, he had won passage of the Civil Rights Act, overcoming a southern filibuster for the first time in Senate history, but wanted to wait before submitting voting rights legislation. Now Johnson deftly allowed pressure to build. Pickets ringed the White House, demanding action, but he resisted their calls. "If I just send in federal troops with their big black boots and rifles, it'll look like Reconstruction all over again," he told aides. Then Alabama Governor George Wallace, a virulent segregationist, asked for a meeting. In the Oval Office, as later recounted by speechwriter Richard Goodwin, Johnson browbeat Wallace for two hours:

> Now listen, George, don't think about 1968; you think about 1988. You and me, we'll be dead and gone then, George. Now you've got a lot of poor people down there in Alabama, a lot of ignorant people. You can do a lot for them, George. Your president will help you. What do you want left after when you die? Do you want a Great...Big...Marble monument that reads, 'George Wallace—He Built'?...Or do you want a little piece of scrawny pine board lying across that harsh, caliche soil, that reads, 'George Wallace—He Hated'?

Wallace meekly agreed to ask for federal help. (He told reporters, "Hell, if I'd stayed in there much longer, he'd have had me coming out for civil rights.") Johnson quickly arranged to be invited to speak before a joint session of Congress.

Arriving at work late the next morning, Richard Goodwin was met by a frantic presidential aide, Jack Valenti. A different writer had been assigned the speech, and when Johnson found out, he exploded: he wanted the passionate Goodwin. "Don't you know a liberal Jew has his hand on the pulse of America?" he roared. Goodwin had eight hours to produce a first and final draft. As soon as each page was taken from his typewriter, it was immediately brought to Johnson. There was no time for editing and no time to feed the text to the teleprompter. Goodwin recalled in his memoir, *Remembering America*, that the president called him to remind him to write about Johnson's days teaching Mexican-Americans in his first job after college. "It never even occurred to me in my fondest dreams that I might have the chance to help the sons and daughters of those students and to help people like them all over this country," Johnson would say. "But now I do have that chance—and I'll let you in on a secret—I mean to use it."

Johnson was legendarily persuasive in private, but his public style was often wooden and bombastic. This time his slow southern solemnity seemed appropriate. He linked the civil rights struggle to the nation's basic values, and outlined a voting rights bill he would now send to Congress. "It is not just Negroes, but really it is all of us, who must overcome the crippling legacy of bigotry and injustice."

Johnson paused; he later remembered that images of the protestors flashed through his mind as he opened his arms wide and said: "And…we…shall…overcome."

Lawmakers gasped and then cheered as they realized the southern president had adopted the protest hymn as his own. Tears streamed down the face of the Senate majority leader. Watching at the home of a supporter in Selma, Martin Luther King Jr. wept as well.

Doris Kearns Goodwin astutely wrote, "It had been that rare thing in politics, rarer still for Lyndon Johnson—a speech that shaped the course of events. For once, Americans would honor him for a greatness of spirit as well as a mastery of technique. For on this issue he was more than a giver of gifts; he had become a moral leader."

Two weeks later, protected by federal troops, King led hundreds of marchers to the state capitol in Montgomery, Alabama. Johnson signed the Voting Rights Act into law on August 6, 1965. As he did, he told his press secretary Bill Moyers, "We just lost the South." Johnson was right: the shift of anti–civil rights white southerners to the Republican Party did produce presidential victories for the GOP for most of the next thirty years. At the same time, voting rights changed American politics. In Alabama in 1965, only 19 percent of blacks were registered to vote; by 1988, 68 percent were. In Mississippi, black voter registration rates increased tenfold. And while in 1964, no blacks sat in the state legislatures of the deep South, by 1992 nearly three hundred did. For all the remaining problems, the Voting Rights law worked.

A family watches Johnson's televised address to Congress on the black right to vote

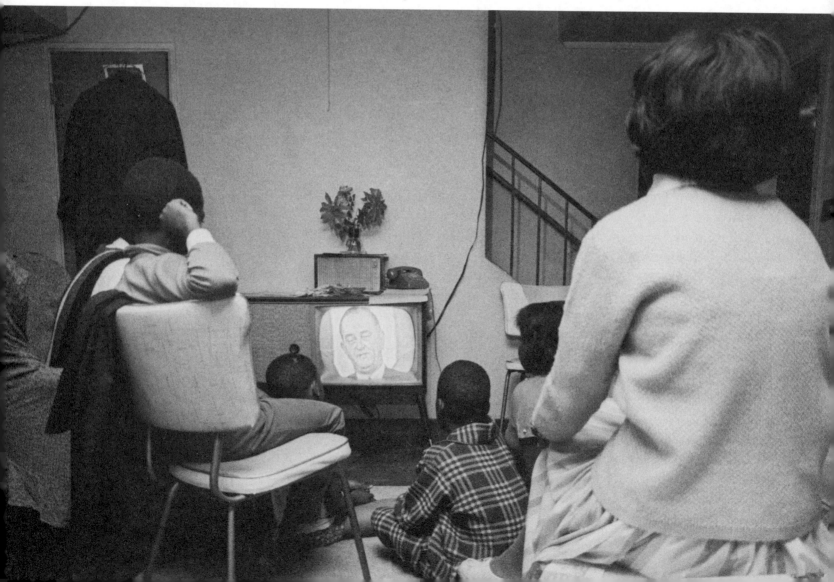

Lyndon B. Johnson's
ADDRESS TO CONGRESS
ON VOTING RIGHTS

Washington, D.C. • March 15, 1965

disc 2
track 5

Mr. Speaker, Mr. President, Members of the Congress:

I speak tonight for the dignity of man and the destiny of democracy.

I urge every member of both parties, Americans of all religions and of all colors, from every section of this country, to join me in that cause.

At times history and fate meet at a single time in a single place to shape a turning point in man's unending search for freedom. So it was at Lexington and Concord. So it was a century ago at Appomattox. So it was last week in Selma, Alabama.

There, long-suffering men and women peacefully protested the denial of their rights as Americans. Many were brutally assaulted. One good man, a man of God, was killed.

There is no cause for pride in what has happened in Selma. There is no cause for self-satisfaction in the long denial of equal rights of millions of Americans. But there is cause for hope and for faith in our democracy in what is happening here tonight.

For the cries of pain and the hymns and protests of oppressed people have summoned into convocation all the majesty of this great Government—the Government of the greatest Nation on earth.

Our mission is at once the oldest and the most basic of this country: to right wrong, to do justice, to serve man.

> *"At times history and fate meet at a single time in a single place to shape a turning point in man's unending search for freedom."*

In our time we have come to live with moments of great crisis. Our lives have been marked with debate about great issues; issues of war and peace, issues of prosperity and depression. But rarely in any time does an issue lay bare the secret heart of America itself. Rarely are we met with a challenge, not to our growth or abundance, our welfare or our security, but rather to the values and the purposes and the meaning of our beloved Nation.

> *"Should we defeat every enemy, should we double our wealth and conquer the stars, and still be unequal to this issue, then we will have failed as a people and as a nation."*

The issue of equal rights for American Negroes is such an issue. And should we defeat every enemy, should we double our wealth and conquer the stars, and still be unequal to this issue, then we will have failed as a people and as a nation.

For with a country as with a person, "What is a man profited, if he shall gain the whole world, and lose his own soul?"

There is no Negro problem. There is no Southern problem. There is no Northern problem. There is only an American problem. And we are met here tonight as Americans—not as Democrats or Republicans—we are met here as Americans to solve that problem.

This was the first nation in the history of the world to be founded with a purpose. The great phrases of that purpose still sound in every American heart, North and South: "All men are created equal"—"government by consent of the governed"—"give me liberty or give me death." Well, those are not just clever words, or those are not just empty theories. In their name Americans have fought and died for two centuries, and tonight around the world they stand there as guardians of our liberty, risking their lives.

Those words are a promise to every citizen that he shall share in the dignity of man. This dignity cannot be found in a man's possessions; it cannot be found in his power, or in his position. It really rests on his right to be treated as a man equal in opportunity to all others. It says that he shall share in freedom, he shall choose his leaders, educate his children, and provide for his family according to his ability and his merits as a human being.

> ## "About this there can and should be no argument. Every American citizen must have an equal right to vote."

To apply any other test—to deny a man his hopes because of his color or race, his religion or the place of his birth—is not only to do injustice, it is to deny America and to dishonor the dead who gave their lives for American freedom.

THE RIGHT TO VOTE

Our fathers believed that if this noble view of the rights of man was to flourish, it must be rooted in democracy. The most basic right of all was the right to choose your own leaders. The history of this country, in large measure, is the history of the expansion of that right to all of our people.

Many of the issues of civil rights are very complex and most difficult. But about this there can and should be no argument. Every American citizen must have an equal right

to vote. There is no reason which can excuse the denial of that right. There is no duty which weighs more heavily on us than the duty we have to ensure that right.

Yet the harsh fact is that in many places in this country men and women are kept from voting simply because they are Negroes.

Every device of which human ingenuity is capable has been used to deny this right. The Negro citizen may go to register only to be told that the day is wrong, or the hour is late, or the official in charge is absent. And if he persists, and if he manages to present himself to the registrar, he may be disqualified because he did not spell out his middle name or because he abbreviated a word on the application.

And if he manages to fill out an application he is given a test. The registrar is the sole judge of whether he passes this test. He may be asked to recite the entire Constitution, or explain the most complex provisions of State law. And even a college degree cannot be used to prove that he can read and write.

For the fact is that the only way to pass these barriers is to show a white skin.

Experience has clearly shown that the existing process of law cannot overcome systematic and ingenious discrimination. No law that we now have on the books—and I have helped to put three of them there—can ensure the right to

President Johnson and Martin Luther King Jr. after Johnson has signed the voter rights bill. At center is Indiana Representative Ray Madden.

vote when local officials are determined to deny it.

In such a case our duty must be clear to all of us. The Constitution says that no person shall be kept from voting because of his race or his color. We have all sworn an oath before God to support and to defend that Constitution. We must now act in obedience to that oath.

"This bill will strike down restrictions to voting in all elections...which have been used to deny Negroes the right to vote."

GUARANTEEING THE RIGHT TO VOTE

Wednesday I will send to Congress a law designed to eliminate illegal barriers to the right to vote.

The broad principles of that bill will be in the hands of the Democratic and Republican leaders tomorrow. After they have reviewed it, it will come here formally as a bill. I am grateful for this opportunity to come here tonight at the invitation of the leadership to reason with my friends, to give them my views, and to visit with my former colleagues.

I have had prepared a more comprehensive analysis of the legislation which I had intended to transmit to the clerk tomorrow but which I will submit to the clerks tonight. But I want to really discuss with you now briefly the main proposals of this legislation.

This bill will strike down restrictions to voting in all elections—Federal, State, and local—which have been used to deny Negroes the right to vote.

This bill will establish a simple, uniform standard which cannot be used, however ingenious the effort, to flout our Constitution.

It will provide for citizens to be registered by officials of the United States Government if the State officials refuse to register them.

It will eliminate tedious, unnecessary lawsuits which delay the right to vote.

"Outside chamber is the outraged conscience of a nation."

Finally, this legislation will ensure that properly registered individuals are not prohibited from voting.

I will welcome the suggestions from all of the Members of Congress—I have no doubt that I will get some—on ways and means to strengthen this law and to make it effective. But experience has plainly shown that this is the only path to carry out the command of the Constitution.

To those who seek to avoid action by their National Government in their own communities; who want to and who seek to maintain purely local control over elections, the answer is simple:

Open your polling places to all your people.

Allow men and women to register and vote whatever the color of their skin.

Extend the rights of citizenship to every citizen of this land.

THE NEED FOR ACTION

There is no constitutional issue here. The command of the Constitution is plain.

There is no moral issue. It is wrong—deadly wrong—to deny any of your fellow Americans the right to vote in this country.

There is no issue of States rights or national rights. There is only the struggle for human rights.

I have not the slightest doubt what will be your answer.

The last time a President sent a civil rights bill to the Congress it contained a provision to protect voting rights in Federal elections. That civil rights bill was passed after 8 long months of debate. And when that bill came to my desk from the Congress for my signature, the heart of the voting provision had been eliminated.

This time, on this issue, there must be no delay, no hesitation and no compromise with our purpose.

We cannot, we must not, refuse to protect the right of every American to vote in every election that he may desire to participate in. And we ought not and we cannot and we must not wait another 8 months before we get a bill. We have already waited a hundred years and more, and the time for waiting is gone.

So I ask you to join me in working long hours—nights and weekends, if necessary—to pass this bill. And I don't make that request lightly. For from the window where I sit with the problems of our country I recognize that outside this chamber is the outraged conscience of a nation, the grave concern of many nations, and the harsh judgment of history on our acts.

WE SHALL OVERCOME

But even if we pass this bill, the battle will not be over. What happened in Selma is part of a far larger movement which reaches into every section and State of America. It is the effort of American Negroes to secure for themselves the full blessings of American life.

Their cause must be our cause too. Because it is not just Negroes, but really it is all of us, who must overcome the crippling legacy of bigotry and injustice.

And we shall overcome.

As a man whose roots go deeply into Southern soil I know how agonizing racial feelings are. I know how difficult it is to reshape the attitudes and the structure of our society.

But a century has passed, more than a hundred years, since the Negro was freed. And he is not fully free tonight.

It was more than a hundred years ago that Abraham Lincoln, a great President of another party, signed the Emancipation Proclamation, but emancipation is a proclamation and not a fact.

A century has passed, more than a hundred years, since equality was promised. And yet the Negro is not equal.

A century has passed since the day of promise. And the promise is unkept.

The time of justice has now come. I tell you that I believe sincerely that no force can hold it back. It is right in the eyes of man and God that it should come. And when it does, I think that day will brighten the lives of every American.

For Negroes are not the only victims. How many white children have gone uneducated, how many white families have lived in stark poverty, how many white lives have been scarred by fear, because we have wasted our energy and our substance to maintain the barriers of hatred and terror?

So I say to all of you here, and to all in the Nation tonight, that those who appeal to you to hold on to the past do so at the cost of denying you your future.

This great, rich, restless country can offer opportunity and education and hope to all: black and white, North and South, sharecropper and city dweller. These are the enemies: poverty, ignorance, disease. They are the enemies and not our fellow man, not our neighbor. And these enemies too, poverty, disease and ignorance, we shall overcome.

AN AMERICAN PROBLEM

Now let none of us in any sections look with prideful righteousness on the troubles in another section, or on the problems of our neighbors. There is really no part of America where the promise of equality has been fully kept. In Buffalo as well as in Birmingham, in Philadelphia as well as in Selma, Americans are struggling for the fruits of freedom.

This is one Nation. What happens in Selma or in Cincinnati is a matter of legitimate concern to every American. But let each of us look within our own hearts and our own communities, and let each of us put our shoulder to the wheel to root out injustice wherever it exists.

As we meet here in this peaceful, historic chamber tonight, men from the South, some of whom were at Iwo Jima, men from the North who have carried Old Glory to far corners of the world and brought it back without a stain on it, men from the East and from the West, are all fighting together without regard to religion, or color, or region, in Viet-Nam. Men from every region fought for us across the world 20 years ago.

And in these common dangers and these common sacrifices the South made its contribution of honor and gallantry no less than any other region of the great Republic—and in some instances, a great many of them, more.

Lyndon B. Johnson

And I have not the slightest doubt that good men from everywhere in this country, from the Great Lakes to the Gulf of Mexico, from the Golden Gate to the harbors along the Atlantic, will rally together now in this cause to vindicate the freedom of all Americans. For all of us owe this duty; and I believe that all of us will respond to it.

Your President makes that request of every American.

PROGRESS THROUGH THE DEMOCRATIC PROCESS

The real hero of this struggle is the American Negro. His actions and protests, his courage to risk safety and even to risk his life, have awakened the conscience of this Nation. His demonstrations have been designed to call attention to injustice, designed to provoke change, designed to stir reform.

He has called upon us to make good the promise of America. And who among us can say that we would have made the same progress were it not for his persistent bravery, and his faith in American democracy.

For at the real heart of battle for equality is a deep seated belief in the democratic process. Equality depends not on the force of arms or tear gas but upon the force of moral right; not on recourse to violence but on respect for law and order.

There have been many pressures upon your President and there will be others as the days come and go. But I pledge you tonight that we intend to fight this battle where it should be fought: in the courts, and in the Congress, and in the hearts of men.

We must preserve the right of free speech and the right of free assembly. But the right of free speech does not carry with it, as has been said, the right to holler fire in a crowded theater. We must preserve the right to free assembly, but free assembly does not carry with it the right to block public thoroughfares to traffic.

We do have a right to protest, and a right to march under conditions that do not infringe the constitutional rights of our neighbors. And I intend to protect all those rights as long as I am permitted to serve in this office.

Selma police, Alabama state patrolmen, and Dallas County deputies block the road out of a black neighborhood in Selma. Civil rights marchers, planning to march to Montgomery, wait in the neighborhood for President Johnson to call in the army for protection.

Dr. Martin Luther King Jr. leads thousands of civil rights demonstrators on the last leg of their Selma to Montgomery 50-mile hike, March 26, 1965

We will guard against violence, knowing it strikes from our hands the very weapons which we seek—progress, obedience to law, and belief in American values.

In Selma as elsewhere we seek and pray for peace. We seek order. We seek unity. But we will not accept the peace of stifled rights, or the order imposed by fear, or the unity that stifles protest. For peace cannot be purchased at the cost of liberty.

In Selma tonight, as in every—and we had a good day there—as in every city, we are working for just and peaceful settlement. We must all remember that after this speech I am making tonight, after the police and the FBI and the Marshals have all gone, and after you have promptly passed this bill, the people of Selma and the other cities of the Nation must still live and work together. And when the attention of the Nation has gone elsewhere they must try to heal the wounds and to build a new community.

This cannot be easily done on a battleground of violence, as the history of the South itself shows. It is in recognition of this that men of both races have shown such an outstandingly impressive responsibility in recent days—last Tuesday, again today.

RIGHTS MUST BE OPPORTUNITIES

The bill that I am presenting to you will be known as a civil rights bill. But, in a larger sense, most of the program I am recommending is a civil rights program. Its object is to open the city of hope to all people of all races.

Because all Americans just must have the right to vote. And we are going to give them that right.

All Americans must have the privileges of citizenship regardless of race. And they are going to have those privileges of citizenship regardless of race.

> *"It is not just Negroes, but really it is all of us, who must overcome the crippling legacy of bigotry and injustice. And we shall overcome."*

But I would like to caution you and remind you that to exercise these privileges takes much more than just legal right. It requires a trained mind and a healthy body. It requires a decent home, and the chance to find a job, and the opportunity to escape from the clutches of poverty.

Of course, people cannot contribute to the Nation if they are never taught to read or write, if their bodies are stunted from hunger, if their sickness goes untended, if their life is spent in hopeless poverty just drawing a welfare check.

So we want to open the gates to opportunity. But we are also going to give all our people black and white, the help that they need to walk through those gates.

THE PURPOSE OF THIS GOVERNMENT

My first job after college was as a teacher in Cotulla, Tex., in a small Mexican-American school. Few of them could speak English, and I couldn't speak much Spanish. My students were poor and they often came to class without breakfast, hungry. They knew even in their youth the pain of prejudice. They never seemed to know why people disliked them. But they knew it was so, because I saw it in their eyes. I often walked home late in the afternoon, after the classes were finished, wishing there was more that I could do. But all I knew was to teach them the little that I knew, hoping that it might help them against the hardships that lay ahead.

Somehow you never forget what poverty and hatred can do when you see its scars on the hopeful face of a young child.

I never thought then, in 1928, that I would be standing here in 1965. It never even occurred to me in my fondest dreams that I might have the chance to help the sons and daughters of those students and to help people like them all over this country.

But now I do have that chance—and I'll let you in on a secret—I mean to use it. And I hope that you will use it with me.

This is the richest and most powerful country which ever occupied the globe. The might of past empires is little compared to ours. But I do not want to be the President who built empires, or sought grandeur, or extended dominion.

I want to be the President who educated young children to the wonders of their world. I want to be the President who helped to feed the hungry and to prepare them to be taxpayers instead of taxeaters.

I want to be the President who helped the poor to find their own way and who protected the right of every citizen to vote in every election.

I want to be the President who helped to end hatred among his fellow men and who promoted love among the people of all races and all regions and all parties.

I want to be the President who helped to end war among the brothers of this earth.

And so at the request of your beloved Speaker and the Senator from Montana; the majority leader, the Senator from Illinois; the minority leader, Mr. McCulloch, and other Members of both parties, I came here tonight—not as President Roosevelt came down one time in person to veto a bonus bill, not as President Truman came down one time to urge the passage of a railroad bill—but I came down here to ask you to share this task with me and to share it with the people that we both work for. I want this to be the Congress,

Republicans and Democrats alike, which did all these things for all these people.

Beyond this great chamber, out yonder in 50 States, are the people that we serve. Who can tell what deep and unspoken hopes are in their hearts tonight as they sit there and

"But now I do have that chance—and I'll let you in on a secret—I mean to use it."

listen. We all can guess, from our own lives, how difficult they often find their own pursuit of happiness, how many problems each little family has. They look most of all to themselves for their futures. But I think that they also look to each of us.

Above the pyramid on the great seal of the United States it says—in Latin—"God has favored our undertaking."

God will not favor everything that we do. It is rather our duty to divine His will. But I cannot help believing that He truly understands and that He really favors the undertaking that we begin here tonight.

29

LYNDON B. JOHNSON

"I SHALL NOT SEEK, AND I WILL NOT ACCEPT, THE NOMINATION OF MY PARTY"

THE VIETNAM WAR was agony for America, for Vietnam, and for Lyndon Johnson. John F. Kennedy had sent sixteen thousand "advisors" to South Vietnam, to help that government combat a communist insurgency. His successor, bound to Kennedy's policies and fearful that a loss in Vietnam would turn Asia to the communists, slowly increased the commitment. In 1965, the United States began to bomb North Vietnam, an assault that lasted with few interruptions for three years. Johnson grew obsessed with the war, worrying about the safety of troops and personally picking targets. But he also chose to deceive the public about the cost of the conflict and the depth of the government's commitment, creating what was known as a "credibility gap."

Protest mounted on college campuses, at the Pentagon, and in the streets. Chants taunted: "Hey, Hey, LBJ /

How many kids did you kill today?" The government still argued we were winning (that, in General William Westmoreland's memorable phrase, we could see "the light at the end of the tunnel"), and most Americans believed those claims. Then, in February 1968, during the lunar new year of Tet, communist guerillas attacked throughout South Vietnam. They even broke into the American embassy. Later that month, Johnson nearly lost the New Hampshire Democratic presidential primary to Eugene McCarthy. Then what he described as "a nightmare" came true: Robert F. Kennedy, the slain president's brother, announced his own challenge.

The military urgently asked for two hundred thousand new troops, and Johnson decided to make a major television speech three weeks hence to announce his intentions

Johnson before a press conference

for the war. This was another instance when the writing of a major speech forced a president to reassess and change policy. Clark Clifford, the silky Washington lawyer who had helped draft the Truman Doctrine, was newly installed as secretary of defense. He was determined to steer Johnson from further involvement in Vietnam. Clifford brought in the "Wise Men"—foreign policy mandarins who had served in earlier administrations—who now counseled Johnson to seek peace. Johnson fumed at what he saw as the cowardice of the Establishment, but their pessimism about the war's course had its desired impact. Still, most of Johnson's current aides were for expanding America's commitment in Vietnam.

Clifford found an ally in White House speechwriter Harry McPherson. Together, Clifford recalled, they "agreed to make an all-out effort to soften the speech and turn it around." McPherson prepared two drafts—a speech defending the war, and one launching a peace initiative and halting the bombing. One began, "I speak to you tonight in a time of grave challenge to our country." The other started, "Tonight I want to speak to you of the prospects for peace in Vietnam and Southeast Asia." The next morning, Johnson phoned McPherson and began discussing changes. The writer realized that the president had chosen to edit the peace draft. When the call was over, he phoned Clifford. "We've won," he shouted. "The president is working from our draft!"

When Johnson spoke, his old colleagues who saw him on television were shocked. "The face was deeply lined and sagging," one wrote, "the drawl occasionally cracked and wavered." He announced a halt to attacks on nearly all of North Vietnam, other than the "demilitarized zone" near the border. Johnson had told McPherson not to spend too much effort on the speech's peroration. "I may even add one of my own," he said slyly. After a half hour discussing the war, he looked at his wife, Lady Bird, and raised his arm in a prearranged signal. Clued-in aides phoned political leaders to tell them the news. "With America's sons in the fields far away, with America's future under challenge right here at home, with our hopes and the world's hopes for peace in the balance every day, I do not believe that I should devote an hour or a day of my time to any personal partisan causes," he said. He would not run for reelection. It was so shocking, so unexpected, that the scene was transformed. Two days later, the U.S. and North Vietnam agreed to begin peace talks.

Johnson was euphoric, but that joy was short-lived. Five days later, an assassin killed Martin Luther King Jr. in Memphis. Cities burned. In June, on the night he won the California presidential primary, Robert Kennedy was murdered. The Democratic convention in Chicago fractured in a riot as police clubbed protestors outside the hotels where delegates were staying. Johnson could not even attend for fear of being booed. Peace talks dragged on, and in the end, they were sabotaged by presidential candidate Richard Nixon, whose supporters convinced South Vietnamese leaders they would get a better deal with a new administration. The war would continue for another four years.

Lyndon B. Johnson's

SPEECH ON THE VIETNAM WAR

Washington, D.C. • March 31, 1968

hear...
disc 2
track 6

Good evening, my fellow Americans:

Tonight I want to speak to you of peace in Vietnam and Southeast Asia.

No other question so preoccupies our people. No other dream so absorbs the 250 million human beings who live in that part of the world. No other goal motivates American policy in Southeast Asia.

For years, representatives of our Government and others have traveled the world—seeking to find a basis for peace talks.

Since last September, they have carried the offer that I made public at San Antonio.

That offer was this:

That the United States would stop its bombardment of North Vietnam when that would lead promptly to productive discussions—and that we would assume that North Vietnam would not take military advantage of our restraint.

Hanoi denounced this offer, both privately and publicly. Even while the search for peace was going on, North Vietnam rushed their preparations for a savage assault on the people, the government, and the allies of South Vietnam.

"Tonight I want to speak to you of peace in Vietnam and Southeast Asia."

Their attack—during the Tet holidays—failed to achieve its principal objectives.

It did not collapse the elected government of South Vietnam or shatter its army—as the Communists had hoped.

It did not produce a "general uprising" among the people of the cities as they had predicted.

The Communists were unable to maintain control of any of the more than 30 cities that they attacked. And they took very heavy casualties.

But they did compel the South Vietnamese and their allies to move certain forces from the countryside into the cities.

"There is no need to delay the talks that could bring an end to this long and this bloody war."

They caused widespread disruption and suffering. Their attacks, and the battles that followed, made refugees of half a million human beings.

The Communists may renew their attack any day.

They are, it appears, trying to make 1968 the year of decision in South Vietnam—the year that brings, if not final victory or defeat, at least a turning point in the struggle.

This much is clear:

If they do mount another round of heavy attacks, they will not succeed in destroying the fighting power of South Vietnam and its allies.

But tragically, this is also clear: Many men—on both sides of the struggle—will be lost. A nation that has already suffered 20 years of warfare will suffer once again. Armies on both sides will take new casualties. And the war will go on.

There is no need for this to be so.

There is no need to delay the talks that could bring an end to this long and this bloody war.

Tonight, I renew the offer I made last August—to stop the bombardment of North Vietnam. We ask that talks begin promptly, that they be serious talks on the substance of peace. We assume that during those talks Hanoi will not take advantage of our restraint.

We are prepared to move immediately toward peace through negotiations.

So, tonight, in the hope that this action will lead to early talks, I am taking the first step to deescalate the conflict. We are reducing—substantially reducing—the present level of hostilities.

And we are doing so unilaterally, and at once.

Tonight, I have ordered our aircraft and our naval vessels to make no attacks on North Vietnam, except in the area north of the demilitarized zone where the continuing enemy buildup directly threatens allied forward positions and where the movements of their troops and supplies are clearly related to that threat.

The area in which we are stopping our attacks includes almost 90 percent of North Vietnam's population, and most of its territory. Thus there will be no attacks around the principal populated areas, or in the food-producing areas of North Vietnam.

Even this very limited bombing of the North could come to an early end—if our restraint is matched by restraint in Hanoi. But I cannot in good conscience stop all bombing so long as to do so would immediately and directly endanger the lives of our men and our allies. Whether a complete bombing halt becomes possible in the future will be determined by events.

Our purpose in this action is to bring about a reduction in the level of violence that now exists.

Johnson addresses the nation, March 31, 1968

It is to save the lives of brave men—and to save the lives of innocent women and children. It is to permit the contending forces to move closer to a political settlement.

And tonight, I call upon the United Kingdom and I call upon the Soviet Union—as cochairmen of the Geneva Conferences, and as permanent members of the United Nations Security Council—to do all they can to move from the unilateral act of deescalation that I have just announced toward genuine peace in Southeast Asia.

"One day, my fellow citizens, there will be peace in Southeast Asia."

Now, as in the past, the United States is ready to send its representatives to any forum, at any time, to discuss the means of bringing this ugly war to an end.

I am designating one of our most distinguished Americans, Ambassador Averell Harriman, as my personal representative for such talks. In addition, I have asked Ambassador Llewellyn Thompson, who returned from Moscow for consultation, to be available to join Ambassador Harriman at Geneva or any other suitable place—just as soon as Hanoi agrees to a conference.

I call upon President Ho Chi Minh to respond positively, and favorably, to this new step toward peace.

But if peace does not come now through negotiations, it will come when Hanoi understands that our common resolve is unshakable, and our common strength is invincible.

Tonight, we and the other allied nations are contributing 600,000 fighting men to assist 700,000 South Vietnamese troops in defending their little country.

Our presence there has always rested on this basic belief: The main burden of preserving their freedom must be carried out by them—by the South Vietnamese themselves.

We and our allies can only help to provide a shield behind which the people of South Vietnam can survive and can grow and develop. On their efforts—on their determination and resourcefulness—the outcome will ultimately depend.

That small, beleaguered nation has suffered terrible punishment for more than 20 years.

I pay tribute once again tonight to the great courage and endurance of its people. South Vietnam supports armed forces tonight of almost 700,000 men—and I call your attention to the fact that this is the equivalent of more than 10 million in our own population. Its people maintain their firm determination to be free of domination by the North.

There has been substantial progress, I think, in building a durable government during these last 3 years. The South Vietnam of 1965 could not have survived the enemy's Tet offensive of 1968. The elected government of South Vietnam survived that attack—and is rapidly repairing the devastation that it wrought.

The South Vietnamese know that further efforts are going to be required:
—to expand their own armed forces,
—to move back into the countryside as quickly as possible,
—to increase their taxes,
—to select the very best men that they have for civil and military responsibility
—to achieve a new unity within their constitutional government, and
—to include in the national effort all those groups who wish to preserve South Vietnam's control over its own destiny.

"As in times before, it is true that a house divided against itself by the spirit of faction, of party, of region, of religion, of race, is a house that cannot stand."

Last week President Thieu ordered the mobilization of 135,000 additional South Vietnamese. He plans to reach—as soon as possible—a total military strength of more than 800,000 men.

To achieve this, the Government of South Vietnam started the drafting of 19-year-olds on March 1st. On May 1st, the Government will begin the drafting of 18-year-olds.

Last month, 10,000 men volunteered for military service—that was two and a half times the number of volunteers during the same month last year. Since the middle of January, more than 48,000 South Vietnamese have joined the armed forces—and nearly half of them volunteered to do so.

All men in the South Vietnamese armed forces have had their tours of duty extended for the duration of the war, and reserves are now being called up for immediate active duty.

President Thieu told his people last week:

"We must make greater efforts and accept more sacrifices because, as I have said many times, this is our country. The existence of our nation is at stake, and this is mainly a Vietnamese responsibility."

He warned his people that a major national effort is required to root out corruption and incompetence at all levels of government.

We applaud this evidence of determination on the part of South Vietnam. Our first priority will be to support their effort....

One day, my fellow citizens, there will be peace in Southeast Asia.

> *"I do not believe that I should devote an hour or a day of my time to any personal partisan causes or to any duties other than the awesome duties of this office."*

It will come because the people of Southeast Asia want it—those whose armies are at war tonight, and those who, though threatened, have thus far been spared.

Peace will come because Asians were willing to work for it—and to sacrifice for it—and to die by the thousands for it.

But let it never be forgotten: Peace will come also because America sent her sons to help secure it.

It has not been easy—far from it. During the past four and a half years, it has been my fate and my responsibility to be Commander in Chief. I have lived—daily and nightly—with the cost of this war. I know the pain that it has inflicted. I know, perhaps better than anyone, the misgivings that it has aroused.

Throughout this entire, long period, I have been sustained by a single principle: that what we are doing now, in Vietnam, is vital not only to the security of Southeast Asia, but it is vital to the security of every American.

Surely we have treaties which we must respect. Surely we have commitments that we are going to keep. Resolutions of the Congress testify to the need to resist aggression in the world and in Southeast Asia.

But the heart of our involvement in South Vietnam—under three different Presidents, three separate administrations—has always been America's own security.

And the larger purpose of our involvement has always been to help the nations of Southeast Asia become independent and stand alone, self-sustaining, as members of a great world community—at peace with themselves, and at peace with all others.

With such an Asia, our country—and the world—will be far more secure than it is tonight.

I believe that a peaceful Asia is far nearer to reality because of what America has done in Vietnam. I believe that the men who endure the dangers of battle—fighting there for us tonight—are helping the entire world avoid far greater conflicts, far wider wars, far more destruction, than this one.

The peace that will bring them home someday will come. Tonight I have offered the first in what I hope will be a series of mutual moves toward peace.

I pray that it will not be rejected by the leaders of North Vietnam. I pray that they will accept it as a means by which the sacrifices of their own people may be ended. And I ask your help and your support, my fellow citizens, for this effort to reach across the battlefield toward an early peace.

Finally, my fellow Americans, let me say this:

Of those to whom much is given, much is asked. I cannot say and no man could say that no more will be asked of us.

Yet, I believe that now, no less than when the decade began, this generation of Americans is willing to "pay any price, bear any burden, meet any hardship, support any friend, oppose any foe to assure the survival and the success of liberty."

Since those words were spoken by John F. Kennedy, the people of America have kept that compact with mankind's noblest cause.

And we shall continue to keep it.

Yet, I believe that we must always be mindful of this one thing, whatever the trials and the tests ahead. The ultimate strength of our country and our cause will lie not in powerful weapons or infinite resources or boundless wealth, but will lie in the unity of our people.

This I believe very deeply.

Throughout my entire public career I have followed the personal philosophy that I am a free man, an American, a public servant, and a member of my party, in that order always and only.

For 37 years in the service of our Nation, first as a Congressman, as a Senator, and as Vice President, and now as your President, I have put the unity of the people first. I have put it ahead of any divisive partisanship.

And in these times as in times before, it is true that a house divided against itself by the spirit of faction, of party, of region, of religion, of race, is a house that cannot stand.

There is division in the American house now. There is divisiveness among us all tonight. And holding the trust that is mine, as President of all the people, I cannot disregard the peril to the progress of the American people and the hope and the prospect of peace for all peoples.

So, I would ask all Americans, whatever their personal interests or concern, to guard against divisiveness and all its ugly consequences.

Fifty-two months and 10 days ago, in a moment of tragedy and trauma, the duties of this office fell upon me. I asked then for your help and God's, that we might continue America on its course, binding up our wounds, healing our history,

moving forward in new unity, to clear the American agenda and to keep the American commitment for all of our people.

United we have kept that commitment. United we have enlarged that commitment.

Through all time to come, I think America will be a stronger nation, a more just society, and a land of greater opportunity and fulfillment because of what we have all done together in these years of unparalleled achievement.

Our reward will come in the life of freedom, peace, and hope that our children will enjoy through ages ahead.

> ## *"I shall not seek, and I will not accept, the nomination of my party for another term as your President."*

What we won when all of our people united just must not now be lost in suspicion, distrust, selfishness, and politics among any of our people.

Believing this as I do, I have concluded that I should not permit the Presidency to become involved in the partisan divisions that are developing in this political year.

With America's sons in the fields far away, with America's future under challenge right here at home, with our hopes and the world's hopes for peace in the balance every day, I do not believe that I should devote an hour or a day of my time to any personal partisan causes or to any duties other than the awesome duties of this office—the Presidency of your country.

Accordingly, I shall not seek, and I will not accept, the nomination of my party for another term as your President.

But let men everywhere know, however, that a strong, a confident, and a vigilant America stands ready tonight to seek an honorable peace—and stands ready tonight to defend an honored cause—whatever the price, whatever the burden, whatever the sacrifice that duty may require.

Thank you for listening.

Good night and God bless all of you.

Richard M.
NIXON

37TH PRESIDENT: 1969–1974

Born: January 9, 1913, in Yorba Linda, California
Died: April 22, 1994, in New York, New York

Disc 2, Tracks 7–8

30

"THE GREAT SILENT MAJORITY"

ON OCTOBER 15, 1969, twenty thousand antiwar protestors marched near the White House, singing, chanting, and carrying candles. That night, alone in his office, Richard Nixon was writing a major television address on Vietnam. Across the top of his yellow pad, he wrote: "Don't Get Rattled—Don't Waver—Don't React."

The upheaval of 1968 produced much abrupt change in America, but nothing more improbable than the election of Richard Nixon. After losing the presidency in 1960 and then the California governorship two years later, he told reporters, "This is my last press conference. You won't have Nixon to kick around anymore." But after riots and assassinations, he represented stability and a yearning for "law and order." Nixon hinted he had a plan to end the war in Vietnam, and narrowly defeated Vice President Hubert Humphrey.

In his first months in office, Nixon kept his intentions on Vietnam deliberately murky. Soon, however, the movement that had brought down Johnson now seemed ready to wash over Nixon. *Washington Post* columnist David Broder wrote, "The men and the movement that broke Lyndon Johnson's authority in 1968 are out to break Richard M. Nixon in 1969. The likelihood is great that they will succeed again, for breaking a president is, like most feats, easier to accomplish the second time around." Two days before the massive Vietnam Moratorium protest, Nixon announced he would make a major address. He would now reveal his course on Vietnam.

What would he say? November 1, 1969, was the anniversary of Johnson's bombing halt, and Nixon had set it as a deadline for diplomacy to pay off. His national security advisor, Henry Kissinger, asked his staff to plan a "savage, punishing blow" to win the war outright. At the same time, U.S. Senate majority leader Mike Mansfield sent Nixon a memo, warning, "The continuance of the war in Vietnam, in my judgment, endangers the future of this nation." Many inside and outside the White House assumed that was Nixon's choice: escalate or withdraw.

The president wrote the speech himself. "President Nixon was in his element," author and columnist Richard Reeves wrote. "Alone. Alone with his yellow pads and his thoughts." He once had told his speechwriter, William Safire, quoting Charles DeGaulle, "Silence is power." By keeping mute, he let suspense build. "I worked through the night," Nixon remembered. "About four A.M. I wrote a paragraph calling for the support of 'the great silent majority of Americans.' I went to bed, but after two hours of restless sleep I was wide awake, so I got up and began work again. By eight A.M. the speech was finished. I called [chief of staff H.R.] Haldeman, and when he answered, I said, 'The baby's just been born.'"

At eight P.M. on November 3, to a huge audience of seventy-two million people, Nixon spoke for half an hour about Vietnam. He revealed a series of failed diplomatic moves. He talked about the dangers of U.S. withdrawal. It became clear that Nixon, faced with the choice of sharp escalation or decisive withdrawal, had chosen…neither. American troops would remain, though in declining numbers. The war would continue as before.

Then, at the end of the speech, he turned to the demonstrators and the threat he believed they posed to the country. "North Vietnam cannot defeat or humiliate the United States. Only Americans can do that," he said. According to Safire, Nixon and Vice President Spiro Agnew had used the phrase "silent majority" before, with

little impact. Now the words signaled an all-out political assault, not on the North Vietnamese, but on the antiwar movement. His purpose was to polarize the debate and marginalize the opposition.

Within minutes, the White House began to orchestrate an outpouring of support. In his diary, Haldeman wrote of one plea from the president. "If only do one thing get 100 vicious dirty calls to *New York Times* and *Washington Post* about their editorials (even though no idea what they'll be)." Nixon piled supportive telegrams on his desk, declaring to photographers, "The great silent majority has spoken." Nixon had in fact tapped an inchoate opposition to

the peace movement and its excesses. The typical American was, in the influential words of political analysts Richard Scammon and Ben Wattenberg, "unyoung, unpoor, unblack." Nixon himself believed that this speech blunted the political momentum of the antiwar movement.

The war would drag on for another three and a half years, with thousands more American casualties. On January 23, 1973, President Nixon announced he had negotiated "peace with honor" in Vietnam. Two years later, the North Vietnamese swept across the south. The last Americans were evacuated by helicopter, and the U.S. involvement in Vietnam was over.

Richard M. Nixon's
ADDRESS TO THE NATION
ON VIETNAM

Washington, D.C. • November 3, 1969

hear...
disc 2
track 7

Good evening, my fellow Americans:

Tonight I want to talk to you on a subject of deep concern to all Americans and to many people in all parts of the world—the war in Vietnam.

I believe that one of the reasons for the deep division about Vietnam is that many Americans have lost confidence in what their Government has told them about our policy. The American people cannot and should not be asked to support a policy which involves the overriding issues of war and peace unless they know the truth about that policy.

Tonight, therefore, I would like to answer some of the questions that I know are on the minds of many of you listening to me.

How and why did America get involved in Vietnam in the first place?

How has this administration changed the policy of the previous administration?

What has really happened in the negotiations in Paris and on the battlefront in Vietnam?

What choices do we have if we are to end the war?

What are the prospects for peace?

Now, let me begin by describing the situation I found when I was inaugurated on January 20.

—The war had been going on for 4 years.

—31,000 Americans had been killed in action.

—The training program for the South Vietnamese was behind schedule.

—540,000 Americans were in Vietnam with no plans to reduce the number.

—No progress had been made at the negotiations in Paris and the United States had not put forth a comprehensive peace proposal.

—The war was causing deep division at home and criticism from many of our friends as well as our enemies abroad.

In view of these circumstances there were some who urged that I end the war at once by ordering the immediate withdrawal of all American forces.

> *"The American people cannot and should not be asked to support a policy which involves the overriding issues of war and peace unless they know the truth about that policy."*

From a political standpoint this would have been a popular and easy course to follow. After all, we became involved in the war while my predecessor was in office. I could blame the defeat which would be the result of my action on him and come out as the peacemaker. Some put it to me quite bluntly: This was the only way to avoid allowing Johnson's war to become Nixon's war.

But I had a greater obligation than to think only of the years of my administration and of the next election. I had to think of the effect of my decision on the next generation and on the future of peace and freedom in America and in the world.

Let us all understand that the question before us is not whether some Americans are for peace and some Americans are against peace. The question at issue is not whether Johnson's war becomes Nixon's war.

The great question is: How can we win America's peace?

Well, let us turn now to the fundamental issue. Why and how did the United States become involved in Vietnam in the first place?

Fifteen years ago North Vietnam, with the logistical support of Communist China and the Soviet Union, launched a campaign to impose a Communist government on South Vietnam by instigating and supporting a revolution.

In response to the request of the Government of South Vietnam, President Eisenhower sent economic aid and military equipment to assist the people of South Vietnam in their efforts to prevent a Communist takeover. Seven years ago, President Kennedy sent 16,000 military personnel to Vietnam as combat advisers. Four years ago, President Johnson sent American combat forces to South Vietnam.

Now, many believe that President Johnson's decision to send American combat forces to South Vietnam was wrong. And many others—I among them—have been strongly critical of the way the war has been conducted.

But the question facing us today is: Now that we are in the war, what is the best way to end it?...

For the future of peace, precipitate withdrawal would...be a disaster of immense magnitude.

—A nation cannot remain great if it betrays its allies and lets down its friends.

—Our defeat and humiliation in South Vietnam without question would promote recklessness in the councils of those great powers who have not yet abandoned their goals of world conquest.

—This would spark violence wherever our commitments help maintain the peace—in the Middle East, in Berlin, eventually even in the Western Hemisphere.

Ultimately, this would cost more lives.

It would not bring peace; it would bring more war.

For these reasons, I rejected the recommendation that I should end the war by immediately withdrawing all of our forces. I chose instead to change American policy on both the negotiating front and battlefront.

In order to end a war fought on many fronts, I initiated a pursuit for peace on many fronts.

In a television speech on May 14, in a speech before the United Nations, and on a number of other occasions I set forth our peace proposals in great detail.

"What are the prospects for peace?"

—We have offered the complete withdrawal of all outside forces within 1 year.

—We have proposed a cease-fire under international supervision.

—We have offered free elections under international supervision with the Communists participating in the organization and conduct of the elections as an organized political force. And the Saigon Government has pledged to accept the result of the elections.

We have not put forth our proposals on a take-it-or-leave-it basis. We have indicated that we are willing to discuss the proposals that have been put forth by the other side. We have declared that anything is negotiable except the right of the people of South Vietnam to determine their own future. At the Paris peace conference, Ambassador Lodge has demonstrated our flexibility and good faith in 40 public meetings.

Hanoi has refused even to discuss our proposals. They demand our unconditional acceptance of their terms, which are that we withdraw all American forces immediately and unconditionally and that we overthrow the Government of South Vietnam as we leave.

We have not limited our peace initiatives to public forums and public statements. I recognized, in January, that a long and bitter war like this usually cannot be settled in a public forum. That is why in addition to the public statements and negotiations I have explored every possible private avenue that might lead to a settlement.

Tonight I am taking the unprecedented step of disclosing to you some of our other initiatives for peace—initiatives we undertook privately and secretly because we thought we

Richard M. Nixon

thereby might open a door which publicly would be closed.

I did not wait for my inauguration to begin my quest for peace.

—Soon after my election, through an individual who is directly in contact on a personal basis with the leaders of North Vietnam, I made two private offers for a rapid, comprehensive settlement. Hanoi's replies called in effect for our surrender before negotiations.

—Since the Soviet Union furnishes most of the military equipment for North Vietnam, Secretary of State Rogers, my Assistant for National Security Affairs, Dr. Kissinger, Ambassador Lodge, and I, personally, have met on a number of occasions with representatives of the Soviet Government to enlist their assistance in getting meaningful negotiations started. In addition, we have had extended discussions directed toward that same end with representatives of other governments which have diplomatic relations with North Vietnam. None of these initiatives have to date produced results.

—In mid-July, I became convinced that it was necessary to make a major move to break the deadlock in the Paris

talks. I spoke directly in this office, where I am now sitting, with an individual who had known Ho Chi Minh [President, Democratic Republic of Vietnam] on a personal basis for 25 years. Through him I sent a letter to Ho Chi Minh.

I did this outside of the usual diplomatic channels with the hope that with the necessity of making statements for propaganda removed, there might be constructive progress toward bringing the war to an end. Let me read from that letter to you now.

"*There were some who urged that I end the war at once.*"

"Dear Mr. President:

"I realize that it is difficult to communicate meaningfully across the gulf of four years of war. But precisely because of this gulf, I wanted to take this opportunity to reaffirm in all solemnity my desire to work for a just peace. I deeply believe that the war in Vietnam has gone on too long and delay in bringing it to an end can benefit no one—least of all the people of Vietnam....

"The time has come to move forward at the conference table toward an early resolution of this tragic war. You will find us forthcoming and open-minded in a common effort to bring the blessings of peace to the brave people of Vietnam. Let history record that at this critical juncture, both sides turned their face toward peace rather than toward conflict and war."

I received Ho Chi Minh's reply on August 30, 3 days before his death. It simply reiterated the public position North Vietnam had taken at Paris and flatly rejected my initiative.

The full text of both letters is being released to the press.

—In addition to the public meetings that I have referred to, Ambassador Lodge has met with Vietnam's chief negotiator in Paris in 11 private sessions.

—We have taken other significant initiatives which must remain secret to keep open some channels of communication which may still prove to be productive.

But the effect of all the public, private, and secret negotiations which have been undertaken since the bombing halt a year ago and since this administration came into office on January 20, can be summed up in one sentence: No progress whatever has been made except agreement on the shape of the bargaining table.

Well now, who is at fault?

It has become clear that the obstacle in negotiating an end to the war is not the President of the United States. It is not the South Vietnamese Government.

The obstacle is the other side's absolute refusal to show the least willingness to join us in seeking a just peace. And it will not do so while it is convinced that all it has to do is to wait for our next concession, and our next concession after that one, until it gets everything it wants.

There can now be no longer any question that progress in negotiation depends only on Hanoi's deciding to negotiate, to negotiate seriously.

I realize that this report on our efforts on the diplomatic front is discouraging to the American people, but the American people are entitled to know the truth—the bad news as well as the good news—where the lives of our young men are involved.

Now let me turn, however, to a more encouraging report on another front.

"*The question at issue is not whether Johnson's war becomes Nixon's war.*"

At the time we launched our search for peace I recognized we might not succeed in bringing an end to the war through negotiation. I, therefore, put into effect another plan to bring peace—a plan which will bring the war to an end regardless of what happens on the negotiating front.

It is in line with a major shift in U.S. foreign policy which I described in my press conference at Guam on July 25. Let me briefly explain what has been described as the

Nixon Doctrine—a policy which not only will help end the war in Vietnam, but which is an essential element of our program to prevent future Vietnams.

We Americans are a do-it-yourself people. We are an impatient people. Instead of teaching someone else to do a job, we like to do it ourselves. And this trait has been carried over into our foreign policy.

In Korea and again in Vietnam, the United States furnished most of the money, most of the arms, and most of the men to help the people of those countries defend their freedom against Communist aggression.

Before any American troops were committed to Vietnam, a leader of another Asian country expressed this opinion to me when I was traveling in Asia as a private citizen. He said: "When you are trying to assist another nation defend its freedom, U.S. policy should be to help them fight the war but not to fight the war for them."

Well, in accordance with this wise counsel, I laid down in Guam three principles as guidelines for future American policy toward Asia:

—First, the United States will keep all of its treaty commitments.

—Second, we shall provide a shield if a nuclear power threatens the freedom of a nation allied with us or of a nation whose survival we consider vital to our security.

—Third, in cases involving other types of aggression, we shall furnish military and economic assistance when requested in accordance with our treaty commitments. But we shall look to the nation directly threatened to assume the primary responsibility of providing the manpower for its defense.

After I announced this policy, I found that the leaders of the Philippines, Thailand, Vietnam, South Korea, and other nations which might be threatened by Communist aggression, welcomed this new direction in American foreign policy.

The defense of freedom is everybody's business—not just America's business. And it is particularly the responsibility of the people whose freedom is threatened. In the previous administration, we Americanized the war in Vietnam.

In this administration, we are Vietnamizing the search for peace.

The policy of the previous administration not only resulted in our assuming the primary responsibility for fighting the war, but even more significantly did not adequately stress the goal of strengthening the South Vietnamese so that they could defend themselves when we left.

"No progress whatever has been made except agreement on the shape of the bargaining table."

The Vietnamization plan was launched following Secretary Laird's visit to Vietnam in March. Under the plan, I ordered first a substantial increase in the training and equipment of South Vietnamese forces.

In July, on my visit to Vietnam, I changed General Abrams' orders so that they were consistent with the objectives of our new policies. Under the new orders, the primary mission of our troops is to enable the South Vietnamese forces to assume the full responsibility for the security of South Vietnam.

Our air operations have been reduced by over 20 percent.

And now we have begun to see the results of this long overdue change in American policy in Vietnam.

—After 5 years of Americans going into Vietnam, we are finally bringing American men home. By December 15, over 60,000 men will have been withdrawn from South Vietnam—including 20 percent of all of our combat forces.

—The South Vietnamese have continued to gain in strength. As a result they have been able to take over combat responsibilities from our American troops.

Two other significant developments have occurred since this administration took office.

—Enemy infiltration, infiltration which is essential if they are to launch a major attack, over the last 3 months is less than 20 percent of what it was over the same period last year.

Nixon with stacks of letters and telegrams in support of his policy in Vietnam

—Most important—United States casualties have declined during the last 2 months to the lowest point in 3 years.

Let me now turn to our program for the future.

We have adopted a plan which we have worked out in cooperation with the South Vietnamese for the complete withdrawal of all U.S. combat ground forces, and their replacement by South Vietnamese forces on an orderly scheduled timetable. This withdrawal will be made from strength and not from weakness. As South Vietnamese forces become stronger, the rate of American withdrawal can become greater.

I have not and do not intend to announce the timetable for our program. And there are obvious reasons for this decision which I am sure you will understand. As I have indicated on several occasions, the rate of withdrawal will depend on developments on three fronts.

One of these is the progress which can be or might be made in the Paris talks. An announcement of a fixed timetable for our withdrawal would completely remove any incentive for the enemy to negotiate an agreement. They would simply wait until our forces had withdrawn and then move in.

The other two factors on which we will base our withdrawal decisions are the level of enemy activity and the progress of the training programs of the South Vietnamese forces. And I am glad to be able to report tonight progress on both of these fronts has been greater than we anticipated when we started the program in June for withdrawal. As a result, our timetable for withdrawal is more optimistic now than when we made our first estimates in June. Now, this clearly demonstrates why it is not wise to be frozen in on a fixed timetable.

We must retain the flexibility to base each withdrawal decision on the situation as it is at that time rather than on estimates that are no longer valid.

Along with this optimistic estimate, I must—in all candor—leave one note of caution.

If the level of enemy activity significantly increases we might have to adjust our timetable accordingly.

However, I want the record to be completely clear on one point.

At the time of the bombing halt just a year ago, there was some confusion as to whether there was an understanding on the part of the enemy that if we stopped the bombing of North Vietnam they would stop the shelling of cities in South Vietnam. I want to be sure that there is no misunderstanding on the part of the enemy with regard to our withdrawal program.

> ## "As President of the United States, I would be untrue to my oath of office if I allowed the policy of this Nation to be dictated by the minority."

We have noted the reduced level of infiltration, the reduction of our casualties, and are basing our withdrawal decisions partially on those factors.

If the level of infiltration or our casualties increase while we are trying to scale down the fighting, it will be the result of a conscious decision by the enemy.

Hanoi could make no greater mistake than to assume that an increase in violence will be to its advantage. If I conclude that increased enemy action jeopardizes our remaining forces in Vietnam, I shall not hesitate to take strong and effective measures to deal with that situation.

> ## "And so tonight—to you, the great silent majority of my fellow Americans— I ask for your support."

This is not a threat. This is a statement of policy, which as Commander in Chief of our Armed Forces, I am making in meeting my responsibility for the protection of American fighting men wherever they may be.

My fellow Americans, I am sure you can recognize from what I have said that we really only have two choices open to us if we want to end this war.

—I can order an immediate, precipitate withdrawal of all Americans from Vietnam without regard to the effects of that action.

—Or we can persist in our search for a just peace through a negotiated settlement if possible, or through continued implementation of our plan for Vietnamization if necessary—a plan in which we will withdraw all of our forces from Vietnam on a schedule in accordance with our program, as the South Vietnamese become strong enough to defend their own freedom.

I have chosen this second course.

It is not the easy way.

It is the right way.

It is a plan which will end the war and serve the cause of peace—not just in Vietnam but in the Pacific and in the world.

In speaking of the consequences of a precipitate withdrawal, I mentioned that our allies would lose confidence in America.

Far more dangerous, we would lose confidence in ourselves. Oh, the immediate reaction would be a sense of relief that our men were coming home. But as we saw the consequences of what we had done, inevitable remorse and divisive recrimination would scar our spirit as a people.

We have faced other crises in our history and have become stronger by rejecting the easy way out and taking the right way in meeting our challenges. Our greatness as a nation has been our capacity to do what had to be done when we knew our course was right.

I recognize that some of my fellow citizens disagree with the plan for peace I have chosen. Honest and patriotic Americans have reached different conclusions as to how peace should be achieved.

In San Francisco a few weeks ago, I saw demonstrators carrying signs reading: "Lose in Vietnam, bring the boys home."

Well, one of the strengths of our free society is that any American has a right to reach that conclusion and to advocate that point of view. But as President of the United States, I would be untrue to my oath of office if I allowed the policy of this Nation to be dictated by the minority who hold that point of view and who try to impose it on the Nation by mounting demonstrations in the street.

For almost 200 years, the policy of this Nation has been made under our Constitution by those leaders in the Congress and the White House elected by all of the people. If a vocal minority, however fervent its cause, prevails over reason and the will of the majority, this Nation has no future as a free society.

And now I would like to address a word, if I may, to the young people of this Nation who are particularly concerned, and I understand why they are concerned, about this war.

I respect your idealism.

I share your concern for peace.

I want peace as much as you do.

There are powerful personal reasons I want to end this war. This week I will have to sign 83 letters to mothers, fathers, wives, and loved ones of men who have given their lives for America in Vietnam. It is very little satisfaction to me that this is only one-third as many letters as I signed the first week in office. There is nothing I want more than to see the day come when I do not have to write any of those letters.

> ## "North Vietnam cannot defeat or humiliate the United States. Only Americans can do that."

—I want to end the war to save the lives of those brave young men in Vietnam.

—But I want to end it in a way which will increase the chance that their younger brothers and their sons will not have to fight in some future Vietnam someplace in the world.

—And I want to end the war for another reason. I want to end it so that the energy and dedication of you, our young people, now too often directed into bitter hatred against those responsible for the war, can be turned to the great challenges of peace, a better life for all Americans, a better life for all people on this earth.

I have chosen a plan for peace. I believe it will succeed.

If it does succeed, what the critics say now won't matter. If it does not succeed, anything I say then won't matter.

I know it may not be fashionable to speak of patriotism or national destiny these days. But I feel it is appropriate to do so on this occasion.

Two hundred years ago this Nation was weak and poor. But even then, America was the hope of millions in the world. Today we have become the strongest and richest nation in the world. And the wheel of destiny has turned so that any hope the world has for the survival of peace and freedom will be determined by whether the American people have the moral stamina and the courage to meet the challenge of free world leadership.

Let historians not record that when America was the most powerful nation in the world we passed on the other side of the road and allowed the last hopes for peace and freedom of millions of people to be suffocated by the forces of totalitarianism.

And so tonight—to you, the great silent majority of my fellow Americans—I ask for your support.

I pledged in my campaign for the Presidency to end the war in a way that we could win the peace. I have initiated a plan of action which will enable me to keep that pledge.

The more support I can have from the American people, the sooner that pledge can be redeemed; for the more divided we are at home, the less likely the enemy is to negotiate at Paris.

Let us be united for peace. Let us also be united against defeat. Because let us understand: North Vietnam cannot defeat or humiliate the United States. Only Americans can do that.

Fifty years ago, in this room and at this very desk, President Woodrow Wilson spoke words which caught the imagination of a war-weary world. He said: "This is the war to end war." His dream for peace after World War I was shattered on the hard realities of great power politics and Woodrow Wilson died a broken man.

Tonight I do not tell you that the war in Vietnam is the war to end wars. But I do say this: I have initiated a plan which will end this war in a way that will bring us closer to that great goal to which Woodrow Wilson and every American President in our history has been dedicated—the goal of a just and lasting peace.

As President I hold the responsibility for choosing the best path to that goal and then leading the Nation along it.

I pledge to you tonight that I shall meet this responsibility with all of the strength and wisdom I can command in accordance with your hopes, mindful of your concerns, sustained by your prayers.

Thank you and goodnight.

31

"WE HAVE DONE SOME THINGS WRONG"

Watergate was a constitutional crisis, a mesmerizing saga of criminality, corruption, and abuse. More than that, it was also the personal story of Richard Nixon, whose demons drove him to destroy his presidency at the peak of his power and public esteem.

The scandal began on June 17, 1972, when police arrested five burglars planting wiretapping equipment at Democratic Party headquarters. The men were tied to the Committee to Reelect the President, but stayed silent even when convicted. Nixon was reelected with 60.7 percent of the vote, winning forty-nine of fifty states. But in the spring of 1973, the scandal broke wide. The country was shocked by an avalanche of disclosures—White House enemies lists, break-ins, illegal payments, perjury. Nixon's top aides, including Chief of Staff H.R. Haldeman, resigned. White House counsel John Dean testified he had warned of a "cancer on the presidency," and had discussed hush-money payments to the burglars in the Oval Office. Nixon denied Dean's charge. Then an aide revealed that all Oval Office conversations were recorded. Nixon refused to turn over the tapes, fired the special prosecutor who sought them, then released edited transcripts confirming many of the charges. Through it all, the president battled on, proclaiming in the Rose Garden, "Let others wallow in Watergate," declaring at another news conference, "I am not a crook."

Events hurtled to their conclusion in the summer of 1974. On July 24, in *United States v. Nixon,* the Supreme Court unanimously ordered the president to turn over subpoenaed tapes as evidence. That night, the House Judiciary Committee began impeachment deliberations, voting out charges three days later. Nixon's defenders demanded:

where was the "smoking gun"? On Monday, August 4, the White House released it: a transcript of a tape in which Nixon and Haldeman, just six days after the break-in, briskly launched the cover-up. The president's remaining political support melted away. Nixon knew he would have to become the first American president to resign.

Now, as historian Stephen Ambrose noted, the drama would come in the way the president would leave—and this was one performance Nixon scripted and directed himself. He set chief speechwriter Raymond Price to work on a resignation talk, but veered back and forth on whether to act. As the president walked to his "hideaway" office to work on the speech, crowds pressed against the White House gates and jeered, "Jail to the chief." Orders went from the Pentagon to forestall any coup attempt by a desperate president. Even though the whole country knew what Nixon was likely to say, tension was excruciating.

"This is the thirty-seventh time I have spoken to you from this office," Nixon began his televised address. "I have never been a quitter. To leave office before my term is completed is abhorrent to every instinct in my body." But his political situation was impossible: "In the past few days, however, it has become evident to me that I no longer have a strong enough political base in the Congress to justify continuing that effort.…Therefore, I shall resign the Presidency effective at noon tomorrow. Vice President Ford will be sworn in as president at that hour in this office." He then devoted the rest of the speech to a review of the administration's accomplishments and hopes.

The next day he spoke again. If the speech from the Oval Office was mannered kabuki, the talk the next day was its own sort of theater: raw, compelling, the presidency

Richard M. Nixon

as exposed nerve. Americans saw a man wrestling with his own fears and resentments. In the East Room of the White House, members of the administration gathered for a farewell. Nixon and his family waited outside, as an aide told them where the battery of television cameras would be. "Oh, Dick," First Lady Pat Nixon implored, "you can't have it televised." Nixon replied, "That's the way it has to be. We owe it to our supporters. We owe it to the people." He would play out his most personal, wrenching moment before the whole nation.

He talked about his parents. "I remember my old man. I think that they would have called him sort of a little man, common man," he said. "He had a lemon ranch. It was the poorest lemon ranch in California, I can assure you. He sold it before they found oil on it." His mother "will have no books written about her. But she was a saint." Nixon pulled out his glasses—which the public had never before seen—and read a passage from Theodore Roosevelt. The words had been written not after a political defeat, much less a self-inflicted wound like Watergate, but after the death of his young wife.

He finished by encouraging his staff—and by the end of the sentence, he was clearly admonishing himself. "Always give your best, never get discouraged, never be petty; always remember, others may hate you, but those who hate you don't win unless you hate them," he said. "And then you destroy yourself."

With that, Nixon walked to the presidential helicopter and thrust his arms in his trademark double "V for victory" salute.

Nixon's farewell speech, August 9, 1974

Richard M. Nixon's
FAREWELL ADDRESS TO WHITE HOUSE STAFF

Washington, D.C. • August 9, 1974

hear...
disc 2
track 8

Members of the Cabinet, members of the White House Staff, all of our friends here:

I think the record should show that this is one of those spontaneous things that we always arrange whenever the president comes in to speak, and it will be so reported in the press, and we don't mind, because they have to call it as they see it.

But on our part, believe me, it is spontaneous.

You are here to say good-bye to us, and we don't have a good word for it in English—the best is *au revoir*. We will see you again.

I just met with the members of the White House staff, you know, those who serve here in the White House day in and day out, and I asked them to do what I ask all of you to do to the extent that you can and, of course, are requested to do so: to serve our next president as you have served me and previous presidents—because many of you have been here for many years—with devotion and dedication, because this office, great as it is, can only be as great as the men and women who work for and with the president.

This house, for example—I was thinking of it as we walked down this hall, and I was comparing it to some of the great houses of the world that I have been in. This isn't the biggest house. Many, and most, in even smaller countries, are much bigger. This isn't the finest house. Many in Europe, particularly, and in China, Asia, have paintings of great, great value, things that we just don't have here and, probably, will never have until we are one thousand years old or older.

But this is the best house. It is the best house because it has something far more important than numbers of people who serve, far more important than numbers of rooms or how big it is, far more important than numbers of magnificent pieces of art.

This house has a great heart, and that heart comes from those who serve. I was rather sorry they didn't come down. We said good-bye to them upstairs. But they are really great. And I recall after so many times I have made speeches, and some of them pretty tough, yet, I always come back, or after a hard day—and my days usually have run rather long—I would always get a lift from them, because I might be a little down but they always smiled.

"Sure, we have done some things wrong in the administration."

And so it is with you. I look around here, and I see so many on this staff that, you know, I should have been by your offices and shaken hands, and I would love to have talked to you and found out how to run the world—everybody wants to tell the president what to do, and boy, he needs to be told many times—but I just haven't had the time. But I want you to know that each and every one of you, I know, is indispensable to this government.

I am proud of this Cabinet. I am proud of all the members who have served in our Cabinet. I am proud of our sub-Cabinet. I am proud of our White House staff. As I pointed out last night, sure, we have done some things wrong in this administration, and the top man always takes the responsibility, and I have never ducked it. But I want to say one thing: we can be proud of it—five and a half years. No man or no woman came into this administration and left it with more of this world's goods than when he came in. No man or no woman ever profited at the public expense or the public till. That tells something about you.

The above text is a transcript of the speech as it was given from the East Room of the White House.

Mistakes, yes. But for personal gain, never. You did what you believed in. Sometimes right, sometimes wrong. And I only wish that I were a wealthy man—at the present time, I have got to find a way to pay my taxes—[laughter]—and if I were, I would like to recompense you for the sacrifices that all of you have made to serve in government.

But you are getting something in government—and I want you to tell this to your children, and I hope the nation's children will hear it, too—something in government service that is far more important than money. It is a cause bigger than yourself. It is the cause of making this the greatest nation in the world, the leader of the world, because without our leadership, the world will know nothing but war, possibly starvation, or worse, in the years ahead. With our leadership it will know peace, it will know plenty.

We have been generous, and we will be more generous in the future as we are able to. But most important, we must be strong here, strong in our hearts, strong in our souls, strong in our belief, and strong in our willingness to sacrifice, as you have been willing to sacrifice, in a pecuniary way, to serve in government.

There is something else I would like for you to tell your young people. You know, people often come in and say, "What will I tell my kids?" They look at government and say, sort of a rugged life, and they see the mistakes that are made. They get the impression that everybody is here for the purpose of feathering his nest. That is why I made this earlier point—not in this administration, not one single man or woman.

And I say to them, there are many fine careers. This country needs good farmers, good businessmen, good plumbers, good carpenters.

I remember my old man. I think that they would have called him sort of a little man, common man. He didn't consider himself that way. You know what he was? He was a streetcar motorman first, and then he was a farmer, and then he had a lemon ranch. It was the poorest lemon ranch in California, I can assure you. He sold it before they found oil on it. [Laughter] And then he was a grocer. But he was a great man, because he did his job, and every job counts up to the hilt, regardless of what happens.

Nobody will ever write a book, probably, about my mother. Well, I guess all of you would say this about your mother—my mother was a saint. And I think of her, two boys dying of tuberculosis, nursing four others in order that she could take care of my older brother for three years in

Arizona, and seeing each of them die, and when they died, it was like one of her own.

Yes, she will have no books written about her. But she was a saint.

Now, however, we look to the future. I had a little quote in the speech last night from T.R. As you know, I kind of like to read books. I am not educated, but I do read books—[laughter]—and the T.R. quote was a pretty good one.

"We think that when we lose an election, we think that when we suffer a defeat that all is ended."

Here is another one I found as I was reading, my last night in the White House, and this quote is about a young man. He was a young lawyer in New York. He had married a beautiful girl, and they had a lovely daughter, and then suddenly she died, and this is what he wrote. This was in his diary.

He said, "She was beautiful in face and form and lovelier still in spirit. As a flower she grew and as a fair young flower she died. Her life had been always in the sunshine. There had never come to her a single great sorrow. None ever knew her who did not love and revere her for her bright and sunny temper and her saintly unselfishness. Fair, pure and joyous as a maiden, loving, tender and happy as a young wife. When she had just become a mother, when her life seemed to be just begun and when the years seemed so bright before her, then by a strange and terrible fate death came to her. And when my heart's dearest died, the light went from my life forever."

That was T.R. in his twenties. He thought the light had gone from his life forever—but he went on. And he not only became president but, as an ex-president, he served his country, always in the arena, tempestuous, strong, sometimes wrong, sometimes right, but he was a man.

And as I leave, let me say, that is an example I think all of us should remember. We think sometimes when things happen that don't go the right way; we think that when you

don't pass the bar exam the first time—I happened to, but I was just lucky; I mean, my writing was so poor the bar examiner said, "We have just got to let the guy through." We think that when someone dear to us dies, we think that when we lose an election, we think that when we suffer a defeat that all is ended. We think, as T.R. said, that the light had left his life forever.

Not true. It is only a beginning, always. The young must know it; the old must know it. It must always sustain us, because the greatness comes not when things go always good for you, but the greatness comes and you are really tested, when you take some knocks, some disappointments, when sadness comes, because only if you have been in the deepest valley can you ever know how magnificent it is to be on the highest mountain.

And so I say to you on this occasion, as we leave, we leave proud of the people who have stood by us and worked for us and served this country.

We want you to be proud of what you have done. We want you to continue to serve in government, if that is your wish. Always give your best, never get discouraged, never be petty; always remember, others may hate you, but those who hate you don't win unless you hate them, and then you destroy yourself.

"Others may hate you, but those who hate you don't win unless you hate them."

And so, we leave with high hopes, in good spirit, and with deep humility, and with very much gratefulness in our hearts. I can only say to each and every one of you, we come from many faiths, we pray perhaps to different gods—but really the same God in a sense—but I want to say for each and every one of you, not only will we always remember you, not only will we always be grateful to you but always you will be in our hearts and you will be in our prayers.

Thank you very much.

Gerald R.
FORD

38ᵀᴴ PRESIDENT: 1974–1977

Born: July 14, 1913, in Omaha, Nebraska

Disc 2, Track 9

32

"OUR LONG NATIONAL NIGHTMARE IS OVER"

NOBODY HAD EVER become president under circumstances as bizarre as Gerald Ford. He had never been elected to national office, serving as vice president because his predecessor, Spiro Agnew, resigned to avoid jail. Now, amid deep national disaffection, he followed the first president to resign from office. Secretary of State Henry Kissinger recalled in his memoirs, "The presidency was in a shambles....The balance between the executive and legislative branches was shifting dramatically to a point where the basic authority of the presidency was in question." With his brief inaugural remarks, Ford did much to reestablish calm and order. As it turned out, nothing he did later was more important than these words delivered in the first minutes of his term.

Gerald Ford had not sought office in any constituency larger than his congressional district in Grand Rapids, Michigan. In 1966, he became minority leader of the House of Representatives. He was regarded as steady, stolid, and a stout partisan. (Democrat Lyndon Johnson cruelly remarked that Ford played football too many times without his helmet.) It appeared highly likely he would finish out his congressional career as a loyal Republican lieutenant in Congress. Then came Watergate.

Spiro Agnew was Nixon's first vice president, but in 1973, prosecutors began to probe charges he had taken bribes, first as a local official and then in his White House office. Agnew pleaded nolo contendere (no contest) and resigned on October 10, 1973. Under a recently enacted constitutional provision, Nixon could choose a new vice president, but the pick would have to be approved by both houses of Congress. Nixon

desperately hoped to tap John Connally, the Treasury secretary and former Democrat, whom he was grooming as his successor, but congressional leaders told him the choice could not pass. Instead, they forcefully urged Nixon to pick the honest and dependable Ford. Congress confirmed him easily. During the difficult months of Watergate, he delicately displayed loyalty without drawing too close to Nixon.

When White House Chief of Staff Alexander Haig realized Nixon must resign, he urgently met with Ford and told him to prepare to take office. (According to Ford's memoirs, Haig also raised the subject of a possible presidential pardon.) Ford asked his longtime aide, Robert Hartmann, to draft remarks. Amid the crisis, as aides planned a hurried transition, the writer worked through the night. Hartmann recalled, "Pulling the rough draft from his pocket, [Ford] said he wouldn't change a word—except for one thing that troubled him. His finger pointed to the sentence 'Our long national nightmare is over.'

"'Isn't that a little hard on Dick?' he asked.

"'No, no, no!' I cried in genuine anguish. 'Don't you see, that's your whole speech!...Maybe it isn't yet quite true, but saying it will make it come true.'" Hartmann begged, "Junk all the rest of the speech if you want to, but not that." Ford reluctantly agreed.

Ford spoke in the same East Room where Nixon had poured out his heart just hours earlier. After bitter struggles between Congress and the White House, which included measures restricting the president's ability to wage war and set budgets, Ford made much of his friendship with lawmakers, even asking to meet with them after the ceremony.

Ford addresses assembled guests in the East Room of the White House after being sworn in as the 38th President, August 9, 1974

He evoked Alexander Hamilton's remark about Congress: "Here, sir, the people rule."

One line that gained significance in retrospect was Ford's promise that he had made no deal for office. A month later, believing Watergate would dog his term if he did not act, Ford granted Nixon a "full, free, and absolute pardon." Ford's press secretary resigned in protest, and the president's public opinion poll ratings plummeted. Ford's term was soon engulfed with the problems that had mounted in Nixon's last months, including inflation and the final loss of South Vietnam. Conservative California Governor Ronald Reagan tried to deny him the Republican nomination. But Ford had won the affection of the public, and he wiped out a fifteen-point deficit in the polls to come within two percentage points of being elected on his own in 1976.

History has treated Ford kindly. In 2001, the John F. Kennedy Library gave him the Profile in Courage award for his pardon of Nixon.

Mr. Chief Justice, my dear friends, my fellow Americans:

The oath that I have taken is the same oath that was taken by George Washington and by every President under the Constitution. But I assume the Presidency under extraordinary circumstances never before experienced by Americans. This is an hour of history that troubles our minds and hurts our hearts.

Therefore, I feel it is my first duty to make an unprecedented compact with my countrymen. Not an inaugural address, not a fireside chat, not a campaign speech—just a little straight talk among friends. And I intend it to be the first of many.

I am acutely aware that you have not elected me as your President by your ballots, and so I ask you to confirm me as your President with your prayers. And I hope that such prayers will also be the first of many.

"I assume the Presidency under extraordinary circumstances never before experienced by Americans."

If you have not chosen me by secret ballot, neither have I gained office by any secret promises. I have not campaigned either for the Presidency or the Vice Presidency. I have not subscribed to any partisan platform. I am indebted to no man, and only to one woman—my dear wife—as I begin this very difficult job.

I have not sought this enormous responsibility, but I will not shirk it. Those who nominated and confirmed me as Vice President were my friends and are my friends. They were of both parties, elected by all the people and acting under the Constitution in their name. It is only fitting then that I should pledge to them and to you that I will be the President of all the people.

Thomas Jefferson said the people are the only sure reliance for the preservation of our liberty. And down the years, Abraham Lincoln renewed this American article of faith asking, "Is there any better way or equal hope in the world?"

"You have not elected me as your President by your ballots."

I intend, on Monday next, to request of the Speaker of the House of Representatives and the President pro tempore of the Senate the privilege of appearing before the Congress to share with my former colleagues and with you, the American people, my views on the priority business of the Nation and to solicit your views and their views. And may I say to the Speaker and the others, if I could meet with you right after these remarks, I would appreciate it.

Even though this is late in an election year, there is no way we can go forward except together and no way anybody can win except by serving the people's urgent needs. We cannot stand still or slip backwards. We must go forward now together.

To the peoples and the governments of all friendly nations, and I hope that could encompass the whole world, I pledge an uninterrupted and sincere search for peace. America will remain strong and united, but its strength will remain dedicated to the safety and sanity of the entire family of man, as well as to our own precious freedom.

I believe that truth is the glue that holds government together, not only our Government but civilization itself. That bond, though strained, is unbroken at home and abroad.

In all my public and private acts as your President, I expect to follow my instincts of openness and candor with full confidence that honesty is always the best policy in the end.

My fellow Americans, our long national nightmare is over.

Our Constitution works; our great Republic is a government of laws and not of men. Here the people rule. But there is a higher Power, by whatever name we honor Him, who ordains not only righteousness but love, not only justice but mercy.

As we bind up the internal wounds of Watergate, more painful and more poisonous than those of foreign wars, let us restore the golden rule to our political process, and let brotherly love purge our hearts of suspicion and of hate.

In the beginning, I asked you to pray for me. Before closing, I ask again your prayers, for Richard Nixon and for his family. May our former President, who brought peace to millions, find it for himself. May God bless and comfort his wonderful wife and daughters, whose love and loyalty will forever be a shining legacy to all who bear the lonely burdens of the White House.

"My fellow Americans, our long national nightmare is over."

I can only guess at those burdens, although I have witnessed at close hand the tragedies that befell three Presidents and the lesser trials of others.

With all the strength and all the good sense I have gained from life, with all the confidence my family, my friends, and my dedicated staff impart to me, and with the good will of countless Americans I have encountered in recent visits to 40 States, I now solemnly reaffirm my promise I made to you last December 6: to uphold the Constitution, to do what is right as God gives me to see the right, and to do the very best I can for America.

God helping me, I will not let you down. Thank you.

Jimmy
CARTER

39TH PRESIDENT: 1977–1981

Born: October 1, 1924, in Plains, Georgia

Disc 2, Track 10

33

JIMMY CARTER

"A CRISIS OF CONFIDENCE"

America's innate optimism was put to severe test by the energy crisis of the 1970s, a situation that worsened during the presidency of Jimmy Carter. A key episode was the so-called "malaise" speech.

Carter was a little-known former governor of Georgia when he won the presidency in 1976 with a pledge that he would "never lie" to the American people. A devout Baptist, he connected with voters weary of the disappointments and neuroses of Kennedy, Johnson, and Nixon. His finest voice was that of a preacher, his best speeches sermons. But in office, Carter, trained as an engineer, seemed to lose his touch, unable to wrest control over government and unsure of what he wanted to do. In an influential article, his former speechwriter James Fallows dubbed it a "Passionless Presidency."

The economy already had been shaken by oil shocks earlier in the decade. An oil embargo imposed by Arab states in 1973 caused massive inflation; by 1979, high prices were joined by economic recession in a new combination that puzzled economists called "stagflation." In early 1979, an Islamic revolution in Iran caused world oil prices to spike again; gas lines and shortages spread across America as inflation reached double digits. Earlier Carter had called the energy crisis the "moral equivalent of war" in a televised fireside chat (he wore a sweater to demonstrate his resolve to lower thermostats and thus save energy), but Congress failed to act. Pollsters found only 25 percent of citizens approved of Carter's performance, and his television speeches drew ever-smaller audiences. Now he again planned to talk to the nation on energy and national goals, in a speech scheduled for July 5.

Then, the day before the talk was due to be given, Carter abruptly canceled it without explanation and remained at Camp David, the presidential retreat in the Maryland mountains. Puzzled speculation ensued. Over eleven days, Carter invited more than one hundred people—eight governors, civic leaders, academics, and ordinary citizens seemingly chosen at random—to Camp David, where they lectured him on his failings.

Jimmy Carter, July 1979

Meanwhile, the president's advisors warred over what the speech should say. Pollster Pat Caddell had sent Carter a 107-page memo warning of a loss of faith in the nation's institutions. Caddell said he detected a spiritual "malaise" in the country. He urged a thematic, emotional talk that eschewed policy and spoke of a national crisis of confidence. Vice President Walter Mondale and policy advisor Stuart Eizenstat were aghast at the prospect of a content-free talk, insisting on new initiatives on energy instead. Carter decided to take both approaches. The first part of the speech, in Carter's own words, spoke of what he heard in the previous week, including what his speechwriter Hendrik Hertzberg called "the most excoriating self-criticism ever heard from any American president." Then Carter turned to the crisis of confidence he saw among the people, drawing from his pollster. He denounced government, called Washington "an island," and sought to recapture the voice of his insurgent presidential campaign. Only in the last fifth of the talk did he turn to steps that could restore confidence by acting on energy shortages, adding six new initiatives to his list of already-stalled policy proposals.

At first the speech was a strong public success. Carter's approval rating in the polls shot up by nine to twelve points. Editorial reaction was decidedly mixed, but commentators noted his firm tone and clenched fist. Two days later, however, after the stock market had closed, he asked his entire cabinet to quit, and accepted the resignations of five of its members (including the secretaries of the Treasury; Health, Education, and Welfare; Energy; and the attorney general). The purge undercut confidence in the stability of Carter's government, and public support dropped to below where it had been before.

Carter's address never used the word "malaise." Pat Caddell used the word in a background briefing for reporters. But it is how the speech was remembered, and for years, Republican orators warned of a "return to the days of malaise." Meanwhile, Carter, defeated for reelection, became a highly productive advocate for peace and human rights. In 2002, he was awarded the Nobel Peace Prize.

Jimmy Carter's
SPEECH ON ENERGY AND NATIONAL GOALS

Washington, D.C. • July 15, 1979

Good evening.

This is a special night for me. Exactly 3 years ago, on July 15, 1976, I accepted the nomination of my party to run for President of the United States. I promised you a President who is not isolated from the people, who feels your pain, and who shares your dreams and who draws his strength and his wisdom from you.

During the past 3 years I've spoken to you on many occasions about national concerns, the energy crisis, reorganizing the Government, our Nation's economy, and issues of war and especially peace. But over those years the subjects of the speeches, the talks, and the press conferences have become increasingly narrow, focused more and more on what the isolated world of Washington thinks is important. Gradually, you've heard more and more about what the Government thinks or what the Government should be doing and less and less about our Nation's hopes, our dreams, and our vision of the future.

"I promised you a President who is not isolated from the people, who feels your pain."

Ten days ago I had planned to speak to you again about a very important subject—energy. For the fifth time I would have described the urgency of the problem and laid out a series of legislative recommendations to the Congress. But as I was preparing to speak, I began to ask myself the same question that I now know has been troubling many of you. Why have we not been able to get together as a nation to resolve our serious energy problem?

It's clear that the true problems of our Nation are much deeper—deeper than gasoline lines or energy shortages, deeper even than inflation or recession. And I realize more than ever that as President I need your help. So, I decided to reach out and listen to the voices of America.

"I left Camp David to listen to other Americans, men and women like you…and I want to share with you what I've heard."

I invited to Camp David people from almost every segment of our society—business and labor, teachers and preachers, Governors, mayors, and private citizens. And then I left Camp David to listen to other Americans, men and women like you. It has been an extraordinary 10 days, and I want to share with you what I've heard.

First of all, I got a lot of personal advice. Let me quote a few of the typical comments that I wrote down.

This from a southern Governor: "Mr. President, you are not leading this Nation—you're just managing the Government."

"You don't see the people enough any more."

"Some of your Cabinet members don't seem loyal. There is not enough discipline among your disciples."

"Don't talk to us about politics or the mechanics of government, but about an understanding of our common good."

"Mr. President, we're in trouble. Talk to us about blood and sweat and tears."

"If you lead, Mr. President, we will follow."

Many people talked about themselves and about the condition of our Nation. This from a young woman in Pennsylvania: "I feel so far from government. I feel like ordinary people are excluded from political power."

And this from a young Chicano: "Some of us have suffered from recession all our lives."

"Some people have wasted energy, but others haven't had anything to waste."

And this from a religious leader: "No material shortage can touch the important things like God's love for us or our love for one another."

And I like this one particularly from a black woman who happens to be the mayor of a small Mississippi town: "The big-shots are not the only ones who are important. Remember, you can't sell anything on Wall Street unless someone digs it up somewhere else first."

This kind of summarized a lot of other statements: "Mr. President, we are confronted with a moral and a spiritual crisis."

"'Mr. President, we're in trouble. Talk to us about blood and sweat and tears.'"

Several of our discussions were on energy, and I have a notebook full of comments and advice. I'll read just a few.

"We can't go on consuming 40 percent more energy than we produce. When we import oil we are also importing inflation plus unemployment."

"We've got to use what we have. The Middle East has only 5 percent of the world's energy, but the United States has 24 percent."

And this is one of the most vivid statements: "Our neck is stretched over the fence and OPEC has a knife."

"There will be other cartels and other shortages. American wisdom and courage right now can set a path to follow in the future."

This was a good one: "Be bold, Mr. President. We may make mistakes, but we are ready to experiment."

And this one from a labor leader got to the heart of it: "The real issue is freedom. We must deal with the energy problem on a war footing."

And the last that I'll read: "When we enter the moral equivalent of war, Mr. President, don't issue us BB guns."

These 10 days confirmed my belief in the decency and the strength and the wisdom of the American people, but it also bore out some of my longstanding concerns about our Nation's underlying problems.

I know, of course, being President, that government actions and legislation can be very important. That's why I've worked hard to put my campaign promises into law—and I have to admit, with just mixed success. But after listening to the American people I have been reminded again that all the legislation in the world can't fix what's wrong with America. So, I want to speak to you first tonight about a subject even more serious than energy or inflation. I want to talk to you right now about a fundamental threat to American democracy.

I do not mean our political and civil liberties. They will endure. And I do not refer to the outward strength of America, a nation that is at peace tonight everywhere in the world, with unmatched economic power and military might.

The threat is nearly invisible in ordinary ways. It is a crisis of confidence. It is a crisis that strikes at the very heart and soul and spirit of our national will. We can see this crisis in the growing doubt about the meaning of our own lives and in the loss of a unity of purpose for our Nation.

The erosion of our confidence in the future is threatening to destroy the social and the political fabric of America.

The confidence that we have always had as a people is not simply some romantic dream or a proverb in a dusty book that we read just on the Fourth of July. It is the idea which founded our Nation and has guided our development as a people. Confidence in the future has supported everything else—public institutions and private enterprise, our own families, and the very Constitution of the United

States. Confidence has defined our course and has served as a link between generations. We've always believed in something called progress. We've always had a faith that the days of our children would be better than our own.

"'If you lead, Mr. President, we will follow.'"

Our people are losing that faith, not only in government itself but in the ability as citizens to serve as the ultimate rulers and shapers of our democracy. As a people we know our past and we are proud of it. Our progress has been part of the living history of America, even the world. We always believed that we were part of a great movement of humanity itself called democracy, involved in the search for freedom, and that belief has always strengthened us in our purpose. But just as we are losing our confidence in the future, we are also beginning to close the door on our past.

In a nation that was proud of hard work, strong families, close-knit communities, and our faith in God, too many of us now tend to worship self-indulgence and consumption. Human identity is no longer defined by what one does, but by what one owns. But we've discovered that owning things and consuming things does not satisfy our longing for meaning. We've learned that piling up material goods cannot fill the emptiness of lives which have no confidence or purpose.

The symptoms of this crisis of the American spirit are all around us. For the first time in the history of our country a majority of our people believe that the next 5 years will be worse than the past 5 years. Two-thirds of our people do not even vote. The productivity of American workers is actually dropping, and the willingness of Americans to save for the future has fallen below that of all other people in the Western world.

As you know, there is a growing disrespect for government and for churches and for schools, the news media, and other institutions. This is not a message of happiness or reassurance, but it is the truth and it is a warning.

These changes did not happen overnight. They've come upon us gradually over the last generation, years that were filled with shocks and tragedy.

We were sure that ours was a nation of the ballot, not the bullet, until the murders of John Kennedy and Robert Kennedy and Martin Luther King Jr. We were taught that our armies were always invincible and our causes were always just, only to suffer the agony of Vietnam. We respected the Presidency as a place of honor until the shock of Watergate.

We remember when the phrase "sound as a dollar" was an expression of absolute dependability, until 10 years of inflation began to shrink our dollar and our savings. We believed that our Nation's resources were limitless until 1973, when we had to face a growing dependence on foreign oil.

These wounds are still very deep. They have never been healed.

Looking for a way out of this crisis, our people have turned to the Federal Government and found it isolated from the mainstream of our Nation's life. Washington, D.C., has become an island. The gap between our citizens and our Government has never been so wide. The people are looking for honest answers, not easy answers; clear leadership, not false claims and evasiveness and politics as usual.

"These wounds are still very deep. They have never been healed."

What you see too often in Washington and elsewhere around the country is a system of government that seems incapable of action. You see a Congress twisted and pulled in every direction by hundreds of well-financed and powerful special interests. You see every extreme position defended to the last vote, almost to the last breath by one unyielding group or another. You often see a balanced and a fair approach that demands sacrifice, a little sacrifice from everyone, abandoned like an orphan without support and without friends.

Often you see paralysis and stagnation and drift. You don't like it, and neither do I. What can we do?

First of all, we must face the truth, and then we can change our course. We simply must have faith in each other, faith in our ability to govern ourselves, and faith in the future of this Nation. Restoring that faith and that confidence to America is now the most important task we face. It is a true challenge of this generation of Americans.

One of the visitors to Camp David last week put it this way: "We've got to stop crying and start sweating, stop talking and start walking, stop cursing and start praying. The strength we need will not come from the White House, but from every house in America."

We know the strength of America. We are strong. We can regain our unity. We can regain our confidence. We are the heirs of generations who survived threats much more powerful and awesome than those that challenge us now. Our fathers and mothers were strong men and women who shaped a new society during the Great Depression, who fought world wars, and who carved out a new charter of peace for the world.

We ourselves are the same Americans who just 10 years ago put a man on the Moon. We are the generation that dedicated our society to the pursuit of human rights and equality. And we are the generation that will win the war on the energy problem and in that process rebuild the unity and confidence of America....[*Carter then set out a six-part proposal on energy conservation and production.*]

So, the solution of our energy crisis can also help us to conquer the crisis of the spirit in our country. It can rekindle our sense of unity, our confidence in the future, and give our Nation and all of us individually a new sense of purpose.

You know we can do it. We have the natural resources. We have more oil in our shale alone than several Saudi Arabias. We have more coal than any nation on Earth. We have the world's highest level of technology. We have the most skilled work force, with innovative genius, and I firmly believe that we have the national will to win this war.

I do not promise you that this struggle for freedom will be easy. I do not promise a quick way out of our Nation's problems, when the truth is that the only way out is an all-out effort. What I do promise you is that I will lead our fight, and I will enforce fairness in our struggle, and I will ensure honesty. And above all, I will act.

We can manage the short-term shortages more effectively and we will, but there are no short-term solutions to our long-range problems. There is simply no way to avoid sacrifice.

"We must face the truth.... There is simply no way to avoid sacrifice."

Twelve hours from now I will speak again in Kansas City, to expand and to explain further our energy program. Just as the search for solutions to our energy shortages has now led us to a new awareness of our Nation's deeper problems, so our willingness to work for those solutions in energy can strengthen us to attack those deeper problems.

I will continue to travel this country, to hear the people of America. You can help me to develop a national agenda for the 1980's. I will listen and I will act. We will act together. These were the promises I made 3 years ago, and I intend to keep them.

Little by little we can and we must rebuild our confidence. We can spend until we empty our treasuries, and we may summon all the wonders of science. But we can succeed only if we tap our greatest resources—America's people, America's values, and America's confidence.

I have seen the strength of America in the inexhaustible resources of our people. In the days to come, let us renew that strength in the struggle for an energy-secure nation.

In closing, let me say this: I will do my best, but I will not do it alone. Let your voice be heard. Whenever you have a chance, say something good about our country. With God's help and for the sake of our Nation, it is time for us to join hands in America. Let us commit ourselves together to a rebirth of the American spirit. Working together with our common faith we cannot fail.

Thank you and good night.

Ronald
REAGAN

40TH PRESIDENT: 1981–1989

Born: February 6, 1911, in Tampico, Illinois

Disc 2, Tracks 11–14

34

RONALD REAGAN

"GOVERNMENT IS NOT THE SOLUTION TO OUR PROBLEM; GOVERNMENT IS THE PROBLEM"

RONALD REAGAN, THE actor and California governor, won the presidential election of 1980 over incumbent Jimmy Carter and would go on to serve two terms as president, becoming known as the "Great Communicator." Carter's last year in office—the election year—was marred by the hostage crisis in Iran, when militant students seized fifty-two Americans at the U.S. embassy and held them captive. Inflation and recession gripped the economy. In a televised debate, Reagan asked viewers, "Are you better off now than you were four years ago?" He won an electoral landslide and carried a Republican Senate into office.

Far more than any other recent president, Reagan entered office with a firm and fixed set of beliefs, views he had honed and argued for years. As a spokesman for General Electric, he estimated, he spoke for four thousand hours to audiences around the country. His conservative vision burst forth in 1964, when he gave a televised speech for Barry Goldwater. "The Speech"—which he wrote himself—galvanized supporters and launched him into a political career. Reagan wrote hundreds of radio commentaries in the 1970s. By the time he came into office, his speechwriters had a huge body of Reagan's own thought, usually written in his own hand, to feed back to him. His philosophy had two stark tenets: opposition to communism abroad, and a desire to shrink "big government" at home.

Reagan's swearing in marked the surge to power of a backlash against government that had begun during the 1960s. A new network of political activists and policy institutes nourished the movement, producing critiques of taxation, regulation, and governmental activism. "We

Reagan during the inaugural address, January 20, 1981

fought a war on poverty," Reagan was to say, "and poverty won." Inaugural week saw a return of glamour and ostentation to Washington, as Reagan's California backers clogged the streets.

Reagan's inaugural address served two distinct functions. The first part of the speech was a ripping repudiation of Carter's policies and approach. Columnist and former Nixon speechwriter William Safire noted that Reagan had issued an "FDR-style warning of economic peril," but that this time government, not business, was to blame. Indeed, where Roosevelt chastised businessmen as moneychangers who had defiled civilization's temple, Reagan extolled them as "heroes." Reagan's chief domestic proposal was a massive tax cut, known as "supply-side economics" for its belief that lower tax rates would stimulate higher tax receipts by spurring productive enterprise. His attack on government was broad—for example, in arguing that the states created the national government, his approach was at odds with the stance taken by Lincoln in his first inaugural.

The second half displays more of Reagan's rhetorical high style. He conveyed a deep optimism about America and its potential, in contrast to Carter's dour pessimism. (Compare this inaugural with the "malaise" speech.) Reagan was lucky: the Iranians released the American hostages just as he finished talking. He liked to invoke American history, a device also used by other presidents proposing controversial departures (such as Lincoln and Roosevelt). In earlier speeches, he had quoted Roosevelt even as he argued against the New Deal—a reflection both of his identification with FDR's jaunty spirit, and also his bid for the support of disaffected Democrats. In this speech, Reagan also took advantage of the vista before him, since the

podium for the first time faced west toward the Mall and the nation beyond rather than east.

Kenneth Khachigian, a former Nixon speechwriter who worked with Reagan on the campaign, drafted the speech. Reagan then took the draft and, on a plane ride across the country, wrote out a new and revised version in longhand. He added a typical touch: a friend had sent him the story of Martin Treptow, a World War I soldier who pledged to fulfill his duty. Staff aides discovered that Treptow had not in fact been buried at Arlington Cemetery, as Reagan had written, but in Wisconsin. Reagan decided to keep the reference anyway, adding the ambiguous language about how Arlington was filled with tombstones, and Treptow rests "under one such marker." After the speech, his aides willingly took the blame in public. Khachigian recalled to journalist Lou Cannon, "Ronald Reagan has a sense of theater that propels him to tell stories in their most theatrically imposing manner. He knew it would break up the story to say that Treptow was buried in Wisconsin." Reagan himself suggested the speech's closing phrase, "Why shouldn't we? We are Americans." He remembered the line from a movie about Bataan that he had seen during World War II.

Reagan formally proposed the tax cut in February. Two months later, he was shot outside a Washington hotel; the bullet missed his heart by an inch. He recovered and fought for the plan, winning the support of sixty-nine Democrats, and signing the tax cut into law in August of that year. The deficit quickly exploded to $128 billion the first year and over $200 billion per year after that. The American economy swooned into a recession, but recovered strongly in 1984. Most significantly, the conservative political era—which saw Reagan's critique of big government, articulated in this inaugural address—began.

Ronald Reagan's FIRST INAUGURAL ADDRESS

Washington, D.C. • January 20, 1981

*hear…* disc 2 track 11

Senator Hatfield, Mr. Chief Justice, Mr. President, Vice President Bush, Vice President Mondale, Senator Baker, Speaker O'Neill, Reverend Moomaw, and my fellow citizens:

To a few of us here today this is a solemn and most momentous occasion, and yet in the history of our nation it is a commonplace occurrence. The orderly transfer of authority as called for in the Constitution routinely takes place, as it has for almost two centuries, and few of us stop to think how unique we really are. In the eyes of many in the world, this every-4-year ceremony we accept as normal is nothing less than a miracle.

Mr. President, I want our fellow citizens to know how much you did to carry on this tradition. By your gracious cooperation in the transition process, you have shown a watching world that we are a united people pledged to maintaining a political system which guarantees individual liberty to a greater degree than any other, and I thank you and your people for all your help in maintaining the continuity which is the bulwark of our Republic.

"*These United States are confronted with an economic affliction of great proportions.*"

The business of our nation goes forward. These United States are confronted with an economic affliction of great proportions. We suffer from the longest and one of the worst sustained inflations in our national history. It distorts our economic decisions, penalizes thrift, and crushes the struggling young and the fixed-income elderly alike. It threatens to shatter the lives of millions of our people.

Idle industries have cast workers into unemployment, human misery, and personal indignity. Those who do work are denied a fair return for their labor by a tax system which penalizes successful achievement and keeps us from maintaining full productivity.

"*We must act today in order to preserve tomorrow. And let there be no misunderstanding: We are going to begin to act, beginning today.*"

But great as our tax burden is, it has not kept pace with public spending. For decades, we have piled deficit upon deficit, mortgaging our future and our children's future for the temporary convenience of the present. To continue this long trend is to guarantee tremendous social, cultural, political, and economic upheavals.

You and I, as individuals, can, by borrowing, live beyond our means, but for only a limited period of time. Why, then, should we think that collectively, as a nation, we're not bound by that same limitation? We must act today in order to preserve tomorrow. And let there be no misunderstanding: We are going to begin to act, beginning today.

The economic ills we suffer have come upon us over several decades. They will not go away in days, weeks, or months, but they will go away. They will go away because we as Americans have the capacity now, as we've had in the past, to do whatever needs to be done to preserve this last and greatest bastion of freedom.

247

President and Mrs. Ronald Reagan wave from their bulletproof limousine as the inaugural parade begins, January 20, 1981

In this present crisis, government is not the solution to our problem; government is the problem. From time to time, we've been tempted to believe that society has become too complex to be managed by self-rule, that government by an elite group is superior to government for, by, and of the people. Well, if no one among us is capable of governing himself, then who among us has the capacity to govern someone else? All of us together, in and out of government, must bear the burden. The solutions we seek must be equitable, with no one group singled out to pay a higher price.

We hear much of special interest groups. Well, our concern must be for a special interest group that has been too long neglected. It knows no sectional boundaries or ethnic and racial divisions, and it crosses political party lines. It is made up of men and women who raise our food, patrol our streets, man our mines and our factories, teach our children, keep our homes, and heal us when we're sick—professionals, industrialists, shopkeepers, clerks, cabbies, and truck-drivers. They are, in short, "We the people," this breed called Americans.

Well, this administration's objective will be a healthy, vigorous, growing economy that provides equal opportunities for all Americans, with no barriers born of bigotry or discrimination. Putting America back to work means putting all Americans back to work. Ending inflation means freeing all Americans from the terror of runaway living costs. All must share in the productive work of this "new beginning," and all must share in the bounty of a revived economy. With the idealism and fair play which are the core of our system and our strength, we can have a strong and prosperous America, at peace with itself and the world.

"Government is not the solution to our problem; government is the problem."

So, as we begin, let us take inventory. We are a nation that has a government—not the other way around. And this makes us special among the nations of the Earth. Our government has no power except that granted it by the people. It is time to check and reverse the growth of government, which shows signs of having grown beyond the consent of the governed.

It is my intention to curb the size and influence of the Federal establishment and to demand recognition of the distinction between the powers granted to the Federal Government and those reserved to the States or to the people. All of us need to be reminded that the Federal Government did not create the States; the States created the Federal Government.

Now, so there will be no misunderstanding, it's not my intention to do away with government. It is rather to make it work—work with us, not over us; to stand by our side, not ride on our back. Government can and must provide opportunity, not smother it; foster productivity, not stifle it.

If we look to the answer as to why for so many years we achieved so much, prospered as no other people on Earth, it was because here in this land we unleashed the energy and individual genius of man to a greater extent than has ever been done before. Freedom and the dignity of the individual have been more available and assured here than in any other place on Earth. The price for this freedom at times has been high, but we have never been unwilling to pay that price.

It is no coincidence that our present troubles parallel and are proportionate to the intervention and intrusion in our lives that result from unnecessary and excessive growth of government. It is time for us to realize that we're too great a nation to limit ourselves to small dreams. We're not, as some would have us believe, doomed to an inevitable decline. I do not believe in a fate that will fall on us no matter what we do. I do believe in a fate that will fall on us if we do nothing. So, with all the creative energy at our command, let us begin an era of national renewal. Let us renew our determination, our courage, and our strength. And let us renew our faith and our hope.

We have every right to dream heroic dreams. Those who say that we're in a time when there are not heroes, they just don't know where to look. You can see heroes every day going in and out of factory gates. Others, a handful in number, produce enough food to feed all of us and then the world beyond. You meet heroes across a counter, and they're on both sides of that counter. There are entrepreneurs with faith in themselves and faith in an idea who create new jobs, new wealth and opportunity. They're individuals and families whose taxes support the government and whose voluntary gifts support church, charity, culture, art, and education. Their patriotism is quiet, but deep. Their values sustain our national life.

"If no one among us is capable of governing himself, then who among us has the capacity to govern someone else?"

Now, I have used the words "they" and "their" in speaking of these heroes. I could say "you" and "your," because I'm addressing the heroes of whom I speak—you, the citizens of this blessed land. Your dreams, your hopes, your goals are going to be the dreams, the hopes, and the goals of this administration, so help me God.

We shall reflect the compassion that is so much a part of your makeup. How can we love our country and not love our countrymen; and loving them, reach out a hand when they fall, heal them when they're sick, and provide opportunity to make them self-sufficient so they will be equal in fact and not just in theory?

"The Federal Government did not create the States; the States created the Federal Government."

Can we solve the problems confronting us? Well, the answer is an unequivocal and emphatic "yes." To paraphrase Winston Churchill, I did not take the oath I've just taken with the intention of presiding over the dissolution of the world's strongest economy.

In the days ahead I will propose removing the roadblocks that have slowed our economy and reduced productivity. Steps will be taken aimed at restoring the balance between the various levels of government. Progress may be slow, measured in inches and feet, not miles, but we will progress. Is it time to reawaken this industrial giant, to get government back within its means, and to lighten our punitive tax burden. And these will be our first priorities, and on these principles there will be no compromise.

On the eve of our struggle for independence a man who might have been one of the greatest among the Founding Fathers, Dr. Joseph Warren, president of the Massachusetts Congress, said to his fellow Americans, "Our country is in danger, but not to be despaired of....On you depend the fortunes of America. You are to decide the important questions upon which rests the happiness and the liberty of millions yet unborn. Act worthy of yourselves."

Well, I believe we, the Americans of today, are ready to act worthy of ourselves, ready to do what must be done to ensure happiness and liberty for ourselves, our children, and our children's children. And as we renew ourselves here in our own land, we will be seen as having greater strength throughout the world. We will again be the exemplar of freedom and a beacon of hope for those who do not now have freedom.

To those neighbors and allies who share our freedom, we will strengthen our historic ties and assure them of our support and firm commitment. We will match loyalty with loyalty. We will strive for mutually beneficial relations. We will not use our friendship to impose on their sovereignty, for our own sovereignty is not for sale.

As for the enemies of freedom, those who are potential adversaries, they will be reminded that peace is the highest aspiration of the American people. We will negotiate for it, sacrifice for it; we will not surrender for it, now or ever.

Our forbearance should never be misunderstood. Our reluctance for conflict should not be misjudged as a failure of will. When action is required to preserve our national security, we will act. We will maintain sufficient strength to prevail if need be, knowing that if we do so we have the best chance of never having to use that strength.

"No weapon in the arsenals of the world is so formidable as the will and moral courage of free men and women. Let that be understood by those who practice terrorism and prey upon their neighbors."

Above all, we must realize that no arsenal or no weapon in the arsenals of the world is so formidable as the will and moral courage of free men and women. It is a weapon our adversaries in today's world do not have. It is a weapon that we as Americans do have. Let that be understood by those who practice terrorism and prey upon their neighbors.

I'm told that tens of thousands of prayer meetings are being held on this day, and for that I'm deeply grateful. We are a nation under God, and I believe God intended for us to be free. It would be fitting and good, I think, if on each Inaugural Day in future years it should be declared a day of prayer.

This is the first time in our history that this ceremony has been held, as you've been told, on this West Front of the Capitol. Standing here, one faces a magnificent vista, opening up on this city's special beauty and history. At the end of this open mall are those shrines to the giants on whose shoulders we stand.

Directly in front of me, the monument to a monumental man, George Washington, father of our country. A man of humility who came to greatness reluctantly. He led America out of revolutionary victory into infant nationhood. Off to one side, the stately memorial to Thomas Jefferson. The Declaration of Independence flames with his eloquence. And then, beyond the Reflecting Pool, the dignified columns of the Lincoln Memorial. Whoever would understand in his heart the meaning of America will find it in the life of Abraham Lincoln.

"Under one such marker lies a young man, Martin Treptow."

Beyond those monuments to heroism is the Potomac River, and on the far shore the sloping hills of Arlington National Cemetery, with its row upon row of simple white markers bearing crosses or Stars of David. They add up to only a tiny fraction of the price that has been paid for our freedom.

Each one of those markers is a monument to the kind of hero I spoke of earlier. Their lives ended in places called Belleau Wood, The Argonne, Omaha Beach, Salerno, and halfway around the world on Guadalcanal, Tarawa, Pork Chop Hill, the Chosin Reservoir, and in a hundred rice paddies and jungles of a place called Vietnam.

"With God's help, we can and will resolve the problems which now confront us. And, after all, why shouldn't we believe that? We are Americans."

Under one such marker lies a young man, Martin Treptow, who left his job in a small town barbershop in 1917 to go to France with the famed Rainbow Division. There, on the western front, he was killed trying to carry a message between battalions under heavy artillery fire.

We're told that on his body was found a diary. On the flyleaf under the heading, "My Pledge," he had written these words: "America must win this war. Therefore I will work, I will save, I will sacrifice, I will endure, I will fight cheerfully and do my utmost, as if the issue of the whole struggle depended on me alone."

The crisis we are facing today does not require of us the kind of sacrifice that Martin Treptow and so many thousands of others were called upon to make. It does require, however, our best effort and our willingness to believe in ourselves and to believe in our capacity to perform great deeds, to believe that together with God's help we can and will resolve the problems which now confront us.

And after all, why shouldn't we believe that? We are Americans.

God bless you, and thank you.

35

"LEAVE MARXISM-LENINISM ON THE ASH-HEAP OF HISTORY"

EVEN BEFORE RONALD REAGAN took office, superpower tensions were rising, as the Soviet Union invaded Afghanistan and both nations increased spending on the arms race. The Solidarity movement in Poland showed rising disaffection within the Eastern bloc until a military takeover crushed it in 1981. But communism and the Cold War seemed permanent. In his first press conference as president, Reagan said of the Soviet Union, "the only morality they recognize is what will further their cause, meaning they reserve unto themselves the right to commit any crime, to lie, to cheat." This was indeed a new tone for talking about the Cold War, and marked a shift from the "détente" of the 1970s.

In June 1982, Reagan was invited to speak to the members of the British Parliament during a European trip. (Prime Minister Margaret Thatcher, Reagan's ideological ally, had not consulted the Labour opposition, so the address was not a formal legislative session.) It was to be Reagan's first major presidential address on foreign policy, and it was the occasion for his broadest assault on the Soviet Union. Seen at the time as bold and even extreme, it is remembered as a prescient assault on Soviet communism that presaged its fall later in the decade.

Reagan belittled the economic inefficiency and lack of freedom in the Soviet Union. At the same time, he portrayed the rival superpower as an aggressive threat to peace. A strong protest movement was demanding a freeze on new nuclear weapons and sought to block new U.S. missiles in Europe. Where previous presidents had stressed the security threat, and sought ways to contain Soviet power without upsetting the delicate nuclear balance, Reagan focused on the intrinsic immorality of the repressive Soviet system.

Reagan remembered, "In retrospect, I am amazed that our national leaders had not philosophically and intellectually taken on the principles of Marxism-Leninism. We were always too worried we would offend the Soviets if we struck at anything so basic. Well, so what? Marxist-Leninist thought is an empty cupboard. Everyone knew it by the 1980s, but no one was saying it." He paraphrased Leon Trotsky when he said that Marxism-Leninism would end on "the ash-heap of history" (where Trotsky said the rival Mensheviks would land). Frequently, he appealed to British memories of World War II (the phrase "crusade for freedom" was the name Dwight D. Eisenhower gave to that war), implicitly equating the Soviets with the Nazis, and he overruled some aides by backing the British troops fighting a war against Argentina over the Falkland Islands. The speech gave rise to the "Reagan Doctrine"—the idea that the U.S. would work to roll back communist regimes and their allies where they now existed. This doctrine encompassed everything from support for the Mujahideen in Afghanistan to the Contras seeking to overthrow the government of Nicaragua.

Originally, the speech was even tougher. A draft from the State Department focused generally on support for democracy (rather than pointed opposition to communism). A different draft was written by White House speechwriter Tony Dolan, a Pulitzer Prize–winning former journalist; it used the word "evil" five times to describe the Soviet Union. The State Department balked, and aides fought over how sweeping the philosophical claims should be. Reagan combined Dolan's draft with language sent by newspaper columnist George Will. ("Regimes planted by bayonet do not take root," Will wrote.)

One fervent passage in an early draft referred to the Soviet Union as "the focus of evil." It was cut out. But the phrase was not itself thrown on the ash-heap of history. Speechwriters and conservative-minded aides on the White House staff slipped the phrase into a speech before evangelical Christians in Orlando, Florida, nine months later. In that speech, he called the Soviet Union the "focus of evil in the modern world." The Westminster first draft said, "Those clichés of conquest we have heard so often from the East are…part of a sad, bizarre, dreadfully evil episode in history, but an episode that is dying, a chapter whose last pages even now are being written." In Orlando, Reagan said, "I believe that communism is another sad, bizarre chapter in human history whose last pages even now are being written." He denounced the "the aggressive impulses of an evil empire"—reminding the public of Darth Vader's empire in the *Star Wars* movies.

Did Reagan actually intend to bring the Soviet Union down by forcing it into unsustainable military expenditure? Hindsight is perilously easy. It is hard to credit Reagan with such clairvoyance, despite how things turned out. He did, however, see the moral rot at communism's core. This speech is remembered for returning the note of American idealism into a superpower contest that had become tired and jaded.

"MR. GORBACHEV, TEAR DOWN THIS WALL!"

Reagan's Speech at the Brandenburg Gate, West Berlin
June 12, 1987

Chancellor Kohl, Governing Mayor Diepgen, ladies and gentlemen:

Twenty-four years ago, President John F. Kennedy visited Berlin, speaking to the people of this city and the world at the City Hall. Well, since then two other presidents have come, each in his turn, to Berlin. And today I, myself, make my second visit to your city.

We come to Berlin, we American presidents, because it's our duty to speak, in this place, of freedom. But I must confess, we're drawn here by other things as well: by the feeling of history in this city, more than 500 years older than our own nation; by the beauty of the Grunewald and the Tiergarten; most of all, by your courage and determination. Perhaps the composer Paul Lincke understood something about American presidents. You see, like so many presidents before me, I come here today because wherever I go, whatever I do: *Ich hab noch einen Koffer in Berlin* [I still have a suitcase in Berlin]….

…We welcome change and openness; for we believe that freedom and security go together, that the advance of human liberty can only strengthen the cause of world peace. There is one sign the Soviets can make that would be unmistakable, that would advance dramatically the cause of freedom and peace.

General Secretary Gorbachev, if you seek peace, if you seek prosperity for the Soviet Union and Eastern Europe, if you seek liberalization: Come here to this gate! Mr. Gorbachev, open this gate! Mr. Gorbachev, tear down this wall!

Ronald Reagan's
ADDRESS TO MEMBERS OF BRITISH PARLIAMENT

London, England • June 8, 1982

hear…

disc 2
track 12

My Lord Chancellor, Mr. Speaker:

The journey of which this visit forms a part is a long one. Already it has taken me to two great cities of the West, Rome and Paris, and to the economic summit at Versailles. And there, once again, our sister democracies have proved that even in a time of severe economic strain, free peoples can work together freely and voluntarily to address problems as serious as inflation, unemployment, trade, and economic development in a spirit of cooperation and solidarity.

Other milestones lie ahead. Later this week, in Germany, we and our NATO allies will discuss measures for our joint defense and America's latest initiatives for a more peaceful, secure world through arms reductions.

Each stop of this trip is important, but among them all, this moment occupies a special place in my heart and in the hearts of my countrymen—a moment of kinship and home-coming in these hallowed halls.

Speaking for all Americans, I want to say how very much at home we feel in your house. Every American would, because this is, as we have been so eloquently told, one of democracy's shrines. Here the rights of free people and the processes of representation have been debated and refined.

"The Berlin Wall, that dreadful gray gash across the city, is in its third decade."

It has been said that an institution is the lengthening shadow of a man. This institution is the lengthening shadow of all the men and women who have sat here and all those who have voted to send representatives here.

This is my second visit to Great Britain as President of the United States. My first opportunity to stand on British soil occurred almost a year and a half ago when your Prime Minister graciously hosted a diplomatic dinner at the British Embassy in Washington. Mrs. Thatcher said then that she hoped I was not distressed to find staring down at me from the grand staircase a portrait of His Royal Majesty King George III. She suggested it was best to let bygones be bygones, and in view of our two countries' remarkable friendship in succeeding years, she added that most Englishmen today would agree with Thomas Jefferson that "a little rebellion now and then is a very good thing." [*Laughter*]

"It was easier to believe in the march of democracy in Gladstone's day—in that high noon of Victorian optimism."

Well, from here I will go to Bonn and then Berlin, where there stands a grim symbol of power untamed. The Berlin Wall, that dreadful gray gash across the city, is in its third decade. It is the fitting signature of the regime that built it.

And a few hundred kilometers behind the Berlin Wall, there is another symbol. In the center of Warsaw, there is a sign that notes the distances to two capitals. In one direction it points toward Moscow. In the other it points toward Brussels, headquarters of Western Europe's tangible unity. The marker says that the distances from Warsaw to Moscow and Warsaw to Brussels are equal. The sign makes this point: Poland is not East or West. Poland is at

On June 8, 1982, Reagan poses with British guards in Westminister Palace, London, before addressing both Houses of Parliament

the center of European civilization. It has contributed mightily to that civilization. It is doing so today by being magnificently unreconciled to oppression.

Poland's struggle to be Poland and to secure the basic rights we often take for granted demonstrates why we dare not take those rights for granted. Gladstone, defending the Reform Bill of 1866, declared, "You cannot fight against the future. Time is on our side." It was easier to believe in the march of democracy in Gladstone's day—in that high noon of Victorian optimism.

We're approaching the end of a bloody century plagued by a terrible political invention—totalitarianism. Optimism comes less easily today, not because democracy is less vigorous, but because democracy's enemies have refined their instruments of repression. Yet optimism is in order, because day by day democracy is proving itself to be a not-at-all-fragile flower. From Stettin on the Baltic to Varna on the Black Sea, the regimes planted by totalitarianism have had more than 30 years to establish their legitimacy. But none—not one regime—has yet been able to risk free elections. Regimes planted by bayonets do not take root.

The strength of the Solidarity movement in Poland demonstrates the truth told in an underground joke in the Soviet Union. It is that the Soviet Union would remain a one-party nation even if an opposition party were permitted, because everyone would join the opposition party. [*Laughter*]

America's time as a player on the stage of world history has been brief. I think understanding this fact has always made you patient with your younger cousins—well, not always patient. I do recall that on one occasion, Sir Winston Churchill said in exasperation about one of our most distinguished diplomats: "He is the only case I know of a bull who carries his china shop with him." [*Laughter*]

"*Regimes planted by bayonets do not take root.*"

But witty as Sir Winston was, he also had that special attribute of great statesmen—the gift of vision, the willingness to see the future based on the experience of the past. It is this sense of history, this understanding of the past that I want to talk with you about today, for it is in remembering what we share of the past that our two nations can make common cause for the future.

We have not inherited an easy world. If developments like the Industrial Revolution, which began here in England, and the gifts of science and technology have made life much easier for us, they have also made it more dangerous. There are threats now to our freedom, indeed to our very existence, that other generations could never even have imagined.

There is first the threat of global war. No President, no Congress, no Prime Minister, no Parliament can spend a day entirely free of this threat. And I don't have to tell you that in today's world the existence of nuclear weapons could mean, if not the extinction of mankind, then surely the end of civilization as we know it. That's why negotiations on intermediate-range nuclear forces now underway in Europe and the START talks—Strategic Arms Reduction Talks—which will begin later this month, are not just critical to American or Western policy; they are critical to mankind. Our commitment to early success in these negotiations is firm and unshakable, and our

purpose is clear: reducing the risk of war by reducing the means of waging war on both sides.

At the same time there is a threat posed to human freedom by the enormous power of the modern state. History teaches the dangers of government that overreaches—political control taking precedence over free economic growth, secret police, mindless bureaucracy, all combining to stifle individual excellence and personal freedom.

Now, I'm aware that among us here and throughout Europe there is legitimate disagreement over the extent to which the public sector should play a role in a nation's economy and life. But on one point all of us are united—our abhorrence of dictatorship in all its forms, but most particularly totalitarianism and the terrible inhumanities it has caused in our time—the great purge, Auschwitz and Dachau, the Gulag, and Cambodia.

Historians looking back at our time will note the consistent restraint and peaceful intentions of the West. They will note that it was the democracies who refused to use the threat of their nuclear monopoly in the forties and early fifties for territorial or imperial gain. Had that nuclear monopoly been in the hands of the Communist world, the map of Europe—indeed, the world—would look very different today. And certainly they will note it was not the democracies that invaded Afghanistan or suppressed Polish Solidarity or used chemical and toxin warfare in Afghanistan and Southeast Asia.

If history teaches anything it teaches self-delusion in the face of unpleasant facts is folly. We see around us today the marks of our terrible dilemma—predictions of doomsday, antinuclear demonstrations, an arms race in which the West must, for its own protection, be an unwilling participant. At the same time we see totalitarian forces in the world who seek subversion and conflict around the globe to further their barbarous assault on the human spirit. What, then, is our course? Must civilization perish in a hail of fiery atoms? Must freedom wither in a quiet, deadening accommodation with totalitarian evil?

Sir Winston Churchill refused to accept the inevitability of war or even that it was imminent. He said, "I do not believe that Soviet Russia desires war. What they desire is the fruits of war and the indefinite expansion of their power and doctrines. But what we have to consider here today while time remains is the permanent prevention of war and the establishment of conditions of freedom and democracy as rapidly as possible in all countries."

Well, this is precisely our mission today: to preserve freedom as well as peace. It may not be easy to see; but I believe we live now at a turning point.

In an ironic sense Karl Marx was right. We are witnessing today a great revolutionary crisis, a crisis where the demands of the economic order are conflicting directly with those of the political order. But the crisis is happening not in the free, non-Marxist West, but in the home of Marxist-Leninism, the Soviet Union. It is the Soviet Union that runs against the tide of history by denying human freedom and human dignity to its citizens. It also is in deep economic difficulty. The rate of growth in the national product has been steadily declining since the fifties and is less than half of what it was then.

> *"The Soviet Union would remain a one-party nation even if an opposition party were permitted, because everyone would join the opposition party."*

The dimensions of this failure are astounding: A country which employs one-fifth of its population in agriculture is unable to feed its own people. Were it not for the private sector, the tiny private sector tolerated in Soviet agriculture, the country might be on the brink of famine. These private plots occupy a bare 3 percent of the arable land but account for nearly one-quarter of Soviet farm output and nearly one-third of meat products and vegetables. Overcentralized, with little or no incentives, year after year the Soviet system pours its best resource into the making of instruments of destruction. The constant shrinkage of economic growth combined with the growth of military production is putting a heavy strain on the Soviet people. What we see here is a political structure that no longer corresponds to its economic base, a society where productive forces are hampered by political ones.

The decay of the Soviet experiment should come as no surprise to us. Wherever the comparisons have been made between free and closed societies—West Germany and East Germany, Austria and Czechoslovakia, Malaysia and Vietnam—it is the democratic countries that are prosperous and responsive to the needs of their people. And one of the simple but overwhelming facts of our time is this: Of all the millions of refugees we've seen in the modern world, their flight is always away from, not toward the Communist world. Today on the NATO line, our military forces face east to prevent a possible invasion. On the other side of the line, the Soviet forces also face east to prevent their people from leaving.

The hard evidence of totalitarian rule has caused in mankind an uprising of the intellect and will. Whether it is the growth of the new schools of economics in America or England or the appearance of the so-called new philosophers in France, there is one unifying thread running through the intellectual work of these groups—rejection of the arbitrary power of the state, the refusal to subordinate the rights of the individual to the superstate, the realization that collectivism stifles all the best human impulses.

Since the exodus from Egypt, historians have written of those who sacrificed and struggled for freedom—the stand at Thermopylae, the revolt of Spartacus, the storming of the Bastille, the Warsaw uprising in World War II. More recently we've seen evidence of this same human impulse in one of the developing nations in Central America. For months and months the world news media covered the fighting in El Salvador. Day after day we were treated to stories and film slanted toward the brave freedom-fighters battling oppressive government forces in behalf of the silent, suffering people of that tortured country.

And then one day those silent, suffering people were offered a chance to vote, to choose the kind of government they wanted. Suddenly the freedom-fighters in the hills were exposed for what they really are—Cuban-backed guerrillas who want power for themselves, and their backers, not democracy for the people. They threatened death to any who voted, and destroyed hundreds of buses and trucks to keep the people from getting to the polling places. But on election day, the people of El Salvador, an unprecedented 1.4 million of them, braved ambush and gunfire, and trudged for miles to vote for freedom.

They stood for hours in the hot sun waiting for their turn to vote. Members of our Congress who went there as observers told me of a woman who was wounded by rifle fire on the way to the polls, who refused to leave the line to have her wound treated until after she had voted. A grandmother, who had been told by the guerrillas she would be killed when she returned from the polls, and she told the guerrillas, "You can kill me, you can kill my family, kill my neighbors, but you can't kill us all." The real freedom-fighters of El Salvador turned out to be the people of that country—the young, the old, the in-between.

> "It is not the democracies that invaded Afghanistan or suppressed Polish Solidarity or used chemical and toxin warfare in Afghanistan and Southeast Asia."

Strange, but in my own country there's been little if any news coverage of that war since the election. Now, perhaps they'll say it's—well, because there are newer struggles now.

On distant islands in the South Atlantic young men are fighting for Britain. And, yes, voices have been raised protesting their sacrifice for lumps of rock and earth so far away. But those young men aren't fighting for mere real estate. They fight for a cause—for the belief that armed aggression must not be allowed to succeed, and the people must participate in the decisions of government—the decisions of government under the rule of law. If there had been firmer support for that principle some 45 years ago, perhaps our generation wouldn't have suffered the bloodletting of World War II.

In the Middle East now the guns sound once more, this time in Lebanon, a country that for too long has had to endure the tragedy of civil war, terrorism, and foreign intervention and occupation. The fighting in Lebanon on the part of all parties must stop, and Israel should bring its forces home. But this is not enough. We must all work to stamp out the scourge of terrorism that in the Middle East makes war an ever-present threat.

But beyond the troublespots lies a deeper, more positive pattern. Around the world today, the democratic revolution is gathering new strength. In India a critical test has been passed with the peaceful change of governing political parties. In Africa, Nigeria is moving in remarkable and unmistakable ways to build and strengthen its democratic institutions. In the Caribbean and Central America, 16 of 24 countries have freely elected governments. And in the United Nations, 8 of the 10 developing nations which have joined that body in the past 5 years are democracies.

In the Communist world as well, man's instinctive desire for freedom and self-determination surfaces again and again. To be sure, there are grim reminders of how brutally the police state attempts to snuff out this quest for self-rule—1953 in East Germany, 1956 in Hungary, 1968 in Czechoslovakia, 1981 in Poland. But the struggle continues in Poland. And we know that there are even those who strive and suffer for freedom within the confines of the Soviet Union itself. How we conduct ourselves here in the Western democracies will determine whether this trend continues.

No, democracy is not a fragile flower. Still it needs cultivating. If the rest of this century is to witness the gradual growth of freedom and democratic ideals, we must take actions to assist the campaign for democracy.

> *"The crisis is happening not in the free, non-Marxist West, but in the home of Marxist-Leninism, the Soviet Union. It is the Soviet Union that runs against the tide of history by denying human freedom and human dignity to its citizens."*

Some argue that we should encourage democratic change in right-wing dictatorships, but not in Communist regimes. Well, to accept this preposterous notion—as some well-meaning people have—is to invite the argument that once countries achieve a nuclear capability, they should be allowed an undisturbed reign of terror over their own citizens. We reject this course.

As for the Soviet view, Chairman Brezhnev repeatedly has stressed that the competition of ideas and systems must continue and that this is entirely consistent with relaxation of tensions and peace.

Well, we ask only that these systems begin by living up to their own constitutions, abiding by their own laws, and complying with the international obligations they have undertaken. We ask only for a process, a direction, a basic code of decency, not for an instant transformation.

We cannot ignore the fact that even without our encouragement there has been and will continue to be repeated explosions against repression and dictatorships. The Soviet Union itself is not immune to this reality. Any system is inherently unstable that has no peaceful means to legitimize its leaders. In such cases, the very repressiveness of the state ultimately drives people to resist it, if necessary, by force.

While we must be cautious about forcing the pace of change, we must not hesitate to declare our ultimate objectives and to take concrete actions to move toward them. We must be staunch in our conviction that freedom is not the sole prerogative of a lucky few, but the inalienable and universal right of all human beings. So states the United Nations Universal Declaration of Human Rights, which, among other things, guarantees free elections.

The objective I propose is quite simple to state: to foster the infrastructure of democracy, the system of a free press, unions, political parties, universities, which allows a people to choose their own way to develop their own culture, to reconcile their own differences through peaceful means.

This is not cultural imperialism, it is providing the means for genuine self-determination and protection for diversity. Democracy already flourishes in countries with very different cultures and historical experiences. It would be cultural condescension, or worse, to say that any people prefer dictatorship to democracy. Who would voluntarily choose not to have the right to vote, decide to purchase government propaganda handouts instead of independent newspapers, prefer government to worker-controlled unions, opt for land to be owned by the state instead of those who till it, want government repression of religious liberty, a single political party instead of a free choice, a rigid cultural orthodoxy instead of democratic tolerance and diversity?

Since 1917 the Soviet Union has given covert political training and assistance to Marxist-Leninists in many countries. Of course, it also has promoted the use of violence and subversion by these same forces. Over the past several decades, West European and other Social Democrats, Christian Democrats, and leaders have offered open assistance to fraternal, political, and social institutions to bring about peaceful and democratic progress. Appropriately, for a vigorous new democracy, the Federal Republic of Germany's political foundations have become a major force in this effort.

We in America now intend to take additional steps, as many of our allies have already done, toward realizing this same goal. The chairmen and other leaders of the national Republican and Democratic Party organizations are initiating a study with the bipartisan American political foundation to determine how the United States can best contribute as a nation to the global campaign for democracy now gathering force. They will have the cooperation of congressional leaders of both parties, along with representatives of business, labor, and other major institutions in our society. I look forward to receiving their recommendations and to working with these institutions and the Congress in the common task of strengthening democracy throughout the world.

> *"Of all the millions of refugees we've seen in the modern world, their flight is always away from, not toward the Communist world."*

It is time that we committed ourselves as a nation—in both the pubic and private sectors—to assisting democratic development.

We plan to consult with leaders of other nations as well. There is a proposal before the Council of Europe to invite parliamentarians from democratic countries to a meeting next year in Strasbourg. That prestigious gathering could consider ways to help democratic political movements.

This November in Washington there will take place an international meeting on free elections. And next spring there will be a conference of world authorities on constitutionalism and self-government hosted by the Chief Justice of the United States. Authorities from a number of developing and developed countries—judges, philosophers, and politicians with practical experience—have agreed to explore how to turn principle into practice and further the rule of law.

At the same time, we invite the Soviet Union to consider with us how the competition of ideas and values—which it is committed to support—can be conducted on a peaceful and reciprocal basis. For example, I am prepared to offer President Brezhnev an opportunity to speak to the American people on our television if he will allow me the same opportunity with the Soviet people. We also suggest that panels of our newsmen periodically appear on each other's television to discuss major events.

Now, I don't wish to sound overly optimistic, yet the Soviet Union is not immune from the reality of what is going on in the world. It has happened in the past—a small ruling elite either mistakenly attempts to ease domestic unrest through greater repression and foreign adventure, or it chooses a wiser course. It begins to allow its people a voice in their own destiny. Even if this latter process is not realized soon, I believe the renewed strength of the democratic movement, complemented by a global campaign for freedom, will strengthen the prospects for arms control and a world at peace.

I have discussed on other occasions, including my address on May 9th, the elements of Western policies toward the Soviet Union to safeguard our interests and protect the peace. What I am describing now is a plan and a hope for the long term—the march of freedom and democracy which will leave Marxism-Leninism on the ash-heap of history as it has left other tyrannies which stifle the freedom and muzzle the self-expression of the people. And that's why we must continue our efforts to strengthen NATO even as we move forward with our Zero-Option initiative in the negotiations on intermediate-range forces and our proposal for a one-third reduction in strategic ballistic missile warheads.

> *"Some argue that we should encourage democratic change in the right-wing dictatorships, but not in the Communist regimes…We reject this course."*

Our military strength is a prerequisite to peace, but let it be clear we maintain this strength in the hope it will never be used, for the ultimate determinant in the struggle that's now going on in the world will not be bombs and rockets, but a test of wills and ideas, a trial of spiritual resolve, the values we hold, the beliefs we cherish, the ideals to which we are dedicated.

"The march of freedom and democracy which will leave Marxist-Leninism on the ash-heap of history."

The British people know that, given strong leadership, time and a little bit of hope, the forces of good ultimately rally and triumph over evil. Here among you is the cradle of self-government, the Mother of Parliaments. Here is the enduring greatness of the British contribution to mankind, the great civilized ideas: individual liberty, representative government, and the rule of law under God.

I've often wondered about the shyness of some of us in the West about standing for these ideals that have done so much to ease the plight of man and the hardships of our imperfect world. This reluctance to use those vast resources at our command reminds me of the elderly lady whose home was bombed in the Blitz. As the rescuers moved about, they found a bottle of brandy she'd stored behind the staircase, which was all that was left standing. And since she was barely conscious, one of the workers pulled the cork to give her a taste of it. She came around immediately and said, "Here now— there now, put it back. That's for emergencies." [*Laughter*]

Well, the emergency is upon us. Let us be shy no longer. Let us go to our strength. Let us offer hope. Let us tell the world that a new age is not only possible but probable.

During the dark days of the Second World War, when this island was incandescent with courage, Winston Churchill exclaimed about Britain's adversaries, "What kind of a people do they think we are?" Well, Britain's adversaries found out what extraordinary people the British are. But all the democracies paid a terrible price for allowing the dictators to underestimate us. We dare not make that mistake again. So, let us ask ourselves, "What kind of people do we think we are?" And let us answer, "Free people, worthy of freedom and determined not only to remain so but to help others gain their freedom as well."

Sir Winston led his people to great victory in war and then lost an election just as the fruits of victory were about to be enjoyed. But he left office honorably, and, as it turned out, temporarily, knowing that the liberty of his people was more important than the fate of any single leader. History recalls his greatness in ways no dictator will ever know. And he left us a message of hope for the future, as timely now as when he first uttered it, as opposition leader in the Commons nearly 27 years ago, when he said, "When we look back on all the perils through which we have passed and at the mighty foes that we have laid low and all the dark and deadly designs that we have frustrated, why should we fear for our future? We have," he said, "come safely through the worst."

"So let us ask ourselves, What kind of people do we think we are?"

Well, the task I've set forth will long outlive our own generation. But together, we too have come through the worst. Let us now begin a major effort to secure the best— a crusade for freedom that will engage the faith and fortitude of the next generation. For the sake of peace and justice, let us move toward a world in which all people are at last free to determine their own destiny.

Thank you.

36

"SLIPPED THE SURLY BONDS OF EARTH"

THE UNITED STATES space program had captured and captivated public attention for years, with the thrilling series of launches culminating in *Apollo 11* and Neil Armstrong's first steps on the moon. Then the public got bored. In 1981, the routinization of space travel became complete, with the start of the space shuttle program. Instead of highly expensive rockets that were used once and allowed to plummet into the ocean, the space shuttle boosters were reusable. As for the shuttle craft itself, instead of barreling through the atmosphere and landing with parachutes, as earlier command modules had done, the shuttle would be piloted and would land at an airfield like a large, ungainly glider. By January 1986, 125 men and women had flown on the shuttle on twenty-four missions.

The National Aeronautics and Space Administration (NASA) had something special planned for the launch of the shuttle *Challenger*. A nationwide contest had chosen a schoolteacher, Christa McAuliffe from Concord, New Hampshire, to serve as an astronaut. Children had followed her training for months. Now classrooms in schools across the country would watch her shuttle's launch live on cable news television. The crew included two women, an African-American man, an Asian man, as well as a scientist, and two engineers—a far cry from the crew-cut fighter pilots who had been the nation's first astronauts.

At first the launch, viewed on television, seemed routine. "Go at throttle up," the ground controller said in the laconic tone of so many missions. Then, one minute and thirteen seconds into flight, the shuttle exploded, sending debris and plumes of smoke streaming into the Atlantic. Viewers saw the horror as McAuliffe's family and others realized what had happened. In an instant, every crew member aboard the *Challenger* had perished.

The Challenger crew walks out of the Operations Building on their way to launch Pad-39B. Crew members include (front to back): Commander Francis R. Scobee, Mission Specialists Judith A. Resnik and Ronald E. McNair, Pilot Michael J. Smith, Payload Specialist Christa McAuliffe, Mission Specialist Ellison Onizuka, and Payload Specialist Gregory B. Jarvis

Debris in the sky above the Kennedy Space Center in Florida after the explosion of the space shuttle Challenger, January 28, 1986

President Ronald Reagan had been scheduled to deliver the State of the Union address that night. Instead, he waited for the search to be called off, and then briefly addressed the country on television from the Oval Office. Reagan recognized the importance of the ceremonial nature of the public presidency: there were times when the most important leadership came not from policies but from leading the nation in common mourning. Reagan delivered a classic eulogy. It is neither fulsome nor grand; we hear formal eloquence only in brief flashes. Religion plays little role. The president had been meeting with the network television anchors to preview his State of the Union, and their questions and his impromptu answers (What should we tell the children? Will the space program go on?) formed the basis of the speech.

Witnesses of the explosion of the space shuttle Challenger, January 28, 1986, Cape Canaveral, Florida

Even an emotional talk like this makes policy and political points. Reagan noted that the U.S. space program publicizes its launches, in implied contrast to the space program of the Soviet Union (where accidents were hidden from view). He also pledged that the space program would go forward. Reagan also placed the tragedy in the context of history. He referred to the loss of astronauts in *Apollo 1*, in a launch-pad fire during rehearsals in 1967, as well as to the death at sea of Sir Francis Drake. Reagan conjured the hopeful scene of the astronauts happily waving good-bye to replace the painful image of the shuttle exploding that had played for hours on television.

Peggy Noonan, a former radio copywriter who became one of Reagan's most celebrated writers, drafted the speech. At the end, Reagan quotes from "High Flight," a poem memorized by pilots and well known to the president's generation. By deftly borrowing, Reagan made the words his own.

"HIGH FLIGHT"
by John Magee

Oh! I have slipped the surly bonds of earth
And danced the skies on laughter-silvered wings;
Sunward I've climbed, and joined the tumbling mirth
Of sun-split clouds—and done a hundred things
You have not dreamed of—wheeled and soared and swung
High in the sunlit silence. Hov'ring there,
I've chased the shouting wind along, and flung
My eager craft through footless halls of air.
Up, up the long, delirious burning blue
I've topped the wind-swept heights with easy grace
Where never lark, or even eagle flew—
And, while with silent lifting mind I've trod
The high untrespassed sanctity of space,
Put out my hand and touched the face of God.

Ronald Reagan's
ADDRESS TO THE NATION ON THE CHALLENGER EXPLOSION

Washington, D.C. • January 28, 1986

hear....
disc 2
track 13

Ladies and gentlemen,

I'd planned to speak to you tonight to report on the state of the Union, but the events of earlier today have led me to change those plans. Today is a day for mourning and remembering. Nancy and I are pained to the core by the tragedy of the shuttle Challenger. We know we share this pain with all of the people of our country. This is truly a national loss.

Nineteen years ago, almost to the day, we lost three astronauts in a terrible accident on the ground. But we've never lost an astronaut in flight; we've never had a tragedy like this. And perhaps we've forgotten the courage it took for the crew of the shuttle. But they, the *Challenger* Seven, were aware of the dangers, but overcame them and did their jobs brilliantly. We mourn seven heroes: Michael Smith,

Reagan addresses the nation after the Challenger explosion

Dick Scobee, Judith Resnik, Ronald McNair, Ellison Onizuka, Gregory Jarvis, and Christa McAuliffe. We mourn their loss as a nation together.

"I want to say something to schoolchildren of America who were watching…"

For the families of the seven, we cannot bear, as you do, the full impact of this tragedy. But we feel the loss, and we're thinking about you so very much. Your loved ones were daring and brave, and they had that special grace, that special spirit that says, "Give me a challenge, and I'll meet it with joy." They had a hunger to explore the universe and discover its truths. They wished to serve, and they did. They served all of us. We've grown used to wonders in this century. It's hard to dazzle us. But for 25 years the United States space program has been doing just that. We've grown used to the idea of space, and perhaps we forget that we've only just begun. We're still pioneers. They, the members of the *Challenger* crew, were pioneers.

"The future doesn't belong to the fainthearted; it belongs to the brave."

And I want to say something to the schoolchildren of America who were watching the live coverage of the shuttle's take-off. I know it is hard to understand, but sometimes painful things like this happen. It's all part of the process of exploration and discovery. It's all part of taking a chance and expanding man's horizons. The future doesn't belong to the fainthearted; it belongs to the brave. The *Challenger* crew was pulling us into the future, and we'll continue to follow them.

I've always had great faith in and respect for our space program, and what happened today does nothing to diminish it. We don't hide our space program. We don't keep secrets and cover things up. We do it all up front and in public. That's the way freedom is, and we wouldn't change it for a minute. We'll continue our quest in space. There will be more shuttle flights and more shuttle crews and, yes, more volunteers, more civilians, more teachers in space. Nothing ends here; our hopes and our journeys continue. I want to add that I wish I could talk to every man and woman who works for NASA or who worked on this mission and tell them: "Your dedication and professionalism have moved and impressed us for decades. And we know of your anguish. We share it."

"We will never forget them, not the last time we saw them, this morning, as they prepared for the journey and waved goodbye and 'slipped the surly bonds of earth' to 'touch the face of God.'"

There's a coincidence today. On this day 390 years ago, the great explorer Sir Francis Drake died aboard ship off the coast of Panama. In his lifetime the great frontiers were the oceans, and an historian later said, "He lived by the sea, died on it, and was buried in it." Well, today we can say of the *Challenger* crew: Their dedication was, like Drake's, complete.

The crew of the space shuttle *Challenger* honored us by the manner in which they lived their lives. We will never forget them, nor the last time we saw them, this morning, as they prepared for their journey and waved goodbye and "slipped the surly bonds of earth" to "touch the face of God."

Thank you.

37

RONALD REAGAN

"I CANNOT ESCAPE RESPONSIBILITY"

THE CONVOLUTED WEB of schemes known as Iran-Contra was a significant scandal, and more important, a constitutional crisis. It laid bare deep problems with Ronald Reagan's style of management. Yet it also showed a masterful effort to extract a chief executive from trouble of his own making.

During the 1980s, American citizens had been kidnapped and held hostage by radical Muslims in Lebanon.

The United States loudly proclaimed it did not negotiate with kidnappers, and denounced Iran as a source of terrorism. But at the same time, Reagan's aides secretly sold missiles to Iran in an effort to trade arms for hostages. The elaborate covert scheme, involving shady middlemen, mysterious arms dealers, and a secret trip by the White House National Security Advisor to Teheran, freed no

Reagan tells reporters on May 15, 1987, that he might have approved a covert plan to pay $2 million to get the American hostages in Lebanon released

hostages and actually encouraged further kidnappings. Reagan approved the plan and kept track of its progress.

At the same time, the U.S. was supporting the Contra guerillas seeking to overthrow the Sandinista government of Nicaragua. Reagan had called the Contras "Freedom Fighters" and likened them to America's own Founding Fathers. But the Congress passed a law, known as the Boland Amendment, explicitly barring the U.S. from funding the rebels. Reagan's aides decided to take the profits from the arms sales to Iran to fund the Contras, in clear violation of the law. It seemed, as Colonel Oliver North, a White House aide, recalled, "a neat idea." When the scheme began to unravel, the officials covered up, lied to Congress, and destroyed documents in what they called a White House "shredding party."

The scandal emerged when an obscure Arab language newspaper revealed the arms for hostages swap in early November 1986. At first, President Reagan misled the public. In an Oval Office address, he insisted that he sent only small amounts of weapons and spare parts that "could easily fit into a single cargo plane. We did not—repeat—did not trade weapons or anything else for hostages, nor will we." Then Attorney General Edwin Meese announced that his own investigation had discovered the diversion of funds to the Contras. A criminal investigation was launched, congressional probes planned, Reagan fired several aides, and a full Washington scandal erupted. Soon Reagan conceded that "mistakes were made," though he did not say who made them.

In what proved to be a savvy move, Reagan appointed a three-person panel, headed by former Senator John Tower, to investigate. (The president gave the group shifting stories about whether he remembered authorizing the arms sales, but denied knowing of the plainly illegal "diversion" to the Contras.) The Tower Commission issued a harsh report on February 26, 1987. It showed a president ignorant of details, unable to remember, and a staff running secret operations with little oversight. It blamed Reagan for "the chaos that descended on the White House," and euphemistically cited Reagan's "detached management style." On the surface, it seemed devastating. In fact, it was his salvation, blaming him not for criminality but for sloth—and it gave Reagan the chance to "clean house" by firing his chief of staff, Donald Regan. In a television address on March 4, 1987, he accepted the verdict of the report. He declared that even though his "heart and [his] best intentions" say otherwise, he did in fact trade arms for hostages. He took "full responsibility" for actions of his subordinates, while still asserting he did not know about them. Theodore Draper, in the authoritative history of the controversy, writes, "It was a strange explanation. In effect, Reagan assumed responsibility for irresponsibility." Still, the speech marked the beginning of his recovery from the scandal, even as congressional hearings and prosecutions continued for years. "By meeting the crisis head on, especially in the press, Reagan gradually rearranged the political landscape so he could govern again," concludes former Reagan aide David Gergen.

In the end, Reagan recovered his standing by negotiating arms agreements with the reformist new leader of the Soviet Union, Mikhail Gorbachev. Many of his top aides were charged with crimes, including his defense secretary, Caspar Weinberger; his national security advisor, Robert McFarlane; and an assistant secretary of state, Elliot Abrams. At the end of his term as president, George H.W. Bush pardoned each of them as he left office.

My fellow Americans:

I've spoken to you from this historic office on many occasions and about many things. The power of the Presidency is often thought to reside within this Oval Office. Yet it doesn't rest here; it rests in you, the American people, and in your trust. Your trust is what gives a President his powers of leadership and his personal strength, and it's what I want to talk to you about this evening.

For the past 3 months, I've been silent on the revelations about Iran. And you must have been thinking: "Well, why doesn't he tell us what's happening? Why doesn't he just speak to us as he has in the past when we've faced troubles or tragedies?" Others of you, I guess, were thinking: "What's he doing hiding out in the White House?" Well, the reason I haven't spoken to you before now is this: You deserve the truth. And as frustrating as the waiting has been, I felt it was improper to come to you with sketchy reports, or possibly even erroneous statements, which would then have to be corrected, creating even more doubt and confusion. There's been enough of that. I've paid a price for my silence in terms of your trust and confidence. But I've had to wait, as you have, for the complete story. That's why I appointed Ambassador David Abshire as my Special Counsellor to help get out the thousands of documents to the various investigations. And I appointed a Special Review Board, the Tower board, which took on the chore of pulling the truth together for me and getting to the bottom of things. It has now issued its findings.

I'm often accused of being an optimist, and it's true I had to hunt pretty hard to find any good news in the Board's report. As you know, it's well-stocked with criticisms, which I'll discuss in a moment; but I was very relieved to read this sentence: "...the Board is convinced

that the President does indeed want the full story to be told." And that will continue to be my pledge to you as the other investigations go forward. I want to thank the members of the panel: former Senator John Tower, former Secretary of State Edmund Muskie, and former national security adviser Brent Scowcroft. They have done the Nation, as well as me personally, a great service by submitting a report of such integrity and depth. They have my genuine and enduring gratitude.

"Others of you...were thinking: What's he doing hiding out in the White House?"

I've studied the Board's report. Its findings are honest, convincing, and highly critical; and I accept them. And tonight I want to share with you my thoughts on these findings and report to you on the actions I'm taking to implement the Board's recommendations. First, let me say I take full responsibility for my own actions and for those of my administration. As angry as I may be about activities undertaken without my knowledge, I am still accountable for those activities. As disappointed as I may be in some who served me, I'm still the one who must answer to the American people for this behavior. And as personally distasteful as I find secret bank accounts and diverted funds—well, as the Navy would say, this happened on my watch.

Let's start with the part that is the most controversial. A few months ago I told the American people I did not trade arms for hostages. My heart and my best intentions still tell me that's true, but the facts and the evidence tell me it is not. As the Tower board reported, what began as a strategic opening to Iran deteriorated, in its implementation, into trading arms for hostages. This runs counter to my own beliefs, to administration policy, and to the original strategy we had in mind. There are reasons why it happened, but no excuses. It was a mistake. I undertook the original Iran initiative in order to develop relations with those who might assume leadership in a post-Khomeini government.

"I've paid a price for my silence in terms of your trust and confidence."

It's clear from the Board's report, however, that I let my personal concern for the hostages spill over into the geopolitical strategy of reaching out to Iran. I asked so many questions about the hostages' welfare that I didn't ask enough about the specifics of the total Iran plan. Let me say to the hostage families: We have not given up. We never

will. And I promise you we'll use every legitimate means to free your loved ones from captivity. But I must also caution that those Americans who freely remain in such dangerous areas must know that they're responsible for their own safety.

Now, another major aspect of the Board's findings regards the transfer of funds to the Nicaraguan *contras*. The Tower board wasn't able to find out what happened to this money, so the facts here will be left to the continuing investigations of the court-appointed Independent Counsel and the two congressional investigating committees. I'm confident the truth will come out about this matter, as well. As I told the Tower board, I didn't know about any diversion of funds to the *contras*. But as President, I cannot escape responsibility.

"Its findings are honest, convincing, and highly critical; and I accept them."

Much has been said about my management style, a style that's worked successfully for me during 8 years as Governor of California and for most of my Presidency. The way I work is to identify the problem, find the right individuals to do the job, and then let them go to it. I've found this invariably brings out the best in people. They seem to rise to their full capability, and in the long run you get more done. When it came to managing the NSC staff, let's face it, my style didn't match its previous track record. I've already begun correcting this. As a start, yesterday I met with the entire professional staff of the National Security Council. I defined for them the values I want to guide the national security policies of this country. I told them that I wanted a policy that was as justifiable and understandable in public as it was in secret. I wanted a policy that reflected the will of the Congress as well as of the White House. And I told them that there'll be no more freelancing by individuals when it comes to our national security.

Reagan admits in this televised address on March 4, 1987, that he and his staff traded arms for hostages with Iran and funneled profits to the Nicaraguan Contras armies

You've heard a lot about the staff of the National Security Council in recent months. Well, I can tell you, they are good and dedicated government employees, who put in long hours for the Nation's benefit. They are eager and anxious to serve their country. One thing still upsetting me, however, is that no one kept proper records of meetings or decisions. This led to my failure to recollect whether I approved an arms shipment before or after the fact. I did approve it; I just can't say specifically when. Well, rest assured, there's plenty of recordkeeping now going on at 1600 Pennsylvania Avenue.

> ## *"As angry as I may be about activities undertaken without my knowledge, I am still accountable for those activities."*

For nearly a week now, I've been studying the Board's report. I want the American people to know that this wrenching ordeal of recent months has not been in vain. I endorse every one of the Tower board's recommendations. In fact, I'm going beyond its recommendations so as to put the house in even better order. I'm taking action in three basic areas: personnel, national security policy, and the process for making sure that the system works.

First, personnel—I've brought in an accomplished and highly respected new team here at the White House. They bring new blood, new energy, and new credibility and experience. Former Senator Howard Baker, my new Chief of Staff, possesses a breadth of legislative and foreign affairs skills that's impossible to match. I'm hopeful that his experience as minority and majority leader of the Senate can help us forge a new partnership with the Congress, especially on foreign and national security policies. I'm genuinely honored that he's given up his own Presidential aspirations to serve the country as my Chief of Staff. Frank Carlucci, my new national security adviser, is respected for his experience in government and trusted for his judgment

and counsel. Under him, the NSC staff is being rebuilt with proper management discipline. Already, almost half the NSC professional staff is comprised of new people.

Yesterday I nominated William Webster, a man of sterling reputation, to be Director of the Central Intelligence Agency. Mr. Webster has served as Director of the FBI and as a U.S. District Court judge. He understands the meaning of "rule of law." So that his knowledge of national security matters can be available to me on a continuing basis, I will also appoint John Tower to serve as a member of my Foreign Intelligence Advisory Board. I am considering other changes in personnel, and I'll move more furniture, as I see fit, in the weeks and months ahead.

Second, in the area of national security policy, I have ordered the NSC to begin a comprehensive review of all covert operations. I have also directed that any covert activity be in support of clear policy objectives and in compliance with American values. I expect a covert policy that, if Americans saw it on the front page of their newspaper, they'd say, "That makes sense." I have had issued a directive prohibiting the NSC staff itself from undertaking covert operations—no ifs, ands, or buts. I have asked Vice President Bush to reconvene his task force on terrorism to review our terrorist policy in light of the events that have occurred.

> ## *"Much has been said about my management style... When it came to managing the NSC staff, let's face it, my style didn't match its previous track record."*

Third, in terms of the process of reaching national security decisions, I am adopting in total the Tower report's model of how the NSC process and staff should work. I am directing Mr. Carlucci to take the necessary steps to make that happen. He will report back to me on further reforms that might be needed. I've created the post of NSC legal adviser to assure a greater sensitivity to matters of law. I am also determined to make the congressional oversight process work. Proper procedures for consultation with the Congress will be followed, not only in letter but in spirit. Before the end of March, I will report to the Congress on all the steps I've taken in line with the Tower board's conclusions.

"I did approve it; I just can't say specifically when."

Now, what should happen when you make a mistake is this: You take your knocks, you learn your lessons, and then you move on. That's the healthiest way to deal with a problem. This in no way diminishes the importance of the other continuing investigations, but the business of our country and our people must proceed. I've gotten this message from Republicans and Democrats in Congress, from allies around the world, and—if we're reading the signals right—even from the Soviets. And of course, I've heard the message from you, the American people. You know, by the time you reach my age, you've made plenty of mistakes. And if you've lived your life properly—so, you learn. You put things in perspective. You pull your energies together. You change. You go forward.

My fellow Americans, I have a great deal that I want to accomplish with you and for you over the next 2 years. And the Lord willing, that's exactly what I intend to do.

Good night, and God bless you.

"By the time you reach my age, you've made plenty of mistakes. And if you've lived your life properly—so, you learn."

George H.W.
BUSH

41ST PRESIDENT: 1989–1993

Born: June 12, 1924, in Milton, Massachusetts

Disc 2, Track 15

38

"A KINDER AND GENTLER NATION"

GEORGE BUSH WAS Ronald Reagan's vice president. Like many who held that office, Bush found his image diminished. He was seen as an elitist, a preppy with no strong views of his own. *Doonesbury* gibed he had placed his "manhood" in a blind trust. *Newsweek* published a cover story entitled "Fighting the Wimp Factor." After the Democratic Convention, Bush trailed 17 percent behind Massachusetts governor Michael Dukakis.

Yet at the Republican gathering in New Orleans, Bush was able to revive his candidacy with a convention acceptance speech that changed his public image and framed the contest in terms he could win. Rarely has a single speech so shifted an election.

Peggy Noonan, one of Ronald Reagan's skilled writers, mostly crafted the speech. She realized Bush was uneasy referring to himself—his mother had long admonished her children not to "brag." "I became adept at pronounless sentences," Noonan recalled. "Instead of 'I moved to Texas and soon we joined the Republican party,' it was, 'Moved to Texas, joined the Republican party, raised a family.'" Out of his very verbal awkwardness, she fashioned an appealing, laconic persona for the man who was best known to voters as a cautious public official.

The speech, like the best political orations, set up a sharp contrast between the way Bush wanted voters to see him and the way he wanted them to see his opponent. (Campaign workers call this a "message grid.") Dukakis had declared to the Democratic Convention, "This election isn't about ideology. It's about competence." Bush countered, "Competence makes the trains run on time but doesn't know where they're going." He wanted to show a sharp philosophical split—that he was the heir to the conservative Reagan Revolution. So he hammered Dukakis as a product of the culturally permissive 1960s, focusing on issues such as the governor's veto on constitutional grounds of a requirement that schoolchildren say the Pledge of Allegiance. While Reagan had ended his 1980 convention speech with a silent prayer, Bush closed by leading delegates in recitation of the patriotic pledge.

Bush subtly sought distance from Reagan, too. The incumbent president was not popular at the end of his second term as he was at the end of his first. He was seen as too rigid, dogmatic, and harsh toward the poor; economic growth was accompanied by widening inequality and newly visible homeless on city streets. Bush vowed to build a "kinder and gentler nation." First Lady Nancy Reagan, watching from the gallery, understood the dig, even if rapturous delegates did not. "Kinder and gentler than who?" she asked icily. Bush painted a vivid word-picture of the array of voluntary associations that he believed could best solve social problems—groups in every community, "a brilliant diversity spread like stars, like a thousand points of light in a broad and peaceful sky." Noonan writes in her memoir, *What I Saw at the Revolution*, that the line was not consciously drawn from a particular poem or piece of literature, though it is evocative of phrases from writers as diverse as Thomas Wolfe and Alexander Hamilton.

Most significantly, Bush talked about taxes. At the suggestion of Representative Jack Kemp, Noonan wanted the vice president to make a Clint Eastwood-esque vow never to raise them. (In the 1983 movie *Sudden Impact*, Eastwood, as Detective "Dirty" Harry Callahan, had pointed his gun at a miscreant and growled, "Go ahead, make my day." Reagan had adopted the quote soon after, aiming it at Democrats in Congress, and Bush used a variation of it in his speech, replacing "day" with "twenty-four-hour time period" for comic effect. "Read my lips" evoked the spirit, if not the exact phrasing of Dirty Harry.) But Bush's economic advisor Richard Darman thought such a pledge "stupid and irresponsible," wrote Bob Woodward in the *Washington Post*, since budget rules and the looming failure of hundreds of savings and loans would likely require a tax hike to close a yearly deficit of nearly two hundred billion dollars. Darman added, Bush is no Clint Eastwood. Exactly, countered Roger Ailes, Bush's media advisor. The wimp factor must be banished forever. So in gunslinger style, Bush said to huge cheers, "And the Congress will push me to raise taxes, and I'll say no, and they'll push, and I'll say no, and they'll push again. And I'll say to them: Read my lips. No new taxes."

The forcefully delivered speech lifted Bush past Dukakis in the polls, and the Democrat never recovered. Probably Bush was most helped by the sense that he represented Reagan's third term—despite Reagan's detractors, the conservative surge had not yet abated. "Read my lips" lived on long after the ballots were counted. As Darman feared, Bush soon was forced to agree to raise taxes as part of a budget agreement in 1990. Questioned by reporters about the reversal while jogging, Bush pointed at his behind and said, "Read my hips." As the economy soured in 1991 and 1992, Democrats used Bush's very visible broken promise against him. Campaign ads for Governor Bill Clinton repeatedly played footage of Bush's 1988 convention talk. To win, did Bush have to overrule his economic advisors and make such a dramatic, vivid pledge? Perhaps. But if the speech could be said to have won him the presidency, it could also be said to have lost it four years later.

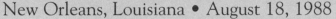

George H. W. Bush's

ACCEPTANCE SPEECH, REPUBLICAN CONVENTION

New Orleans, Louisiana • August 18, 1988

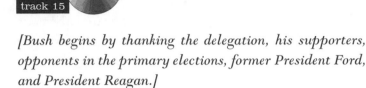

hear...
disc 2
track 15

[Bush begins by thanking the delegation, his supporters, opponents in the primary elections, former President Ford, and President Reagan.]

I accept your nomination for president. I mean to run hard, to fight hard, to stand on the issues—and I mean to win.

There are a lot...there are a lot of great stories in politics about the underdog winning—and this is going to be one of them....

Many of you have asked, "When will this campaign really begin?" Well, I've come to this hall to tell you, and to tell America: Tonight is the night.

For seven and a half years I've helped the president conduct the most difficult job on Earth. Ronald Reagan asked for, and received, my candor. He never asked for, but he did receive, my loyalty. And those of you who saw the president's speech last week, and listened to the simple truth of his words, will understand my loyalty all these years.

And now...now you must see me for what I am: the Republican candidate for president of the United States.

And now I turn to the American people to share my hopes and intentions, and why and where I wish to lead.

And so tonight is for big things. But I'll try to be fair to the other side. I'll try to hold my charisma in check. I reject the temptation to engage in personal references. My approach this evening is, as Sergeant Joe Friday used to say, "Just the facts, ma'am."

And after all...after all, the facts are on our side.

I seek the presidency for a single purpose, a purpose that has motivated millions of Americans across the years and the ocean voyages. I seek the presidency to build a better America. It's that simple—and that big.

I'm a man who sees life in terms of missions—missions defined and missions completed.

And when I was a torpedo bomber pilot they defined the mission for us. And before we took off, we all understood that no matter what, you try to reach the target. And there have been other missions for me—Congress, and China, the CIA. But I'm here tonight, and I am your candidate, because the most important work of my life is to complete the mission that we started in 1980. And how, and how do we complete it? We build upon it.

The stakes are high this year and the choice is crucial, for the differences between the two candidates are as deep and wide as they have ever been in our long history.

Not only two very different men, but two very different ideas of the future will be voted on this Election Day.

And what it all comes down to is this: my opponent's view of the world sees a long slow decline for our country, an inevitable fall mandated by impersonal historical forces. But America is not in decline. America is a rising nation.

> ## "I'm here tonight, and I am your candidate, because the most important work of my life is to complete the mission that we started in 1980."

He sees America as another pleasant country on the UN roll call, somewhere between Albania and Zimbabwe. And I see America as the leader—a unique nation with a special role in the world.

And this has been called the American century, because in it we were the dominant force for good in the world. We

---

The above text is a transcript of the speech as it was given in New Orleans.

saved Europe, cured polio, went to the moon, and lit the world with our culture. And now we are on the verge of a new century, and what country's name will it bear? I say it will be another American century.

"He sees America as another pleasant country on the UN roll call, somewhere between Albania and Zimbabwe."

Our work is not done, our force is not spent.

There are those…there are those who say there isn't much of a difference this year. But America, don't let 'em fool ya.

Two parties this year ask for your support. Both will speak of growth and peace. But only one has proved it can deliver. Two parties this year ask for your trust, but only one has earned it. Eight years ago…eight years ago, I stood here with Ronald Reagan and we promised, together, to break with the past and return America to her greatness. Eight years later, look at what the American people have produced: the highest level of economic growth in our entire history—and the lowest level of world tensions in more than fifty years.

You know, some say this isn't an election about ideology, it's an election about competence. Well, it's nice of them to want to play on our field. But this election isn't only about competence, for competence is a narrow ideal.

Competence makes the trains run on time but doesn't know where they're going. Competence…competence is the creed of the technocrat who makes sure the gears mesh but doesn't for a second understand the magic of the machine.

The truth is…the truth is, this election is about the beliefs we share, the values that we honor and the principles that we hold dear….

Our economy is strong but not invulnerable, and the peace is broad but can be broken. And now we must decide.

We will surely have change this year, but will it be change that moves us forward? Or change that risks retreat?

In 1940, when I was barely more than a boy, Franklin Roosevelt said we shouldn't change horses in midstream.

My friends, these days the world moves even more quickly, and now, after two great terms, a switch will be made. But when you have to change horses in midstream, doesn't it make sense to switch to one who's going the same way?

An election that is about ideas and values is also about philosophy. And I have one.

At the bright center is the individual. And radiating out from him or her is the family, the essential unit of closeness and of love. For it is the family that communicates to our children—to the twenty-first century—our culture, our religious faith, our traditions and history.

From the individual to the family to the community, and then on out to the town, the church and the school, and, still echoing out, to the county, the state, and the nation—each doing only what it does well, and no more. And I believe that power must always be kept close to the individual, close to the hands that raise the family and run the home.

I am guided by certain traditions. One is that there is a God and He is good, and His love, while free, has a self-imposed cost: we must be good to one another.

"We saved Europe, cured polio, went to the moon, and lit the world with our culture."

I believe in another tradition that is, by now, imbedded in the national soul. It is that learning is good in and of itself. You know, the mothers of the Jewish ghettoes of the East would pour honey on a book so the children would know that learning is sweet. And the parents who settled hungry Kansas would take their children in from the fields when a teacher came. That is our history.

And there is another tradition. And that is the idea of community—a beautiful word with a big meaning. Though liberal Democrats have an odd view of it. They see "community" as a limited cluster of interest groups, locked in odd conformity. And in this view, the country waits passive while Washington sets the rules.

But that's not what community means—not to me.

For we're a nation of communities, of thousands and tens of thousands of ethnic, religious, social, business, labor union, neighborhood, regional, and other organizations—all of them varied, voluntary, and unique.

This is America: the Knights of Columbus, the Grange, Hadassah, the Disabled American Veterans, the Order of AHEPA [American Hellenic Educational Progressive Association], the Business and Professional Women of America, the union hall, the Bible study group, LULAC [League of United Latin American Citizens], "Holy Name"—a brilliant diversity spread like stars, like a thousand points of light in a broad and peaceful sky.

Does government have a place? Yes. Government is part of the nation of communities—not the whole, just a part.

And I don't hate government. A government that remembers that the people are its master is a good and needed thing.

And I respect old-fashioned common sense, and have no great love...and I have no great love for the imaginings of the social planners. You see, I like what's been tested and found to be true.

For instance:

Should public school teachers be required to lead our children in the pledge of allegiance? My opponent says no—and I say yes.

Should society be allowed to impose the death penalty on those who commit crimes of extraordinary cruelty and violence? My opponent says no—but I say yes.

Vice President George Bush speaks at the 1988 Republican National Convention in New Orleans, Louisiana, on August 18, 1988

And should our children…should our children have the right to say a voluntary prayer, or even observe a moment of silence in the schools? My opponent says no—but I say yes.

"Competence makes the trains run on time but doesn't know where they're going."

And should free men and women have a right to own a gun to protect their home? My opponent says no—but I say yes.

And is it right to believe in the sanctity of life and protect the lives of innocent children? My opponent says no—but I say yes.

You see, we must…we must change, we've got to change from abortion to adoption. And let me tell you this: Barbara and I have an adopted granddaughter. And the day of her christening we wept with joy. I thank God that her parents chose life.

I'm the one who believes it is a scandal to give a weekend furlough to a hardened first-degree killer who hasn't even served enough time to be eligible for parole.

I'm the one who says a drug dealer who is responsible for the death of a policeman should be subject to capital punishment.

And I'm the one who will not raise taxes. My opponent now says…my opponent now says he'll raise them as a last resort, or a third resort. Well, when a politician talks like that, you know that's one resort he'll be checking into. And, my opponent won't rule out raising taxes. But I will.

And the Congress will push me to raise taxes, and I'll say no, and they'll push, and I'll say no, and they'll push again. And I'll say to them: Read my lips. No new taxes.…

It seems to me the presidency provides an incomparable opportunity for "gentle persuasion."

And I hope to stand for a new harmony, a greater tolerance. We've come far, but I think we need a new harmony among the races in our country. And we're on a journey into a new century, and we've got to leave that tired old baggage of bigotry behind.

Some people who are enjoying our prosperity have forgotten what it's for. But they diminish our triumph when they act as if wealth is an end in itself.

And there are those who have dropped their standards along the ways, as if ethics were too heavy and slowed their rise to the top. There's graft in city hall, and there's greed on Wall Street; there's influence-peddling in Washington, and the small corruptions of everyday ambition.

But you see, I believe public service is honorable. And every time I hear that someone has breached the public trust it breaks my heart.

And I wonder sometimes if we've forgotten who we are. But we're the people who sundered a nation rather than allow a sin called slavery—and we're the people who rose from the ghettoes and the deserts.

And we weren't saints, but we lived by standards. We celebrated the individual, but we weren't self-centered. We were practical, but we didn't live only for material things. We believed in getting ahead, but blind ambition wasn't our way.

"I'm the one who believes it is a scandal to give a weekend furlough to a hardened first-degree killer who hasn't even served enough time to be eligible for parole."

The fact is prosperity has a purpose. It is to allow us to pursue "the better angels," to give us time to think and grow. Prosperity with a purpose means taking your idealism and making it concrete by certain acts of goodness.

It means helping a child from an unhappy home learn how to read—and I thank my wife Barbara for all her work in helping people to read and all her work for literacy in this country.

It means teaching troubled children through your presence that there is such a thing as reliable love. Some would say it's soft and insufficiently tough to care about these things. But where is it written that we must act as if we do not care, as if we are not moved?

"And the Congress will push me to raise taxes, and I'll say no, and they'll push, and I'll say no, and they'll push again. And I'll say to them: Read my lips. No new taxes."

Well, I am moved. I want a kinder and gentler nation.

Two men this year ask for your support. And you must know us.

As for me, I have held high office and done the work of democracy day by day. Yes, my parents were prosperous; and their children sure were lucky. But there were lessons we had to learn about life.

John Kennedy discovered poverty when he campaigned in West Virginia; there were children who had no milk. And young Teddy Roosevelt met the new America when he roamed the immigrant streets of New York. And I learned a few things about life in a place called Texas.

And when I—and when I was…when I was working on this part of the speech, Barbara came in and asked what I was doing. And I looked up, and I said I'm working hard. And she said: "Oh dear, don't worry, relax, sit back, take off your shoes and put up your silver foot."

Now, we moved to West Texas forty years ago—forty years ago this year. The war was over, and we wanted to get out and make it on our own. Those were exciting days. We lived in a little shotgun house, one room for the three of us. Worked in the oil business, and then started my own.

And in time we had six children. Moved from the shotgun to a duplex apartment to a house. And lived the dream—high school football on Friday nights, Little League, neighborhood barbecue.

People don't see their own experience as symbolic of an era—but of course we were.

And so was everyone else who was taking a chance and pushing into unknown territory with kids and a dog and a car.

But the big thing I learned is the satisfaction of creating jobs, which meant creating opportunity, which meant happy families, who in turn could do more to help others and enhance their own lives.

I learned that the good done by a single good job can be felt in ways you can't imagine.

It's been said that I'm not the most compelling speaker, and there are actually those who claim that I don't always communicate in the clearest, most concise way. But I dare them to keep it up—go ahead: Make my twenty-four-hour time period!

Well, I may not be the most eloquent, but I learned that, early on, that eloquence won't draw oil from the ground.

And I may sometimes be a little awkward. But there's nothing self-conscious in my love of country.

And I am a quiet man, but I hear the quiet people others don't. The ones who raise the family, pay the taxes, meet the mortgages.

And I hear them and I am moved, and their concerns are mine.

A president must be many things.

He must be a shrewd protector of America's interests; and he must be an idealist who leads those who move for a freer and more democratic planet.

And he must see to it that government intrudes as little as possible in the lives of the people; and yet remember that it is right and proper that a nation's leader take an interest in the nation's character.

And he must be able to define—and lead—a mission.

For seven and a half years, I have worked with a great president—I have seen what crosses that big desk. I have seen the unexpected crisis that arrives in a cable in a young aide's hand. And I have seen the problems that simmer on for decades and suddenly demand resolution. And I have seen modest decisions made with anguish, and crucial decisions made with dispatch.

"I want a kinder and gentler nation."

And so I know that what it all comes down to, this election…what it all comes down to, after all the shouting and the cheers—is the man at the desk. And who should sit at that desk.

My friends, I am that man.

I say it without boast or bravado.

I've fought for my country, I've served, I've built—and I'll go from the hills to the hollows, from the cities to the suburbs to the loneliest town on the quietest street to take our message of hope and growth for every American to every American.

I will keep America moving forward, always forward, for a better America, for an endless enduring dream and a thousand points of light.

This is my mission. And I will complete it.

Thank you.

You know…you know it is customary to end an address with a pledge or a saying that holds a special meaning. And I've chosen one that we all know by heart. One that we all learned in school. And I ask everyone in this great hall to stand and join me in this—we all know it.

I pledge allegiance to the flag of the United States of America and to the republic for which it stands, one nation under God, indivisible, with liberty and justice for all.

Thank you.

Bill
CLINTON

42ND PRESIDENT: 1993–2001

Born: August 19, 1946, in Hope, Arkansas

Disc 2, Tracks 16–18

39

BILL CLINTON

"WHAT WOULD MARTIN LUTHER KING SAY?"

WILLIAM SAFIRE, the former Nixon speechwriter who now writes a column for the *New York Times*, once asked Bill Clinton which speech he thought was his best. "Memphis?" Safire asked. Clinton agreed instantly. His speech to five thousand black ministers from the very pulpit where Martin Luther King Jr. gave his last sermon is remembered as a courageous challenge to address social problems—and a high form of Clinton's personal, often improvised style.

Clinton was the first baby boomer president. While very different from Reagan, he found a way to be a master communicator in the age of omnipresent, twenty-four–hour media. At the podium, he was less formal and more intimate than other modern presidents. He likened his approach to that of a jazz musician; he used a speech text as a score but also improvised, "soloing" and responding to audience emotions.

Clinton's most thoughtful speeches often came on the subject of race. As a young man growing up in the segregated South, he memorized King's "I Have a Dream" speech. When Clinton ran for president, Bill Moyers asked him on which issue, if any, the famously pragmatic politician would refuse to bend. His answer: "Racial justice." But perhaps because he felt so comfortable with black audiences, he was more willing than most white politicians to speak candidly about social problems. In the early 1990s, record crime devastated inner-city neighborhoods. Clinton was heavily influenced by a new wave of social scientists who argued that the problems of persistent poverty and lawlessness were due less to racism than to failures of education, economics, and social order.

The Memphis speech was not billed as a major address. Clinton was working hard to pass NAFTA, the free-trade pact with Mexico and Canada. Speechwriter Carolyn Curiel, the first Latina to write for a president, was assigned to produce a draft speech. She realized it would be given at the church where King had prophesied, the eve of his assassination, "I've seen the promised land. I may not get there with you." She knew, too, that Clinton had been to this gathering before. "It felt like one of those speeches where the president was not going to stick to a script, because he knew these people." So she gave him a few talking points, and passed on a *Washington Post* article about a young girl so afraid of gang gunfire that she planned her own funeral. As the trip approached, other aides insisted Clinton talk about NAFTA, too. On the flight to Memphis, the speechwriter recalled, the president's only question was whether there was enough material in the speech about trade. In the end, he relied almost entirely on his own scrawled notes.

The church was packed and steaming. Ministers rose and sermonized, spurred by the crowd and each other. Parishioners fanned themselves with their programs. Then a lone saxophonist played a wrenching "Amazing Grace." The church was silent as Clinton rose to speak.

He won the crowd with humor, finding a personal connection—teasing the bishops by name, reminding the audience of his African-American appointments. He talked about his record, and made a perfunctory pitch for NAFTA. Then he turned to the nation's "great crisis of spirit." His rhetorical device was risky but effective: an imaginary conversation with King himself. The civil rights leader would be proud, Clinton said, of the progress toward equality—with segregation gone, a rising black middle class, African-Americans in positions of power.

285

But, Clinton said, King would be appalled by the social decay plaguing the very community he was trying to help. "My fellow Americans, he would say, I fought to stop white people from being so filled with hate that they would wreak violence on black people. I did not fight for the right of black people to murder other black people with reckless abandon." Clinton knew the innate social conservatism of his audience—and coupled a call for greater family responsibility with a call for more jobs and wider economic opportunity.

The speech was immediately hailed as a highly effective use of the bully pulpit. The *Atlanta Constitution* called it "a brave speech; most politicians these days only dance around the topic of race. Clinton risked being criticized as blaming the victim, of relieving white Americans of any responsibility. But he understood it was a timely message, as demonstrated by his audience's enthusiastic response." One black leader angrily charged it was wrong for Clinton to link King with crime in his address.

Clinton continued to speak out on racially charged social issues throughout his term, with mixed effect. The crime bill that won applause at the church passed the Congress the next year; while its impact was unclear, community policing measures helped bring crime down dramatically. In 1995, with Congress seeking to scale back affirmative action, Clinton spoke at the National Archives. He conceded that set-aside programs were flawed and needed reform, but concluded, "Our slogan should be: mend it, don't end it." More provocatively, federal poverty policy was recast with a new focus on work. He signed legislation doubling the tax credit for the working poor. In 1996, he signed into law welfare reform passed by the Republican-controlled Congress. He spoke about racism at length in his second inaugural, and even mounted a yearlong discussion on race (called "One America"). His support in the black community grew strong, even when he signed legislation, such as welfare reform, widely opposed by black leaders. When he faced impeachment in 1998, the black community was his rock of support. Novelist Toni Morrison hyperbolized that Clinton was "our first black president." After leaving office, Clinton located his post-presidential office in Harlem.

Clinton speaking in Memphis, November 13, 1993

Bill Clinton's
REMARKS TO THE CHURCH OF GOD IN CHRIST IN MEMPHIS

Memphis, Tennessee • November 13, 1993

hear...
disc 2
track 16

Bishop Ford, Mrs. Mason, Bishop Owens, and Bishop Anderson; my bishops, Bishop Walker and Bishop Lindsey:

Now, if you haven't had Bishop Lindsey's barbecue, you haven't had barbecue. And if you haven't heard Bishop Walker attack one of my opponents, you have never heard a political speech. [Laughter]

I am glad to be here. You have touched my heart. You've brought tears to my eyes and joy to my spirit. Last year, I was with you over at the convention center. Two years ago, your bishops came to Arkansas, and we laid a plaque at the point in Little Rock, Arkansas, at 8th and Gaines, where Bishop Mason received the inspiration for the name of this great church. Bishop Brooks said from his pulpit that I would be elected president when most people thought I wouldn't survive. I thank him, and I thank your faith, and I thank your works, for without you I would not be here today as your president....

You know, in the last ten months, I've been called a lot of things, but nobody's called me a bishop yet. [Laughter] When I was about nine years old, my beloved and now departed grandmother, who was a very wise woman, looked at me and she said, "You know, I believe you could be a preacher if you were just a little better boy." [Laughter]

Proverbs says, "A happy heart doeth good like medicine, but a broken spirit dryeth the bone." This is a happy place, and I'm happy to be here. I thank you for your spirit.

By the grace of God and your help, last year I was elected president of this great country. I never dreamed that I would ever have a chance to come to this hallowed place where Martin Luther King gave his last sermon. I ask you to think today about the purpose for which I ran and the purpose for which so many of you worked to put me in this great office. I have worked hard to keep faith with our common efforts: to restore the economy, to reverse the politics of helping only those at the top of our totem pole and not the hard-working middle class or the poor; to bring our people together across racial and regional and political lines, to make a strength out of our diversity instead of letting it tear us apart; to reward work and family and community and try to move us forward into the twenty-first century. I have tried to keep faith.

[Clinton discusses the country's economic progress and his push for NAFTA, the free trade pact with Canada and Mexico.]

"If Martin Luther King... were to reappear by my side today and give us a report card on the last twenty-five years, what would he say?"

But I guess what I really want to say to you today, my fellow Americans, is that we can do all of this and still fail unless we meet the great crisis of the spirit that is gripping America today....

If Martin Luther King, who said, "Like Moses, I am on the mountaintop, and I can see the promised land, but I'm not going to be able to get there with you, but we will get there"—if he were to reappear by my side today and give us a report card on the last twenty-five years, what would he say? You did a good job, he would say, voting and electing people who formerly were not electable because of the color of their skin. You have more political power, and that is good. You did a good job, he would say, letting people who

The above text is a transcript of the speech as it was given in Memphis, Tennessee.

Excerpt from Bill Clinton's handwritten notes for his Memphis speech:

MLK didn't die → 13 yr old the freedom to get semi auto shoot 9 yr old → teenage girls freedom to have children & watch father of their child to walk away → young freedom destroy lives w/ drugs or bld pers. fortunes destroying lives of others → Am Soc liberated black ppl [unintelligible] permit family & country to be destroyed → <u>wrong</u>—Do what I can w/ you to

have the ability to do so live wherever they want to live, go wherever they want to go in this great country. You did a good job, he would say, elevating people of color into the ranks of the United States Armed Forces to the very top or into the very top of our government. You did a very good job, he would say. He would say, you did a good job creating a black middle class of people who really are doing well, and the middle class is growing more among African-Americans than among non-African-Americans. You did a good job; you did a good job in opening opportunity.

But he would say, I did not live and die to see the American family destroyed. I did not live and die to see thirteen-year-old boys get automatic weapons and gun down nine-year-olds just for the kick of it. I did not live and die to see young people destroy their own lives with drugs and then build fortunes destroying the lives of others. That is not what I came here to do. I fought for freedom, he would say, but not for the freedom of people to kill each other with reckless abandon, not for the freedom of children to have children and the fathers of the children to walk away from them and abandon them as if they don't amount to anything. I fought for people to have the right to work but not to have whole communities and people abandoned. This is not what I lived and died for.

My fellow Americans, he would say, I fought to stop white people from being so filled with hate that they would wreak violence on black people. I did not fight for the right of black

people to murder other black people with reckless abandon.

The other day the mayor of Baltimore, a dear friend of mine, told me a story of visiting the family of a young man who had been killed—eighteen years old—on Halloween. He always went out with little bitty kids so they could trick-or-treat safely. And across the street from where they were walking on Halloween, a fourteen-year-old boy gave a thirteen-year-old boy a gun and dared him to shoot the eighteen-year-old boy, and he shot him dead. And the mayor had to visit the family.

In Washington, D.C., where I live, your nation's capital, the symbol of freedom throughout the world, look how that freedom is being exercised. The other night a man came along the street and grabbed a one-year-old child and put the child in his car. The child may have been the child of the man. And two people were after him, and they chased him in the car, and they just kept shooting with reckless abandon, knowing that baby was in the car. And they shot the man dead, and a bullet went through his body into the baby's body, and blew the little bootie off the child's foot.

The other day on the front page of our paper, the nation's capital, are we talking about world peace or world conflict? No, big article on the front page of the *Washington Post* about an eleven-year-old child planning her funeral: "These are the hymns I want sung. This is the dress I want to wear. I know I'm not going to live very long." That is not the freedom, the freedom to die before you're a teenager is not what Martin Luther King lived and died for.

More than thirty-seven thousand people die from gunshot wounds in this country every year. Gunfire is the leading cause of death in young men. And now that we've all gotten so cool that everybody can get a semiautomatic weapon, a person shot now is three times more likely to die than fifteen years ago, because they're likely to have three bullets in them. A hundred and sixty thousand children stay home from school every day because they are scared they will be hurt in their schools.

The other day, I was in California at a town meeting, and a handsome young man stood up and said, "Mr. President, my brother and I, we don't belong to gangs. We don't have guns. We don't do drugs. We want to go to school. We want to be professionals. We want to work hard. We want to do well. We want to have families. And we changed our school because the school we were in was so dangerous. So when we showed up to the new school to register, my brother and I were standing in line and somebody ran into the school and started shooting a gun. My brother was shot down standing right in front of me at the safer school." The freedom to do that kind of thing is not what Martin Luther King lived and died for, not what people gathered in this hallowed church for the night before he was assassinated in April of 1968. If you had told anybody who was here in that church on that night that we would abuse our freedom in that way, they would have found it hard to believe. And I tell you, it is our moral duty to turn it around.

And now I think finally we have a chance. Finally, I think, we have a chance. We have a pastor here from New Haven, Connecticut. I was in his church with Reverend Jackson when I was running for president on a snowy day in Connecticut to mourn the death of children who had been killed in that city. And afterward we walked down the street for more than a mile in the snow. Then, the American people were not ready. People would say, "Oh, this is a terrible thing, but what can we do about it?"

Now when we read that foreign visitors come to our shores and are killed at random in our fine state of Florida, when we see our children planning their funerals, when the American people are finally coming to grips with the accumulated weight of crime and violence and the breakdown of family and community and the increase in drugs and the decrease in jobs, I think finally we may be ready to do something about it.

And there is something for each of us to do. There are changes we can make from the outside in; that's the job of the president and the Congress and the governors and the mayors and the social service agencies. And then there's some changes

> *"We cannot…restore the American family until we provide the structure, the values, the discipline, and the reward that work gives."*

we're going to have to make from the inside out, or the others won't matter. That's what that magnificent song was about, isn't it? Sometimes there are no answers from the outside-in; sometimes all the answers have to come from the values and the stirrings and the voices that speak to us from within.

So we are beginning. We are trying to pass a bill to make our people safer, to put another hundred thousand police officers on the street, to provide boot camps instead of prisons for young people who can still be rescued, to provide more safety in our schools, to restrict the availability of these awful assault weapons, to pass the Brady bill and at least require people to have their criminal background checked before they get a gun, and to say, if you're not old enough to vote and you're not old enough to go to war, you ought not to own a handgun, and you ought not to use one unless you're on a target range.

We want to pass a health-care bill that will make drug treatment available for everyone. And we also have to do it, we have to have drug treatment and education available to everyone and especially those who are in prison who are coming out….But I say to you, my fellow Americans, we need some other things as well. I do not believe we can repair the basic fabric of society until people who are willing to work have work. Work organizes life. It gives structure and discipline to life. It gives meaning and self-esteem to people who are parents. It gives a role model to children.

The famous African-American sociologist William Julius Wilson has written a stunning book called *The Truly Disadvantaged* in which he chronicles in breathtaking terms how the inner cities of our country have crumbled as work has disappeared. And we must find a way, through public and private sources, to enhance the attractiveness of the American people who live there to get investment there. We cannot, I submit to you, repair the American community and restore the American family until we provide the structure, the values, the discipline, and the reward that work gives.

I read a wonderful speech the other day given at Howard University in a lecture series funded by Bill and Camille Cosby, in which the speaker said, "I grew up in Anacostia years ago. Even then it was all black, and it was a very poor neighborhood. But you know, when I was a child in Anacostia, a 100 percent African-American neighborhood, a very poor neighborhood, we had a crime rate that was lower than the average of the crime rate of our city. Why? Because we had coherent families. We had coherent communities. The people who filled the church on Sunday lived in the same place they went to church. The guy that owned the drugstore lived down the street. The person that owned the grocery store lived in our community. We were whole." And I say to you, we have to make our people whole again.

This church has stood for that. Why do you think you have five million members in this country? Because people know you are filled with the spirit of God to do the right thing in this life by them. So I say to you, we have to make a partnership, all the Government agencies, all the business folks; but where there are no families, where there is no order, where there is no hope, where we are reducing the size of our armed services because we have won the Cold War, who will be there to give structure, discipline, and love to these children? You must do that. And we must help you.

Scripture says, you are the salt of the Earth and the light of the world, that if your light shines before men they will give glory to the Father in heaven. That is what we must do.

That is what we must do. How would we explain it to Martin Luther King if he showed up today and said, yes, we won the Cold War. Yes, the biggest threat that all of us grew up under, communism and nuclear war, communism gone, nuclear war receding. Yes, we developed all these miraculous technologies. Yes, we all have got a VCR in our home; it's interesting. Yes, we get fifty channels on the cable. Yes, without regard to race, if you work hard and play by the rules, you can get into a service academy or a good college, you'll do just great. How would we explain to him all these kids getting killed and killing each other? How would we justify the things that we permit that no other country in the world would permit? How could we explain that we gave people the freedom to succeed, and we created conditions in which millions abuse that freedom to destroy the things that make life worth living and life itself? We cannot.

And so I say to you today, my fellow Americans, you gave me this job, and we're making progress on the things you hired me to do. But unless we deal with the ravages of crime and drugs and violence and unless we recognize that it's due to the breakdown of the family, the community, and the disappearance of jobs, and unless we say some of this cannot be done by government, because we have to reach deep inside to the values, the spirit, the soul, and the truth of human nature, none of the other things we seek to do will ever take us where we need to go.

So in this pulpit, on this day, let me ask all of you in your heart to say: We will honor the life and the work of Martin Luther King. We will honor the meaning of our church. We will, somehow, by God's grace, we will turn this around. We will give these children a future. We will take away their guns and give them books. We will take away their despair and give them hope. We will rebuild the families and the neighborhoods and the communities. We won't make all the work that has gone on here benefit just a few. We will do it together by the grace of God.

40

"IN THE FACE OF DEATH, LET US HONOR LIFE"

ON APRIL 19, 1995, a Ryder truck pulled up in front of the Alfred P. Murrah Federal Building in Oklahoma City. At 9:03 A.M., the truck—crammed with chemical fertilizer—exploded, ripping off the front of the nine-story building. The blast killed 167 people, including nineteen children from a day care center on the ground floor. It was the most devastating act of terrorism on American soil up to that point.

It came at a time when Bill Clinton was languishing politically. His party lost control of both houses of Congress the prior November. The night before the bombing, he had been reduced to insisting at a news conference (broadcast by only one television network), "The Constitution gives me relevance....The president is relevant here." Clinton had become viewed as a partisan, polarizing figure. With word of the bombing, his response lifted him to a new level—a country united in grief saw him for the first time as "president of all the people." He showed, as Reagan had done, the importance of the president's role as "mourner in chief."

That afternoon, he denounced the attack as the work of "evil cowards." He spoke to children in a radio address on Saturday morning. The next day, he flew to Oklahoma City, where he spoke to the grieving families and rescue workers at the state fairgrounds. A skilled eulogist cannot promise to salve the psyche of grieving families. Instead, when a president leads a tribute, he must subtly use it to turn the audience's attention to the tasks of statecraft ahead. (Think of Lincoln at Gettysburg, or Reagan's remarks after the *Challenger* explosion.) Clinton worked with his chief speechwriter, Donald Baer, a former journalist who had met him during the campaign; Baer called in a talented speechwriter, Jonathan Prince. They had just one day to craft remarks. "It was a tenuous moment," Baer recalled. "We knew he had to try to heal the nation even when many were doubting his political strength." A wide group of clergy and advisors added ideas. In the end, Clinton stayed up late rewriting the eulogy, which was still being polished in the traveling office on Air Force One on the way to Oklahoma City.

In urging the citizens to reject hate, Clinton subtly evoked a larger political purpose. At first, many suspected foreign terrorists. But by the memorial service, authorities had arrested a young Gulf War veteran, Timothy McVeigh. He was linked to anti-government radical groups, known as "militias," that had sprung up around the country. When

Clinton speaking in Oklahoma City nearly a year after the bombing, April 5, 1996

arrested, McVeigh was wearing a T-shirt quoting Thomas Jefferson. The attack, it was later surmised, was in retaliation for the federal government's siege at a cult compound in Waco, Texas, two years before, which itself killed eighty-six people. It came on the anniversary of the battle of Lexington and Concord, which sparked the American Revolution—and one day before Adolf Hitler's birthday.

The ardent anti-government views expressed by McVeigh through violence were heard that spring in harsh words on talk radio, and even in the halls of Congress. Three weeks later, Clinton spoke at Michigan State University, near where the paramilitary groups trained. "If you appropriate our sacred symbols for paranoid purposes and compare yourselves to colonial militias who fought for the democracy you now rail against, you are wrong," he said with unusual passion. "How dare you suggest that we in the freest nation on earth live in tyranny? How dare you call

yourselves patriots and heroes?" Clinton did not link the argument to current political battles—he did not have to. The next year, at his State of the Union address, he introduced a survivor of the bombing. In budget battles, the Congress had sought to force Clinton's hand by shutting down the government. On behalf of the federal worker, who had rescued two people from the ruins, Clinton demanded, "Never shut the government down again."

Historian Carol Gelderman, in her book *All the Presidents' Words*, wrote, "Despite distortions of what he had said from the mainstream press and from political opponents who accused him of scapegoating and of trying to stifle criticism of the government, he dominated the national response to the bombing tragedy....After Clinton's response to this crisis, no one spoke of his relevance or irrelevance again. He had clearly established his national voice, as he would again and again in the future."

The devastation on the north side of the Alfred P. Murrah Federal Building in Oklahoma City caused by a fuel and fertilizer truck bomb on April 19, 1995

Bill Clinton's

EULOGY FOR THE VICTIMS OF THE OKLAHOMA CITY BOMBING

Oklahoma City, Oklahoma • April 23, 1995

hear...
disc 2
track 17

Thank you very much. Governor Keating and Mrs. Keating, Reverend Graham, to the families of those who have been lost and wounded, to the people of Oklahoma City, who have endured so much, and the people of this wonderful state, to all of you who are here as our fellow Americans.

I am honored to be here today to represent the American people.

But I have to tell you that Hillary and I also come as parents, as husband and wife, as people who were your neighbors for some of the best years of our lives. Today our nation joins with you in grief. We mourn with you. We share your hope against hope that some may still survive. We thank all those who have worked so heroically to save lives and to solve this crime—those here in Oklahoma and those who are all across this great land, and many who left their own lives to come here to work hand in hand with you.

> ## "We pledge to do all we can to help you heal the injured, to rebuild this city, and to bring to justice those who did this evil."

We pledge to do all we can to help you heal the injured, to rebuild this city, and to bring to justice those who did this evil.

This terrible sin took the lives of our American family, innocent children in that building, only because their parents were trying to be good parents as well as good workers; citizens in the building going about their daily business; and many there who served the rest of us—who worked to help the elderly and the disabled, who worked to support our farmers and our veterans, who worked to enforce our laws and to protect us. Let us say clearly, they served us well, and we are grateful.

But for so many of you they were also neighbors and friends. You saw them at church or the PTA meetings, at the civic clubs, at the ball park. You know them in ways that all the rest of America could not.

And to all the members of the families here present who have suffered loss, though we share your grief, your pain is unimaginable, and we know that. We cannot undo it. That is God's work.

Our words seem small beside the loss you have endured. But I found a few I wanted to share today. I've received a lot of letters in these last terrible days. One stood out because it came from a young widow and a mother of three whose own husband was murdered with over 200 other Americans when Pan Am 103 was shot down. Here is what that woman said I should say to you today:

> The anger you feel is valid, but you must not allow yourselves to be consumed by it. The hurt you feel must not be allowed to turn into hate, but instead into the search for justice. The loss you feel must not paralyze your own lives. Instead, you must try to pay tribute to your loved ones by continuing to do all the things they left undone, thus ensuring they did not die in vain.

Wise words from one who also knows.

You have lost too much, but you have not lost everything. And you have certainly not lost America, for we will stand with you for as many tomorrows as it takes.

> *"If anybody thinks Americans have lost the capacity for love and caring and courage, they ought to come to Oklahoma."*

If ever we needed evidence of that, I could only recall the words of Governor and Mrs. Keating. If anybody thinks that Americans are mostly mean and selfish, they ought to come to Oklahoma. If anybody thinks Americans have lost the capacity for love and caring and courage, they ought to come to Oklahoma.

To all my fellow Americans beyond this hall, I say, one thing we owe those who have sacrificed is the duty to purge ourselves of the dark forces which gave rise to this evil. They are forces that threaten our common peace, our freedom, our way of life.

Let us teach our children that the God of comfort is also the God of righteousness. Those who trouble their own house will inherit the wind. Justice will prevail.

Let us let our own children know that we will stand against the forces of fear. When there is talk of hatred, let us stand up and talk against it.

When there is talk of violence, let us stand up and talk against it. In the face of death, let us honor life. As St. Paul admonished us, let us not be overcome by evil, but overcome evil with good.

Yesterday Hillary and I had the privilege of speaking with some children of other federal employees—children like those who were lost here. And one little girl said something we will never forget. She said, we should all plant a tree in memory of the children. So this morning before we got on the plane to come here, at the White House, we planted a tree in honor of the children of Oklahoma.

It was a dogwood with its wonderful spring flower and its deep, enduring roots. It embodies the lesson of the Psalms—that the life of a good person is like a tree whose leaf does not wither.

> *"Those who are lost now belong to God. Some day we will be with them. But until that happens, their legacy must be our lives."*

My fellow Americans, a tree takes a long time to grow, and wounds take a long time to heal. But we must begin. Those who are lost now belong to God. Some day we will be with them. But until that happens, their legacy must be our lives.

Thank you all, and God bless you.

41

BILL CLINTON

"LET THAT BE OUR GIFT TO THE TWENTY-FIRST CENTURY"

"I WANT TO say one thing to the American people. I want you to listen to me. I'm going to say this again," President Bill Clinton looked into the camera and shook his finger angrily, "I did not have sexual relations with that woman, Miss Lewinsky."

It was the most bizarre eruption yet of the controversies that dogged the Clinton presidency. A long-dormant investigation of Clinton's personal finances by an independent counsel, Kenneth Starr, exploded with news that the prosecutor was probing Clinton's personal life. In particular, he was zeroing in on the charge that Clinton lied when he denied under oath an affair with a young White House intern, Monica Lewinsky. The news broke first on a gossip website on the Internet, then on the front page of the *Washington Post*, and then consumed the news media in an astounding frenzy.

Clinton's presidency hung by a thread. Television commentators speculated on impeachment and agreed his resignation, in the words of one, was not a matter of whether but when. By a quirk of the schedule, he was due to give the annual State of the Union address days later. It would be a chance to save his presidency, or see it collapse along with his personal credibility. (This author was in the middle of it, as Clinton's chief speechwriter, charged with writing the address.)

Work on the speech proceeded in a surreal atmosphere of siege and crisis. Frantic TV camera crews followed speechwriters and staff as they trekked in to work. Meanwhile, Clinton mulled its phrases in an oasis of eerie calm. An observer might conclude nothing was amiss. Rehearsing a critical passage at a podium in the

family theater, he wrote a new line, to the approval of his aides. "See? I haven't totally lost it." (Meanwhile, sheepish aides combed the text, looking for double entendres. He couldn't say America was strong "abroad"—just "around the world.")

The speech came at a critical policy moment, too. In 1993, on taking office, Clinton had inherited a budget deficit of $290 billion per year. Clinton had won a tax increase, and cut the deficit dramatically. In 1997, the Democratic president and Republican-led Congress agreed to a plan that would balance the budget. Indeed, the economy was growing so fast that there would now be a budget surplus. Welfare rolls and crime were dropping, too. This was a chance to reverse the public distrust of government

On January 26, 1998, Clinton addresses reporters, denying an alleged affair with former White House intern Monica Lewinsky

that had boiled for three decades. Working late at night in the White House residence, Clinton mused to his staff, "FDR saved capitalism from itself," echoing a common analysis. "Our mission is to save government from its own excesses. So that it can again be a progressive force." Republican lawmakers hoped to use the surplus for a new, large tax cut—a politically potent proposal. Administration aides met secretly in the Cabinet room, in sessions designated "Special Issues" to foil press leaks, to plot a response. Clinton decided to urge that the surplus be set aside—no tax cuts until Social Security, due to go bankrupt in the new century, was saved. Clinton wasn't sure the proposal would succeed in blocking the tax cut, but it was his party's only hope.

The pressure built as the speech approached. The day before the address, Clinton spoke in the Roosevelt Room of the West Wing. The topic was education. At the end, as reporters bellowed questions about the scandal, Clinton furrowed his brow and issued his now infamous denial. He would not speak about the scandal in the address to Congress. The evening of the speech, as the presidential motorcade idled, Clinton's chief political advisor, Mark Penn, said to me, "Here's what I think. If the speech is a success, the presidency is saved. If it's a failure, the presidency is over." (This is not something to tell a speechwriter if the goal is to keep his blood pressure down.) The motorcade glided past the federal courthouse, where a dozen camera trucks were camped out, following the day's comings and goings before the grand jury.

When Clinton strode into the well of the Congress, applause was mixed with an almost palpable sense of scrutiny. What would he say? More important, how would he seem? Would he collapse within himself, or would he pull it off? Clinton was smiling, chin out. This marathon speech, crammed with policy initiatives, was his favorite forum. His addresses usually ran an hour or more. This night, he began with a litany of facts—drumming home the success of the economy. Then he unveiled his gambit to stop the tax cut. "What should we do with this projected surplus? I have a simple four-word answer," he said. "Save

Social Security first." Journalist Joe Klein described the reaction:

> The Democrats were up, out of their seats with a roar. Newt Gingrich, the Republican speaker of the House, who sat directly above and behind the President, was applauding too, but reluctantly, and he was still seated. Slowly, Gingrich seemed to understand that he had been snookered yet again by Bill Clinton—that the nation would see Democrats vigorously supporting the most popular federal program, Social Security, while the Republicans were still seated, glumly—and he hauled himself to his feet and joined in a standing ovation for the president of the United States.

At a moment when his personal credibility was in tatters, Clinton had found a way to use the presidential megaphone to shift policy—and, not incidentally, save his presidency.

The performance reminded the public of what they liked about Clinton. After the speech, his approval ratings in public opinion polls shot up to 79 percent. Voters were dismayed by Clinton's ongoing personal problems. But they approved of his conduct of the public business of office. Over the coming weeks, citizens began to see his foes as too relentless and driven to bring Clinton down. All year, there was cognitive dissonance on a mass scale, with Clinton's public actions lifting him up as his personal troubles pulled him down.

On August 17, 1998, Clinton testified before a grand jury. That night he spoke to the American people, and confessed that his earlier denials had been false. His speech admitted much, but its defensive tone infuriated his critics. Clinton never said, "I'm sorry," either to the public or to Monica Lewinsky. That came several weeks later, in a tearful talk at a prayer breakfast. Starr released a 445-page report, outlining Clinton's peccadilloes in lurid, footnoted detail. Yet in the mid-term elections, the president's party gained seats, a historically unprecedented rebuke by voters to the congressional majority. Within a

Bill Clinton

month, both Speaker Gingrich and his successor, Representative Robert Livingston, stepped down (the latter in a sex scandal of his own). Still, on December 19, the House of Representatives voted to impeach Clinton—the first time an elected president was impeached. The Senate began a trial. In the middle of the proceeding, the Senate adjourned, its members marching over to the House chamber to hear yet another improbably timed, jauntily delivered State of the Union address. On February 12, 1999, the Senate voted to acquit Clinton.

PRESIDENT'S ADDRESS TO THE NATION ON THE LEWINSKY AFFAIR

August 17, 1998

This afternoon in this room, from this chair, I testified before the Office of Independent Counsel and the grand jury. I answered their questions truthfully, including questions about my private life, questions no American citizen would ever want to answer. Still, I must take complete responsibility for all my actions, both public and private....I did have a relationship with Miss Lewinsky that was not appropriate. In fact, it was wrong. It constituted a critical lapse in judgment and a personal failure on my part for which I am solely and completely responsible. But I told the grand jury today, and I say to you now, that at no time did I ask anyone to lie, to hide or destroy evidence or to take any other unlawful action. I know that my public comments and my silence about this matter gave a false impression. I misled people, including even my wife. I deeply regret that....This has gone on too long, cost too much and hurt too many innocent people. Now, this matter is between me, the two people I love most—my wife and our daughter—and our God. I must put it right, and I am prepared to do whatever it takes to do so. Nothing is more important to me personally. But it is private, and I intend to reclaim my family life for my family. It's nobody's business but ours. Even presidents have private lives. It is time to stop the pursuit of personal destruction and the prying into private lives and get on with our national life.

297

Bill Clinton's
STATE OF THE UNION ADDRESS

Mr. Speaker, Mr. Vice President, members of the 105th Congress, distinguished guests, my fellow Americans:

For 209 years it has been the President's duty to report to you on the state of the Union. Because of the hard work and high purpose of the American people, these are good times for America. We have more than 14 million new jobs; the lowest unemployment in 24 years; the lowest core inflation in 30 years; incomes are rising; and we have the highest homeownership in history. Crime has dropped for a record five years in a row. And the welfare rolls are at their lowest levels in 27 years. Our leadership in the world is unrivaled. Ladies and gentlemen, the state of our Union is strong.

"With barely 700 days left in the 20th century, this is not a time to rest."

With barely 700 days left in the 20th century, this is not a time to rest. It is a time to build, to build the America within reach: an America where everybody has a chance to get ahead with hard work; where every citizen can live in a safe community; where families are strong, schools are good and all young people can go to college; an America where scientists find cures for diseases from diabetes to Alzheimer's to AIDS; an America where every child can stretch a hand across a keyboard and reach every book ever written, every painting ever painted, every symphony ever composed; where government provides opportunity and citizens honor the responsibility to give something back to their communities; an America which leads the world to new heights of peace and prosperity.

This is the America we have begun to build; this is the America we can leave to our children—if we join together to finish the work at hand. Let us strengthen our nation for the 21st century.

"We have the smallest government in 35 years, but a more progressive one."

Rarely have Americans lived through so much change, in so many ways, in so short a time. Quietly, but with gathering force, the ground has shifted beneath our feet as we have moved into an Information Age, a global economy, a truly new world.

For five years now we have met the challenge of these changes as Americans have at every turning point—by renewing the very idea of America: widening the circle of opportunity, deepening the meaning of our freedom, forging a more perfect union.

We shaped a new kind of government for the Information Age. I thank the Vice President for his leadership and the Congress for its support in building a government that is leaner, more flexible, a catalyst for new ideas—and most of all, a government that gives the American people the tools they need to make the most of their own lives.

We have moved past the sterile debate between those who say government is the enemy and those who say government is the answer. My fellow Americans, we have found a third way. We have the smallest government in 35 years, but a more progressive one. We have a smaller government, but a stronger nation. We are moving steadily toward an even stronger America in the 21st century: an economy that offers opportunity, a society rooted in responsibility and a nation that lives as a community.

First, Americans in this chamber and across our nation have pursued a new strategy for prosperity: fiscal discipline to cut interest rates and spur growth; investments in education and skills, in science and technology and transportation, to prepare our people for the new economy; new markets for American products and American workers.

When I took office, the deficit for 1998 was projected to be $357 billion, and heading higher. This year, our deficit is projected to be $10 billion, and heading lower. For three decades, six Presidents have come before you to warn of the damage deficits pose to our nation. Tonight, I come before you to announce that the federal deficit—once so incomprehensibly large that it had 11 zeroes—will be, simply, zero. I will submit to Congress for 1999 the first balanced budget in 30 years. And if we hold fast to fiscal discipline, we may balance the budget this year—four years ahead of schedule.

You can all be proud of that, because turning a sea of red ink into black is no miracle. It is the product of hard work by the American people, and of two visionary actions in Congress—the courageous vote in 1993 that led to a cut in the deficit of 90 percent, and the truly historic bipartisan balanced budget agreement passed by this Congress. Here's the really good news: If we maintain our resolve, we will produce balanced budgets as far as the eye can see.

We must not go back to unwise spending or untargeted tax cuts that risk reopening the deficit. Last year, together we enacted targeted tax cuts so that the typical middle class family will now have the lowest tax rates in 20 years. My plan to balance the budget next year includes both new investments and new tax cuts targeted to the needs of working families: for education, for child care, for the environment.

But whether the issue is tax cuts or spending, I ask all of you to meet this test: Approve only those priorities that can actually be accomplished without adding a dime to the deficit.

Now, if we balance the budget for next year, it is projected that we'll then have a sizeable surplus in the years

Clinton's State of the Union address, January 27, 1998

that immediately follow. What should we do with this projected surplus? I have a simple four-word answer: Save Social Security first.

Tonight, I propose that we reserve 100 percent of the surplus—that's every penny of any surplus—until we have taken all the necessary measures to strengthen the Social Security system for the 21st century. Let us say to all Americans watching tonight—whether you're 70 or 50, or whether you just started paying into the system—Social Security will be there when you need it. Let us make this commitment: Social Security first. Let's do that together....

> *"The federal deficit—once so incomprehensibly large that it had 11 zeroes—will be, simply, zero. I will submit to Congress for 1999 the first balanced budget in 30 years."*

The Information Age is, first and foremost, an education age, in which education must start at birth and continue throughout a lifetime. Last year, from this podium, I said that education has to be our highest priority. I laid out a 10-point plan to move us forward and urged all of us to let politics stop at the schoolhouse door. Since then, this Congress, across party lines, and the American people have responded, in the most important year for education in a generation—expanding public school choice, opening the way to 3,000 new charter schools, working to connect every classroom in the country to the Information Superhighway, committing to expand Head Start to a million children, launching America Reads, sending literally thousands of college students into our elementary schools to make sure all our 8-year-olds can read.

Last year I proposed, and you passed, 220,000 new Pell Grant scholarships for deserving students. Student loans, already less expensive and easier to repay, now you get to deduct the interest. Families all over America now can put their savings into new tax-free education IRAs. And this year, for the first two years of college, families will get a $1,500 tax credit—a HOPE Scholarship that will cover the cost of most community college tuition. And for junior and senior year, graduate school, and job training, there is a lifetime learning credit. You did that and you should be very proud of it.

And because of these actions, I have something to say to every family listening to us tonight: Your children can go on to college. If you know a child from a poor family, tell her not to give up—she can go on to college. If you know a young couple struggling with bills, worried they won't be able to send their children to college, tell them not to give up—their children can go on to college. If you know somebody who's caught in a dead-end job and afraid he can't afford the classes necessary to get better jobs for the rest of his life, tell him not to give up—he can go on to college. Because of the things that have been done, we can make college as universal in the 21st century as high school is today. And, my friends, that will change the face and future of America....

As we enter the 21st century, the global economy requires us to seek opportunity not just at home, but in all the markets of the world. We must shape this global economy, not shrink from it. In the last five years, we have led the way in opening new markets, with 240 trade agreements that remove foreign barriers to products bearing the proud stamp "Made in the USA." Today, record high exports account for fully one-third of our economic growth. I want to keep them going, because that's the way to keep America growing and to advance a safer, more stable world.

> *"We must not go back to unwise spending or untargeted tax cuts that risk reopening the deficit."*

All of you know whatever your views are that I think this a great opportunity for America. I know there is opposition to more comprehensive trade agreements. I have listened carefully and I believe that the opposition is rooted in two fears: first, that our trading partners will have lower environmental and labor standards which will give them an unfair advantage in our market and do their own people no favors, even if there's more business; and, second, that if we have more trade, more of our workers will lose their jobs and have to start over. I think we should seek to advance worker and environmental standards around the world. I have made it abundantly clear that it should be a part of our trade agenda. But we cannot influence other countries' decisions if we send them a message that we're backing away from trade with them.

This year, I will send legislation to Congress, and ask other nations to join us, to fight the most intolerable labor practice of all—abusive child labor. We should also offer help and hope to those Americans temporarily left behind by the global marketplace or by the march of technology, which may have nothing to do with trade. That's why we have more than doubled funding for training dislocated workers since 1993—and if my new budget is adopted, we will triple funding. That's why we must do more, and more quickly, to help workers who lose their jobs for whatever reason.

You know, we help communities in a special way when their military base closes. We ought to help them in the same way if their factory closes. Again, I ask the Congress to continue its bipartisan work to consolidate the tangle of training programs we have today into one single G.I. Bill for Workers, a simple skills grant so people can, on their own, move quickly to new jobs, to higher incomes and brighter futures.

> *"What should we do with this projected surplus? I have a simple four-word answer: Save Social Security first."*

We all know in every way in life change is not always easy, but we have to decide whether we're going to try to hold it back and hide from it or reap its benefits. And remember the big picture here: While we've been entering into hundreds of new trade agreements, we've been creating millions of new jobs.

So this year we will forge new partnerships with Latin America, Asia, and Europe. And we should pass the new African Trade Act—it has bipartisan support. I will also renew my request for the fast track negotiating authority necessary to open more new markets, create more new jobs, which every President has had for two decades.

> *"Because of the things that have been done, we can make college as universal in the 21st century as high school is today."*

You know, whether we like it or not, in ways that are mostly positive, the world's economies are more and more interconnected and interdependent. Today, an economic crisis anywhere can affect economies everywhere. Recent months have brought serious financial problems to Thailand, Indonesia, South Korea, and beyond.

Now, why should Americans be concerned about this? First, these countries are our customers. If they sink into recession, they won't be able to buy the goods we'd like to sell them. Second, they're also our competitors. So if their currencies lose their value and go down, then the price of their goods will drop, flooding our market and others with much cheaper goods, which makes it a lot tougher for our people to compete. And, finally, they are our strategic partners. Their stability bolsters our security.

The American economy remains sound and strong, and I want to keep it that way. But because the turmoil in Asia will have an impact on all the world's economies, including ours, making that negative impact as small as possible is the right thing to do for America—and the right thing to do for a safer world.

Our policy is clear: No nation can recover if it does not reform itself. But when nations are willing to undertake serious economic reform, we should help them do it. So I call on Congress to renew America's commitment to the International Monetary Fund. And I think we should say to all the people we're trying to represent here that preparing for a far-off storm that may reach our shores is far wiser than ignoring the thunder until the clouds are just overhead....

"Preparing for a far-off storm that may reach our shores is far wiser than ignoring the thunder until the clouds are just overhead."

Nearly 200 years ago, a tattered flag, its broad stripes and bright stars still gleaming through the smoke of a fierce battle, moved Francis Scott Key to scribble a few words on the back of an envelope—the words that became our national anthem. Today, that Star Spangled Banner, along with the Declaration of Independence, the Constitution and the Bill of Rights, are on display just a short walk from here. They are America's treasures and we must also save them for the ages.

"Let that be our gift to the 21st century."

I ask all Americans to support our project to restore all our treasures so that the generations of the 21st century can see for themselves the images and the words that are the old and continuing glory of America; an America that has continued to rise through every age, against every challenge, of people of great works and greater possibilities, who have always, always found the wisdom and strength to come together as one nation—to widen the circle of opportunity, to deepen the meaning of our freedom, to form that "more perfect union." Let that be our gift to the 21st century.

God bless you, and God bless the United States.

George W.
BUSH

43RD PRESIDENT: 2001–

Born: July 6, 1946, in New Haven, Connecticut

Disc 2, Tracks 19–20

42

GEORGE W. BUSH

"FREEDOM AND FEAR, JUSTICE AND CRUELTY, HAVE ALWAYS BEEN AT WAR"

THE POWER OF the presidential pulpit was proven anew after September 11, 2001. The attacks that day on the World Trade Center and Pentagon by three hijacked airliners killed nearly three thousand people. The transportation system was shut down. Phones stopped working. Citizens watched as firefighters, police officers, and soldiers rushed toward the burning buildings and their own death. Not in a generation had America's sense of security been so undermined, its psyche so rattled.

In crisis, instinct tells us to look to the leader—to reassure, rally, and guide. That morning, President George W. Bush was in Florida, visiting a school classroom. At first his touch was unsure. He declared the "folks who did this" would be caught, then jetted off to military bases before returning to the capital for a tentative Oval Office address. Within days, he vowed a "crusade" (a word with unhappy memories for Muslims) and called for the capture of terrorist mastermind Osama bin Laden, dead or alive. Even his father, former President George H.W. Bush, urged him to cool his rhetoric. Fortunately for Bush, the adage, "You only get one chance to make a first impression," was wrong. Nine days after the attack, he delivered an address to Congress that was as forceful and eloquent as any president had ever delivered, calming the country and firming its resolve.

Bush worked with two trusted aides: chief speechwriter Michael Gerson (presidential nickname: "the Scribe") and Karen Hughes, a Texas confidante who was once a TV reporter. On Monday morning, September 16, Hughes asked for a draft by seven that evening. Gerson and two colleagues gathered around a word processor, producing a text filled with lofty language. "Freedom is at war with fear," they wrote, tweaking it to, "Freedom and fear are at war." A National Security Council writer passed on language from the White House's terror expert, explaining the enemy and its motives. Over days, the draft would be reshaped and rewritten—with Hughes working to make it more conversational, clearer to viewers watching at home. What goals would the speech set? In a security meeting at Camp David, Secretary of State Colin Powell urged a focus on the terrorists, with catching bin Laden the main goal; Pentagon official Paul Wolfowitz wanted to target Iraq, too. Bush chose the narrower approach, and the State Department drafted a section of the speech, leaden prose that Gerson then rewrote.

Presidents had gone before Congress twenty-one times to discuss war, the *Washington Post* reported, "But rare as such events are, this one had no precedent." Government officials believed the Capitol building itself may have been the target of the fourth hijacked plane, and was saved only when passengers, alerted by cell phone of the fate of the other planes, stood up to their hijackers, causing the jet to crash where it could not harm those on the ground. (Todd Beamer, one of the passengers who stood up to the hijackers and died in the crash, was praised by Bush during the speech. His widow, Lisa, was a guest of honor at the address.) Now the grand building was ringed by uniformed troops; fighter planes screamed overhead; ambulances stood by in case of a new attack. Vice President Richard Cheney stayed away, the first such absence ever for security reasons, according to the Senate historian. British Prime Minister Tony Blair looked on from the First Lady's gallery. Even the normally poker-faced Supreme Court justices cheered key lines.

The World Trade Center south tower (left) burst into flames after being struck by hijacked United Airlines Flight 175 as the north tower burns following an earlier attack by a hijacked airliner in New York City, September 11, 2001

Bush's address alternated between ringing eloquence and conversational talk explaining the new world. He adroitly began by recalling the State of the Union ritual, declaring the state of the nation still strong. (Once, joint session addresses on a single topic were common, but the last one had been Clinton's 1993 speech proposing a national health plan; instead, the annual address in January is the only time presidents typically come before Congress.) The speech sought balance—giving voice to the anger and thirst for justice widely felt by Americans, while reassuring other nations that our response would be measured.

Bush chose to describe the attack and response as part of a war (not, say, a police action). In previous wars, the enemy was visible: whom was America fighting now? Bush framed the foe by describing "a fringe form of Islamic extremism" and declaring a "war on terror." Since attacks would hit Afghanistan, he outlined the repressive Taliban regime's role in hosting bin Laden. He denounced bigotry against Muslims and stressed that the U.S. sought no clash of civilizations. Yet he likened the terrorists to "fascism, Nazism, and totalitarianism." ("Imperial communism" was struck from early drafts due to Russian sensitivities.) "And they will follow that path all the way to where it ends: in history's unmarked grave of discarded lies." This evoked a century of genocide, as well as Ronald Reagan's borrowing of Leon Trotsky's vow that communism's foes would end on the "ash-heap of history."

The outlines of a new security strategy took shape. Bush declared, "Either you are with us, or you are with the terrorists. From this day forward, any nation that continues to harbor or support terrorism will be regarded by the U.S. as a hostile regime." Reporters quickly called this the "Bush doctrine," echoing Truman. Such a stark approach would prove hard to follow to the letter. But these words undergirded our invasion of Iraq a year and a half later.

In contrast to the first-person, folksy style of recent political speeches, this one had a magisterial tone throughout, a president speaking for the nation. Only at the end did Bush speak in personal terms. Brandishing the shield of a fallen New York City police officer, Bush vowed in Churchillian cadences, "I will not forget the wound to our country and those who inflicted it. I will not yield. I will not rest. I will not relent." When Bush finished, amid strong applause, Democratic Senate Leader Tom Daschle hugged him.

The speech lacked the lasting line; the nation heard no "ask not" or "day of infamy." But it was itself an act of strong statesmanship. The public rallied to the president, a bond that did not break through the attack on Afghanistan and the long search for bin Laden.

Smoldering World Trade Center on September 11, 2001, with two sport utility vehicles seen bottom center among unidentifiable rubble

George W. Bush's
ADDRESS TO CONGRESS AFTER THE ATTACKS OF SEPTEMBER 11

Washington, D.C. • September 20, 2001

Mr. Speaker, Mr. President Pro Tempore, members of Congress, and fellow Americans:

In the normal course of events, Presidents come to this chamber to report on the state of the Union. Tonight, no such report is needed. It has already been delivered by the American people.

We have seen it in the courage of passengers, who rushed terrorists to save others on the ground—passengers like an exceptional man named Todd Beamer. And would you please help me to welcome his wife, Lisa Beamer, here tonight.

We have seen the state of our Union in the endurance of rescuers, working past exhaustion. We have seen the unfurling of flags, the lighting of candles, the giving of blood, the saying of prayers—in English, Hebrew, and Arabic. We have seen the decency of a loving and giving people who have made the grief of strangers their own.

My fellow citizens, for the last nine days, the entire world has seen for itself the state of our Union—and it is strong.

> ## "We have seen the decency of a loving and giving people who have made the grief of strangers their own."

Tonight we are a country awakened to danger and called to defend freedom. Our grief has turned to anger, and anger to resolution. Whether we bring our enemies to justice, or bring justice to our enemies, justice will be done.

I thank the Congress for its leadership at such an important time. All of America was touched on the evening of the tragedy to see Republicans and Democrats joined together on the steps of this Capitol, singing "God Bless America." And you did more than sing; you acted, by delivering $40 billion to rebuild our communities and meet the needs of our military.

> ## "For the last nine days, the entire world has seen for itself the state of our Union—and it is strong."

Speaker Hastert, Minority Leader Gephardt, Majority Leader Daschle and Senator Lott, I thank you for your friendship, for your leadership and for your service to our country.

And on behalf of the American people, I thank the world for its outpouring of support. America will never forget the sounds of our National Anthem playing at Buckingham Palace, on the streets of Paris, and at Berlin's Brandenburg Gate.

We will not forget South Korean children gathering to pray outside our embassy in Seoul, or the prayers of sympathy offered at a mosque in Cairo. We will not forget moments of silence and days of mourning in Australia and Africa and Latin America.

Nor will we forget the citizens of 80 other nations who died with our own: dozens of Pakistanis; more than 130 Israelis; more than 250 citizens of India; men and women from El Salvador, Iran, Mexico and Japan; and hundreds of British citizens. America has no truer friend than Great Britain. Once again, we are joined together in a great cause—so honored the British Prime Minister has crossed an ocean to show his unity of purpose with America. Thank you for coming, friend.

On September the 11th, enemies of freedom committed an act of war against our country. Americans have known wars—but for the past 136 years, they have been wars on foreign soil, except for one Sunday in 1941. Americans have known the casualties of war—but not at the center of a great city on a peaceful morning. Americans have known surprise attacks—but never before on thousands of civilians. All of this was brought upon us in a single day—and night fell on a different world, a world where freedom itself is under attack.

Americans have many questions tonight. Americans are asking: Who attacked our country? The evidence we have gathered all points to a collection of loosely affiliated terrorist organizations known as al Qaeda. They are the same murderers indicted for bombing American embassies in Tanzania and Kenya, and responsible for bombing the USS *Cole*.

Al Qaeda is to terror what the mafia is to crime. But its goal is not making money; its goal is remaking the world—and imposing its radical beliefs on people everywhere.

"Whether we bring our enemies to justice, or bring justice to our enemies, justice will be done."

The terrorists practice a fringe form of Islamic extremism that has been rejected by Muslim scholars and the vast majority of Muslim clerics—a fringe movement that perverts the peaceful teachings of Islam. The terrorists' directive commands them to kill Christians and Jews, to kill all Americans, and make no distinction among military and civilians, including women and children.

This group and its leader—a person named Osama bin Laden—are linked to many other organizations in different countries, including the Egyptian Islamic Jihad and the Islamic Movement of Uzbekistan. There are thousands of these terrorists in more than 60 countries. They are recruited from their own nations and neighborhoods and brought to camps in places like Afghanistan, where they are trained in the tactics of terror. They are sent back to their homes or sent to hide in countries around the world to plot evil and destruction.

The leadership of al Qaeda has great influence in Afghanistan and supports the Taliban regime in controlling most of that country. In Afghanistan, we see al Qaeda's vision for the world.

"America will never forget the sounds of our National Anthem playing at Buckingham Palace, on the streets of Paris, and at Berlin's Brandenburg Gate."

Afghanistan's people have been brutalized—many are starving and many have fled. Women are not allowed to attend school. You can be jailed for owning a television. Religion can be practiced only as their leaders dictate. A man can be jailed in Afghanistan if his beard is not long enough.

The United States respects the people of Afghanistan—after all, we are currently its largest source of humanitarian aid—but we condemn the Taliban regime. It is not only repressing its own people, it is threatening people everywhere by sponsoring and sheltering and supplying terrorists. By aiding and abetting murder, the Taliban regime is committing murder.

And tonight, the United States of America makes the following demands on the Taliban: Deliver to United States authorities all the leaders of al Qaeda who hide in your land. Release all foreign nationals, including American citizens, you have unjustly imprisoned. Protect foreign journalists, diplomats and aid workers in your country. Close immediately and permanently every terrorist training camp in Afghanistan, and hand over every terrorist, and every person in their support structure, to appropriate authorities. Give the United States full access to terrorist training camps, so we can make sure they are no longer operating.

"On September the 11th, enemies of freedom committed an act of war against our country."

These demands are not open to negotiation or discussion. The Taliban must act, and act immediately. They will hand over the terrorists, or they will share in their fate.

I also want to speak tonight directly to Muslims throughout the world. We respect your faith. It's practiced freely by many millions of Americans, and by millions more in countries that America counts as friends. Its teachings are good and peaceful, and those who commit evil in the name of Allah blaspheme the name of Allah. The terrorists are traitors to their own faith, trying, in effect, to hijack Islam itself. The enemy of America is not our many Muslim friends; it is not our many Arab friends. Our enemy is a radical network of terrorists, and every government that supports them.

Our war on terror begins with al Qaeda, but it does not end there. It will not end until every terrorist group of global reach has been found, stopped and defeated.

Americans are asking, why do they hate us? They hate what we see right here in this chamber—a democratically elected government. Their leaders are self-appointed. They hate our freedoms—our freedom of religion, our freedom of speech, our freedom to vote and assemble and disagree with each other.

They want to overthrow existing governments in many Muslim countries, such as Egypt, Saudi Arabia, and Jordan. They want to drive Israel out of the Middle East. They want to drive Christians and Jews out of vast regions of Asia and Africa.

These terrorists kill not merely to end lives, but to disrupt and end a way of life. With every atrocity, they hope that America grows fearful, retreating from the world and forsaking our friends. They stand against us, because we stand in their way.

We are not deceived by their pretenses to piety. We have seen their kind before. They are the heirs of all the murderous ideologies of the 20th century. By sacrificing human life to serve their radical visions—by abandoning every value except the will to power—they follow in the path of fascism, and Nazism, and totalitarianism. And they will follow that path all the way, to where it ends: in history's unmarked grave of discarded lies.

Americans are asking: How will we fight and win this war? We will direct every resource at our command—every means of diplomacy, every tool of intelligence, every instrument of law enforcement, every financial influence, and every necessary weapon of war—to the disruption and to the defeat of the global terror network.

This war will not be like the war against Iraq a decade ago, with a decisive liberation of territory and a swift conclusion. It will not look like the air war above Kosovo two years ago, where no ground troops were used and not a single American was lost in combat.

Our response involves far more than instant retaliation and isolated strikes. Americans should not expect one battle, but a lengthy campaign, unlike any other we have ever seen. It may include dramatic strikes, visible on TV, and covert operations, secret even in success. We will starve terrorists of funding, turn them one against another, drive them from place to place, until there is no refuge or no rest. And we will pursue nations that provide aid or safe haven to terrorism. Every nation, in every region, now has a decision to make. Either you are with us, or you are with the terrorists. From this day forward, any nation that continues to harbor or support terrorism will be regarded by the United States as a hostile regime.

"In Afghanistan, we see al Qaeda's vision for the world."

Our nation has been put on notice: We are not immune from attack. We will take defensive measures against terrorism to protect Americans. Today, dozens of federal departments and agencies, as well as state and local governments, have responsibilities affecting homeland security.

Bush vows to use "every resource" to combat global terrorism in a televised address to a joint session of Congress on September 20, 2001

Forces to alert, and there is a reason. The hour is coming when America will act, and you will make us proud.

This is not, however, just America's fight. And what is at stake is not just America's freedom. This is the world's fight. This is civilization's fight. This is the fight of all who believe in progress and pluralism, tolerance and freedom.

We ask every nation to join us. We will ask, and we will need, the help of police forces, intelligence services, and banking systems around the world. The United States is grateful that many nations and many international organizations have already responded—with sympathy and with support. Nations from Latin America, to Asia, to Africa, to Europe, to the Islamic world. Perhaps the NATO Charter reflects best the attitude of the world: An attack on one is an attack on all.

"Americans are asking, why do they hate us?"

The civilized world is rallying to America's side. They understand that if this terror goes unpunished, their own cities, their own citizens may be next. Terror, unanswered, can not only bring down buildings, it can threaten the stability of legitimate governments. And you know what—we're not going to allow it.

Americans are asking: What is expected of us? I ask you to live your lives, and hug your children. I know many citizens have fears tonight, and I ask you to be calm and resolute, even in the face of a continuing threat.

I ask you to uphold the values of America, and remember why so many have come here. We are in a fight for our principles, and our first responsibility is to live by them. No one should be singled out for unfair treatment or unkind words because of their ethnic background or religious faith.

I ask you to continue to support the victims of this tragedy with your contributions. Those who want to give can go to a central source of information, libertyunites.org, to find the names of groups providing direct help in New York, Pennsylvania, and Virginia.

These efforts must be coordinated at the highest level. So tonight I announce the creation of a Cabinet-level position reporting directly to me—the Office of Homeland Security.

And tonight I also announce a distinguished American to lead this effort, to strengthen American security: a military veteran, an effective governor, a true patriot, a trusted friend—Pennsylvania's Tom Ridge. He will lead, oversee and coordinate a comprehensive national strategy to safeguard our country against terrorism, and respond to any attacks that may come.

These measures are essential. But the only way to defeat terrorism as a threat to our way of life is to stop it, eliminate it, and destroy it where it grows.

Many will be involved in this effort, from FBI agents to intelligence operatives to the reservists we have called to active duty. All deserve our thanks, and all have our prayers. And tonight, a few miles from the damaged Pentagon, I have a message for our military: Be ready. I've called the Armed

The thousands of FBI agents who are now at work in this investigation may need your cooperation, and I ask you to give it.

I ask for your patience, with the delays and inconveniences that may accompany tighter security; and for your patience in what will be a long struggle.

I ask your continued participation and confidence in the American economy. Terrorists attacked a symbol of American prosperity. They did not touch its source. America is successful because of the hard work, and creativity, and enterprise of our people. These were the true strengths of our economy before September 11th, and they are our strengths today.

And, finally, please continue praying for the victims of terror and their families, for those in uniform, and for our great country. Prayer has comforted us in sorrow, and will help strengthen us for the journey ahead.

Tonight I thank my fellow Americans for what you have already done and for what you will do. And ladies and

"Either you are with us, or you are with the terrorists. From this day forward, any nation that continues to harbor or support terrorism will be regarded by the United States as a hostile regime."

gentlemen of the Congress, I thank you, their representatives, for what you have already done and for what we will do together.

Tonight, we face new and sudden national challenges. We will come together to improve air safety, to dramatically expand the number of air marshals on domestic flights, and

Bush is applauded while preparing to address a Joint Session of Congress at the Capitol Building on September 20, 2001 regarding the terrorist attacks of September 11. Behind the president are House Speaker Dennis Hastert (left) and Senate President Pro Tempore Robert Byrd (right).

take new measures to prevent hijacking. We will come together to promote stability and keep our airlines flying, with direct assistance during this emergency.

We will come together to give law enforcement the additional tools it needs to track down terror here at home. We will come together to strengthen our intelligence capabilities to know the plans of terrorists before they act, and find them before they strike.

We will come together to take active steps that strengthen America's economy, and put our people back to work.

Tonight we welcome two leaders who embody the extraordinary spirit of all New Yorkers: Governor George Pataki, and Mayor Rudolph Giuliani. As a symbol of America's resolve, my administration will work with Congress, and these two leaders, to show the world that we will rebuild New York City.

After all that has just passed—all the lives taken, and all the possibilities and hopes that died with them—it is natural to wonder if America's future is one of fear. Some speak of an age of terror. I know there are struggles ahead, and dangers to face. But this country will define our times, not be defined by them. As long as the United States of America is determined and strong, this will not be an age of terror; this will be an age of liberty, here and across the world.

"I will not yield; I will not rest; I will not relent."

Great harm has been done to us. We have suffered great loss. And in our grief and anger we have found our mission and our moment. Freedom and fear are at war. The advance of human freedom—the great achievement of our time, and the great hope of every time—now depends on us. Our nation—this generation—will lift a dark threat of violence from our people and our future. We will rally the world to this cause by our efforts, by our courage. We will not tire, we will not falter, and we will not fail.

It is my hope that in the months and years ahead, life will return almost to normal. We'll go back to our lives and routines, and that is good. Even grief recedes with time and grace. But our resolve must not pass. Each of us will remember what happened that day, and to whom it happened. We'll remember the moment the news came—where we were and what we were doing. Some will remember an image of a fire, or a story of rescue. Some will carry memories of a face and a voice gone forever.

"Freedom and fear, justice and cruelty, have always been at war."

And I will carry this: It is the police shield of a man named George Howard, who died at the World Trade Center trying to save others. It was given to me by his mom, Arlene, as a proud memorial to her son. This is my reminder of lives that ended, and a task that does not end.

I will not forget this wound to our country or those who inflicted it. I will not yield; I will not rest; I will not relent in waging this struggle for freedom and security for the American people.

The course of this conflict is not known, yet its outcome is certain. Freedom and fear, justice and cruelty, have always been at war, and we know that God is not neutral between them.

Fellow citizens, we'll meet violence with patient justice—assured of the rightness of our cause, and confident of the victories to come. In all that lies before us, may God grant us wisdom, and may He watch over the United States of America.

Thank you.

43

"THE DAY OF YOUR LIBERATION IS NEAR"

"HERE'S AN ASSIGNMENT," Michael Gerson, President Bush's chief speechwriter, told his colleague David Frum. "Can you sum up, in a sentence or two, our best case for going against Iraq?" It was December 2001—just a month after the fall of Afghanistan. Frum wrote a draft charging that Iraq and Iran, in league with terrorists, constituted an "axis of hatred." Gerson thought "evil" sounded more theological, Frum recalled. With North Korea added to the list, in his State of the Union address the next month, Bush issued a remarkable challenge. "States like these, and their terrorist allies, constitute an axis of evil, arming to threaten the peace of the world. By seeking weapons of mass destruction, these regimes pose a grave and growing danger."

One year later, the United States invaded Iraq and ousted the dictator Saddam Hussein. Not since World War II had a conflict been so debated in advance. In a series of key speeches, Bush articulated a dramatically new American foreign policy—every bit as consequential, and controversial, as the doctrines that guided the Cold War. For half a century, as the United States and Soviet Union faced off, presidents focused on building formal institutions and alliances, such as NATO, to contain communism. After the end of the Cold War, with Washington the capital of the only superpower left, presidents George Bush and Bill Clinton focused on linking the world through global alliances. In an address to a joint session of Congress, the first President Bush had declared the goal of a "new world order"—"a world where the rule of law supplants the rule of the jungle. A world in which nations recognize the shared responsibility for freedom and justice. A world where the strong respect the rights of the weak."

Speaking at West Point on June 1, 2002, the younger Bush rejected the earlier doctrine. "For much of the last century, America's defense relied on the Cold War doctrines of deterrence and containment," he told graduating cadets.

In some cases, those strategies still apply. But new threats also require new thinking. Deterrence—the promise of massive retaliation against nations—means nothing against shadowy terrorist networks with no nation or citizens to defend. Containment is not possible when unbalanced dictators with weapons of mass destruction can deliver those weapons on missiles or secretly provide them to terrorist allies.

We cannot defend America and our friends by hoping for the best. We cannot put our faith in the word of tyrants, who solemnly sign non-proliferation treaties, and then systemically break them. If we wait for threats to fully materialize, we will have waited too long.

By summer, it was clear the United States would likely move against Iraq. Urged by Great Britain's Prime Minister Tony Blair, however, Bush went to the United Nations. He spoke before the General Assembly on September 12, 2002. Aides battled over whether the administration would seek UN authorization for force. The night before, Bush decided to make the request. But the text on the teleprompter left the line off. Bush ad-libbed: "We will work with the UN Security Council for the necessary resolutions." His apparent call for multiple votes would prove highly significant later—a slip of the tongue with dramatic consequences, as France demanded that war go forward only with a second resolution.

President Bush addresses the nation from the White House Cross Hall, giving a forty-eight-hour ultimatum to Iraqi leader Saddam Hussein on Monday, March 17, 2003

The UN Security Council backed a new push to disarm Saddam. In an extraordinary minuet of diplomacy and force, the United States argued for "regime change," while UN inspectors combed through Iraq. Many rationales for war slipped in and out of view—alleged links with terrorists; the human rights abuses perpetrated by Saddam and his regime; the impact on democracy and reform throughout the Arab world if Saddam were to fall; even, as Bush told an audience at a fundraiser, "This is a guy that tried to kill my dad," referring to a plot hatched a decade before. But above all was the danger of Iraq's purported arsenal of chemical and biological weapons, and the charge that it was seeking to build nuclear bombs. In his 2003 State of the Union address, Bush outlined specific, precise amounts

of banned material he charged was in Iraq. Secretary of State Colin Powell made a forceful presentation to the Security Council.

But the inspectors found nothing. Led by France, major nations including Germany, Russia, and China turned against a war, a view backed strongly by public opinion in most lands. At a prime-time press conference, President Bush vowed to call a Security Council vote anyway. "And so, you bet," he said. "It's time for people to show their cards, to let the world know where they stand when it comes to Saddam." France announced it would issue a veto. Bush flew to meet with Prime Minister Tony Blair in the Azores. Gerson traveled with him, as did Karen Hughes (retired from government but still helping with speeches). The next day, he called off the Security Council vote—and that night he addressed the world from the foyer of the White House.

It was a moment of compressed drama. The United States would act: without new United Nations authority, with only Great Britain, among major traditional allies, providing help. Bush was brief and emphatic. He set out the new doctrine to the widest audience—words now punctuated by action.

Bush issued a stark ultimatum. Saddam Hussein—and his sons—must leave Iraq within forty-eight hours. The speech was extraordinary in several respects. It was directed at specific people within Iraq: the military was urged not to obey Saddam's possible orders to use chemical or biological weapons against American troops, or to destroy oil wells. He spoke to the Iraqi people, and told them their liberation was at hand. It was eloquent, as Bush's formal public statements often are; the language was simple, propelled by alliteration ("day of decision") and parallelisms ("shift our attention with panic and weaken our morale with fear"). Still, for all its muscularity, it reflected the unfamiliar logic of preemption, saying we act to forestall what "might" happen.

By summer, controversy boiled over Bush's prewar speeches. The White House admitted that in Bush's 2003 State of the Union he should not have charged that Iraq had sought uranium in Africa. *Time* magazine examined his talks in a cover story, "Untruth and Consequences." Defenders countered the withdrawn uranium charge took only sixteen words in nearly an hour-long speech.

Complex events would continue to cascade. Where, after all, were Iraq's weapons? Would the resounding image be that of disorder and looting, and throngs of Muslims demanding that the U.S. leave? Or would it be the image of a crowd of Iraqis cheering, as American soldiers pulled down a statue of the dictator who had suppressed his own people—the most recent example of the best of America's tradition?

Fire and smoke can be seen over Baghdad the night of Thursday, March 27, 2003, as strong explosions from U.S. air strikes shake the city's center

George W. Bush's
ADDRESS ON IRAQ

Washington, D.C. • March 17, 2003

*hear...
disc 2
track 20

My fellow citizens:

Events in Iraq have now reached the final days of decision. For more than a decade, the United States and other nations have pursued patient and honorable efforts to disarm the Iraqi regime without war. That regime pledged to reveal and destroy all its weapons of mass destruction as a condition for ending the Persian Gulf War in 1991.

Since then, the world has engaged in 12 years of diplomacy. We have passed more than a dozen resolutions in the United Nations Security Council. We have sent hundreds of weapons inspectors to oversee the disarmament of Iraq. Our good faith has not been returned.

The Iraqi regime has used diplomacy as a ploy to gain time and advantage. It has uniformly defied Security Council resolutions demanding full disarmament. Over the years, U.N. weapon inspectors have been threatened by Iraqi officials, electronically bugged, and systematically deceived. Peaceful efforts to disarm the Iraqi regime have failed again and again—because we are not dealing with peaceful men.

Intelligence gathered by this and other governments leaves no doubt that the Iraq regime continues to possess and conceal some of the most lethal weapons ever devised. This regime has already used weapons of mass destruction against Iraq's neighbors and against Iraq's people.

"Events in Iraq have now reached the final days of decision."

The regime has a history of reckless aggression in the Middle East. It has a deep hatred of America and our friends. And it has aided, trained and harbored terrorists, including operatives of al Qaeda.

The danger is clear: using chemical, biological or, one day, nuclear weapons, obtained with the help of Iraq, the terrorists could fulfill their stated ambitions and kill thousands or hundreds of thousands of innocent people in our country, or any other.

"Peaceful efforts to disarm the Iraqi regime have failed again and again—because we are not dealing with peaceful men."

The United States and other nations did nothing to deserve or invite this threat. But we will do everything to defeat it. Instead of drifting along toward tragedy, we will set a course toward safety.

Before the day of horror can come, before it is too late to act, this danger will be removed.

The United States of America has the sovereign authority to use force in assuring its own national security. That duty falls to me, as Commander-in-Chief, by the oath I have sworn, by the oath I will keep.

Recognizing the threat to our country, the United States Congress voted overwhelmingly last year to support the use of force against Iraq. America tried to work with the United Nations to address this threat because we wanted to resolve the issue peacefully. We believe in the mission of the United Nations. One reason the U.N. was founded after the second world war was to confront aggressive dictators, actively and early, before they can attack the innocent and destroy the peace.

In the case of Iraq, the Security Council did act, in the early 1990s. Under Resolutions 678 and 687—both still in effect—the United States and our allies are authorized to use force in ridding Iraq of weapons of mass destruction. This is not a question of authority, it is a question of will.

Last September, I went to the U.N. General Assembly and urged the nations of the world to unite and bring an end to this danger. On November 8th, the Security Council unanimously passed Resolution 1441, finding Iraq in material breach of its obligations, and vowing serious consequences if Iraq did not fully and immediately disarm.

> ## "This is not a question of authority, it is a question of will."

Today, no nation can possibly claim that Iraq has disarmed. And it will not disarm so long as Saddam Hussein holds power. For the last four-and-a-half months, the United States and our allies have worked within the Security Council to enforce that Council's long-standing demands. Yet, some permanent members of the Security Council have publicly announced they will veto any resolution that compels the disarmament of Iraq. These governments share our assessment of the danger, but not our resolve to meet it. Many nations, however, do have the resolve and fortitude to act against this threat to peace, and a broad coalition is now gathering to enforce the just demands of the world. The United Nations Security Council has not lived up to its responsibilities, so we will rise to ours.

In recent days, some governments in the Middle East have been doing their part. They have delivered public and private messages urging the dictator to leave Iraq, so that disarmament can proceed peacefully. He has thus far refused. All the decades of deceit and cruelty have now reached an end. Saddam Hussein and his sons must leave Iraq within 48 hours. Their refusal to do so will result in military conflict, commenced at a time of our choosing. For their own safety, all foreign nationals—including journalists and inspectors—should leave Iraq immediately.

Many Iraqis can hear me tonight in a translated radio broadcast, and I have a message for them. If we must begin a military campaign, it will be directed against the lawless men who rule your country and not against you. As our coalition takes away their power, we will deliver the food and medicine you need. We will tear down the apparatus of terror and we will help you to build a new Iraq that is prosperous and free. In a free Iraq, there will be no more wars of aggression against your neighbors, no more poison factories, no more executions of dissidents, no more torture chambers and rape rooms.

The tyrant will soon be gone. The day of your liberation is near.

It is too late for Saddam Hussein to remain in power. It is not too late for the Iraqi military to act with honor and protect your country by permitting the peaceful entry of coalition forces to eliminate weapons of mass destruction. Our forces will give Iraqi military units clear instructions on actions they can take to avoid being attacked and destroyed. I urge every member of the Iraqi military and intelligence services, if war comes, do not fight for a dying regime that is not worth your own life.

> ## "The United Nations Security Council has not lived up to its responsibilities, so we will rise to ours."

And all Iraqi military and civilian personnel should listen carefully to this warning. In any conflict, your fate will depend on your action. Do not destroy oil wells, a source of wealth that belongs to the Iraqi people. Do not obey any command to use weapons of mass destruction against anyone, including the Iraqi people. War crimes will be prosecuted. War criminals will be punished. And it will be no defense to say, "I was just following orders."

A British tank, seen in this television image, topples a statue of Iraqi President Saddam Hussein in Basra, Iraq, April 5, 2003

Should Saddam Hussein choose confrontation, the American people can know that every measure has been taken to avoid war, and every measure will be taken to win it. Americans understand the costs of conflict because we have paid them in the past. War has no certainty, except the certainty of sacrifice.

Yet, the only way to reduce the harm and duration of war is to apply the full force and might of our military, and we are prepared to do so. If Saddam Hussein attempts to cling to power, he will remain a deadly foe until the end. In desperation, he and terrorists groups might try to conduct terrorist operations against the American people and our friends. These attacks are not inevitable. They are, however, possible. And this very fact underscores the reason we cannot live under the threat of blackmail. The terrorist threat to America and the world will be diminished the moment that Saddam Hussein is disarmed.

Our government is on heightened watch against these dangers. Just as we are preparing to ensure victory in Iraq, we are taking further actions to protect our homeland. In recent days, American authorities have expelled from the country certain individuals with ties to Iraqi intelligence services. Among other measures, I have directed additional security of our airports, and increased Coast Guard patrols of major seaports. The Department of Homeland Security is working closely with the nation's governors to increase armed security at critical facilities across America.

Should enemies strike our country, they would be attempting to shift our attention with panic and weaken our morale with fear. In this, they would fail. No act of theirs can alter the course or shake the resolve of this country. We are a peaceful people—yet we're not a fragile people, and we will not be intimidated by thugs and killers.

If our enemies dare to strike us, they and all who have aided them, will face fearful consequences.

We are now acting because the risks of inaction would be far greater. In one year, or five years, the power of Iraq to inflict harm on all free nations would be multiplied many times over. With these capabilities, Saddam Hussein and his terrorist allies could choose the moment of deadly conflict when they are strongest. We choose to meet that threat now, where it arises, before it can appear suddenly in our skies and cities.

"Saddam Hussein and his sons must leave Iraq within 48 hours."

The cause of peace requires all free nations to recognize new and undeniable realities. In the 20th century, some chose to appease murderous dictators, whose threats were allowed to grow into genocide and global war. In this century, when evil men plot chemical, biological and nuclear terror, a policy of appeasement could bring destruction of a kind never before seen on this earth.

Terrorists and terror states do not reveal these threats with fair notice, in formal declarations—and responding to such enemies only after they have struck first is not self-defense, it is suicide. The security of the world requires disarming Saddam Hussein now.

"The tyrant will soon be gone. The day of your liberation is near."

As we enforce the just demands of the world, we will also honor the deepest commitments of our country. Unlike Saddam Hussein, we believe the Iraqi people are deserving and capable of human liberty.

And when the dictator has departed, they can set an example to all the Middle East of a vital and peaceful and self-governing nation.

The United States, with other countries, will work to advance liberty and peace in that region. Our goal will not be achieved overnight, but it can come over time. The power and appeal of human liberty is felt in every life and every land. And the greatest power of freedom is to overcome hatred and violence, and turn the creative gifts of men and women to the pursuits of peace.

That is the future we choose. Free nations have a duty to defend our people by uniting against the violent. And tonight, as we have done before, America and our allies accept that responsibility.

Good night, and may God continue to bless America.

NOTES

George Washington
First Inaugural Address: "The American Experiment"

3   *Washington's trip north:* James MacGregor Burns, *The Vineyard of Liberty* (New York: Vintage Books, 1982) p. 64–67.

3   *Madison noted ruefully:* James Thomas Flexner, *Washington: The Indispensable Man* (Boston: Little, Brown and Company, 1994) p. 214.

3   *Fisher Ames:* Barry Schwartz, *George Washington: The Making of an American Symbol* (New York: Free Press, 1987) p. 152.

3   *Lost his composure:* Ibid., p. 150–155.

3   *Warm public approval:* See Jeffrey K. Tulis, *The Rhetorical Presidency* (Princeton: Princeton University Press, 1987).

3   *Washington as deist:* Flexner, *Washington: The Indispensable Man,* p. 216.

Farewell Address: "These Counsels of an Old and Affectionate Friend"

9   *New Hampshire paper:* Joseph J. Ellis, *Founding Brothers: The Revolutionary Generation* (New York: Knopf, 2000) p. 181.

9   *King George III:* Garry Wills, *Cincinatus* (Garden City, NY: Doubleday & Company, 1984) p. 13.

9   *Use of bully pulpit:* Ibid., p. 88.

9   *Hamilton and Madison:* Felix Gilbert, *To The Farewell Address: Ideas of Early American Foreign Policy* (Princeton: Princeton University Press 1970) p. 126.

9   *Us rather than them:* Ellis, *Founding Brothers,* p. 155–156.

10   *Washington's desire to retire:* James Thomas Flexner, *George Washington, Anguish and Farewell* (Boston: Little, Brown and Company, 1972) p. 304.

10   *Jefferson at inaugural:* Richard Brookhiser, *Founding Father: Rediscovering George Washington* (New York: Free Press, 1996) p. 103.

Thomas Jefferson
First Inaugural Address: "We Are All Republicans, We Are All Federalists"

17   *Revolution of 1800:* Richard J. Ellis, ed., *Speaking to the People: The Rhetorical Presidency in Historical Perspective* (Amherst: University of Massachusetts Press, 1998) p. 37.

17   *House votes for Jefferson:* Noble E. Cunningham, *In Pursuit of Reason: The Life of Thomas Jefferson* (New York: Ballantine Books, 1988 [paperback ed.]) p. 221–237.

17   *Burr and Hamilton:* See Joseph J. Ellis, *Founding Brothers,* p. 20–47.

17   *Adams leaves by coach:* David McCullough, *John Adams,* (New York: Simon & Schuster, 2001) p. 564.

17   *Address published by end of ceremony:* Frank Van Der Linden, *The Turning Point: Jefferson's Battle for the Presidency* (New York: Van Rees Press, 1962) p. 319.

17   *Could hardly hear him:* Bernard A. Weisberger, *America Afire: Jefferson, Adams, and the Revolutionary Election of 1800* (New York: William Morrow, 2000) p. 279.

17   *Party names not capitalized:* Joseph J. Ellis, *American Sphinx: The Character of Thomas Jefferson* (New York: Vintage, 1998) p. 215–216.

17   *Wooing moderate Federalists:* Frank Van Der Linden, *The Turning Point,* p. 321.

17   *Political tolerance:* Wayne Fields, *Union of Words: A History of Presidential Eloquence* (New York: Free Press, 1996) p. 121.

Andrew Jackson
Veto of the Bank of the United States: "The Rich and Powerful Too Often Bend the Acts of Government to Their Selfish Purposes"

25   *Public appeals improper:* See Tulis, *The Rhetorical Presidency.*

25   *Voter turnout:* Lyn Ragsdale, *Vital Statistics on the Presidency: Washington to Clinton* rev. ed. (Washington D.C.: Congressional Quarterly, 1998) p. 132.

25   *"The bank, Mr. Van Buren":* Robert V. Remini, *Andrew Jackson and the Course of American Freedom, 1822–1832* (New York: Harper & Row, 1981) p. 366.

25   *Decision to veto:* Ibid., p. 365.

25   *Reach their minds and hearts:* Robert V. Remini, *Andrew Jackson* (New York: Twayne Publishers Inc., 1966) p. 150.

25   *"Demagogic":* Arthur M. Schlesinger Jr., *The Age of Jackson* (Boston: Little Brown, 1945) (paperback ed.) p. 90.

25   *Jackson used party machine:* Tulis, *The Rhetorical Presidency,* p. 75.

25   *Bank ruled constitutional:* McCullough v. Maryland: 17 U.S. (4 Wheat.) 316, 4 L. Ed. 579 (1819).

26   *Bank closed:* Robert V. Remini, *Andrew Jackson and the Course of American Democracy, 1833–1845* (New York: HarperCollins, 1984) passim.

Proclamation on Nullification:
"Disunion by Armed Force Is Treason"

30 *Dinner toast*: Remini, *Andrew Jackson and the Course of American Freedom, 1822–1832*, p. 234–237.

30 *Southerners feared*: By 1830, most South Carolinians were enslaved. See Harry L. Watson, *Liberty and Power* (New York: Hill & Wang, 1990) p. 115.

30 *"I will die with the Union"*: Remini, *Andrew Jackson*, p. 133.

31 *On drafting of proclamation and Jackson's marking the pages*: Remini, *Andrew Jackson and the Course of American Democracy, 1833–1845*, p. 17–20.

31 *On reaction to proclamation*: Donald B. Cole, *The Presidency of Andrew Jackson* (Lawrence: University of Kansas Press, 1993) p. 162; Robert V. Remini, *The Life of Andrew Jackson* (New York: HarperCollins Perennial, 2001) p. 244.

Abraham Lincoln
Address to the State Republican Convention: "A House Divided Against Itself Cannot Stand"

37 *Dred Scott v. Sandford*: 60 U.S. (19 How.) 393 (1857) Stephen B. Oates, *With Malice Toward None: A Life of Abraham Lincoln* (New York: HarperPerennial, 1994) p. 144.

37 *From memory*: David Herbert Donald, *Lincoln* (New York: Simon & Schuster, 1995) p. 206.

37 *For a summary of Lincoln's shifting views*: Mario Cuomo and Harold Holzer, eds., *Lincoln on Democracy* (New York: Harper Collins, 1990) p. 59–61.

37 *"radical" and "dangerous"*: Oates, *With Malice Toward None* p. 142.

37 *Echoes of Webster*: Don E. Fehrenbacher, *Prelude to Greatness: Lincoln in the 1850's* (Palo Alto, CA: Stanford University Press, 1962) p. 180.

37 *Used twice in scripture*: Matthew 12:25, Mark 3:25.

37 *Earlier speech*: Donald, *Lincoln*, p. 206.

38 *Syllogism*: Ibid., p. 209.

38 *"Clear cut decision"*: Fehrenbacher, *Prelude to Greatness*, p. 95.

38 *Lincoln believed*: Cuomo and Holzer, *Lincoln on Democracy*, p. 99.

First Inaugural Address: "The Better Angels of Our Nature"

43 *"Taste is in my mouth"*: Abraham Lincoln, Letter to Lyman Trumbull, April 29, 1860, http://showcase.netins.net/web/creative/lincoln/speeches/trumbull.htm.

43 *"Neglected back room"*: Oates, *With Malice Toward None*, p 206.

45 *Seven states*: Donald, *Lincoln* p. 276.

Gettysburg Address: "A New Birth of Freedom"

53 *51,000 dead or wounded*: James M. McPherson, *Battle Cry of Freedom* (New York: Oxford University Press, 1988) p. 653–665.

53 *"a few appropriate remarks"*: Garry Wills, *Lincoln at Gettysburg* (New York: Simon & Schuster, 1992) p. 25.

53 *determined to attend*: Oates, *With Malice Toward None*, p. 364.

54 *slavery in the Declaration*: See Pauline Maier, *American Scripture* (New York: Vintage Books, 1998) p. 146.

54 *birth, death, and resurrection*: George P. Fletcher, *Our Secret Constitution: How Lincoln Redefined American Democracy* (New York: Oxford University Press, 2001) p. 39–40.

55 *Copied by hand*: Donald, *Lincoln*, p. 465.

Second Inaugural Address: "With Malice Toward None"

57 *Approach to the South*: Garry Wills, "Lincoln's Greatest Speech?" *The Atlantic Monthly*, September 1999, Volume 284, No. 3, p. 60–70.

57 *One syllable long*: Ronald C. White Jr., *Lincoln's Greatest Speech: The Second Inaugural* (New York: Simon & Schuster, 2001) p.48.

58 *Scripture*: Matthew 7:1, Matthew 18:7, Psalms 19:9—Glenn E. Thurow, *Abraham Lincoln and American Political Religion* (Albany, NY: State University of New York Press, 1976) p. 15.

58 *New York Herald*: Garry Wills, "Lincoln's Greatest Speech"

Theodore Roosevelt
Dedication of the House Office Building: "The Man with the Muck-rake"

63 *"That madman"*: H.W. Brands, *TR: The Last Romantic* (New York: Basic Books, 1997) p. 396.

63 *Prolific author*: Edmund Morris, *The Rise of Theodore Roosevelt* (New York: Ballantine Books, 1979) p. 7.

63 *"Bride at every wedding"*: Nathan Miller, *Theodore Roosevelt: A Life* (New York: Morrow, 1992) p. 411.

63 *TR held back*: Tulis, *The Rhetorical Presidency*, p.106–107.

63 *"Millionaire's Club"*: David Graham Phillips, *The Treason of the Senate* (New York: Monthly Review Press reprint, 1953).

64 *"Man with the muck-rake"*: John Bunyan, *The Pilgrim's Progress* (New York: Payson & Clarke Ltd., 1928).

Speech at Osawatomie, Kansas: "The New Nationalism"

68 *Two lesser*: James Reston, "The Evil of 2 Lessers," *The New York Times*, September 27, 1980, Section 4, p. 21.

68 *"Prophet business"*: John A. Gable, *The Bull Moose Years: Theodore Roosevelt and the Progressive Party* (Port Washington: Kennikat Press, 1978) p. ix.

68 *Book*: Herbert Croly, *The Promise of American Life* (New York: Capricorn Books, 1964).

69 *"Confession of Faith"*: reprinted in Mario R. DiNunzio, ed., *Theodore Roosevelt: An American Mind—Selected Writings* (New York: Penguin Books, 1994) p. 150–160.

69 *Roosevelt shot*: Brands, *TR: The Last Romantic*, p. 721–722.

Woodrow Wilson

Declaration of War: "The World Must Be Made Safe for Democracy"

79   *Classic book*: Woodrow Wilson, *Congressional Government* (Boston: Houghton, Mifflin and Company, 1885).

79   *"National voice"*: Woodrow Wilson, *Constitutional Government in the United States* (New York: Columbia University Press, 1917) p. 68.

79   *"Jealous power"*: Supplement to the Messages and Papers of the Presidents, Covering the First Term of Woodrow Wilson (Bureau of National Literature, 1917) p. 7871.

79   *"Put one over on Teddy"*: Carol Gelderman, *All The Presidents' Words* (New York: Walker & Co., 1997) p.7.

79   *"Too proud to fight"*: Address to a Gathering of 4,000 Naturalized American Citizens, Philadelphia, PA, May 10, 1915, in Supplement to the Messages and Papers of the Presidents Covering the First Term of Woodrow Wilson (Bureau of National Literature, 1917) p. 8068.

79   *Demands for war*: Arthur S. Link, *Woodrow Wilson and the Progressive Era* (New York: Harper & Brothers, 1954) p. 274–277.

79   *"not by words"*: August Heckscher, *Woodrow Wilson* (New York: Collier Books, 1991) p. 438.

79   *Peroration*: Ibid., p. 440.

80   *Walter Lippmann*: Ibid., p. 439–440.

Address to Congress on Peace Terms: "The Fourteen Points"

87   *Secret Treaties*: Ronald Steel, *Walter Lippmann and the American Century* (New York: Vintage Books, 1981) p. 132.

87   *Lippmann's role*: Steel, *Walter Lippmann and the American Century*, p. 609.

87   *Surprised cabinet and diplomatic corps*: Heckscher, *Woodrow Wilson*, p. 471.

89   *Wilson's moral principles*: John Morton Blum, *The Progressive Presidents* (New York: W.W. Norton and Company, 1980) p. 99.

89   *Fourteen Points as moral standard*: Arthur S. Link, *Woodrow Wilson: Revolution, War and Peace* (Wheeling, IL: Harlan Davidson, 1982) p. 84.

Franklin Delano Roosevelt

First Inaugural Address: "The Only Thing We Have to Fear Is Fear Itself"

95   *Depression statistics*: David M. Kennedy, *Freedom from Fear* (New York: Oxford University Press, 1999) p. 163.

96   *A line he added*: Kenneth S. Davis, *FDR: The New Deal Years* (New York: Random House, 1986) p. 29.

96   *Moley's role*: Halford R. Ryan, *Franklin D. Roosevelt's Rhetorical Presidency* (Westport, CT: Greenwood Press, 1988) p. 76–79; Raymond Moley, *The First New Deal* (New York: Harcourt, Brace & World, Inc., 1966) p. 96–120.

96   *Eleanor Roosevelt*: Samuel Rosenman, *Working With Roosevelt* (New York: Harper & Row, 1952) p. 91.

96   *Howe*: See also Davis W. Houck, *FDR and Fear Itself: The First Inaugural Address* (College Station: Texas A&M University Press, 2002) p. 119–122.

96   *Lippmann*: Davis, *FDR: The New Deal Years*, 1986 p. 36.

96   *Terrifying*: James MacGregor Burns, *The Lion and the Fox* (New York: Harcourt, Brace & World, 1956) p. 165.

96   *Fireside chat*: Public Papers and Addresses of Franklin Delano Roosevelt, Volume Two, p. 64.

97   *"Capitalism was saved"*: Raymond Moley, *After Seven Years* (New York: Harper & Brothers Publisher, 1939) p. 155.

97   *FDR explained*: Public Papers and Addresses of Franklin Delano Roosevelt, Volume Two, p. 16.

Acceptance Speech for Renomination: "A Rendezvous with Destiny"

102   *Republican platform*: http://www.presidency.ucsb.edu/docs/ platforms/republicans/R1936.htm

102   *Militant, bare fisted*: Rosenman, *Working With Roosevelt*, p. 104.

102   *Pale and shaken*: Arthur M. Schlesinger Jr., *The Politics of Upheaval* (New York: Houghton Mifflin, 1974 edition) p. 583.

103   *End of reform*: See Alan Brinkley, *The End of Reform: New Deal Liberalism in Recession and War* (New York: Knopf, 1995).

1941 Annual Message to Congress: "The Four Freedoms"

109   *Agony of neutrality*: Kennedy, *Freedom From Fear*, p. 426–464.

109   *Perkins*: Doris Kearns Goodwin, *No Ordinary Time* (New York: Simon & Schuster, 1994) p. 193.

109   *Gallup Poll*: Kenneth S. Davis, *FDR: The War President 1940–1943* (New York: Random House, 2000) p. 85.

109   *Arsenal of democracy*: Robert E. Sherwood, *Roosevelt and Hopkins: An Intimate History* (New York: Harper and Brothers, 1948) p. 225.

110   *Hopkins caution*: Rosenman, *Working With Roosevelt*, p. 263–264.

110   *Norman Rockwell*: Maureen Hart Hennessey and Anne Knutson, *Rockwell: Pictures for the American People* (New York: Harry N. Abrams, 1999) p. 95–96.

Request for Declaration of War Against Japan: "A Date Which Will Live in Infamy"

118   *FDR in his study*: Davis, *FDR: The War President*, p. 99.

118   *Pearl Harbor attack*: Kennedy, *Freedom From Fear*, p. 519–522.

118   *Angry congressional meeting*: Frank Freidel, *Roosevelt: A Rendezvous With Destiny* (Boston: Little, Brown and Company, 1990) p. 405.

118   *New reports added*: Rosenman, *Working With Roosevelt*, p. 307.

D-Day Prayer: "Our Sons, Pride of Our Nation"

122 *"A little sleepy"*: Public Papers and Addresses of Franklin Delano Roosevelt, Volume Thirteen, p. 160.

122 *Sons in service*: Freidel, *Roosevelt*, p. 526.

123 *"the kind of speech Hitler would have made"*: Rosenman, *Working With Roosevelt*, p. 433.

Harry S. Truman
Address to Congress on Greece and Turkey: "The Truman Doctrine"

129 *Vandenberg*: James Chase, *Acheson: The Secretary of State Who Created the American World* (New York: Simon & Schuster, 1998) p. 166.

129 *"No hedging"*: Harry S. Truman, *Memoirs: Years of Trial and Hope* (Garden City, NY: Doubleday & Company, 1956) p. 105.

129 *State Department draft*: Clark Clifford with Richard Holbrooke, *Counsel to the President* (New York: Random House, 1991) p.136.

129 *Standing ovation*: Dean Acheson, *Present at the Creation: My Years in the State Department* (New York: W.W. Norton, 1969) p 223.

130 *Newsweek*: Cited in David McCullough, *Truman* (New York: Simon & Schuster, 1992) p. 549.

130 *Belligerent tone*: See Melvin J. Leffler, *A Preponderance of Power* (Stanford University Press, 1992) p. 142–146.

130 *Clearer than truth*: Acheson, *Present at the Creation*, p. 375.

130 *Universalist rhetoric*: Chase, *Acheson*, p. 168.

130 *Policy set forth*: Clifford, *Counsel to the President*, p. 131.

Whistle-Stop Speech: "Do-Nothing Congress"

136 *"You are the one"*: Truman, *Memoirs*, Volume 1, p. 5.

136 *Roper Poll*: McCullough, *Truman*, p. 657—quoting *Time* magazine, September 13, 1948.

137 *"Blackguarding Congress"*: Alonzo Hamby, *Man of the People: A Life of Harry Truman* (New York: Oxford University Press, 1995) p. 443.

137 *Whistle-stop campaign*: Zachary Karabell, *The Last Campaign: How Harry Truman Won the 1948 Election* (New York: Knopf, 2000) p. 252.

137 *Told the truth*: McCullough, *Truman*, p. 664, quoting New York Times, December 27, 1972

137 *Sharp speeches*: Robert J. Donovan, *Conflict and Crisis* (New York: W.W. Norton, 1979) p. 425.

Dwight D. Eisenhower
Address Before the UN General Assembly: "Atoms for Peace"

145 *Appearances deceived*: See Fred I. Greenstein, *The Hidden-Hand Presidency: Eisenhower as Leader* (New York: Basic Books, 1982).

145 *Ike as writer*: Arthur Larson, *Eisenhower: The President Nobody Knew* (New York: Scribner, 1968) p. 145.

145 *"Best clerk"*: Merle Miller, *Ike the Soldier: As They Knew Him* (New York: Putnam, 1987) p. 290.

145 *First hydrogen bomb*: James MacGregor Burns, *The Crosswinds of Freedom: The American Experiment* (New York: Knopf, 1989) p. 257.

145 *ASNE Speech*: Public Papers of the Presidents, Eisenhower, 1953, p. 182.

145 *Operation Candor*: Stephen E. Ambrose, *Eisenhower: Soldier and President* (New York: Simon & Schuster, 1990) p. 339.

145 *"Can't we find some hope here?*: Carol Gelderman, *All the Presidents' Words* (New York: Walker & Co., 1997) p. 47.

145 *"Red lights blinking"*: Ibid., p. 49.

145 *Donating stockpiles*: Dwight D. Eisenhower, *The White House Years: Mandate for Change 1953–1956* (Garden City, NY: Doubleday & Company, 1963) p. 252.

146 *Collating and printing the speech*: Gelderman, *All The Presidents' Words*, p. 51.

146 *Eisenhower prayed*: Geoffrey Perrett, *Eisenhower* (Holbrook, MA: Adams Media Corp., 1999) p. 523.

Farewell Address: "The Military-Industrial Complex"

153 *"To the American Soldier"*: Wayne Fields, *Union of Words* (New York: Free Press, 1996) p. 357.

153 *Norman Cousins*: Stephen E. Ambrose, *Eisenhower* (New York: Touchstone, 1990) p. 536.

153 *Theme of "balance"*: See Martin J. Medhurst, *Dwight D. Eisenhower: Strategic Communicator* (Westport, CT: Greenwood Press, 1993) p. 119–120.

153 *"Military-industrial-congressional"*: Geoffrey Perrett, *Eisenhower*, p. 599.

John F. Kennedy
Inaugural Address: "Ask Not What Your Country Can Do for You"

161 *"Secret" of the Gettysburg Address*: Theodore C. Sorensen, *Kennedy* (New York: Harper and Row, 1965) p. 240.

161 *Handwritten notes*: Sorensen, *Kennedy*, p. 243.

161 *Parallelism*: Actually, "ask not" is a form of chiasmus—a parallelism that switches the meanings of words.

161 *Detroit rally*: Arthur M. Schlesinger Jr., *A Thousand Days* (Boston: Houghton Mifflin, 1965) p. 4.

162 *How Kennedy's Inaugural was Drafted*: Sorensen, *Kennedy*, p. 241–242.

Address to the Nation on the Cuban Missile Crisis: "Missiles in Cuba"

166 *Kennedy stayed away*: Carol Gelderman, *All the Presidents' Words* (New York: Walker & Co., 1997) p. 48.

166 *Sorensen's questions*: Gelderman, *All the Presidents' Words*, p. 48.

166 *Five drafts*: Pierre Salinger, *With Kennedy* (Garden City, NY: Doubleday & Co., 1966) p. 66.

166 *Quarantine*: Gelderman, *All the Presidents' Words*, p. 48.

166 *Invasion draft found*: See Alicia Kolar, "The Two Speeches of the Cuban Missile Crisis," unpublished paper, Center for the Study of the Presidency, 2003.

166 *"Day of Mystery"*: Richard Reeves, *President Kennedy: Profile of Power* (New York: Simon & Schuster, 1994) p. 394.

166 *Most important Cold War address*: Michael R. Beschloss, *The Crisis Years* (New York: HarperCollins, 1991) p. 483.

167 *"Well, that's it"*: Beschloss, *The Crisis Years*, p. 485.

167 *22,000 Soviet personnel*: Raymond L. Garthoff, *Reflections on the Cuban Missile Crisis* (Washington, D.C.: Brookings Institution, 1989) p. 35.

Commencement Address, American University: "Let Us Reexamine Our Attitude Toward the Cold War"

175 *Dean Rusk*: Richard Reeves, *President Kennedy: Profile of Power* (New York: Simon & Schuster, 1993) p. 512.

175 *Background of American University speech*: The public concerns about fallout are described in Richard Reeves', *President Kennedy*, p. 510–513.

176 *Redefined attitude toward Cold War*: Schlesinger, *A Thousand Days*, p. 900.

176 *JFK seeks to reclaim "peace"*: Jeff Shesol, unpublished manuscript, January 2003.

Speech at the Berlin Wall: "Ich Bin Ein Berliner"

181 *"This is terrible"*: Reeves, *President Kennedy*, p. 535.

181 *A few words of German*: Beschloss, *The Crisis Years*, p. 605.

182 *Kennedy's angry poetry*: Ibid.

182 *Ad lib fallout*: Sorensen, *Kennedy*, p. 331–332.

Lyndon B. Johnson
Address to Congress After the Kennedy Assassination: "Let Us Continue"

188 *"The man on the horse"*: Doris Kearns, *Lyndon Johnson and The American Dream* (New York: Harper and Row, 1976) p. 172.

188 *Johnson and Sorensen*: Michael R. Beschloss, *Taking Charge: The Johnson White House Tapes, 1963–1964* (New York: Simon & Schuster, 1997) p. 40–41.

188 *Johnson wrote in pencil*: Brian MacArthur, ed., *The Penguin Book of 20th Century Speeches* (New York: Penguin, 2000) p. 334.

Address to Congress on Voting Rights: "We Shall Overcome"

193 *"Reconstruction all over again"*: Richard N. Goodwin, *Remembering America: A Voice From the Sixties* (New York: Harper and Row, 1989) p. 319.

193 *Wallace meeting*: Goodwin, *Remembering America*, p. 323.

194 *The image of the protestors flashed*: Lyndon B. Johnson, *The Vantage Point* (New York: Holt, Rinehart and Winston, 1971) p. 165–166.

194 *Johnson became a moral leader*: Kearns, *Lyndon Johnson and the American Dream*, p. 230.

194 *Success of voting rights law*: United States Department of Justice, Civil Rights Division, "Introduction to Voting Rights Law," at http://www.usdoj.gov/crt/voting/intro/ intro_c.htm. See also Chandler Davidson and Bernard Grofman, eds., *Quiet Revolution in the South: Impact of the Voting Rights Law, 1965–1990* (Princeton, NJ: Princeton University Press, 1994).

Speech on the Vietnam War: "I Shall Not Seek, and I Will Not Accept, the Nomination of My Party"

204 *"soften the speech"*: Clifford, *Counsel to the President*, p. 519.

204 *Old colleagues were shocked*: Eric F. Goldman, *The Tragedy of Lyndon Johnson* (New York: Random House, 1969) p. 512.

204 *"may even add one of my own"*: Harry McPherson, *A Political Education* (Austin: University of Texas Press, 1995 edition) p. 437.

Richard Nixon
Address to the Nation on Vietnam: "The Great Silent Majority"

213 *Broder*: Quoted in William Safire, *Before the Fall* (New York: Belmont Tower Books, 1975) p. 151.

213 *Vietnam Moratorium*: Walter Isaacson, *Kissinger* (New York: Simon & Schuster, 1992) p. 246.

213 *Kissinger*: Ibid.

213 *Mansfield memo*: Richard M. Nixon, *RN: The Memoirs of Richard Nixon* (New York: Grosset and Dunlap, 1978) p. 408.

213 *"In his element"*: Richard Reeves, *President Nixon: Alone in the White House* (New York: Simon & Schuster, 2001) p. 141.

213 *"The baby's just been born"*: Nixon, *RN*, p. 409.

214 *The typical American*: Richard M. Scammon and Ben J. Wattenberg, *The Real Majority* (New York: Coward, McCann & Geoghegan, Inc., 1970) p. 54–57.

Farewell Address to White House Staff: "We Have Done Some Things Wrong"

224 *"Wallow in Watergate"*: July 20, 1973.

224 *"I am not a crook"*: November 17, 1973.

224 *Nixon staged his own exit*: Stephen E. Ambrose, *Nixon: Ruin and Recovery 1973–1990* (New York: Simon & Schuster, 1991) p. 422.

224 *Writing resignation speech*: Raymond Price, *With Nixon* (New York: The Viking Press, 1977) p. 326–339.

225 *Televising the ceremony*: Ambrose, *Nixon*, p. 439.

Gerald Ford
Remarks upon Taking the Oath of Office: "Our Long National Nightmare Is Over"

231 *Presidency in shambles*: See Henry A. Kissinger, *Years of Upheaval* (Boston: Little, Brown, 1982).

231 *Haig raises pardon*: Gerald R. Ford, *A Time To Heal* (New York: Harper and Row, 1979) p. 4.

231 *"Our long national nightmare"*: Robert T. Hartmann, *Palace Politics: An Inside Account of the Ford Years* (New York: McGraw-Hill, 1980) p. 159–160.

232 *Nixon pardon*: Gerald R. Ford, Public Papers of the Presidents, 1974 (United States Government Printing Office, Washington: 1975) p. 104.

232 *Profile in Courage award*: http://www.cs.umb.edu/jfklibrary/pica_2001_ford_remarks.html

Jimmy Carter
Speech on Energy and National Goals: "A Crisis of Confidence"

237 *Fallows article*: James Fallows, "The Passionless Presidency," *Atlantic Monthly* (May 1979), Vol. 243, No. 5, p. 33–48.

237 *25 percent approval rating*: Joseph Califano, *Governing America* (New York: Simon & Schuster, 1981) p. 427.

237 *Speech scheduled*: Carol Gelderman, *All the Presidents' Words* (New York: Walker & Co., 1997) p. 129.

238 *Caddell and "malaise"*: Elizabeth Drew, "A Reporter at Large (Washington, D.C.)" *The New Yorker*, August 27, 1979, p. 54.

238 *Mondale and Eizenstat appalled*: See Stuart Eizenstat, exit interview on departure from the White House, January 10, 1981, available at: http://carterlibrary.galileo.peachnet.edu/download/exitstu.rtf.

238 *Self-criticism*: Hendrik Hertzberg, "Jimmy Carter," in Robert Wilson, ed., *Character Above All: Ten Presidents from FDR to George Bush* (New York: Simon & Schuster, 1996) p. 191.

Ronald Reagan
First Inaugural Address: "Government Is Not the Solution to the Problem, Government Is the Problem"

245 *Spokesman for GE*: See Ronald Reagan with Richard G. Hubler, *Where's the Rest of Me? The Autobiography of Ronald Reagan* (New York: Duell, Sloan & Pearce, 1965) p.257; See also Garry Wills, *Reagan's America* (Garden City, NY: Doubleday, 1987) p. 332-343.

245 *Radio commentaries*: See Martin Anderson, ed., *Reagan In His Own Hand: The Writings of Ronald Reagan That Reveal His Revolutionary Vision for America* (New York: Free Press, 2001).

246 *FDR style warning*: William Safire, "The Land is Bright" *New York Times*, January 22, 1981, p. A27.

246 *Praise of businessmen*: see William Ker Muir Jr., *The Bully Pulpit: The Presidential Leadership of Ronald Reagan* (San Francisco: Institute for Contemporary Studies, 1992) p. 150.

246 *Reagan contradicting Lincoln*: See William Lee Miller, *Lincoln's Virtues: An Ethical Biography* (New York: Vintage Books, 2003) p. 444.

246 *Treptow in Wisconsin*: Lou Cannon, *President Reagan: The Role of a Lifetime* (New York: Simon & Schuster, 1991) p. 98–100.

Address to Members of British Parliament: "Leave Marxism-Leninism on the Ash-Heap of History"

252 *Reagan's first press* conference: *Time*, January 1, 1984, "Men of the Year: Ronald Reagan and Yuri Andropov" http://www.time.com/time/special/moy/ 1983.html.

252 *In retrospect*: Ronald Reagan, *Speaking My Mind: Selected Speeches* (New York: Simon & Schuster, 1989) p. 108.

252 *"Crusade for Freedom"*: Lou Cannon, "President Calls for 'Crusade'; Reagan Proposes Plan to Counter Soviet Challenge," *Washington Post*, June 9, 1982, p. A1.

252 *Reagan Doctrine*: Charles Krauthammer, "The Reagan Doctrine," *Time* magazine, April 1, 1985.

253 *"evil empire" speech*: Remarks at the Annual Convention of the National Association of Evangelicals in Orlando, Florida, March 8, 1983, Ronald Reagan, The Public Papers of the Presidents, 1983, p. 359.

Address to the Nation on the Challenger Explosion: "Slipped the Surly Bonds of Earth"

262 *Space Shuttle mission summaries*: at http://science.ksc.nasa.gov/shuttle/technology/sts-newsref/stover-missions.html.

262 *Challenger crew*: http://www.challenger.org

263 *Reagan's meeting with TV network anchors*: Peggy Noonan, *What I Saw at the Revolution* (New York: Random House, 1990) p. 263-264.

264 *High flight*: John Magee, *The Pilot Poet* (Cheltenham: This England Books, 1989) p. 79.

Remarks on the Iran-Contra Scandal: "I Cannot Escape Responsibility"

267 *Iran-Contra scandal*: See Lawrence E. Walsh, *Firewall: The Iran-Contra Conspiracy and Cover Up* (New York: W.W. Norton & Company, 1997); Theodore Draper, *A Very Thin Line: The Iran-Contra Affairs* (New York: Hill & Wang, 1991).

268 *Diversion a "neat idea"*: U.S. House of Representatives Select Committee to Investigate Covert Arms Transactions With Iran/U.S. Senate Select Committee On Secret Military Assistance to Iran and the Nicaraguan Opposition, *Report of the Congressional Committees Investigating the Iran-Contra Affair* (Washington, D.C.: U.S. Government Printing Office, 1987) p. 271.

268 *Tower Report*: Report of the President's Special Review Board (New York: Bantam Books, 1987).

268 *Strange explanation*: Draper, *A Very Thin Line*, p. 569–570.

268 *Able to govern again*: David R. Gergen, *Eyewitness to Power* (New York: Simon & Schuster, 2000) p. 188.

268 *Bush pardons Weinberger*: Lawrence E. Walsh, *Firewall*, p. 492–494.

George H.W. Bush

Acceptance Speech, Republican Convention: "A Kinder and Gentler Nation"

275 *"Wimp factor"*: *Newsweek*, October 19, 1997.

275 *Bush's style*: Peggy Noonan, *What I Saw at the Revolution* (New York: Random House, 1990) p. 312–313.

275 *Dukakis acceptance*: http://www.cnn.com/ALLPOLITICS/1996/conventions/chicago/facts/famous.speeches/dukakis.88.shtml

275 *"Kinder and gentler than who?"*: William Safire, "Bush's Gamble," *New York Times*, October 18, 1992.

275 *Origin of "points of light"*: Noonan, *What I Saw at the Revolution*, p. 324–325.

276 *Darman on "read my lips"*: Bob Woodward, "Origin of the Tax Pledge; In '88, Bush Camp Was Split on 'Read My Lips' Vow," *Washington Post*, October 4, 1992, p. A1.

Bill Clinton

Remarks to the Church of God in Christ in Memphis: "What Would Martin Luther King Say?"

285 *"Memphis"*: William Safire, *Lend Me Your Ears* (New York: W.W. Norton and Company, second edition, 1997) p. 538.

285 *"Promised land"*: Martin Luther King Jr., *A Testament of Hope: The Essential Writings of Martin Luther King, Jr.*, edited by James Melvin Washington (San Francisco: Harper & Row, 1986) p. 286.

285 *"He knew these people"*: Carolyn Curiel, interview, March 9, 2003.

286 *Press reaction*: E.J. Dionne, "Clinton's Bully Pulpit," *Washington Post*, November 16, 1993, p. A21.

286 *"Brave"*: "Clinton's Best Shot Against Violence," editorial, *Atlanta Constitution*, November 18, 1993, p. A18.

Eulogy for Victims of Oklahoma City Bombing: "In the Face of Death, Let Us Honor Life"

291 *"relevant"*: See Public Papers of President William J. Clinton, 1995 V. 1.

291 *Writing the speech*: Donald A. Baer, interview, March 17, 2003.

292 *Clinton's response*: Carol Gelderman, *All the Presidents' Words*, p. 166–167.

State of the Union Address: "Let That Be Our Gift to the Twenty-First Century"

295 *Lewinsky media frenzy*: See Marvin Kalb, *One Scandalous Story: Clinton, Lewinsky, and Thirteen Days That Tarnished American Journalism* (New York: Free Press, 2001).

295 *Work on the speech*: I recount this episode in Michael Waldman, *POTUS Speaks: Finding the Words That Defined the Clinton Presidency* (New York: Simon & Schuster, 2000) p. 201–216.

296 *State of the Union*: Joe Klein, *The Natural: The Misunderstood Presidency of Bill Clinton* (New York: Doubleday, 2002) p. 18–19.

George W. Bush

Address to Congress After the Attacks of September 11: "Freedom and Fear, Justice and Cruelty, Have Always Been at War"

305 *Tentative Oval Office speech*: See David Frum, *The Right Man* (New York: Random House, 2003) p. 125.

305 *Bush's father*: D.T. Max, "The Making of the Speech," *New York Times* magazine, October 7, 2001, p. 32.

305 *Writing process*: Ibid.

305 *Presidents before Congress*: Dana Millbank, "On Fortress Capitol Hill, United Roars of Approval" *Washington Post*, September 21, 2001, p. A22.

Address on Iraq: "The Day of Your Liberation Is Near"

314 *"Here's an assignment"*: David Frum, *The Right Man*, p. 224.

314 *Line added the night before*: *Newsweek*, September 15, 2002.

314 *"Necessary resolutions" ad libbed*: David S. Cloud, Jeanne Whalen and Carla Ann Robbins, "Bush Challenges U.N. to Enforce Security Resolutions Against Iraq," *Wall Street Journal*, September 13, 2002.

BIBLIOGRAPHY AND SUGGESTED READING

Several general books focus on presidential speechmaking. Carol Gelderman's *All the Presidents' Words: The Bully Pulpit and the Creation of the Virtual Presidency* (New York: Walker & Co., 1997) is an invaluable look at how presidents craft their words. There is a growing academic literature about the rise of the "rhetorical presidency," including: Jeffrey K. Tulis, *The Rhetorical Presidency* (Princeton, NJ: Princeton University Press, 1987) (arguing it is a relatively recent phenomenon, and not a particularly good one); Richard J. Ellis, ed., *Speaking to the People: The Rhetorical Presidency in Historical Perspective* (Amherst: University of Massachusetts Press, 1998); and Martin J. Medhurst, ed., *Beyond the Rhetorical Presidency* (College Station: Texas A&M University, 1996). Also useful is Wayne Fields, *Union of Words: A History of Presidential Eloquence* (New York: Free Press, 1999). The role of presidential speechwriters is the subject of Kurt Ritter and Martin J. Medhurst, eds., *Presidential Speechwriting: From the New Deal to the Reagan Revolution and Beyond* (College Station: Texas A&M University Press, 2002). Some academic books look at the increased importance of public speechmaking to the presidents: Samuel Kernell, *Going Public: New Strategies of Presidential Leadership* (2nd ed.) (Washington, D.C.: Congressional Quarterly, 1993) (with much data); Kathleen Hall Jamieson, *Eloquence in an Electronic Age: The Transformation of Political Speechmaking* (New York: Oxford University Press, 1988); and *Deeds Done in Words: Presidential Rhetoric and Genres of Governance* (Chicago: University of Chicago Press, 1990).

There are several valuable collections of speeches. Janet Podell and Steven Anzovin, *Speeches of the American Presidents* (New York: The H.W. Wilson Company, 1998) is a thorough compendium. Among the best general collections, which include speeches by presidents: William Safire, ed., *Lend Me Your Ears: Great Speeches in History* (New York: W.W. Norton & Company, 1997); Josh Gottheimer, ed., *Ripples of Hope: Great American Civil Rights Speeches* (New York: Basic Books, 2003); Brian MacArthur, ed., *The Penguin Book of Twentieth Century Speeches* (New York: Penguin USA, 2000); and Lewis Copeland, ed., *World's Greatest Speeches* (4th ed.) (Dover, 2000). The speeches of presidents prior to 1897 were collected and published by the United States government in 1896–1899 (James D. Richardson, ed., *A Compilation of the Messages and Papers of the Presidents, 1789–1897*). The speeches of presidents from Herbert Hoover forward (except for Franklin Roosevelt) are

published in the Public Papers of the Presidents series, published by the Government Printing Offices. The speeches of many recent presidents are available online through the University of California at Santa Barbara, *www.americanpresidency.org* (and we should all thank the site's creators, professors John Woolley and Gerhard Peters). Drafts of some are available at the Library of Congress "American Memory" website, *http://memory.loc.gov*.

Of course, countless books have been written about the presidency. Several were especially illuminating on political leadership and public communication: Stephen Skorownek, *The Politics Presidents Make: Leadership From John Adams to Bill Clinton* (Cambridge, MA: Belknap Press, 1997); Fred I. Greenstein, *The Presidential Difference: Leadership Style from FDR to Clinton* (New York: Free Press, 2001) has a partisan bias, but a valuable summary of source materials on the presidents; Sidney M. Milkis and Michael Nelson, *The American Presidency: Origins and Development 1776–1998* (Washington, D.C.: CQ Press, 1999); Richard E. Neustadt, *Presidential Power and the Modern Presidents* (New York: Free Press, 1991), still valuable in its fourth edition. David R. Gergen, *Eyewitness to Power: The Essence of Leadership, Nixon to Clinton* (New York: Simon & Schuster, 2000)—in the course of discussing the four presidents for whom the author worked—is very thoughtful on the office and its public voice. Also useful were: Dick Morris, *Power Plays: Win or Lose—How History's Great Political Leaders Play the Game* (New York: Regan Books, 2002) (with savvy analyses of Lincoln, FDR, Clinton, and Bush, among others) and Garry Wills, *Certain Trumpets: The Nature of Leadership* (New York: Simon & Schuster, 1994).

GEORGE WASHINGTON

In understanding Washington and his speeches, I have relied on James Thomas Flexner, *Washington: The Indispensable Man* (Boston: Little, Brown & Company, 1994), a single-volume life by the authoritative recent Washington biographer; Flexner, *George Washington and the New Nation 1783–1793* (Boston: Little, Brown & Company, 1970); Flexner, *George Washington, Anguish and Farewell* (Boston: Little, Brown & Company, 1972). Perceptive looks at Washington's leadership, especially his retirement from office, include: Garry Wills, *Cincinatus* (Garden City,

NY: Doubleday & Company, 1984), Richard Brookhiser, *Founding Father: Rediscovering George Washington* (New York: Free Press, 1996), and Barry Schwartz, *George Washington: The Making of an American Symbol* (New York: Free Press, 1987). Washington's first inaugural is described in James MacGregor Burns, *The Vineyard of Liberty* (New York: Vintage Books, 1982). Washington's Farewell Address—and the role played by Alexander Hamilton—is discussed at length in Joseph J. Ellis, *Founding Brothers: The Revolutionary Generation* (New York: Knopf, 2000). The address's emphasis on morality is the subject of Matthew Spalding and Patrick Garrity, *A Sacred Union of Citizens: George Washington's Farewell Address and the American Character* (New York: Rowman & Littlefield, 1998). Its impact is discussed in Felix Gilbert, *To The Farewell Address: Ideas of Early American Foreign Policy* (Princeton, NJ: Princeton University Press, 1970).

THOMAS JEFFERSON

His first inaugural and the tumultuous election of 1800 are described in: Bernard A. Weisberger, *America Afire: Jefferson, Adams, and the Revolutionary Election of 1800* (New York: William Morrow, 2000); Frank Van Der Linden, *The Turning Point: Jefferson's Battle for the Presidency* (New York: Van Rees Press, 1962). There are of course many useful biographies of Jefferson; those that discuss this speech include Noble E. Cunningham, *In Pursuit of Reason: The Life of Thomas Jefferson* (New York: Ballantine Books, 1988 [paperback ed.]) and Joseph J. Ellis, *American Sphinx: The Character of Thomas Jefferson* (New York: Vintage, 1998).

ANDREW JACKSON

Any discussion of Jackson draws heavily on the work of one remarkable scholar, Robert V. Remini. His books: *Andrew Jackson and the Course of American Freedom, 1822–1832* (New York: Harper & Row, 1981); *Andrew Jackson and the Course of American Democracy, 1833–1845* (New York: Harper & Row, 1984); *Andrew Jackson and the Bank War: A Study in the Growth of Presidential Power* (New York: W.W. Norton, 1967), and *Andrew Jackson* (New York: Twayne Publishers Inc., 1966). The three volumes were abridged in *The Life of Andrew Jackson* (New York: HarperPerrenial, 2001). Although it is dated, Arthur M. Schlesinger Jr.'s *The Age of Jackson* (Boston: Little, Brown [paperback reissue], 1988) still is highly useful. A fine history of Jacksonian America is Harry L. Watson, *Liberty and Power* (New York: Hill and Wang, 1990). See also Donald B. Cole, *The Presidency of Andrew Jackson* (Lawrence: University of Kansas Press, 1993), which has a useful bibliographic essay.

ABRAHAM LINCOLN

A search on Amazon.com for books about Abraham Lincoln yields 869 hits. This volume drew on only a fraction of those, naturally. The most useful general Lincoln biographies are: David Herbert Donald, *Lincoln* (New York: Simon & Schuster, 1995) and Stephen B. Oates, *With Malice*

Toward None: A Life of Abraham Lincoln (New York: HarperPerennial, 1994). Lincoln's prose is collected in Don E. Fehrenbacher, ed., *Abraham Lincoln: Speeches and Writings 1832–1858* (New York: Library of America, 1989) and *Abraham Lincoln: Speeches and Writings 1859–1865* (New York: Library of America, 1989). A good sampling, with introductory essays, is found in Mario Cuomo and Harold Holzer, eds., *Lincoln on Democracy* (New York: HarperCollins, 1990). A general history of the Civil War is: James M. McPherson, *Battle Cry of Freedom* (New York: Oxford University Press, 1988). The best source on the "House Divided" speech is Don E. Fehrenbacher, *Prelude to Greatness: Lincoln in the 1850s* (Palo Alto, CA: Stanford University Press, 1962); see also Harry V. Jaffa, *Crisis of the House Divided* (Seattle: University of Washington Press, 1973). The evolution of Lincoln toward his first inaugural is traced in William Lee Miller, *Lincoln's Virtues: An Ethical Biography* (New York: Vintage Books, 2003). The classic discussion of the Gettysburg Address is Garry Wills, *Lincoln at Gettysburg: The Words That Remade America* (New York: Simon & Schuster, 1992). George P. Fletcher, *Our Secret Constitution: How Lincoln Redefined American Democracy* (New York: Oxford University Press, 2001), argues the address led to the "second Constitution" of the Fourteenth Amendment. The legacy of the Declaration of Independence is traced in Pauline Maier, *American Scripture* (New York: Vintage Books, 1998); she argues that Wills gives Lincoln too much personal credit for recognizing the power in the Declaration's ideals. On Lincoln's Second Inaugural, see Ronald C. White Jr., *Lincoln's Greatest Speech: The Second Inaugural* (New York: Simon & Schuster, 2001) and Garry Wills, "Lincoln's Greatest Speech?" *The Atlantic Monthly*, September 1999, Volume 284, No. 3, p. 60–70. On Lincoln's theology as expressed in his speeches, see Glenn E. Thurow, *Abraham Lincoln and American Political Religion* (Albany: State University of New York Press, 1976).

THEODORE ROOSEVELT

The recent surge of interest in Theodore Roosevelt tends to focus more on his zestful personality and less on his presidency. General sources include: H.W. Brands, *TR: The Last Romantic* (New York: Basic Books, 1997); Edmund Morris, *The Rise of Theodore Roosevelt* (New York: Ballantine Books, 1979) and *Theodore Rex* (New York: Random House, 2001); Nathan Miller, *Theodore Roosevelt: A Life* (New York: William Morrow, 1992); and Mario R. DiNunzio, ed., *Theodore Roosevelt: An American Mind—Selected Writings* (New York: Penguin Books, 1994). Roosevelt's post-presidential life is less well-traced; sources include John Morton Blum, *The Progressive Presidents* (W.W. Norton and Company, 1980), which looks at Wilson and FDR, too, and John A. Gable, *The Bull Moose Years: Theodore Roosevelt and the Progressive Party*. (Eagerly awaited is James Chace's forthcoming history of the 1912 election.) For a perspectives on the Progressive Era, see Robert Wiebe, *Search for Order 1877–1920* (New York: Hill & Wang, 1980) and Herbert Croly, *The Promise of American Life* (New

York: Capricorn Books edition, 1964), obscure to modern readers, but still essential.

WOODROW WILSON

A good general biography is August Heckscher, *Woodrow Wilson* (New York: Collier Books, 1991). Short recent biographical essays include Louis Auchincloss, *Woodrow Wilson* (New York: Penguin [Penguin Lives], 2000) and H.W. Brands, *Woodrow Wilson 1913–1921* (New York: Times Books, 2003). The most eminent historian of Wilson is Arthur S. Link, whose books include *Woodrow Wilson and the Progressive Era* (New York: Harper & Brothers, 1954) and *Woodrow Wilson: Revolution, War and Peace* (Wheeling, IL: Harlan Davidson, 1982). Wilson's own books give a sense of his own ideological evolution: *Congressional Government* (Boston: Houghton, Mifflin & Company, 1885) and *Constitutional Government in the United States* (New York: Columbia University Press, 1917). On Walter Lippmann—who, as chronicler and advisor, recurs throughout this book—see Ronald Steel, *Walter Lippmann and the American Century* (Boston: Little, Brown & Company, 1980). On the impact of the Fourteen Points, see Gaddis Smith, *Woodrow Wilson's Fourteen Points After Seventy-Five Years* (New York: Carnegie Council, 1993).

FRANKLIN DELANO ROOSEVELT

FDR's rhetoric is richly documented, in part because his speechwriters began the practice of writing memoirs. Chief writer and close aide Samuel Rosenman's *Working With Roosevelt* (New York: Harper & Row, 1952) is the essential book for understanding Roosevelt's speeches. Raymond Moley—who chaired the "Brain Trust" and was FDR's collaborator on his first Inaugural—wrote two memoirs: *After Seven Years* (New York: Harper & Brothers, 1939), and a less-known and less-reliable volume, *The First New Deal* (New York: Harcourt, Brace & World Inc., 1966). Robert E. Sherwood, the Pulitzer Prize–winning playwright who wrote speeches for FDR, wrote *Roosevelt and Hopkins: An Intimate History* (New York: Harper and Brothers, 1948). Roosevelt's speeches are studied in depth by Halford R. Ryan in *Franklin D. Roosevelt's Rhetorical Presidency* (Westport, CT.: Greenwood Press, 1988). Roosevelt's first inaugural is discussed in Davis W. Houck, *FDR and Fear Itself: The First Inaugural Address* (College Station: Texas A&M University Press, 2002) and will be described in a forthcoming book by Jonathan Alter. For FDR and the effort to "talk" America into war, see Doris Kearns Goodwin, *No Ordinary Time* (New York: Simon & Schuster, 1994). Though it covers the years before the presidency, Kenneth S. Davis, *FDR: The New York Years 1928–1933* (New York: Random House, 1985) focuses on the critical campaign speeches, including the address to the Commonwealth Club, written by Adolph A. Berle, in which Roosevelt expounded his political philosophy. There are of course many histories of FDR's four terms. Most useful for studying his speeches are: Kenneth S. Davis, *FDR: The New Deal Years* (New York: Random House, 1986) and James MacGregor Burns, *The Lion and the Fox* (New

York: Harcourt, Brace & World, 1956). Also valuable are Arthur M. Schlesinger Jr., *The Age of Roosevelt: The Coming of the New Deal* (New York: Mariner Books reprint, 2003) and *The Age of Roosevelt: The Politics of Upheaval* (New York: Houghton Mifflin, 1974 edition); Kenneth S. Davis, *FDR: Into the Storm 1937–1940* (New York: Random House, 1993) and *FDR: The War President 1941–1943* (New York: Random House, 2000); William E. Leuchtenberg, *Franklin D. Roosevelt and the New Deal 1933–1940* (New York: HarperCollins paperback, 1963). A single volume biography is Frank Freidel, *Roosevelt: A Rendezvous with Destiny* (Boston: Little, Brown, 1990). A reliable general reference on the era is David M. Kennedy's Pulitzer Prize–winning *Freedom from Fear* (New York: Oxford University Press, 1999). On the New Deal, the best recent book is Alan Brinkley, *The End of Reform: New Deal Liberalism in Recession and War* (New York: Knopf, 1995). On FDR's foreign policy, including Lend-Lease, see Robert Dallek, *Franklin D. Roosevelt and American Foreign Policy, 1932–1945* (New York: Oxford University Press, 1979). On D-Day: Stephen E. Ambrose, *D-Day: June 6, 1944* (New York: Simon & Schuster, 1994).

HARRY S. TRUMAN

The best chronicle of Truman's life and presidency is David McCullough, *Truman* (New York: Simon & Schuster, 1992). Less colorful but authoritative is Alonzo Hamby, *Man of the People: A Life of Harry Truman,* (New York: Oxford University Press, 1995). An early and engaging book on his presidency is Robert J. Donovan, *Conflict and Crisis* (New York: W.W. Norton, 1979). Among the memoirs of Truman's speechwriters, the most useful was by Clark Clifford, written with Richard Holbrooke, *Counsel to the President* (New York: Random House, 1991). Also enjoyable is Ken Hechler, *Working with Truman: A Personal Memoir of the White House Years* (Columbia: University of Missouri Press, reprint edition, 1996) by a speechwriter who later served for decades in Congress. On the Truman Doctrine speech: Dean Acheson, *Present at the Creation: My Years in the State Department* (New York: W.W. Norton, 1969) and James Chase, *Acheson: The Secretary of State Who Created the American World* (New York: Simon & Schuster, 1998). Historians continue to debate Truman's tone: see Melvin J. Leffler, *A Preponderance of Power,* (Palo Alto, CA: Stanford University Press, 1992) and John Lewis Gaddis, *The United States and the Origins of the Cold War 1941–1947* (New York: Columbia University Press, 1972). The "whistle stop" election is described in Zachary Karabell, *The Last Campaign: How Harry Truman Won the 1948 Election* (New York: Knopf, 2000); Richard Norton Smith, *Thomas E. Dewey and His Times* (New York: Simon & Schuster, 1982), and John C. Culver and John Hyde, *American Dreamer: A Life of Henry A. Wallace* (New York: W.W. Norton, 2001). Many speech drafts (including Truman's handwritten notes for his acceptance speech) are available online from the Truman library: *www.trumanlibrary.org*. Truman's memoirs are *Year of Decisions* and *Year of Trials and Hope* (Garden City, NY: Doubleday, 1955, 1956).

Bibliography and Suggested Reading

DWIGHT D. EISENHOWER

Several biographers have profiled Ike, though most pay more attention to his years in uniform than his years in the White House. Most useful are Stephen E. Ambrose, *Eisenhower: Soldier and President* (New York: Simon & Schuster, 1990) and Fred I. Greenstein, *The Hidden-Hand Presidency: Eisenhower as Leader* (New York: Basic Books, 1982); also see Geoffrey Perrett, *Eisenhower* (Holbrook, MA: Adams Media, 1999). Eisenhower's presidential speeches are examined in Martin J. Medhurst, *Dwight D. Eisenhower: Strategic Communicator* (Westport, CT: Greenwood Press, 1993). His speechwriter Emmett John Hughes wrote a controversial book, *The Ordeal of Power: A Political Memoir of the Eisenhower Years* (New York: Atheneum, 1963). The Atoms for Peace speech is discussed in Ira Chernus, *Eisenhower's Atoms for Peace* (College Station: Texas A&M University Press, 2002) and in Ike's own memoirs: Dwight D. Eisenhower, *The White House Years: Mandate for Change 1953–1956* (Garden City, NY: Doubleday and Company, 1963).

JOHN F. KENNEDY

Gifted writers surrounded Kennedy, and he encouraged them to take notes. Theodore C. Sorensen's *Kennedy* (New York: Harper and Row, 1965) and Arthur M. Schlesinger Jr.'s *A Thousand Days* (Boston: Houghton Mifflin, 1965), written just after JFK died, still are worth reading (though one is aware of their omissions and deep loyalty), as is Richard Goodwin's (see below). Sorensen edited a collection of Kennedy's speeches, *Let the Word Go Forth: The Speeches, Statements and Writings of John F. Kennedy* (New York: Delacorte Press, 1988). Of recent biographies and histories, the best are Richard Reeves, *President Kennedy: Portrait in Power* (New York: Simon & Schuster, 1994) and Robert Dallek, *An Unfinished Life: John F. Kennedy, 1917–1963* (Boston: Little, Brown, 2003). The Cuban Missile Crisis is discussed in Michael R. Beschloss, *The Crisis Years* (New York: HarperCollins, 1991); Raymond L. Garthoff, *Reflections on the Cuban Missile Crisis* (Washington, D.C.: Brookings Institution, 1989); Robert F. Kennedy, *Thirteen Days* (New York: W.W. Norton, reprint, 1999); Ernest D. May and Philip D. Zelikow, *The Kennedy Tapes: Inside the White House During the Cuban Missile Crisis* (Cambridge: Belknap Press, 1997); and Graham Allison, *The Essence of Decision* (Boston: Addison-Wesley, 1999). Kennedy School student Alicia Kolar has unearthed intriguing alternative speech drafts, presented in "The Two Speeches of the Cuban Missile Crisis" (paper presented to the Center for the Study of the Presidency, forthcoming).

LYNDON B. JOHNSON

Robert Dallek's *Flawed Giant: Lyndon Johnson 1961–1973* (New York: Oxford University Press, 1998) is comprehensive. Johnson's speeches and larger-than-life personality burst through several books and memoirs by aides and associates, especially Doris Kearns, *Lyndon Johnson and the American Dream* (New York: Harper and Row, 1976), especially perceptive, based on their private talks as she helped write his memoirs; Richard N. Goodwin, *Remembering America: A Voice From the Sixties* (Boston: Little, Brown, 1988), recounting the civil rights speech, among others. Johnson's moves upon taking office are described by speechwriter and aide Jack Valenti in *A Very Human President* (New York: Pocket Books, paperback, 1977); by Jeff Shesol, *Mutual Contempt: Lyndon Johnson, Robert Kennedy and the Feud That Defined a Decade* (New York: W.W. Norton, 1997), and in Michael Beschloss, *Taking Charge: The Johnson White House Tapes, 1963–1964* (New York: Simon & Schuster, 1997). An interesting analysis of the 1965 address to Congress is Ronald A. Heifetz, *Leadership without Easy Answers* (Cambridge, MA: Belknap Press, 1994). The 1968 renunciation speech is discussed by speechwriter Harry McPherson in *A Political Education* (Austin: University of Texas Press, 1995 edition), as well as by Clark Clifford (above). See also Evan Thomas and Walter Isaacson, *The Wise Men: Six Friends and the World They Made* (New York: Simon & Schuster, 1986). Other valuable memoirs include Joseph A. Califano, *Triumph and Tragedy of Lyndon Johnson: The White House Years* (New York: Simon & Schuster, 1991) and Eric F. Goldman, *The Tragedy of Lyndon Johnson* (New York: Random House, 1969). Johnson's own memoir—reminiscent of one of his stiff speeches—is *The Vantage Point: Perspectives of the Presidency* (New York: Holt, Rinehart & Winston, 1971). Of course, Johnson's rise is chronicled in Robert A. Caro's remarkable series: *The Path to Power, Means of Ascent,* and *Master of the Senate* (New York: Knopf, 1982, 1990, and 2002), and by Robert Dallek's *Lone Star Rising* (New York: Oxford University Press, 1991). A general recent history of the Vietnam War is A.J. Langguth, *Our Vietnam* (New York: Simon & Schuster, 2000); see also Stanley Karnow, *Vietnam: A History* (New York: Penguin, 2nd ed., 1997).

RICHARD M. NIXON

Nixon's presidency was documented to a clinical turn, as recounted in Richard Reeves' *President Nixon: Alone in the White House* (New York: Simon & Schuster, 2001): in addition to the taping system, any aide who talked to Nixon had to send a memorandum of the conversation to his chief of staff, H.R. Haldeman; note takers usually were present; and speechwriters were eventually brought in to record warm anecdotes. Two memoirs by Nixon speechwriters are highly valuable: William Safire's *Before the Fall: An Inside View of the Pre-Watergate White House* (New York: Belmont Tower Books, 1975), and Raymond Price's *With Nixon* (New York: Viking Press, 1977), with a special focus on Nixon's resignation speech. The "silent majority" speech is described in Nixon's own memoir, *RN: The Memoirs of Richard Nixon* (New York: Grosset and Dunlap, 1978); in Walter Isaacson, *Kissinger* (New York: Simon & Schuster, 1992); and in H.R. Haldeman's posthumously published *The Haldeman Diaries: Inside the Nixon White House* (New York: Putnam Group, 1994). Nixon's resignation throes are detailed in Stephen E.

Ambrose, *Nixon: Ruin and Recovery 1973–1990* (New York: Simon & Schuster, 1991), and Bob Woodward and Carl Bernstein, *Final Days* (New York: Simon & Schuster, 1977). General biographies include Stephen E. Ambrose, *Nixon: The Triumph of a Politician, 1962–1972* (New York: Simon & Schuster, 1989); Roger Morris, *Richard Milhous Nixon: The Rise of an American Politician* (New York: Henry Holt & Company, 1989); Tom Wicker, *One of Us: Richard Nixon and the American Dream* (New York: Random House, 1991); and Garry Wills, *Nixon Agonistes* (Boston: Mariner Books, reprint, 2002). On Watergate: Fred Emery, *Watergate: The Corruption of American Politics and the Fall of Richard Nixon* (New York: Times Books, 1994), and, earlier but still gripping, J. Anthony Lukas, *Nightmare: The Underside of the Nixon Years* (New York: Viking Press, 1976). Nixon's tapes, as well as those of Johnson, can be heard at *www.c-span.org*.

GERALD R. FORD

The best book on Ford's presidency, written by his domestic policy advisor, is James Cannon's *Time and Chance: Gerald R. Ford's Appointment with History* (New York: HarperCollins, 1994). The story of his inaugural remarks is told by his speechwriter, Robert T. Hartmann, *Palace Politics: An Inside Account of the Ford Years*, (New York: McGraw-Hill, 1980), as well as by Ford himself, in *A Time To Heal* (New York: Harper and Row, 1979). Also of interest: John J. Casserly, *The Ford White House: Diary of a Speechwriter* (Boulder: University of Colorado Press, 1977).

JIMMY CARTER

As with Ford, surprisingly little has been written of the Carter presidency. The best sympathetic account of Carter's term and personality is the essay by Hendrik Hertzberg, his chief speechwriter, in Robert Wilson, ed., *Character Above All: Ten Presidents from FDR to George Bush*, (New York: Simon & Schuster, 1996). Far more critical, by Hertzberg's predecessor in the job, is James Fallows, "The Passionless Presidency," *Atlantic Monthly* (May 1979), vol. 243, no. 5, p. 33–48. The story of the "malaise" speech is told in detail in Elizabeth Drew, "A Reporter at Large (Washington, D.C.)" *The New Yorker*, August 27, 1999, p. 54. The best full biography of Carter is Peter Bourne, *Jimmy Carter* (New York: Scribner, 1997). Carter's successful post-presidential years are described in Douglas Brinkley, *The Unfinished Presidency: Jimmy Carter's Journey Beyond the White House* (New York: Viking Press, 1998)

RONALD REAGAN

The standard history of his presidency is Lou Cannon, *President Reagan: The Role of a Lifetime* (New York: Simon & Schuster, 1991). Memoirs by Reagan's speechwriters include: Peggy Noonan, *What I Saw at the Revolution: A Political Life in the Reagan Years* (New York: Random House, 1989), and Peter Robinson, *It's My Party: A Republican's Messy Love Affair with the GOP* (New York: Warner Books, 2000), describing how State Depart-

ment functionaries nearly blocked Reagan's call to dismantle the Berlin Wall. Reagan's own writing is collected in Martin Anderson, ed., *Reagan in His Own Hand: The Writings of Ronald Reagan That Reveal His Revolutionary Vision for America* (New York: Free Press, 2001); his speeches are in Ronald Reagan, *Speaking My Mind: Selected Speeches* (New York: Simon & Schuster, 1989). William Ker Muir Jr., *The Bully Pulpit: The Presidential Leadership of Ronald Reagan* (Oakland, CA: Institute for Contemporary Studies, 1992) focuses on the speechwriters. Reagan's official presidential memoir is *An American Life* (New York: Simon & Schuster, 1990); a history of his rise to power as the leading conservative is Matthew Dallek, *The Right Moment: Ronald Reagan's First Victory and the Decisive Turning Point in American Politics* (New York: Free Press, 2000). Other thoughtful books on Reagan's presidency and rhetoric include: Garry Wills, *Reagan's America: Innocents at Home* (New York: Doubleday, 1987); Dinesh D'Souza, *Ronald Reagan* (New York: Free Press, 1997); and Sidney Blumenthal and Thomas Byrne Edsall, eds., *The Reagan Legacy* (New York: Pantheon, 1988). On the Westminster speech: see a June 3, 2002, conference sponsored by the Heritage Foundation, online at *www.heritage.org*, and a thorough study by Patrick Ruffini, available at *www.patrickruffini.com* (and who generously made available the drafts of the speech). On Iran-Contra and Reagan's successful "damage control": Lawrence E. Walsh, *Firewall: The Iran-Contra Conspiracy and Cover Up* (New York: W.W. Norton, 1997); Theodore Draper, *A Very Thin Line: The Iran-Contra Affairs* (New York: Hill & Wang, 1991); Jane Mayer and Doyle McManus, *Landslide: The Unmaking of the President, 1984–1988* (Boston: Houghton Mifflin, 1988); U.S. House of Representatives Select Committee to Investigate Covert Arms Transactions With Iran/U.S. Senate Select Committee on Secret Military Assistance to Iran and the Nicaraguan Opposition, *Report of the Congressional Committees Investigating the Iran-Contra Affair* (Washington, D.C.: U.S. Government Printing Office, 1987). A forthcoming book by David Abshire, Reagan's special counsel on Iran-Contra, should shed new light.

GEORGE H.W. BUSH

The only full-length biography of George H.W. Bush is Herbert S. Parmet, *George Bush: The Life of a Lone Star Yankee* (New York: Scribner, 1997). On Bush's convention speech, see Peggy Noonan, *What I Saw at the Revolution*, above. President Bush never wrote a full-dress memoir. On the first war with Iraq, see George Bush and Brent Scowcroft, *A World Transformed* (New York: Knopf, 1998). On speechwriting in the Bush White House, see a book by a former Reagan and Bush writer, John Podhoretz, *Hell of a Ride: Backstage at the White House Follies 1989–1993* (New York: Simon & Schuster, 1993).

BILL CLINTON

Plainly, for the introductions to the Clinton speeches, I drew heavily on my own experience working seven years for him. His speeches and leadership style are illuminated in several memoirs including my own earlier book, *POTUS Speaks: Finding the Words That Defined the Clinton Presidency* (New York: Simon & Schuster, 2000); Sidney Blumenthal, *The Clinton Wars* (New York: Farrar Straus & Giroux, 2003); George R. Stephanopoulos, *All Too Human* (Boston: Little, Brown, 1997); and Dick Morris, *Behind the Oval Office* (New York: Random House, 1997). Susan Page of *USA Today* was given access to the writing of a Clinton speech in 1999: see "Anatomy of a Speech: 'Pivot' Point in Words," *USA Today*, June 28, 1999, p. 1. The best books on Clinton and his presidency are Joe Klein, *The Natural: The Misunderstood Presidency of Bill Clinton*, (New York: Doubleday, 2002); David Marannis, *First in His Class* (New York: Simon & Schuster, 1993) (which we speechwriters used to remind Clinton of personal anecdotes from his early years); and Martin Walker, *The President We Deserve* (New York: Crown Publishers, 1995). See also a particularly insightful article, Jacob Weisberg, "The Governor-President," *New York Times Magazine*, January 17, 1999. Clinton's pre-presidential speeches are collected by Stephen Smith, ed., *Preface to the Presidency: Selected Speeches of Bill Clinton 1974–1992* (Fayetteville: University of Arkansas Press, 1996), and his presidential speeches are available online: *www.clinton.nara.gov*. Books critical of Clinton's rhetoric include James MacGregor Burns and Georgia Sorenson, *Dead Center: Clinton-Gore Leadership and the Perils of Moderation* (New York: Scribner, 1999) and Benjamin Barber's solipsistic *The Truth of Power* (New York: W.W. Norton, 2002). On Clinton and civil rights: see DeWayne Wickham, *Bill Clinton and Black America* (New York: One World, 2002), and Christopher J. Edley Jr., *Not All Black and White* (New York: Hill & Wang, 1996) (focusing on Clinton's affirmative action review and National Archive speech). On the 1998 State of the Union and impeachment see Marvin L. Kalb, *One Scandalous Story: Thirteen Days That Tarnished American Journalism* (New York: Free Press, 2001); Thomas Rosensteil and Bill Kovach, *Warp Speed* (New York: Century Foundation Press, 1999); *The Starr Report* (New York: Public Affairs Press, 1998); Jeffrey Toobin, *A Vast Conspiracy* (New York: Random House, 1999); and Peter Baker, *The Breach* (New York: Scribner, 2000). The speech in which Clinton admitted to the Lewinsky affair is included in Robert Torricelli and Andrew Carroll, eds., *In Our Own Words: Extraordinary Speeches of the American Century* (New York: Washington Square Books, paperback ed., 2000), along with an unused, more conciliatory draft. On the policy agenda of the 1998 speech, see the forthcoming books by Gene B. Sperling and Robert Rubin.

GEORGE W. BUSH

Bush's speechwriting process has received unusual early attention. His speechwriter David Frum's *The Right Man* (New York: Random House, 2003) is the first of, presumably, many such memoirs. By coincidence, and fortunately for history, a journalist was writing a story on the speechwriters as the September 20, 2001 speech was composed: D.T. Max, "The Making of the Speech," *New York Times Magazine*, October 7, 2001. The 2003 State of the Union was the subject of a *Time* magazine cover story, "Untruth and Consequences," July 21, 2003. President Bush's speeches are online at *www.whitehouse.gov*.

CREDITS

PHOTOGRAPHS

Photographs on the following pages courtesy of Corbis Images: 10, 16, 24, 26, 30, 35, 53, 57, 62, 64, 69, 87, 88, 94, 95, 96, 103, 105, 107, 112, 112, 115, 115, 118, 120, 121, 122, 123, 128, 133, 136, 137, 141, 144, 160, 164, 169, 171, 174, 183, 184, 186, 188, 194, 199, 200, 203, 212, 214, 217, 220, 230, 237, 244, 245, 248, 255, 262, 263, 264, 267, 270, 274, 284, 291, 292, 304, 306, 307, 311. Photographs courtesy of AP/Wide World Photos on pages: 1, 5, 15, 23, 36, 39, 47, 60, 61, 77, 80, 93, 99, 110, 119, 127, 143, 149, 155, 159, 167, 175, 181, 185, 187, 190, 196, 206, 211, 225, 227, 229, 232, 235, 243, 265, 273, 279, 283, 286, 295, 299, 303, 312, 315, 316, 319. Photographs courtesy of the Library of Congress on pages: 2, 7, 18, 43, 44, 45, 48, 49, 51, 54, 56, 82, 86, 89. Photographs courtesy of Truman Presidential Museum and Library on pages 138 and 139. Photographs from the National Security Archive at George Washington University, courtesy of Alicia Kolar Prevost on page 173. Photograph courtesy of National Archives and Records Administration on page 55. Image on page 125 reprinted by permission of *New York Times*.

AUDIO

The audio excerpt from "Gettysburg Eyewitness" is from NPR's Lost & Found Sound and used by permission from William Rathvon's relative, Dennis Siebold, story producer Jay Allison, and The Kitchen Sisters (Davia Nelson & Nikki Silva). Copyright © 1999 The Kitchen Sisters and Jay Allison.

The voices of George Washington and Andrew Jackson were performed by Pat Duke.

The voices of Thomas Jefferson and Abraham Lincoln were performed by Roger Mueller.

Audio excerpts provided by the Truman Presidential Museum and Library, the Jimmy Carter Library and Museum, the Reagan Museum and Library, and the Clinton Presidential Center.

Archival audio research and dubbing by Michael Dolan and Alex Lubertozzi; preliminary audio editing by Alex Lubertozzi and Tara Utsey.

Audio recording, editing, engineering, and mastering by John Larson, Larson Recording, Chicago, Illinois.

Some audio segments have been edited for time and content. While we have attempted to achieve the best possible quality on the archival audio, some audio quality is the result of source limitations.

ACKNOWLEDGMENTS

I first had the idea for this book when I was working in the White House. In 1998, I asked an intern to go to a bookstore to buy a compilation of presidential speeches, and he returned empty-handed. So I began to compile photocopies of the greatest presidential speeches in a three-ring binder. Five years later, that summer project has grown into this book.

I want to thank, first, Alex Lubertozzi, my editor at Sourcebooks, who has worked as a real partner, with avid creativity on so many levels—including assembling the audio and photographs from sources all around the country. My thanks as well to Dominique Raccah, Sourcebooks's publisher; editors Jennifer Fusco, Todd Stocke, and Tara Utsey; editorial intern Sasha TerMaat; designers Jenna Jakubowski and Taylor Poole; Sales Director Jack Perry; and my publicist, Heather Otley. Rafe Sagalyn, my agent, was enthusiastic and helpful.

I want to express appreciation to President Bill Clinton for the opportunity he gave me to serve and to learn, and I would like to thank him, President Gerald Ford, and President Jimmy Carter for offering their thoughts on the speeches that influenced them. Thanks to those in the former presidents' offices who arranged for their participation, including Doug Band, Penny Circle, and Maggie Williams.

George Stephanopoulos, now of ABC News, brought me into the White House, and was generous enough to join in this project—and is a valued friend. David Gergen, who wrote the forward, taught me much at the White House and when we were both instructors together at Harvard.

This book could not have been written without the help of my colleagues at the John F. Kennedy School of Government at Harvard, where I taught full-time while writing it. Alison Kommer, my faculty assistant, provided invaluable assistance over two years—researching, proofreading, supervising students, managing the project's administration, and in countless other ways. Amanda Fuchs was a meticulous researcher, digging through libraries, checking facts, and, among other things, carefully proofreading these speeches. This book was immensely strengthened by their work and friendship. Several students in my class on "rhetorical leadership" tracked down and proofread the texts of presidential speeches: Ric Arthur, Glenn Davis, Kerry Greeley, Kim Levy, Bill McCamley, Julie Piscitelli, Tom Seamonds, and Eileen Toback. (Apologies to any I may have left out.)

My Fellow Americans was written with the support of the Joan Shorenstein Center for Press and Public Policy. Thomas Patterson, a distinguished and generous scholar, lured me to the school and was an unfailingly wise mentor. My thanks go to the Center's director, Alex Jones, and his colleagues Nancy Palmer, Edie Holway, Fred Schauer, Richard Parker and others, and to Walter Shorenstein for supporting that worthy cause. Thanks, as well, to Kennedy School faculty colleagues Marie Danziger and Mimi Goss.

Friends and colleagues commented on all or parts of the draft. Jeff Shesol and Eric Alterman, two gifted historians, were particularly helpful, sharing their knowledge of the presidency and their frank editorial judgments. The comments of Don Baer, Stephen Bowman, Josh Gottheimer, Michael Tomasky, Jonathan Alter, and John Seigal were appreciated as well.

I would also like to thank the staffs of the Truman Presidential Museum and Library, the Jimmy Carter Library and Museum, the Reagan Museum and Library, and the Clinton Presidential Center (especially my friend,

Stephanie Streett) for helping to provide recordings of some of the speeches included on the audio CDs that accompany this book. Others were generous with their research, including Professor Marty Medhurst, Alicia Kolar and Patrick Ruffini; Jon Alter discussed at length his forthcoming book on Franklin Roosevelt.

Thanks as well to my new law partners (and old friends), Jonathan Cuneo and Pamela Gilbert, who have been patient as the finishing touches were added to this book, even as we start an exciting new venture.

Thanks, also, to Robert Rubin, Joann McGrath and Michael Schlein for their support during the time I was writing this.

This volume draws on many years of conversation and guidance from White House alumni of both political parties including Ted Sorensen, Rick Hertzberg, Jim Fallows, Walter Shapiro, Dick Goodwin, Tony Snow, Tony Dolan, Peter Robinson, David Frum, Jon Podhoretz, Don Baer, Jordan Tamagni, Jonathan Prince, Paul Glastris and Carolyn Curiel. Other former colleagues in the Clinton White House, including June Shih, David Kusnet, Alan Stone, Lowell Weiss, David Shipley, Tony Blinken, Bob Boorstin, Bruce Reed, Gene Sperling, Paul Begala, Sidney Blumenthal, Rahm Emanuel, and Mark Penn enriched this through their insights over the years.

Every two years or so, a group of former presidential speechwriters gathers for dinner, convened by William Safire (Nixon) and hosted by Jack Valenti (Johnson). It's called the Judson Welliver Society, puckishly named after the so-called Literary Secretary to President Warren G. Harding. (Unfortunately, none of Mr. Welliver's handiwork appears in this volume.) This dinner is a rare treat—gathering in one room, under a temporary political truce, men and women who served presidents all the way back to FDR. One night in January 2003, George Elsey rose to his feet. He looked fragile, but his voice boomed, as he told us about writing the Truman Doctrine speech that helped launch the Cold War in 1947. Then we heard from Michael Gerson, the gifted writer who was then busy preparing the arguments for the war with Iraq. All the people there share a passion for their country and a deep respect for the men we served. Far more than is probably healthy, we have each learned to drink deeply of the words of the presidents who came before we served, and to keenly assess those who came after. I hope this book succeeds in sharing some of our passion for these words.

Finally, of course, I could not have done this without the love and support of my family. My parents, Sandy and Marty Waldman, and my brother Steve and his wife Amy, were encouraging as ever. My father-in-law, Jonathan Fine, offered early support, urging me to make presidential history more than just a hobby. My children, Benjamin, Susannah, and Joshua were a delight, and on this book, were helpful as well—two of them learned to read while it was being written, and made useful comments. My wife, Liz Fine was both a sharp-eyed editor and a loving best friend. While this book was being written, we moved to a new city (we arrived in New York on September 1, 2001—*So when did you move to Pearl Harbor?*), she started a new job, I was away teaching for much of the time, and still she was generous and joyful. I don't deserve her, but I'm grateful nonetheless.

Michael Waldman
New York City
July 2003

ABOUT THE AUTHOR

Michael Waldman was director of speechwriting for President Clinton from 1995–1999, after serving as Special Assistant to the President for Policy Coordination. He wrote or edited nearly two thousand presidential speeches, including two inaugural addresses and four State of the Unions. Waldman is the author of *POTUS Speaks: Finding the Words That Defined the Clinton Presidency* and *Who Robbed America? A Citizen's Guide to the S&L Scandal.* Since leaving the White House, he has been a lecturer in public policy at Harvard's John F. Kennedy School of Government. He practices law at Cuneo Waldman & Gilbert, LLP. Waldman lives with his family in New York City.

ABOUT THE NARRATOR

George Stephanopoulos is the anchor of ABC's Sunday morning program "This Week with George Stephanopoulos." He appears regularly on "Good Morning America," "World News Tonight," and other ABC News broadcasts. He is the author of the *New York Times* bestseller *All Too Human.* Prior to joining ABC News, he served in the Clinton administration as the senior advisor to the president for policy and strategy.